The Middle East For Dummies®

W9-APG-407

A Map of the Middle East

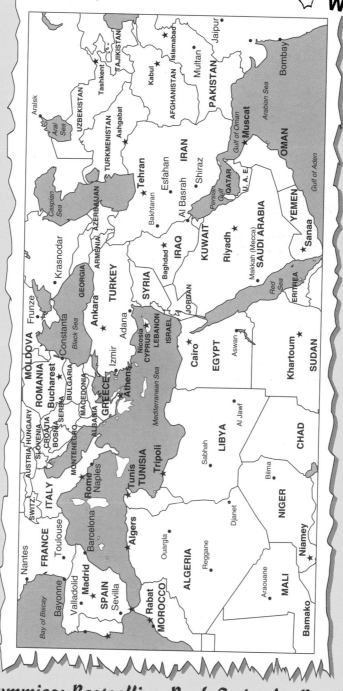

For Dummies: Bestselling Book Series for Beginners

The Middle East For Dummies®

Cheat Sheet

Important Acronyms

FLN: National Liberation Front (Algeria)

IDF: Israeli Defense Forces

ISI: Inter-Service Intelligence (Pakistan)

LOC: Line of Control (Kashmir)

PA: Palestinian Authority

PKK: Kurdistan Workers Party (Turkey)

PLO: The Palestine Liberation Organization

SLA: Southern Lebanese Army

UN: United Nations

UNSCOM: The United Nations Special Commission on Disarmament

Islamic Technical Terms

Fatwa: Islamic injunction

Hadith: Oral Traditions of the Prophet Muhammad

Hajj: Annual pilgrimage to Mecca

Madrasa: Islamic theological schools

Quran: Allah's message revealed to the Prophet Muhammad

Ramadan: Month of Fasting

Shahada: Muslim creed (there is no god, but God)

Sharia: Islamic law

Sunna: Traditions of the Prophet Muhammad

Zakat: Tithe or alms

Middle-Eastern Heads of State

Mahmoud Abbas: Palestinian Prime Minister

Crown Prince Abdullah: First Deputy Prime Minister and next in line for the Saudi throne

King Abdullah: King of Jordan

Yasser Arafat: President of the Palestinian Authority

Bashar al-Assad: President of Syria

Hamid Karzai: President of Afghanistan

Muhammad Khatami: President of Iran

Hosni Mubarak: President of Egypt

Muammar al-Qaddafi: Libyan Chief of State

Pervez Musharraf: President of Pakistan

Ariel Sharon: Prime Minister of Israel

For Dummies: Bestselling Book Series for Beginners

The Middle East

FOR

DUMMIES®

by Craig S. Davis, PhD

WILEY

Wiley Publishing, Inc.

About the Author

Craig S. Davis earned a dual PhD in Near Eastern Languages and Cultures and in Religious Studies from Indiana University in 2002. He has conducted research in Pakistan, Afghanistan, and India on contemporary primary education and medieval history. In the spring of 2002, he published an article on images of violence in Afghan primary education textbooks entitled "'A' is for Allah, 'J' is for Jihad" in *World Policy Journal*. His dissertation focused on a textual analysis of medieval Persian texts from the Mughal Empire. He studied Arabic in Jordan, Urdu and Pashtu in Pakistan, as well as Persian and other regional languages in the United States. Today, he works for the International Child Labor Program at the U.S. Department of Labor's Bureau of International Labor Affairs. Craig lives in Maryland with his wife Mirna and their four children: Helen, Trevor, Tellie, and Cassie.

Dedication

I dedicate this book to two very important individuals who helped to shape my understanding of freedom and justice during my formative years. The first is "Scud" McCrary, my middle school history teacher, who taught me the values of democracy and civil liberties that have stuck with me to this very day. The second is my high school Latin and German teacher, Lester Kerns, who influenced my teen years as much as anyone. I will never forget either.

Author's Acknowledgments

Without the patience and understanding of my wife, Mirna, and my children, Helen, Trevor, Tellie, and Cassie over the past six months, this book would not have been possible. I would also like to thank Kevin Farris and Nick Levintow who lent their support. Jamsheed Choksy's unwavering direction, both technical and otherwise, is always appreciated. I am grateful to Pam Mourouzis who provided assistance in the initial stages of the project. I also wish to thank Tim Gallan and Chad Sievers.

Publisher's Acknowledgments

We're proud of this book; please send us your comments through our Dummies online registration form located at www.dummies.com/register/.

Some of the people who helped bring this book to market include the following:

Acquisitions, Editorial, and Media Development

Senior Project Editor: Tim Gallan

Acquisitions Editor: Norm Crampton

Copy Editor: Chad Sievers

Acquisitions Coordinator: Holly Grimes

Technical Editor: Jamsheed Choksy

Editorial Manager: Christine Meloy Beck

Editorial Assistants: Melissa Bennett, Elizabeth Rea

Cover Photos: © George A. Dillon/Stock, Boston Inc./PictureQuest

Cartoons: Rich Tennant, www.the5thwave.com

Production

Project Coordinator: Nancee Reeves, Ryan Steffen

Layout and Graphics: Karl Brandt, Jennifer Click, Stephanie D. Jumper, Michael Kruzil, Tiffany Muth, Jacque Schneider, Erin Zeltner

Proofreaders: Laura Albert, John Tyler Connoley, Angel Perez, TECHBOOKS Production Services

Indexer: TECHBOOKS Production Services

Publishing and Editorial for Consumer Dummies

    Diane Graves Steele, Vice President and Publisher, Consumer Dummies

    Joyce Pepple, Acquisitions Director, Consumer Dummies

    Kristin A. Cocks, Product Development Director, Consumer Dummies

    Michael Spring, Vice President and Publisher, Travel

    Brice Gosnell, Publishing Director, Travel

    Suzanne Jannetta, Editorial Director, Travel

Publishing for Technology Dummies

    Andy Cummings, Vice President and Publisher, Dummies Technology/General User

Composition Services

    Gerry Fahey, Vice President of Production Services

    Debbie Stailey, Director of Composition Services

Contents at a Glance

Table of Contents

Part IV: Regions in Turmoil *135*

Introduction

*F*or nearly two decades now, I have dedicated myself to the study of the history, languages, and culture of the region loosely called the Middle East. It's been a fascinating journey. I've lived, traveled, studied, and/or conducted research in Egypt, Palestine, Jordan, Pakistan, Afghanistan, and Kashmir. For most of my adult life, I've taught or explained that violence, militancy, and religious extremism are only a small, albeit politically significant, part of everyday life in the region.

The aftermath of September 11, 2001, has affected us all. Those of us who know and love the Middle East have been no less jolted than the rest. Since that fateful day, the Middle East has been on almost everyone's mind. With all that's been written and everything that's appeared on the TV screen — the War on Terrorism and the hunt for Osama bin Laden, a war in Afghanistan, another in Iraq, nuclear neighbors of Pakistan and India squaring off, cycles of violence in Palestine and Israel — I relished the opportunity to draw on my experience and expertise of the region to make sense of it all in this easy-to-understand *The Middle East For Dummies.* This book describes the recent political dynamics that snatch the headlines and weigh on everyone's mind, but it also goes much further. It explains the rich history of the Middle East from ancient Mesopotamia to the formation of the modern state of Israel. The book also details the diverse religious and cultural heritage, showcases the region's literary treasure chest, and explains the Middle East's culinary and familial customs.

About This Book

The Middle East For Dummies provides a window into the Middle East. Whether you're interested in ancient Egypt, the Crusades, Libya's brush with the United States, Arab cuisine, modern film, or literature, suicide bombings, the Taliban, or the peace process in Israel and Palestine, *The Middle East For Dummies* has something for you. This user-friendly book written in the typical *Dummies* fashion provides, at the flip of a page, easily accessible information on very relevant events and pertinent issues.

Conventions Used in This Book

For the purposes of this book, the Middle East refers broadly to the region stretching from Morocco in the west to Pakistan in the east. The region runs from Turkey in the north to the Sudan, Somalia, and Yemen in the south. An area so vast naturally includes a variety of languages — Arabic, Hebrew, and Farsi to name but a few. Reading foreign words is always difficult. To make matters worse, some of the letters in those languages don't have English equivalents. Specialists in the field have adapted sophisticated transliteration systems that include symbols like ' or ` to represent foreign letters, but they don't mean much to nonspecialists. Wading through a paragraph of foreign names and terms filled with odd symbols can be confusing. Therefore, this book has simplified the process by eliminating those symbols almost entirely and replacing foreign words with the English equivalents whenever possible. When certain foreign terms are unavoidable, I provide the simplified foreign word with its trusty English translation at its side (at least a few times until you catch on).

You also notice that the book uses the traditional abbreviations B.C. (before Christ) and A.D. (anno Domini, meaning in the year of the Lord) for dates.

Foolish Assumptions

This book makes the following assumptions about you:

- You've seen something on the TV or radio, read about it, or heard part of a conversation dealing with the Middle East, and now you want to find out more.

- With so many apparent contradictions in the media and diversity of opinion, you're not sure what to believe.

- You like to check things out for yourself. You don't really trust everything you hear.

- You want to fill in the gaps. You understand a lot of the basics about the Middle East but need a reference book to fall back on.

- You read a lot. After September 11, 2001, you rushed out and loaded up on reading material, but got hung up on some of the technical stuff. You've been waiting for a book to provide all the essentials.

This book spans the whole spectrum of topics on the region, including religion. But if you want more on religion, you also may want to check out *Islam For Dummies* by Malcolm Clark, *Judaism For Dummies* by Ted Falcon and David Blatner, and *Religion For Dummies* by Rabbi Marc Gellman and Monsignor Thomas Hartman (all by Wiley Publishing, Inc.).

How This Book Is Organized

This book contains 26 chapters divided into seven parts. You can pick up this reader-friendly book, thumb through it and stop and read what stands out, look up specific topics in the table of contents or index, or read it cover to cover. Take your pick. A brief description of each part follows.

Part I: Getting Acquainted with the Middle East

Part I introduces you to the Middle East. This part provides a variety of reasons why the Middle East is important to you. It spans the geography from Morocco to Pakistan and identifies important rivers, mountains, and deserts located in each area. This part also paints a portrait of the people and their hospitality.

Part II: The History of the Middle East

Part II is where you find the Middle East's historical background. The three chapters in this part detail the Middle East's ancient, medieval, and modern histories. The ancient period starts at about 3000 B.C. and explores the ancient civilizations of Mesopotamia, Egypt, Canaan, Anatolia (Turkey), and Iran up through the mid-sixth century A.D. The Medieval period starts with the birth of Muhammad, the Prophet of Islam, in the late sixth century and runs through the 17th or 18th centuries. The religious and political dynamics of this period paved the way for the Modern period, which picks up where the Medieval period left off and runs through the mid-20th century. The events in the Modern period have set the stage for the Middle East, as we know it in the 21st century.

Part III: Politics, Islam, and Oil: Three Reasons Not to Ignore the Middle East

Part III outlines the region's political, religious, and economic dynamics. This part discusses how the Middle East's political systems have transformed, or remained the same, in some cases. Some nations have dabbled with communism, socialism, democracy, and theocracy. Regardless of the political system, the leadership all too often has become authoritarian.

This part also delves into the question of Islamic militancy, *jihad* (holy war), extremist points of view, and madrasas. You see how the history of extremist interpretations has laid groundwork for militancy in the 21st century. This section also explains a number of reasons for the rocky relationship between Islam and the West. Finally, this part discusses the region's economics in the context of some important factors that come into play: oil, failed strategies, politics, and war.

Part IV: Regions in Turmoil

Part IV deals with four regions currently suffering from conflict. When you speak of conflict in the Middle East, Israel and Palestine first come to mind. This section explains the current crisis and describes the forces at play threatening to pull it apart. Before the Iran-Iraq War in the 1980s, Iraq was one of the region's wealthiest countries. This section outlines Iraq's troubled history from its inception after World War I through the 2003 U.S.-led invasion. The Soviet invasion of Afghanistan set this poverty-stricken nation on a path to destruction from which it has yet to recover. Pakistan, which recently entered the nuclear age, enters the 21st century with a combination of political and social ills that pose a threat to the Muslim country itself and other countries in the vicinity. This section explores the recent history of these two neighbors and provides a down-to-earth assessment of the current turmoil.

Part V: Regions in Repair

This part deals with a number of countries that have had their fair share of suffering but recently moved from a state of turmoil to one of repair. Countries, like Algeria, Sudan, Lebanon, and Somalia, have been entrenched in civil war and have endured unspeakable misery in the past but are now struggling to rebound. The recent histories of Egypt, Libya, Jordan, Syria, Saudi Arabia, Yemen, Iran, and Turkey are filled with violence, intolerance, and suffering no less unsettling. These regions are also attempting to put their pasts behind them and find their way in the 21st century.

Part VI: Cultural Contributions of the Middle East

Part VI lays out the Middle East's contributions to the world. The region's religions almost immediately come to mind. This part highlights various dynamics of the three major religions — Judaism, Christianity, and Islam — while describing numerous religious minorities and mystics' belief systems as well. The cultural contributions also include important family dynamics, like the family unit, marriage, and gender issues. This part also describes essential elements of language in the region and showcases 5,000 years of Middle Eastern literature. The discussion on arts and sciences demonstrates that the Middle East has probably contributed to basic science and philosophy in ways you had never imagined, while the various dimensions of the region's art and entertainment are definitely worth checking out.

Part VII: The Part of Tens

Part VII lays out ten important ethnic groups and ten key militant organizations. These guides are insightful on the first read through, and may come in handy as a reference tool when you get stuck on a particular ethnic or militant group. The last part discusses ten challenges facing the Middle East. These challenges represent common themes for discussion that you'll likely come across again and again in the media or in other literature on the Middle East. So, you may want to look at these chapters more than once.

Icons Used in This Book

Icons are these peculiar little pictures that surface in the margin from time to time in each chapter to let you know that the following topic is special in some way. *The Middle East For Dummies* utilizes the following four icons.

The Check It Out icon alerts you to a truly significant example of something, like art, food, literature, or music, is worth looking into. Go ahead, *check it out.*

The Tip icon provides a suggestion. If you choose to take the tip, you'll probably digest the information a little easier.

I use the Remember icon in two ways. First, this icon flags an item to keep in mind (remember) because that item may come in handy later. Second, I use this icon to refresh your memory, saying, "Hey! You remember this, don't you?"

The Ground Rules icon establishes a time out in the flow of the text so that I can lay down the political *rules of the game.* The rules following the icon let you know that distasteful offenses that the players (rulers, politicians, or tyrants) actually did may not be any worse than other players (rulers, politicians, or tyrants) did because they were just following the ground rules. As long as the players know the rules of the game and play on a level field, then all is fair in love and war (and politics).

Where to Go from Here

I didn't write this book in a linear fashion. Although the chapters in Parts II, IV, and V may read like an historical narrative, you can read the book by topics or in chunks. Basically, you can start anywhere. If, for example, you want to read up on the Camp David Accords or find out more on the history of the Occupied Territories, you can look those topics up in the index and read about them in Chapter 11. Next, you may decide to read about the Taliban or the pyramids. Just flip to your topic and voilá. If you have a more generalized feel for what you're looking for, you may want to run down the Table of Contents until you find it. If, however, you want to brush up on history, you may choose to select a chapter and read the whole thing.

Right now, if you have no idea where to start, I have a few suggestions. Start with Chapter 1 to explore some reasons why the Middle East is important to you. If you like friendly people, check out the part on hospitality in Chapter 3. If you just want to get a feel for current affairs, browse Parts IV and V until something catches your eye.

Part I
Getting Acquainted with the Middle East

The 5th Wave   By Rich Tennant

"I told him we were lost and needed directions. He offered a road map for the former, but suggested the Quran for the latter."

In this part . . .

Part I helps to make sense of it all by explaining why the Middle East should be relevant to you. This part further charts a map of the region, identifying the geography and climate. Finally, this part introduces you to the Middle East's greatest asset: its people, along with their hospitality and cuisine.

Chapter 1

The Middle East's Relevance in the 21st Century

*L*ike it or not, you live in a global society where nearly everything you do affects others, and other people's actions also affect you. Every time you purchase a product made abroad (which is more often than you may imagine), you're contributing to a global network of mechanisms that influence the lives of millions of people you'll never meet. Every time OPEC (Organization of the Petroleum Exporting Countries) raises the price of oil, higher prices make their way to the gas pump, impinging on your budget and reducing your ability to buy items for your family and yourself.

While you were going about your business on September 11, 2001, 19 Arabs hijacked four civilian airliners and flew three of them into the World Trade Center and Pentagon, killing more than 3,000 innocent people. This single event has likely changed your life, your worldview, and your opinions on the Middle East. First, you may have been among the throngs of people who began a concerted effort to educate themselves on the Middle East. Bookstores rushed to keep the shelves stocked with books on the Near East, Islam, and terrorism, while regional experts tirelessly attempted to keep up with requests to speak on TV and radio, give lectures, and participate in panel discussions on Middle Eastern issues. Religious studies and Near East studies departments struggled to answer phones and meet the growing demand of students who suddenly wanted crash courses in Islam and the Near East. Suddenly, the Middle East was relevant.

This chapter discusses the importance of the Middle East to our 21st-century world by highlighting issues relevant to you: oil, economy, terrorism, environment, art, literature, and human rights among them.

Making Sense of It All

With the recent turmoil in the Middle East, many people in the West have tried to find out more about the underlying issues, but this task can be a confusing one. The information they gleaned from the TV, radio, newspapers, magazines, books, and the Internet, at times seemed contradictory or filled with obscure terminology, complex concepts, and scores of foreign names of people and places.

Because I've lived, studied, and traveled in Pakistan, Afghanistan, Kashmir, Palestine, Israel, Jordan, and Egypt, my friends, family, and colleagues often ask me questions about the Taliban, *madrasas* (theological schools), Pashtuns, Hamas, General Pervez Musharraf, martyrdom, *sharia* (Islamic law), and the Quran, along with a whole host of other topics. *The Middle East For Dummies* provides the essentials on religion, politics, society, and history of the Middle East so that you can process all the data that you're downloading from the Internet, TV, newspapers, and other sources.

Following the headlines

The events taking place in the far-off Middle East have a lot to do with you. In fact, the Middle East is so relevant to Westerners that they can no longer afford to ignore it. You read about the region in the headlines everyday, and the most visible reason that the Middle East's events, trends, and politics affect you is the impact that terrorism has had on the West. If you traveled abroad in the past, you probably think twice about flying overseas now, don't you? In fact, you may think twice about flying at all. The tighter restrictions, longer lines, and baggage screening at airports are a direct result of September 11. After the July 2002 murder of three people standing at the El Al airline ticket counter at the Los Angeles International Airport, many people feel even less comfortable just waiting in lines.

Understanding global Islamic militancy

A wave of anti-Western feelings is currently washing over the Muslim World. All too often this anti-Western sentiment has taken the form of deadly violence against innocent civilians. Islamic militancy has struck in many parts of the world. Consider the following in the month of October 2002.

✔ **Bali:** Militants bomb two Bali nightclubs, killing 183 people. Most of the victims are Australian, British, and Indonesian.

✔ **French Oil Tanker Limberg:** Suicide bombers attack a French oil tanker, killing a Bulgarian crewmember in Yemen.

✔ **Moscow:** Approximately 50 Chechen separatists storm the Moscow Palace of Cultural Theater, taking approximately 750 hostages, only three of whom are Americans. More than 100 die when Russian security forces pump an airborne chemical agent into the theater in order to disable the militants.

Unfortunately, Islamic militancy has impacted the West and has dominated the media, much in the same way that violence and conflict fills history books. Other issues, often filled with controversy, also fill the headlines.

Art, architecture, and history

Five millennia of art and architecture telling the region's history saturate the Middle East. Egypt's pyramids, royal tombs, and ancient relics, like mummies, sarcophagi, and statues, and the Holy Land's countless sites held sacred by Jews, Christians, and Muslims, like the Wailing Wall, Church of the Holy Sepulcher, and Dome of the Rock are just glimpses into the Middle East's treasure chest of art, architecture, and history (for more, see Chapter 23). You're probably also aware the region's art has suffered setbacks recently. In 2001, the Taliban destroyed the 50-meter tall Buddhist statues that had endured two millennia in Bamiyan, Afghanistan. During the wars in Iraq in 1991 and 2003, looters decimated holdings, most notably in Iraq's National Museum of Antiquities.

Gender and human rights

Gender in the Middle East is a complex topic. Turkey, Israel, and Pakistan can boast having elected female prime ministers. The highly publicized activities of educated, visible Jordanian queens Nur and Rania represent the more progressive elements in Middle Eastern society. An increase in women-run businesses and improved education for girls in several countries signals a shift in traditional attitudes. Yet women continue to suffer in the region.

The Taliban became the most recent regime in the Middle East to emerge as poster boys for human rights abuses. The most commonly cited infraction was their treatment of women. In many parts of Afghanistan, women were forbidden to work in most jobs and travel outside the home alone or without a *chador* (type of veil). Furthermore, in many areas, girls and women were denied access to education. Women also weren't allowed to drive cars. When found in violation of these Islamic regulations, a special religious police under the Ministry for the Prevention of Vice and the Promotion of Virtue would beat or arrest the perpetrators.

Figure 1-1:
One of several Buddhist statues destroyed by the Taliban in Bamiyan, Afghanistan.

The Taliban didn't create all these practices; many they borrowed from Saudi Arabia. The issue of forbidding women to drive, for instance, came to a head in Saudi Arabia in November 1990 with the arrival of 500,000 Americans to the country for the Gulf War. Hoping to draw international sympathy for their cause (women's rights), 45 Saudi women drove automobiles to downtown Riyadh defying the ban. The Saudi Commission for the Prevention of Vice and Promotion of Virtue arrested the women. The most vociferous of the religious police labeled the women "communist whores." Some of the women lost their jobs. More controversial yet was the incident in March 2002, when religious police blocked an exit of a burning school, preventing the girls from fleeing the fire because the girls weren't wearing the appropriate Islamic attire presentable for the public. Even though 15 girls lie inside dying in the fire, outside the religious police dutifully busied themselves with beating young girls for not wearing the *abaya* (black robe and headdress).

Oil and economy

Because most of the world's oil reserves lie in the Middle East, the global economy hinges on the unimpeded production and flow of that oil. Disturbances of any type — war, rumors of war, or militancy — upset the delicate balance of the global economy and can affect countries for a variety of reasons. For example, since the USS Cole bombing in 2000, Yemen's already ailing economy has been reeling. After a wave of tribal kidnappings, bombings, and other violence, estimates indicate a loss of $7.6 million a month, which is substantial for a small developing nation of 18 million people. The bombing of two Bali nightclubs in October 2002 has had a devastating impact on Indonesia's economy, which relies heavily on tourism. The Jakarta Stock Exchange plunged 10 percent immediately after the bombings because investors worried that the violence may convince foreign firms to pull out.

Ecology and environment

On October 6, 2002, a suicide bomber attacked the French oil tanker Limburg off the coast of Yemen, killing one Bulgarian crewmember and spilling 90 million barrels of oil. The oil spill has caused serious ecological damage to coral reefs, fish, birds, and other marine life. This spill is dwarfed by the destruction wreaked in the eight-year Iran-Iraq War when offshore oil platforms and oil tankers served as military targets. A recent U.N. report found that 25 years of war, drought, and famine have devastated Afghanistan's environment. Deforestation, desertification, water contamination, oil dumps, and soil erosion are among the country's most prominent environmental problems. And you probably remember that Saddam Hussein's soldiers set 1,164 Kuwaiti oil wells ablaze as they were withdrawing in 1991.

Humanitarian issues

Take Lebanon, for instance, where an estimated 100,000 Lebanese were killed, 250,000 maimed or injured, and more than 1 million forced to flee their homes during the civil war. In the Iran-Iraq War, some 500,000 were killed. After 25 years of war, Afghanistan's soil is saturated with land mines, infesting an estimated 344 million square meters of territory. More than 150 people a month, frequently children, fall victim to mines. In 1992, a growing humanitarian crisis in Somalia, brought on by the century's worst drought and exacerbated by civil war, left 300,000 dead. Tribal warlords demanded loyalty from the starving population in return for access to food. Rival factions used military force to strangle U.N. supply routes, raid and hoard food supplies, and extort money from relief agencies. U.S. and U.N. peacekeepers stepped in to lend stability to the suffering Somalis.

Judeo-Christian tradition

If you live in the West, you're a product of Judeo-Christian tradition, which itself was born in the ancient Middle East. The Bible's origins, for instance, lie in Mesopotamia, Egypt, and Canaan. The notion of *hell* that has played an important role in Western religion, culture, and literature, not to mention a central theme in so many Hollywood movies, originated in the Middle East (see Chapter 4). Ever wonder why you get Sunday off? It's a religious day of rest. Christmas, Easter, and Hanukkah are all holidays embedded in our society.

The Middle Eastern story of infant Moses floating down the River Nile or concepts like *sacrifice* and *the golden rule* are so ingrained in our culture that imagining life without them is difficult.

Apart from these few reasons why the Middle East is relevant, I could name many more. Approximately 1.2 billion Muslims populate the globe. Islam is America's fastest-growing religion; an estimated 5 million Muslims live in the United States. If you pay taxes, then you support military and economic aid to both Israel and Egypt, as well as Turkey and many other countries in the region. You probably have friends or family members who have recently served in the military in Afghanistan or Iraq or who have been stationed in the Near East. Middle Eastern work, travel, trade, food, and other elements are woven into the very fabric of our Western society. Our destiny is intertwined with that of the Middle East. The first step in beginning to understand the Middle East is meeting it halfway.

Meeting the Middle East halfway

The issues that I mention in previous sections dominate the headlines, and you've probably already run across many of them. Just as history books and headlines are generally filled with wars and invasions and other brutalities of which humanity is capable, *The Middle East For Dummies* discusses the Middle East's historical and political developments. This political history requires an accounting of revolts, revolutions, wars, torture, invasions, and yes, Islamic militancy. In order to understand the current "mess" that you read about or watch on TV, you have to face some tough issues.

The Middle East's greatest asset

The Middle East's greatest asset — its people along with their customs — is the main reason the Middle East should interest you. Daily life for most people in the Middle East is pretty routine. Parents raise their children, kids go to school and do homework (yuck), and families attend functions, such as weddings and parties. People sing, dance, write poetry, create art, joke and laugh, cook fantastic food, work long hours, pay their bills, have kids, grow old, and do most of the things you do. I have, therefore, reserved a considerable portion of the book to capture various dimensions of Middle Eastern life. The chapters on food, literature, ethnicity, customs, and art provide a window into the Middle East's rich and diverse culture.

Although Islamic militancy and religious and ethnic violence currently snatch the lion's share of headlines, most of the world's Middle Easterners have never participated in any act of violence, nor have they even picked up a firearm or even seen an explosive device in real life. Most have never conspired against any nation, burned effigies of a U.S. president, or shouted

"Death to America." By and large, Middle Easterners are among the kindest, most tolerant, and most hospitable people on earth. Although the vast majority of Middle Eastern people don't actively participate in violence, they still may harbor ill will against the West or sympathize with suicide bombers or people the West labels as "terrorists."

If you're truly going to understand why Islamic militants hate the West and how some Muslims (and Christians) could possibly sympathize with Islamic militants, you need to release the old biases and stereotypes and attempt to look at various Middle Eastern worldviews. This advice doesn't mean sympathizing with any particular group or accepting its justifications, but rather it means you must meet the Middle East halfway. The Middle East is a multifaceted world that can best be fully appreciated with an open mind.

Wiping out the monoliths

Middle Eastern people, whether Jews, Arabs, Muslims, Christians, or whoever, are as diverse as any other religious or ethnic group. You can't lump all Jews or all Muslims into monolithic categories where all members think, walk, and act alike. Like Westerners, members of all these communities disagree, argue, challenge, reconcile, and fight.

In the January 2003 elections in Israel, for instance, the Likud party ran on a platform of stiff resistance against the Palestinians, while the Labor party campaigned to negotiate with the Palestinians and withdraw from the Occupied Territories (see Chapter 11).

You really can't view the controversial Taliban who ruled Afghanistan with a heavy hand as a monolithic entity. Taliban rulers in the capital of Kabul outlawed girls' education, forcing dedicated female teachers to set up clandestine schools in their homes. Yet, in May 2000, just 40 miles from the capital in the Taliban stronghold of Gardez, I visited a number of legal girls' schools filled with daughters of Taliban rank and file.

We're Muslims, not terrorists

If you want to conduct a simple examination of perspectives on terrorism, read a few articles from Pakistani newspapers on violence in Kashmir, and then read a handful on the same events in Indian newspapers. Pakistani articles routinely use the term *freedom fighters* or *mujahideen* (holy warriors) while Indians call the same militants *terrorists*. (I cover this multifaceted debate in more detail in Chapter 8.)

Most of the Muslim community, whether living in the West or in the Muslim World, is a little peeved. The Muslims feel slighted, even offended, that the West now looks at them with suspicious eyes. In an effort to crack the monoliths, try to appreciate the complexities of the term so loosely referred to as *terrorism* in the West. Although all but the most extreme Muslims renounce terrorism, various nuances regarding armed resistance against the enemy deserve special consideration:

- ✔ **Condemning terrorism:** Most Muslims condemn terrorism (including the state variety), which to them means unfair or unacceptable violence against innocent civilians. Interpretation of the categories of acceptable and unacceptable targets becomes tricky.

- ✔ **Denouncing all forms of Islamic terrorism:** Many Muslims, especially those who've been acculturated to the West, condemn all forms of terrorism and militancy.

- ✔ **Interpreting terrorism:** Even among Islamic militants a debate rages on about how best to interpret acceptable acts of armed resistance. Some proponents of Palestinian militancy, for instance, attempt to rationalize harmful actions by arguing that suicide bombings and killing of Israeli civilians is okay only in the Occupied Territories, but not in Israel proper.

- ✔ **Sympathizing with terrorists:** Many Muslims (and Christians) denounce terrorism, but sympathize with the plight of those Muslims they feel are forced through desperation to commit such militant acts.

- ✔ **Understanding state terrorism:** Many Muslims charge that hostile governments have utilized unwarranted, brutal force against civilians that amounts to state terrorism.

- ✔ **Using the terms "terrorism" or "freedom fighting":** Other Muslims condone armed opposition against those they perceive as repressive forces, such as the Indian army in Kashmir or the Israeli Defense Force in Palestine. In such cases, they argue, Muslim resistance should be labeled *freedom fighting*, not *terrorism*.

Do these points seem difficult to understand? You can try to reconcile such a line of thought by trying to imagine Christian fundamentalists who may condemn the bombing of an abortion clinic while sympathizing with the terrorists' cause. Certainly not all demonstrators against abortion are *terrorists* or militants. Because the definition of *terrorism* and *terrorist* becomes increasingly difficult when taking various points of view into account, throughout the remainder of the book, I generally refer to such acts of violence as *militancy*.

Navigating Through the Book

The Middle East For Dummies is organized into seven parts. The rest of Part I acquaints you with the diverse geography and climate of the Middle East as well as its people, their culture, and hospitality. Part II provides the essentials for Middle Eastern history. This part is broken into ancient, medieval, and modern history running to about the mid-20th century. Part III discusses political and economic issues related to current events. Within this part, Chapter 7 treats various types of leadership in the region, as well as experiments in communism, socialism, and democracy. Chapter 8 describes Islamic militancy in a nutshell, while Chapter 9 deals with the stormy romance between Islam and the West. Chapter 10 rounds out this part with a general discussion of oil and economics in the region.

Regions in turmoil is the topic for Part IV. If you really want to get to the meat of Middle Eastern affairs today, this section is for you. It begins with Chapter 11 that digs into the complicated events in Israel and Palestine. The next three chapters describe the history of Iraq, Afghanistan, and Pakistan respectively, laying out the important historical developments leading to the most recent ongoing crises. Part V looks at regions in repair — North Africa, the Fertile Crescent, the Arabian Peninsula, and the non-Arab states — that represent numerous nations attempting to recover from turmoil in their recent pasts.

Next is Part VI, which deals with religion and culture in detail, including major and minor religions in addition to family dynamics, language and literature, and arts and sciences in the Middle Eastern context. The Part of Tens closes out the book in Part VII. These three chapters should be significant to you as they deal with ten key ethnic groups, ten key militant groups, and ten key challenges facing the Middle East in the 21st century.

Chapter 2

Charting a Map

. . . .

In This Chapter

▶ Staking out the Middle East's parameters

▶ Understanding the region's geography

▶ Getting your bearings

. . . .

*I*n the winter of 1983 and 1984, I traveled to Pakistan and Afghanistan for the first time. A number of Afghans befriended me, welcoming me into their homes and lives. One arranged for me to travel into Afghanistan dressed as a *mujahid* (holy warrior). The Afghan Mujahideen were at the time embroiled in a *jihad* (holy war) against Afghan communists and the Soviet Red Army, which felt that the barren Afghan soil was as good as any place to invade.

A couple of months later I left my new friends and returned to the United States with an appreciation for the complexities, not only of the Afghan conflict, but also of the entire region in general. Apart from the Afghan guerrilla resistance against the Soviets, I discovered Afghan communists secretly providing information to their Mujahideen opponents. Relief agencies struggled to keep the medical supplies they were providing to refugee camps from surfacing on the black market. Accusations circled that Pakistan siphoned off substantial portions of U.S. military aid before handing it over to the Mujahideen leaders, who countered by taking a share before passing the aid along to the commanders. I heard stories that Afghan refugee boys and men who had fled to Iran were being conscripted and sent to the front line against Iraq. Arabs in the region were funding, or fighting for, the resistance; the Chinese and Iranians were providing weapons; and the CIA and Soviet intelligence were keeping tabs on it all.

Upon returning to the United States, I naively explained to friends and family that if a Third World War were to erupt, it would originate in the Middle East. Little did I know how the Afghan War would profoundly affect Afghanistan, Pakistan, and Kashmir militarily, politically, and ideologically, and how it would set the stage for Arab Islamic militant attacks against U.S. targets on September 11, 2001. Since those attacks, the world has found out just how Afghanistan and Pakistan are inextricably linked to the Arab World (Saudi Arabia, Palestine, and Egypt, for instance).

Getting Acquainted with the Region

Somewhere on a continent far, far away, a cartographer grappled with the term *Middle East.* This cartographer had to consider how other cartographers, scholars, journalists, and politicians used the term, and that wasn't easy. Often the *Middle East* refers to part of the Arab World as far west as Egypt, as far east as Iran, and as far north as Turkey. Because the rest of the Arab World (Morocco, Algeria, Sudan, Tunisia, and Libya) is in North Africa, some people employ the term MENA (Middle East North Africa). Others coin the term the *Near East* (as opposed to the Far East) to cover this region, and toss in Afghanistan for good measure. This term (*Near East*) didn't really catch on in the media, so today scholars and political analysts are just about the only ones who use it.

To simplify, others stubbornly just use the *Middle East* to refer to all those countries and sometimes lump in Pakistan because it's culturally, politically, and religiously linked. Some people argue that Afghanistan and Pakistan don't belong on the indistinguishable Middle East's map (and that strictly speaking they belong on the map of Central and/or South Asia). But nowadays, more and more people equate these two countries with the Middle East. Since September 11, 2001, separating Afghanistan and Pakistan from the Middle East has been increasingly difficult.

Therefore, I have solved the cartographer's dilemma (and expect to be rewarded handsomely). For the purposes of the *Middle East For Dummies*, the *Middle East* stretches from Morocco in the west to Pakistan in the east (see Figure 2-1). The Middle East extends to Turkey in the north and Yemen, Somalia, and Sudan in the south. Likewise, I occasionally use the term *Near East* interchangeably with *Middle East* (so don't hold it against me).

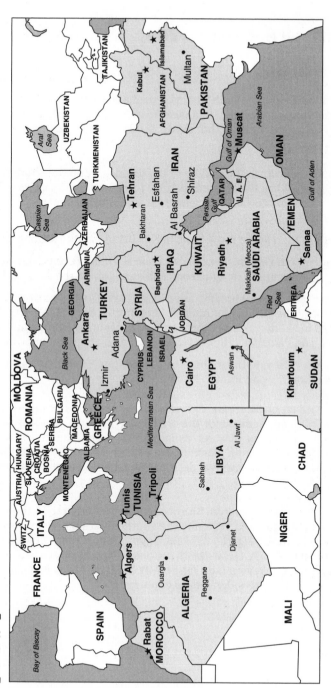

Figure 2-1:
The Middle
East.

Identifying the Countries, the Land, and the Climate

When you think of the Middle East, you probably think of sand dunes, flat-roofed mud houses clustered in a desert, and minarets rising out of a dry, dusty Egyptian city. Well, all that exists, but the Middle East is a little more diverse. Take a look!

- **Nature reserve:** In the middle of the dry desert on the shore of the Dead Sea in Israel lies the Ein Gedi natural reserve: an oasis of waterfalls, fresh water springs, and wildlife refuge for a number of species, including ibex and fox.

- **Rainfall:** Rain in the mountains of Kurdistan is quite significant.

- **Semitropical region:** The Salalah Plain of Oman receives an annual monsoon that creates a unique tropical-like region on the Arabian Peninsula.

- **Snow:** Lebanese mountains have been a favorite for snow skiers for generations. The Elburz Mountains of northern Iran, which are often mentioned in ski magazines, Morocco's Atlas Mountains, Afghanistan's Hindu Kush, and Pakistan's Himalayas also receive abundant snowfall.

- **Verdant valley:** In the mountains of Pakistan, the Hunza Valley makes for a breathtaking panorama.

From the earliest civilizations, dating back thousands of years before the Common Era (a euphemism for the era formerly known as A.D.), people typically lived near sources of water, usually rivers (see Chapter 4). Even today, in the age of desalinization plants and sophisticated underground water systems, the Middle East's survival depends on rivers and other natural sources of water.

The *Arab World* stretches from Morocco in the west to Iraq in the east, and from Syria in the north to Yemen in the southern Arabian Peninsula, encompassing 17 countries: Algeria, Bahrain, Egypt, Iraq, Jordan, Kuwait, Lebanon, Libya, Morocco, Oman, Qatar, Saudi Arabia, Sudan, Syria, Tunisia, the United Arab Emirates, and Yemen (see Figure 2-2). You can throw in Palestine although it's not yet an independent country.

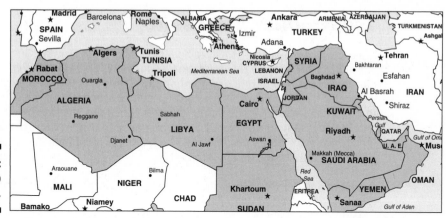

Figure 2-2:
The Arab
World.

North Africa

North Africa runs from the Atlantic Ocean at Mauritania, along the
Mediterranean Sea, and across the Nile River to the Red Sea. Mauritania,
Morocco, Algeria, Tunisia, Libya, Egypt, and Sudan comprise North Africa.
The Sahara Desert stretches across most of North Africa. Sand dunes occupy
about 15 percent of the Sahara, while huge bare plateaus of stone cover ⅔ of
the desert. Temperatures are hot, and the climate is dry. With the exception
of Morocco, which has 18 percent arable land, less than 5 percent of the soil
in North Africa is tillable. The Atlas Mountains stretch from Morocco through
Algeria and into Tunisia. The northern slopes of these mountains form flowing river basins that produce fertile farmland and forests and allow for irrigation. In Morocco, for instance, the majority of the population lives in the Atlas
Mountains foothills and farms the fertile plains, valleys, and plateaus
between the mountains and the coast.

More than 90 percent of Egypt is barren desert. The Nile River sustains life in
the desert throughout Egypt and parts of the Sudan. The Nile also provides
hydroelectric energy. The Sinai Peninsula is east of the Nile, with Mount
Katherine and Mount Sinai at the peninsula's center. Egypt is hot and dry, and
even in the winter, average temperatures are about 70 degrees in the day.
Some parts receive almost no rainfall, while Alexandria boasts a whopping
seven inches a year.

The Arabian Peninsula

Three bodies of water — the Red Sea to the west, the Persian Gulf to the east, and the Arabian Sea to the southeast — surround the Arabian Peninsula. The climate is mostly a harsh, dry uninhabitable sandy desert. Temperatures exceeding 120 degrees from May to September aren't out of the ordinary. Rub al-Khali Desert (or the Empty Quarter) occupies the northwest region and receives almost no rainfall at all compared to other parts that receive six inches per year. Had it not been for the famous well of Zam Zam, the holy city of Mecca could never have sustained life.

A host of smaller Gulf States line the periphery of the peninsula: Bahrain, Qatar, and the United Arab Emirates. Oman and Yemen eclipse a significant portion of the Arabian Peninsula's southern tip. Jordan and Iraq lie to the north of the peninsula. Farmers can work very little of the peninsula, and most of the nations rely on petroleum production. The Asir Mountains run along the southwestern coast of Saudi Arabia and receive 25 times the national average rainfall. The Jebel Akhdar Mountains are a luscious green contrast to the peninsula's overwhelming barrenness. The fertile Batinah Plain runs near Muscat, while the Salalah Plain in the south near Dhofar is a lush semitropical area as a result of the summer monsoon lasting from June to September.

The Fertile Crescent

The Fertile Crescent runs from the Mediterranean Sea along the coast of Israel, Lebanon, and Syria across the Rift Valley through Jordan and over to the Tigris and Euphrates rivers in Iraq in the east. In the summer, the coastline is hot and balmy, and in the winter, rain and snow can fall in Palestine and Israel. The bulk of the region from the Negev and Judean deserts in southern Israel across the Dead Sea and the Jordan Valley reaching into Iraq is hot and dry. About 17 percent of Israel's and Palestine's land is arable, primarily in the north, which receives more rainfall and where you can find a wide range of wildlife. Nestled in the Lebanon Mountains, the Cedars is the famous winter resort where snowfall is so abundant that the French set up a ski resort in the 1930s. After World War II, Lebanon earned a reputation as *The Switzerland of the Middle East* (see Chapter 16).

The Jordan, Tigris, and Euphrates rivers have sustained life in Jordan and Iraq for thousands of years. Very little of Jordanian land and only about 12 percent of Iraqi land can be farmed. Although most of Syrian territory is semi-arid and desert plateau, about a quarter of the land is used for agriculture. The Anti-Lebanon Mountains create a natural border between Lebanon and Syria, just as the Zagros Mountains and the Shatt al-Arab waterway do between Iraq and Iran.

Anatolia

Rising north from Syria is the Anatolian Plateau, which is home to modern-day Turkey. This country extends from Greece and the Mediterranean Sea in the west and southwest, to a narrow strip bordering Bulgaria in the north-west, and to the Black Sea in the north. Turkey borders Armenia and Iran in the east. The terrain and climate contrast the Middle East's other dry desert regions. Turkey has sprawling plains, thick forests, rolling steppes, tall mountains, and powerful rivers and streams. More than a third of the territory is arable. Assorted wildlife is native to Turkey. The winters can be cold with considerable snow in the mountains. Summers are cool on the Black Sea coast and on the Anatolian Plateau but extremely hot in the country's southeast region.

Iranian Plateau

The Zagros Mountains and the Shatt al-Arab waterway in western Iran form a natural border with Iraq. The Elburz Mountains in the north run along the Caspian Sea. Iran shares northern borders with Turkmenistan east of the Caspian and Azerbaijan west of the Caspian. The eastern Iranian frontier runs adjacent to Afghanistan and Pakistan. The Persian Gulf flanks Iran to the south. Although the Caspian coast is subtropical, as a result of heavy rain and snowfall on the northern slope of the Elburz, Iran is mostly arid. Much of Iran's terrain is dry, particularly its two massive deserts — Dasht-i Kavir and Dasht-i Lut — which lie in the eastern and northeastern regions of the country. Iran can be cold in the winter, although summers can reach 105 degrees in the southwest. Iran's oil reserves are significant, but only about 10 percent of the land can be farmed.

Afghanistan and Pakistan

Afghanistan and Pakistan pick up in the west where Iran leaves off. Southwestern Afghanistan is flat and dry, and gives way to the Hindu Kush Mountains occupying most of the remainder of the country. These mountains became famous after 2001 as U.S.-led coalition troops conducted operations against the Taliban and Al-Qaeda forces holed up in sophisticated caves designed with elaborate ventilation systems and generators for electricity. The mountainous region is cool in the summer and extremely cold in the winter. Some regions receive heavy snowfall. Afghanistan shares a border with Turkmenistan, Uzbekistan, and Tajikistan in the north, Pakistan in the south, and a small sliver of China in the east. About 12 percent of the land is arable.

Don't think about traveling alone through Pakistan's western no-man's lands! Extending eastward from the Iranian border are the inhospitable climates of Baluchistan and the Makran coast, where Alexander the Great's army was nearly decimated by the brutal heat and aridity. The Indus River and its five famous river tributaries (Jhelum, Chenab, Ravi, Sutlej, and Beas) offset the bulk of Pakistan's dry and flat terrain, giving the region of the Punjab (five rivers) its name. These rivers flow southwest and have provided life for millennia. Originating high in the mountains of eastern Pakistan near the border with China, these five rivers help to make 28 percent of Pakistan's land farmable. India and the Arabian Sea delineate the southeastern border of Pakistan.

Chapter 3

Middle Eastern Hospitality

*B*y far, the coolest thing about the Middle East is visiting it. After you arrive, you can interact with the people, experience the culture, enjoy the food, witness the sights, share in the customs, listen to the music, and bustle your way through bazaars. This chapter introduces you to the people, the warmth of their hospitality, and the flavor of their cuisine.

Meeting the People

The overwhelming majority of people living in the Middle East are Muslim. Therefore, the tendency to speak in general terms about Middle Eastern culture as if it were Muslim culture is great. For the sake of simplicity, *The Middle East For Dummies* often succumbs to that tendency, because it is impossible to stop at every point made and find suitable examples for each religious minority. With this thought in mind, wherever appropriate, the book also goes to great lengths to highlight the rich diversity of Middle Eastern culture.

Making introductions

Middle Easterners are diverse. Each country, region, subculture, and community has an assortment of music, customs, clothes, languages, religions, and food that are equally diverse. I want to introduce you to just a few Middle Easterners.

✔ **Bedouin:** The Bedouins are Arab nomadic tribes living on the Arabian Peninsula, in Jordan, Israel, Egypt, and elsewhere. They make up about 10 percent of the Arab population. They're traditionally known to herd sheep and camels, moving freely from region to region across borders. In the 20th century, many have abandoned nomadic life and taken up farming or other sedentary occupations (see Chapter 24).

✔ **Berbers:** Throughout Libya, Algeria, Tunisia, and Morocco, approximately 12 million people speak Berber. Most belong to the Berber ethnic group of loosely knit tribes whose heritage in the region stretches back to 2400 B.C. (see Chapter 24).

✔ **Copts:** The Copts are an indigenous Egyptian Christian sect that pre-dates Islam. As a spoken language, Coptic died out in favor of Arabic around the 12th century, but it continues to be used in religious rites. The Copts circumcise their infant sons and have their own pope.

✔ **Druze:** Some 300,000 members of this religious sect survive in Syria, Lebanon, Israel, and Jordan as an offshoot of Islam. Because of their beliefs in God's incarnation in the form of their 12th-century leader al-Hakim, Neo-Platonic tenets, and reincarnation, the Druze have often been persecuted by more orthodox Muslims. As a result, Druze have customarily hidden their identity, blending in among Christians or Muslims (see Chapter 20).

✔ **Hijras:** In South Asia, eunuchs and male crossdressers don attractive female clothing, apply makeup, and attend wedding ceremonies as paid singers, dancers, and musicians. In a society where female participants in such ceremonies are kept separate from the men, the attendance of these pseudo-women performers comes in handy.

✔ **Ismailis of Hunza:** Nestled in the mountainous enclave near the border of China on the Pakistani side is the utopian region of Hunza. The people speak Burushashki, and although this community of Ismailis is an off-shoot of Islam, the people of Hunza are considered neither Muslim nor Pakistanis. With their features and colorful clothing, the people of Hunza resemble the indigenous populations of the Andes (yes, the South American Andes Mountains — on the other side of the world).

✔ **Kurds:** About 25 million Kurds live in Syria, Turkey, Iraq, and Iran, primarily in mountainous regions. The Kurds farm, herd goat and sheep, speak their own language, Kurdish, and have their own customs. In northern Iraq, they were awarded their own autonomous region after the Gulf War. In 2003, as a result of the U.S.-led war in Iraq, the Kurds reclaimed much of the property lost 12 years earlier (see Chapter 24).

✔ **Pashtuns:** The Pashtun-speaking tribes live on both sides of the Afghan-Pakistani border. For centuries the Pashtuns have earned a reputation in the region for their lawlessness and volatility because of their refusal to accept the sovereignty of rulers in Afghanistan and Pakistan and their proclivity toward armed violence. They live according to tribal codes of conduct tempered with Muslim practices they consider Islamic law (see Chapter 24).

✔ **Sephardim/Oriental Jews:** Many Sephardic/Oriental Jews living in Israel today were either born in the Muslim World — Palestine, Iraq, Yemen, and Iran, for example — or descended from Jews who migrated from these regions. Many Arab Jews, for instance, grew up practicing Arab traditions, such as henna ceremonies before weddings, eating Middle Eastern food, like falafel and shawarma, and speaking Arabic as a mother tongue (see Chapter 24).

✔ **Sufis:** From Morocco to Egypt and from Turkey to Kashmir, you can find Islamic mystics called Sufis. These Sufis often gather in mausoleums or shrines of deceased Muslim saints to perform a special type of worship. For instance, in Lahore, Pakistan, holy men, with their long unkempt hair and dirty clothes, meet every Thursday to dance, sing, play music, and drift off into spiritual trances that allow them to experience union with God (see Chapter 20).

With such a rich diversity of Middle Eastern culture, most Middle Easterners seem to have one thing in common: their commitment to hospitality.

Welcoming You into Their Homes

If you visit the Middle East, you'll likely be "duped" by the unique hospitality demonstrated by its people. Whether a Christian family in Syria invites you in for a meal, a Bedouin welcomes you into his tent for coffee, an Iranian takes you home for tea and fruit, or an Afghan Pashtun insists you spend the night, this Middle Eastern conspiracy of hospitality is fooling no one.

An Israeli couple may snag you into their home on the pretext of offering a soft drink, but keep you there all afternoon, filling your cup, and serving tray after tray of olives, cucumber salad, humus and bread, fruit, meat with gravy, fish, and chicken. An Afghan refugee may bring you to his house to meet his brother, and you end up basking in the limelight, amid smiling faces, friendly questions, and enormous trays of Kabuli pilau — rice with raisins and chunks of tender lamb — and bowls of yogurt, and *nan*, foot-long pieces of soft flat bread. Later — and you knew it was coming — they serve green tea and fruit and insist that you spend the night. In the morning, they serve breakfast, and start their "trickery" all over again.

In Jordan and Lebanon, their "sinister" plan involves seizing any opportunity to rope you in. They spend hours in the kitchen preparing stuffed grape leaves, rice and succulent chunks of goat meat, maybe freshly baked bread basted on one side with olive oil and sprinkled with *zattar* (the perfect blend of thyme, marjoram, sumac and other spices). They "get" you with their tiny, powerful cups of delicious Turkish coffee sweetened just as you like. And just when you can't eat another bite, they launch their secret weapon: a coffee-table–size tray *kunafah* — a sweet pastry made of cheese, nuts, and a special syrup that makes you say, "Well maybe just one piece."

Those Egyptians with their *khoshary* — a dish made of pasta, rice, lentils, onions, chilis, and tomatoes — think by snapping you up off the street, buying you a tall glass of thick mango pulp, or with their unrelenting commitment to pick up the bill for the *shawarma* — a succulent roasted chicken or lamb, shaved off a vertical spit and plopped into a pocket of Arab bread dressed with sauce and vegetables — that they can demonstrate their affection for visitors and foreigners.

Don't be embarrassed by all the special treatment you receive when visiting the Middle East. The food and hospitality are superb, and boy do Middle Easterners know how to pour it on. But why are Middle Easterners so hospitable? An Afghan Pashtun once told me that "guests are blessings from God." Some Muslims claim that their customs of friendliness toward visitors (often complete strangers) have roots in Islamic tradition going back to the Prophet and his companions. Maybe! But this theory fails to explain Christian and Jewish hospitality. Other suggestions that special treatment of visitors is exclusively an Arab custom fall short of justifying Persian, Punjabi, and Tajik warmth and generosity. Hospitality must be a deep-rooted tradition woven into the very fabric of Near Eastern society that defies simple explanations. Whatever the source, you can rest assured that when visiting the region, you'll discover what it's like to be treated as a guest.

Trying the Cuisine

Middle Eastern cuisine is as extensive as it is delightful. Most of you are already familiar with traditional Middle Eastern dishes like olives and cucumber salads, kebabs, humus and bread, falafel, baklava, and of course Turkish coffee. The following delicacies may whet your appetite. And you don't even have to travel far to taste them — just visit a nearby Middle Eastern restaurant! (Is it lunchtime yet?)

✔ **Breads:** Each region has its own style of bread. In the Arab World, you can enjoy a variety of *khubz* (bread). The small, pizza-type bread has one side basted with olive oil and sprinkled with *zattar* (the perfect blend of thyme, marjoram, sumac and other spices). You also find thin Arab bread the size of an extra-large pizza sliced up to wrap around your shawarma. In Afghanistan, *nan* usually means the one-foot-long, thin, spongy bread that is a meal in itself. In the Punjab (Pakistan), *qima-vali nan* has ground beef and spices hot enough to set your mouth afire, while *paratha* is thin skillet-size fried bread, sometimes stuffed with potato. *Chapatti (roti)* is the thin tortilla-like bread made on a hot griddle (see Figure 3-1). These breads have become so popular in the West that you can now pick many of them up in a supermarket near you.

✔ **Chicken Tikka:** Charcoal-grilled chicken quarters basted with garlic, chili, ginger, and lime. Popular in Pakistan.

✔ **Kabuli Pilau:** One of the various forms of pilau popular across Iran, Afghanistan, and Pakistan. This particular rice dish is cooked with carrots, raisins, almonds, saffron, other spices, and lamb, and is named after Kabul, Afghanistan where it originated and spread westward.

✔ **Khoshary:** Pasta, rice, lentils, onions, chilis, and tomatoes. Particularly prominent in Egypt.

✔ **Kunafah:** This pastry comprises sweet cheese, nuts, and special syrup. A favorite in Arab countries.

✔ **Mensaf:** This is the national dish of Jordan that originated with the Bedouins. Mensaf contains a tray of rice with mutton cooked in a tangy yogurt sauce. The Bedouins traditionally placed the lamb's head atop the rice.

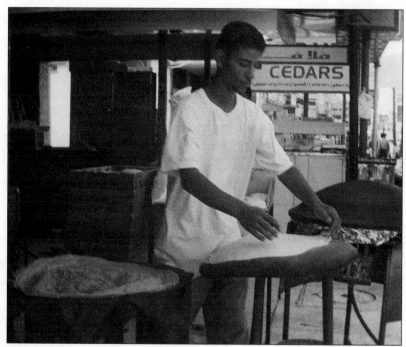

Figure 3-1: A Jordanian making bread.

Photo courtesy of Trevor Davis.

- ✔ **Shawarma:** That succulent roasted chicken or mutton shaved off a vertical spit and plopped into a pocket of Arab bread dressed with vegetables and sauce, dripping down your hand. Popular in the Arab World. (See Figure 3-2.)

- ✔ **Stuffed grape leaves (waraq ainab):** Stuffed with ground meat, rice, and spices. You can find this dish in many parts of the Arab World.

- ✔ **Tabbouleh:** Lebanese national dish of cracked wheat, onions, tomatoes, lemon juice, and spices.

- ✔ **Tea and coffee:** In much of the Arab World and Turkey (for obvious reasons), Turkish coffee is the drink of choice. You can also find hot mint tea made with cardamom in many countries, including Morocco, Jordan, Palestine, and other places. In Iran, hot black tea is a favorite, and in Afghanistan, hot green tea is popular and is often sipped while sucking on a chunk of brown sugar candy. Pakistanis usually prefer sweet black tea boiled with milk and cardamom so that it tastes something like hot chocolate. In Kashmir, salt tea is a favorite.

Wherever you go, you'll likely enjoy the region's people, food, and hospitality, both in the Middle East and among immigrants in the West. Sometimes your hosts may want to exchange addresses (e-mail addresses nowadays) and attempt to keep in touch. On occasion, you and your hosts become good friends. Enjoy.

Figure 3-2:
Shawarma:
Roasted
meat on
a spit.

Photo courtesy of Cassie Davis.

Part II
The History of the Middle East

Though many questioned its claim to be divinely inspired, The First Book of Gossip was a popular item at food stands across Jerusalem during the 1st century B.C.E.

"Not another St. Elvis sighting...?"

In this part . . .

Part II provides the necessary historical background of the Middle East by outlining the developments in three time periods: the ancient, medieval, and modern periods. The discussion of the ancient Middle East includes the fascinating cultures, languages, dynasties, historical developments, and religions of Egypt, Canaan, Mesopotamia, Persia, and Anatolia. The discussion of the Medieval period details the history associated with the rise of Islam, its spread throughout the region, and its effect on the Middle East. The final discussion explains the crucial political dynamics of the Modern period that pave the way for the Middle East in the 21st century.

Chapter 4

The Ancient Middle East

*A*ll ancient civilizations had at least one thing in common: They were addicted to water. In order to drink, bathe, and water their livestock, they needed a reliable water source. Because they didn't have any desalination plants or bottled water trucks, communities often sprung up near major rivers. The rivers also acted as waterways for transportation, provided fresh food (fish), and served as water sources to irrigate fields. You can understand then that ancient civilizations arose on the banks of the Nile River in Egypt, on the Jordan River in Palestine, Israel, and Jordan, near the Tigris and the Euphrates rivers of Mesopotamia (Iraq), and along the Indus River in the Sind (Pakistan). (See Figure 4-1.)

Because today people have retained the habit of drinking water, are you really surprised that modern communities have survived in the same general vicinity as the ancient civilizations, sometimes in the very same spot? Take Jericho, for instance! Just a few miles from the Jordan River, Jericho dates back to about 9,500 B.C., long before the Israelites arrived, and is the world's oldest inhabited city. Modern Jericho with 25,000 people grew up around the ancient site. Like many other ancient communities, Jericho was destroyed, rebuilt, abandoned, and restored many times over, and although many walls fell, archaeology shows that none fell at the time of Joshua.

Later generations found it convenient to construct dwellings at the site of earlier communities because so much of the legwork had already been done. Subsequent societies often built right on top of the older, demolished structures, utilizing the same water sources, farming the same fields, and traveling the same roads. As you may expect, building and rebuilding on older structures over time created a visible hump on the surface of the earth. Archaeologists call these mounds *tell*s. By carefully unearthing the remains in a tell, an archaeologist can study artifacts, which offer insight into these ancient cultures. In this way, scientists have mined a wealth of information about the ancient people, including:

- Approximate dates of settlements
- Customs and practices
- Dietary habits, often discovered by sifting through rubbish heaps (doesn't that smell appetizing?)
- Farming practices and techniques
- Military traditions, defeats, and conquests
- Religious beliefs and rituals

Written records have always been informative archaeological relics. Most ancient Middle Eastern societies left some form of writing on tablets, papyrus, books, stones, or walls of temples and tombs. After scholars found out how to read these ancient — often dead — languages, they unlocked the mysteries of these societies. The written word provides a wealth of details about

- Beliefs in the supernatural and hereafter
- Military campaigns, strategies, and victories
- Names of their kings and their families
- Political and legal systems

The origins of Judeo-Christian tradition

Although you may not realize it, the ancient Middle East has probably influenced you in some way. If you live in the West, you're a product of Judeo-Christian tradition, which itself was born in the ancient Middle East. The Bible's origins, for instance, lie in Mesopotamia, Egypt, and Canaan. The notions of heaven and hell that play such an important role in literature, music, and Hollywood movies was absent in the earliest books of the Bible. It only surfaced after the Ancient Israelites were exposed to Iranian Zoroastrian beliefs while in exile in Babylonia. (See "The Promised Land [Kings, Gods, and Prophets]" section in this chapter.) The story of infant Moses floating down the River Nile is actually a variation of an earlier tale of a Mesopotamian king named Sargon who was set adrift as well.

Furthermore, Judaism, Christianity, and Islam share similar Middle Eastern motifs and features. The Hebrew word for God (*Elohim*), for instance, is related to the name for the earlier Canaanite god *El* and to that of the later Muslim god *Allah*. The biblical accounts of Abraham and Sarah have their parallel versions in Muslim tradition (see Chapter 5). And you can trace many of the gender roles, biases, and practices of the 21st century to beliefs, stories, and traditions arising in the ancient Middle East.

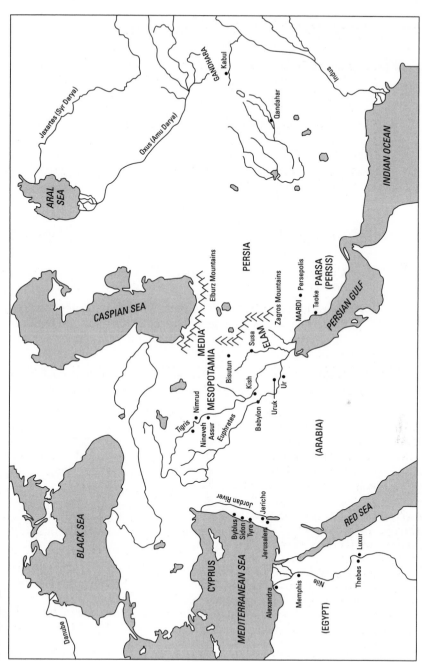

Figure 4-1:
The ancient
Middle East.

The Land Formerly Known as Mesopotamia (Iraq)

Yeah, I know. You remember reading about Mesopotamia in high school or recall hearing the name on a TV documentary, but you never really had the time to locate it on the map. (Now take the time to find it on the map in Figure 4-1.)

The land formerly known as Mesopotamia is today called Iraq. Mesopotamia is an ancient Greek word, meaning the land between two rivers. When the Greeks saw the land between the Tigris and Euphrates rivers, they naturally called it Mesopotamia, and the name stuck.

Mesopotamia was one of the main cultural centers in the ancient world. About 3000 B.C. it began developing a level of cultural sophistication in

- ✔ **Kingship:** An elaborate system of royalty, kingship, and succession evolved.

- ✔ **Literature, art, and architecture:** Written texts, like the Epic of Gilgamesh, vases with depictions of fertility goddesses, and the famous structures called ziggurats are testimonies to the level of Mesopotamian sophistication.

- ✔ **Politics and religion:** A co-reliance between rulers and priests developed, and politics and religions became intermeshed in Mesopotamian society.

- ✔ **Writing system:** Cuneiform developed as the writing system for a number of regional languages.

Elements of Mesopotamia's culture spread to many of the neighboring civilizations, but a group of people called the Sumerians really started the ball rolling.

Sumerians

The earliest coherent political entities to arise in a region were city-states. These city-states were tiny, self-contained kingdoms operating out of a single city. A group of local extended families, known as the Sumerians, ruled the city-states in Sumer, southern Mesopotamia, from about 3000 to 2340 B.C. The Sumerians spoke a Semitic language related to Hebrew. The most important Sumerian cities were

- ✔ Ur, located on the Euphrates River
- ✔ Uruk, located on the Euphrates River
- ✔ Kish, located in the Euphrates Valley

Because succession of kingship was passed on to members of one family, historians consider the Sumerians a dynasty. They devised a system of writing known as *cuneiform* that involved pressing characters of wedges in clay. Neighboring cultures, such as the Elamites in Iran and the Hittites in Turkey, borrowed this writing system. Similar to the way the Latin alphabet has been used for English, French, Spanish, German, and Portuguese, cuneiform was adapted to various ancient Middle Eastern languages.

Babylonians

With time, some kings sought to increase their wealth by asserting political control over a number of other city-states, often through military expansionism or alliances. The successful kings formed larger kingdoms and empires.

Although you probably know about the story of the Tower of Babylon from the Bible, the Babylonians did more than just build towers (called *ziggurats*); they built the world's first empire in Mesopotamia. Around 1750 B.C., a king named Hammurabi formed the empire at the city of Babylon, eclipsing many of the smaller kingdoms. Hammurabi's empire stretched across Southern Mesopotamia and into Persia (western Iran), which was known as Elam then. He also developed a series of laws called Hammurabi's Code.

By the 12th century B.C., the Babylonian Empire was in decline. The Assyrians sacked Babylon about 689 B.C. The Neo-Babylonians regrouped some 60 years later and again consolidated their power in the region. King Nebuchadnezzar conquered Israel in 586 B.C. and brought thousands of ancient Israelite captives back to Babylon. In 538 B.C., the Persian armies of Cyrus defeated Babylonia and set the Israelites free. (See the "Ancient Israelites" section in this chapter.)

Assyrians

Even as the Babylonians ruled southern Mesopotamia, the Assyrians exerted control over the north. Between 1243 B.C. and 612 B.C., they ruled from three important cities on the Tigris:

✔ Assur

✔ Nimrud

✔ Nineveh

The golden age of the Assyria civilization was during Assurbanipal's reign (669–633 B.C.). He collected a library of 22,000 cuneiform tablets, built a splendid palace at his capital, Nineveh, and expanded his empire by capturing Babylon, Susa (Iran), and Egypt.

The principal Assyrian god was Ashur (Ashshur, Assur), the god of war. Religion wasn't just a private matter but played an essential role in politics. For example, during the reign of Tukulti Ninurta I (1243–1207 B.C.), when the Assyrian army sacked Babylon, they carried off a statue of Marduk, demonstrating Ashur's supremacy over the Babylonian god.

"The Big Guy Up There" (Mesopotamian religion)

Mesopotamian cultures revered the sky, mountains, and other high places. This reverence for loftiness and the beings who dwelt there was a forerunner to the Judeo-Christian beliefs that heaven was up, instead of down, and that *the big guy up there* resides *up there*. Yet, they also believed that gods and goddesses could come down here and live in cult statues — so the statues were washed, clothed, and cared for.

Mixing religion and politics: Royal kingship

One rule that you must observe when studying the ancient Middle East is that the intricate link between politics and religion is all fair play. The ancient kings and priests certainly did.

Kings and priests recognized the political advantage in controlling religion as it held enormous sway over the common worshippers. Because lay worshippers generally follow the religious rules, whoever controlled religion could more easily maintain political dominance over those worshippers. Kings and priests developed a variety of politico-religious arrangements that allowed priests to have a say in the politics of a kingdom, and kings to assert influence over religious activities and doctrine.

Royal kingship was one of these arrangements. Accordingly, the gods granted a king authority to rule over his subjects. The priests sanctioned that authority, thereby legitimizing the king's rule. In return, the king provided material and physical security for the priests. So kingship became sacred — given by divinities to men.

The relationship between rulers and religious leaders throughout the Middle East's history has been rocky and has undergone a number of transformations. At times, the clergy refused to be manipulated by the political leaders. On other occasions, rulers sought to minimize the influence of religious leaders. At other times, the political rulers *were* the religious leaders. Keep this relationship in mind as you follow the developments in Middle East in all time periods.

The Mesopotamians didn't believe in just one god though. They had a pantheon of nature gods, including:

✔ Enlil, the storm god

✔ Ishtar, the fertility goddess

✔ Shamash, the sun god

✔ Sin, the moon god

As Babylon became more powerful, the local god Marduk also became more popular. A number of religious customs developed into a religious system, such as:

✔ Babylonians constructed temples and ziggurats.

✔ Cults grew up around certain gods.

✔ Devotees established special rituals.

✔ Myths and legends evolved.

✔ Priests orchestrated the system.

As you may expect, managing and coordinating religious activities and doctrines required the skills of specialists. Priests, temple prostitutes, and caretakers arose and assumed responsibility.

Elements of Mesopotamian religion spread to neighboring cultures even as Mesopotamia absorbed religious elements from those cultures. A sort of cross-pollination of religious beliefs, gods, and goddesses took place, resulting in a rich cultural heritage.

The Promised Land (Kings, Gods, and Prophets)

According to the book of Genesis in the Bible, Abraham migrated from Ur in Mesopotamia westward and settled in Canaan (also known as Palestine and Israel), which God had promised to Abraham's descendents as part of an agreement referred to as the Covenant. Jewish patriarchs, who remained in almost constant conflict with the residents of Canaan, led Abraham's male descendents (Jews) to Canaan. Ironically, many of the enemies of the Hebrew-speaking Israelites were their "cousins."

Ancient Israelites

The term *Ancient Israelites* refers to biblical Jews, Abraham's descendants who lived in Canaan or Israel (see Figure 4-2); whereas, *Jews* designates religious adherents to Judaism during any time period. *Israelis*, on the other hand, indicates citizens of the modern state of Israel.

The Hebrew Bible (known to Christians as the Old Testament) is the most informative source on the legendary history of the Ancient Israelites. It describes a stormy relationship between the Israelites and God. The Bible portrays Israelites as a rebellious people, who despite God's kindness, stubbornly continued to worship pagan gods, making God jealous. He sent Jewish prophets time and again to demand his chosen people (the Jews) worship only Him (see Chapter 19). The prophets warned of the perils that await the disobedient, but time and again God was forced to punish the Israelites, by allowing Israel's enemies to conquer her.

Following a number of Jewish patriarchs who led the Israelites through a minefield of obstacles, King David (c. 1000–961 B.C.) established a unified kingdom of Israel. His son, King Solomon, succeeded him and built the first Jewish temple in the City of David (Jerusalem). Solomon's political and economic policies alienated the northern tribes, and after King Solomon's rule ended in 922 B.C., the kingdom split in two: The northern kingdom of Israel had its capital at Samaria, and the southern kingdom of Judah had its capital at Jerusalem.

The language of Semitic peoples

Linguists have determined family relationships between languages. They categorize certain languages into groups due to grammatical or linguistic similarities. The Semitic language family includes

✔ Hebrew

✔ Arabic

✔ Assyrian

✔ Akkadian

✔ Aramaic

✔ Phoenician

✔ Ugaritic (spoken by the Canaanites)

These findings explain the linguistic relationship between the Canaanite god *El,* ancient Israelite god *Elohim,* and the Arab god *Allah.* Because Semitic languages are related, experts maintain that the people who spoke these languages are in some way related. This theory means that the Assyrians were linguistic "cousins" to the ancient Israelites, Canaanites, and Arabs.

Defining the Diaspora

Diaspora refers to the Jews living outside Palestine. A number of factors created the Diaspora, including the Neo-Babylonian destruction of the first temple and the subsequent Jewish captivity in Babylonia in 586 B.C., and the Roman destruction of the second temple in 70 A.D. Jews lived in Europe (Rome and Greece), North Africa, and all over the Middle East.

Although by WWII the largest Jewish population was in Central and Eastern Europe, Jews lived all over the Arab World, even as far away as China and the Americas. After the Holocaust in the 1940s, the state of Israel was formed in Palestine, and Jews of any nationality were encouraged to return to Israel (see Chapter 6). Even today, the majority of Jews live outside of Israel, primarily in North America, Russia, and the Ukraine.

Located on the trade routes between Mesopotamia and Egypt, Jewish kingdoms were naturally in constant dialog with the surrounding civilizations and a rich exchange of ideas flowed in all directions. The Jewish nations were also vulnerable to invasion by their neighbors. In 721 B.C., the Assyrians defeated the northern kingdom of Israel and deported 27,900 Israelites into exile. When Neo-Babylonian King Nebuchadnezzar conquered Israel in 586 B.C., he destroyed the first temple and took thousands more Israelites back to Babylon as slaves. The Iranian armies of Cyrus defeated Babylonia in 538 B.C., and the Persian king allowed the Jews to return to Israel and supported the reconstruction of the second temple, which was completed in 516 B.C.

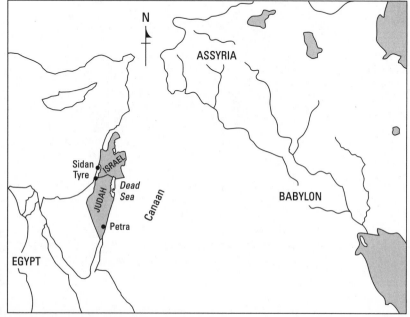

Figure 4-2:
The
Promised
Land.

Petra: The rock city that rocked

Petra is an ancient city beautifully carved into the rocks of Jordan. Just a small portion of it is shown in the photograph in this sidebar. The Edomites, Semite "cousins" of the Canaanites and Israelites, occupied the city. In the Bible, Petra was known as Sela (2 Kings 14:7). Later, an Arab tribe known as the Nabataeans made it their capital from about the fourth century B.C. In the third and second centuries B.C., it became part of the Roman province of Arabia Petraea. The Arabs conquered Petra during their expansion in the seventh century A.D., and in the 12th century, the Crusaders captured it and built a citadel there.

During the Roman occupation, they built a huge amphitheater as only the Romans liked to do throughout the region. Some of the sculpted facades of the buildings, such as the Treasury, are breathtaking. Other locations are ordinary caves that were used as temporary tombs. The wealthy Nabataeans mummified their dead by removing internal organs and pickling the corpse. The poor reused burial caves. After allowing the body to decay in a cave for months, the living boiled bones to remove the flesh, placed the bones in ossuaries, and washed the cave for the next body.

The city was lost to all but a few local Arabs until Johann Burckhardt discovered it in 1812. It now is a major tourist attraction for the Kingdom of Jordan. Even Hollywood got into the action and filmed part of *Indiana Jones and the Last Crusade* in Petra.

Photo courtesy of Mirna Davis

Those revolting Maccabees

The Greeks extended power over the region in the fourth century B.C. A religious family known as the Maccabees led a revolt that succeeded in securing Jewish independence in 142 B.C. Independence was short lived as the Romans established their authority in the region in 63 B.C. Another group of Jewish insurgents revolted against the Roman rule in 66 A.D., and in retaliation, the Romans destroyed the second temple in 70 A.D. As a result, Jews once more fled Palestine. The Romans deported other Jews to Europe — forming the basis for European Jews in the centuries thereafter (see the sidebar "Defining the Diaspora" earlier in this chapter).

Around 30 A.D., another group of Jewish discontents led by Saul (or Paul) splintered off mainstream Judaism and began spreading a religious doctrine of their own throughout the Middle East, Greece, and Rome. The world would never be the same. This Jewish group became known as the Christians (see Chapter 19).

Canaanites

The territory of Canaan consisted of a number of city-states running along the Mediterranean Sea and covering Palestine, Israel, Lebanon, Syria, and Jordan. The Canaanite capital was Ugarit (now called Ras Sharma) in western Syria. In the second millennium B.C., the Canaanites forged an alliance with Egypt to defend against invading neighbors. The civilization reached its zenith in the 15th and 14th centuries B.C. as trade and art flourished. Archaeologists discovered a number of Ugaritic tablets written in cuneiform dating from the 14th century B.C. at Ugarit. This body of literature provided a window into the Canaanite religious culture. The head of the Canaanite pantheon was a deity named El, who unlike traditional gods wasn't a god of the elements. El was awarded many of the epithets later attributed to the God of Judaism, Christianity, and/or Islam, including:

✔ King

✔ Father (of gods)

✔ Kind, the Compassionate

✔ Creator of All

A host of other gods also played a prominent role in Canaanite literature, including Baal who the Hebrew Bible mentions. Anat, Baal's wife and sister, was a violent goddess who wore a necklace of human heads and a belt of human hands, much like the Hindu goddess Kali.

Phoenicians

The Phoenicians were also a Semitic people related to the Canaanites. They were best known for their trading skills, ship building, and navigation. The Phoenicians traded in:

- ✔ Alcohol
- ✔ Olive oil
- ✔ Pottery
- ✔ Silver
- ✔ Slaves

They settled along the coast of Lebanon. They flourished from about the 11th to 8th centuries B.C., establishing trading colonies throughout the Mediterranean. They traded with the Greeks, Egyptians, North Africans, and even reached Cadiz on the Atlantic coast of Spain. Tyre and Sidon in modern Lebanon were two of their main cities.

Egypt (Pharaohs, Gods, and Pyramids)

The Egyptians called their kings pharaohs. These kings had a much different relationship with the gods than the Mesopotamian or Canaanite kings. The Egyptians considered pharaohs as gods incarnate, or at least quasi-gods. Their rule then was uniquely divine, and their administration, architecture, literature, and policies reflected that uniqueness.

Some background on the Three Kingdoms

The long list of 30 dynasties running from 3110 B.C. to 332 B.C. is divided into three periods: Old Kingdom, Middle Kingdom, and New Kingdom, with two intermediate periods worked in for good measure. The intermediate periods were characterized by lack of centralized authority, and local rulers succeeded in snatching up power.

The Old Kingdom: Age of the Pyramids (c. 2700–2200 B.C.)

The capital of the Old Kingdom was Memphis (no Graceland in these parts). The III Dynasty, during the rule of Snefru, experienced a landmark change in Egyptian culture. The elite began sun worship, upper classes started using mummification for the preservation of the dead, and the Egyptians commenced constructing stone monuments. The nobility lost much of its independence while the pharaohs snatched up most of the power and owned all the land. The pyramid building occurred during the IV Dynasty because the pharaohs wanted monumental tombs.

Priests and nobles eventually succeeded in wrestling power from the pharaohs, centralized authority gave way to local rule, and the Old Kingdom fell apart.

Middle Kingdom (c. 2050–1800)

The Middle Kingdom ruled from Thebes (see map of the Middle East). About this time the social structure changed. A huge marsh at El Faiyum was drained, freeing up some 27,000 acres of agricultural land. Lower classes owned the land, and the pharaoh was no longer an absolute monarch, but more of a feudal lord, ruling over these land-owning vassals. The lower classes, as well as the elite, now mummified their dead.

Appreciating the pyramids

The *mastaba* was a prototype of the pyramid. It was a rectangular, flat-roofed tomb with sloping walls. Inside, the *mastaba* chambers were constructed over a mummy pit.

The step pyramid at Saqqara (the left photo) was built about around 2620 B.C. The ziggurats of Mesopotamia and the Mayan pyramids of Mexico and Central America resemble the step pyramid.

The three pyramids of Giza (the right photo), representing the apex of Egyptian architecture, were constructed during the IV Dynasty. The largest, the Great Pyramid of Khufu, or Cheops, is one of the Seven Wonders of the World. It's a mass of solid limestone blocks covering 13 acres, and at one time was more than 750 feet high. It contains several chambers within, including one underground.

Photos courtesy of Cassie Davis and Mirna Davis

New Kingdom (c. 1550–332)

With the dawn of the New Kingdom, radical changes happened. Egyptian dominance was extended to Syria. Thebes became the most magnificent city in the world under the rule of Amenhotep III (ruled c. 1388–1351). The old power struggles between the king and the priests resurfaced. In an effort to offset the priestly authority, Akhenaten (ruled c. 1351–1334) changed the state religion to one of monotheism, declaring that Aten (sun disc) was the only true god. He built a number of temples to Aten. This innovation was as controversial as it was short lived. Akhenaten's successor, King Tutankhamen, reversed those religious policies, reverted the kingdom to its official pantheon of gods, and moved the capital back to Memphis.

Egyptian religion

Like all the other major civilizations of the ancient Middle East, religion in Egypt wasn't a static monolithic component of society, but rather a reflection of the changing and complex fabric of society. The elite's religion wasn't necessarily that of the common people. For most of the dynastic periods, the upper classes worshipped a national pantheon of gods, including:

✔ Amon, chief god of Thebes; ram or ram-headed god; associated with Ra

✔ Aten, sun disc

✔ Horus, sky god; son of Osiris; falcon-headed god

✔ Isis, nature goddess; wife and sister of Osiris

✔ Osiris, god of the underworld; judge of the dead; identified with moon and sun

✔ Ra, sun god; hawk or lion; associated with Amon

The Scorpion King

Thousands of years before Hollywood and The Rock collaborated on the motion picture, a true, live King Scorpion ruled in Egypt. This pharaoh lived around 3250 B.C. and succeeded in raising order out of the chaos created by the lawless Egyptian tribes marauding the desert. He may even have unified Upper and Lower Egypt into one empire. Art and inscriptions depict a victorious king with a scorpion mace head, the falcon symbol of Horus over a scorpion, a bird swallowing its enemy, and on one occasion the King Scorpion gripping a rope around the neck of an enemy king, demonstrating King Scorpion's supremacy. The hieroglyphics of this period may be the earliest known form of writing, predating even that of the Sumerians.

The Egyptians blurred the line between pharaoh and god. They believed some pharaohs were gods while living, and they deified and worshiped other pharaohs after death. Likewise, they believed Ra was the ancestor of the pharaohs or even a deceased king. When Akhenaten established his new monotheistic religion of Aten, he also appointed himself the high priest and claimed to be the deity's son on earth.

Burial practices reveal a great deal about religious beliefs in every culture. The ancient Egyptians were infatuated with the dead. Most Egyptians believed that the preservation of the body was essential for the soul to continue in the afterlife. For this reason, Egyptians mummified the earthly bodies of kings and nobility and carefully preserved them in sarcophagi, tombs, caves, and/or pyramids.

Write like an Egyptian

The Egyptians developed their own writing style called hieroglyphics written from top to bottom or horizontal on tablets, pots, and papyrus made of reeds. Modern scholars couldn't decipher the code until the Rosetta stone was discovered. The priests of Ptolemy V in the second century B.C. had written in hieroglyphics, demotic (a phonetic script), and Greek on the Rosetta stone. Napoleon's army discovered the stone during its invasion of Egypt in 1799 (see Chapter 6). By matching demotic for sound and Greek for meaning, scholars were able to "break the code."

Foreign affairs: Cleopatra and her men

Have you ever had a neighbor that just wouldn't leave? Egypt has. During the final years of the New Kingdom, Egypt fell prey to a series of invasions from its neighbors. The Assyrians invaded in the eighth century B.C. and were ousted only with the help of Greek mercenaries. Then came the Iranians. Cambyses conquered Egypt in 525 B.C. and became a pharaoh of the 27th dynasty. But Alexander the Great's invasion in 332 B.C. ended a string of 30 Egyptian dynasties that spanned nearly 3,000 years. When Alexander died some nine years later, one of his generals, Ptolemy, filled the void. Cleopatra was Ptolemy's descendent.

At the age of 17, Cleopatra married her younger brother, as was the custom. She became queen of Egypt in 52 B.C. when her brother and father died. She married an even younger brother, and when it didn't work out, she sought the aid of Rome to help her out of the marriage. Her newest lover, Julius Caesar, helped her dislodge her brother-husband, and she bore the Roman a child.

After Julius Caesar was killed, Marc Antony fell helplessly in love with Cleopatra, and the two married. Roman Emperor Octavian defeated the couple in Egypt, and the two lovers committed suicide.

Iran

Iran is located on a vast plateau nestled between the Elburz Mountains in the north, the Zagros Mountains in the west, and the low ranges of Pakistan and Afghanistan in the east (see Figure 4-3). A group of seminomadic settlers arrived there about 1500 B.C. and changed the history, language, and religion of the Middle East forever. They were called the Persians. In order to understand how these changes took shape though, you need to become familiar with the earlier civilizations.

Elamites

Susa was the most important Elamite city-state (and the capital of Elam) in the region from about 3000 B.C. Like other surrounding societies, the Elamites were heavily influenced by their Mesopotamian neighbors. Their ability to wage war often led them into conflict with the Babylonians.

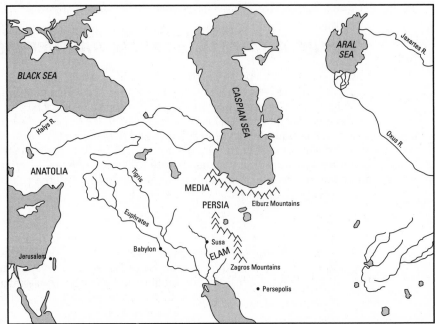

Figure 4-3:
Persia.

In the second millennium B.C., the Elamites captured and controlled parts of Babylonia. They carried off the Hammurabi Code (and in the 20th century, the French returned the favor by carrying it off to Paris and placing it in a museum, where it remains today). Between the 13th and 12th centuries B.C., Elamite culture truly flourished making great accomplishments in art, architecture, and literature. They even built a ziggurat at their religious center at Tchoga-Zanbil. In 646 B.C., the Assyrian king Assurbanipal destroyed Susa. Although the Elamites used cuneiform to write, their language wasn't related to Semitic or Sumerian. Elamite as a language was similar to the Dravidian languages now spoken in South India.

Medes

The Medes began to rise out of the shadow of the Elamites in the eighth century B.C. They ruled from Media in western Iran and spoke a new type of language in the Middle East from the Indo-European language family (see the sidebar, "Indo-Europeans move in," in this chapter), although archeologists haven't discovered any existing written records.

Indo-Europeans move in

The Indo-European language family entered the neighborhood of the ancient Middle East relatively late — around 1500 B.C. This language group earned its name about 3,200 years later when a British scholar named Sir William Jones discovered the link between some Indian languages and European languages while studying Sanskrit in India in the late 1700s.

This discovery revolutionized not only linguistics, but also the fields of history, anthropology, and others. If Latin and Greek were related to Sanskrit, then somewhere in the ancient past, Europeans and Indians must have been "cousins" as well.

By developing a family tree of languages, linguists theorized that at one time, a parent language (long since deceased) had existed. They hypothesized that long ago Indo-Europeans, or Aryan, tribes lived in a homeland north of the Caucus. Over the course of centuries, waves of migrations brought some of these tribes into Europe while others settled in Central Asia, Pakistan, north India, and the Iranian plateau about 1500 B.C.

These new kids on the block called themselves Aryan, from which the term "Iran" comes.

Not all the languages of India and Iran are Indo-European, but the following are:

✔ Hindi

✔ Urdu

✔ Persian/Farsi/Dari

✔ Pashtu

Modern European languages belonging to this family are the following:

✔ English

✔ French

✔ German

✔ Spanish

Incidentally, the Indo-European family is still popular. More than half of the world speaks one of its languages.

In 705 B.C., the Medes extended their rule over Elam (later called Persia) and defeated the Assyrians by seizing Nineveh in 612 B.C. As was customary, they hauled much of the Assyrian population back to Media into slavery. Around 550 B.C., the Persian king Cyrus overthrew the Medes and established the Achaemenian Empire.

The Achaemenids

Among the Iranian tribes that migrated from Central Asia westward were the Medes and the Persians. The Persians moved into Elam and took over. They renamed Elam Persia and introduced their language, Old Persian, from which the modern language of Iran called Persian derives. The Persians then served the Medes to establish dominance in the region.

About 550 B.C., a Persian leader named Cyrus II, whose mother was a Median princess, revolted against the Median king (his grandfather) and took control of the kingdom. When he defeated the Neo-Babylonians in 538 B.C., he allowed the Jews to return and reconstruct the second temple (see the section, "Ancient Israelites" in this chapter). He expanded his empire in all directions: northwest to Anatolia (Turkey), west to Egypt, and east to Sind (Pakistan). Later Achaemenian monarchs, such as Darius I and Xerxes, both well-known for having fought the Greeks, established Zoroastrianism as the official religion that would become the dominant religion in the Middle East until the Arab invasion in the seventh century A.D. (see Chapter 20).

Darius also claimed to be ruling on god's behalf and attributed his successes to god. In this sense, the Iranian kings continued the Akkadian, Babylonian, and Assyrian practice of kicking butt and taking names.

Kicking butt and taking names: The Iranian shahs

The Iranian shahs, or kings, liked to boast about their conquests. In order to rise to power and stay in power, they normally had to squash a number of rebellions. They often commissioned royal rock inscriptions to chronicle their military exploits. The most notable example is the rock relief at Bisutun in western Iran that depicts a long line of rebels with ropes around their necks whom King Darius I (d. 486 B.C.) defeated. The inscription describes Darius's victories over his enemies, one after the other. A few of the hundreds of lines read

- I slew Gaumata.
- I had Acina led to me in chains; then I killed him.
- There I slaughtered the army of Nidintu-Bel with a vengeance.
- Then I executed Nidintu-Bel at Babylon.

Satraps: Iranian governors

Initially the Achaemenids utilized the Assyrian administrative structure already in place. Darius I centralized imperial rule and gave provincial authority to governors called *satrap*s. The shah maintained his authority by offsetting the governor's power with that of a loyal military commander posted at each *satrapy* to ensure obedience and an uninterrupted flow of revenue to the shah.

Alexander the Great

In 336 B.C., Alexander of Macedonia came to power at the age of 19. After establishing rule in Macedonia, he proceeded with his Greek army to conquer much of the Middle East, including:

- ✔ Egypt, where he founded the city of Alexandria
- ✔ Iran, all the way to Afghanistan, Pakistan, and North India
- ✔ Palestine, Syria, and Mesopotamia

After he conquered Iran, Alexander was depicted as a mighty monarch. In Egypt, he became a pharaoh — divinity included.

Legal procedure for stayin' alive

The ancient Middle East didn't have elections. Most kings were in power not because of their popularity but because they were masters of diplomacy, politics, and military prowess. The main goal of a monarch was to stay in power. In order to do so, a ruler relied on revenue: taxes, tribute, and booty. Therefore, to get power and hang onto power, a ruler followed a set of ground rules for stayin' alive, including:

- ✔ Appease potential opponents — with property, revenue, or positions of power

- ✔ Eliminate competition — even if it meant fratricide, patricide, and incest

- ✔ Establish legitimacy — religious and/or dynastic; legitimacy came from the gods or from royal bloodlines

- ✔ Squash rebellions — show who's the boss

- ✔ Use existing administration — make modifications only when needed

The Iranian shahs followed these ground rules. When Darius came to power, he eliminated potential male contenders and married his sisters so that others couldn't stake a claim to the throne by marrying a princess. He established religious legitimacy as a worshipper of Ahura Mazda, the Zoroastrian god (see Chapter 20 for more on Zoroastrians), squashed rebellions throughout the empire, and executed his opponents. He also modified the established administrative structure into an efficient system of governance.

When he died at the age of 33, two of his Greek generals divvied up the spoils. Ptolemy took the western half that included Egypt, Palestine, and Syria, and Seleucid took the eastern half that included Mesopotamia and Iran.

The Parthians

About 250 B.C. the Parthians established rule in eastern Persia and eventually captured the rest of Seleucid's territory. Their empire stretched from the Euphrates to the Indus River (Pakistan). The Parthians are most famous for the "Parthian shot," which refers to the technique of turning and shooting an arrow while riding backwards on a horse. They constantly fought the Romans. In 224 A.D., the Sasanians defeated the Parthians.

The Sasanians

The Sasanians reestablished Zoroastrianism as the official religion when they rose to power in 224 A.D. At its height, this massive empire spanned the Iranian Plateau, reaching Syria and Armenia in the north, Mesopotamia and Palestine in the west, Pakistan and Afghanistan in the east, and the Persian Gulf to the south. For centuries they carried on a love-hate relationship with the other major power in the region, the Byzantine Empire (see "The Byzantines" section later in this chapter). The Sasanians were patrons of the arts, literature, and architecture.

Anatolia (Turkey)

Anatolia is the ancient name for Asia Minor, or Turkey. Three bodies of water — the Mediterranean Sea on the southwest, Aegean Sea on the west, and the Black Sea on the north — surround this great peninsula. Historically, its geographical location linking the Middle East with Europe via Greece in the north has made Anatolia a natural catalyst for cultural, political, military, and commercial interaction.

The Hittites

About the time the Assyrians and the Babylonians were flexing their military muscle in Mesopotamia, a loose confederation of Indo-European tribes called the Hittites came to power on the Anatolian Plateau. By 1800 B.C., they had already made their presence felt by entering Cappadocia. They were a constant nuisance to their neighbors in the Middle East. They invaded the Assyrians, Babylonians, Ancient Israelites, and Phoenicians. Between 1300 and 1200 B.C., they waged war against the Egyptians, who considered them barbarians. The Assyrians finally defeated them around 700 B.C. The Medes also expanded into Anatolia, which was then held by the Achaemenians until Alexander's conquest.

The Byzantines

When the Roman Empire collapsed, power sort of fell into the hands of the Byzantines, who continued to rule the eastern part of the empire, centered in Byzantium (Istanbul). Also known as the Eastern Roman Empire, the Byzantine Empire spanned southeast Europe across Anatolia to North Africa and the border of Persia. Originally a pagan nation, the Byzantines eventually converted to Christianity, following the lead of Emperor Constantine, who changed the name of Byzantium to Constantinople in 330 A.D. For centuries they came into constant conflict with the Persian Empire. The two superpowers fought wars, conquered and lost territory, undertook rich cultural exchange, and maintained trading partners. The Byzantine Empire ruled until the Ottomans defeated them in 1453 A.D.

Five women worth remembering

History is a gender-biased process. Because primarily men were literate and men did most of the conquering, ruling, pillaging, and destroying, male historians spent most of their time writing about the exploits of men, often at the expense of women. Nonetheless, in every time period, history has left some vestiges of women worth remembering. Note these five women who played important roles in the ancient Middle East:

✔ **Cleopatra**: the Egyptian queen (d. 30 B.C.) of Greek descent through Ptolemy, who was probably no more promiscuous than the average king, but nonetheless has earned a place in history because of her soap opera-type exploits with the men in her life, who just happened to be her brothers and famous Roman commanders.

✔ **Esther**: the legendary orphan Jewish concubine of Iranian Shah Artaxerxes I (died circa. 358 B.C.) saves the Jews from certain massacre at the hands of the evil courtier Haman and earns her place as queen.

Although the account is fictional, her name appears in the Bible more often than any other woman. The Purim Festival celebrates Esther's bravery.

✔ **Nefertiti**: the queen (d. c.1350 B.C.) of Pharaoh Akhenaten and aunt of Tutankhamen. She played a central role in the new religion. Contemporary artwork of the queen is in uncharacteristic abundance for the wife of a pharaoh.

✔ **Tomyris**: the violent Central Asian queen (sixth century B.C.) of the Massagetae, the Scythian tribe that killed Persian king Cyrus I. When she found Cyrus's body after battle, she severed his head to avenge her son's death.

✔ **Theodora**: an actress and prostitute before marrying Byzantine Emperor Justinian I and becoming Empress (d. 548 B.C.). As a strong-willed coruler, she saved the throne during the Nika revolt.

Chapter 5

The Medieval Middle East

*A*nytime you hear *medieval,* you probably think of damsels in distress, armored knights on horseback jousting one another or sitting at round tables gobbling up wild fowl, kings defending their castles against invading armies, feudal lords shaking down hard-working peasants, evil priests leading inquisitions, or dark periods of lawlessness when barbarian tribes marauded innocent townspeople. Although these images you conjure up are European, the Middle East had its own version of the Middle Ages that was just as romantic, exotic, and fascinating.

The Middle Ages in the Middle East was a period of kings, palaces, and harems. It was a time when armies fought holy wars, pillaged, and raped. It was an era of piety and morality and honor, as Islam arose in the desert and spread into three continents seemingly over night. The Medieval period saw sweeping political, military, and linguistic changes. The "barbarian" Mongols terrorized the entire region and left destruction, rubble, and mounds of skulls as calling cards. This era also was a period of literary renaissance, artistic inspiration, and a rich cultural, commercial, and intellectual exchange. New religious movements vied for power and rose to prominence, or were stamped out as heresies. The Silk Road, linking China and India in the east to Europe in the west, operated along a network of caravan routes through the Middle East.

In this book, the Medieval period, or Middle Ages, in the Middle East begins with the advent of Islam in the sixth and seventh centuries and ends just before the period of modernization around the 17th and 18th centuries. Because this period is all A.D. (anno Domini, meaning in the year of the Lord), I don't include this distracting two-letter acronym after each date. So 1258 means 1258 A.D. unless otherwise specified. A map of the Medieval Middle East is shown in Figure 5-1.

Figure 5-1:
The
Medieval
Middle East.

Islam's Birth and Adolescence

Imagine Islam's birth almost like a script written in Hollywood. While the most sophisticated and cultured civilizations in the Near East were located in Egypt, Iran, and Byzantium, an illiterate orphan of humble origin arose out of the wilderness as a desert prophet, propagating a new religion that would change the world forever.

In the late sixth century, Mecca was a backwater city. Located on the Arabian Peninsula, Mecca was a key trading center on an important caravan route, an oasis in the middle of the desert, and an important spiritual site for pagan pilgrims. The Meccans had no architecture, written literature, or royal heritage worth mentioning. Socially they were organized into a confederation of desert tribes. In 570, Muhammad was born into the Hashim clan of the ruling Quraysh tribe in Mecca. When his parents died early, he went to live with his cousin Ali where his uncle, Ali's father, raised him.

Undergoing a sort of spiritual crisis at the age of 40, Muhammad was on retreat in a cave at Mt. Hira outside Mecca in search of enlightenment when the Angel Gabriel appeared and whispered revelation from Allah (God) in Muhammad's ear. The Prophet returned to Mecca and began reciting this revelation, known as the Quran. He quickly converted his wife, cousin Ali, and closest friends to Islam, which means *submission* (to Allah). As the religion continued to spread, Muslims didn't see it as a new faith but merely a continuation of the religion of Abraham, the last of the Abrahamic religions after Judaism and Christianity (see Chapter 19).

Hailing (or murdering) the Rightly Guided Caliphs

In 632, Muhammad died without naming a successor. While his cousin and son-in-law Ali was making funeral arrangements, a council of the Prophet's companions convened without him and named the Prophet's closest friend and father-in-law Abu Bakr *caliph,* or successor. The caliph was the spiritual and political leader of the *umma,* or the Muslim community. After Abu Bakr, came Umar, another companion of the Prophet. After a Persian slave murdered Umar in 644, a third of the Prophet's companions named Uthman became caliph. Ali finally had his chance to succeed the Prophet as the fourth caliph after Uthman's execution in 656. Sunni Muslims look back nostalgically upon these four companions of the Prophet who led the *umma* and call them the *Rightly Guided Caliphs.*

Islam: The last Abrahamic religion

Muslims don't see Islam as a new religion at all. Rather, they consider it as the third and final Abrahamic religion, and believe Muhammad was the *seal* of a long list of Judeo-Christian (Muslim from their point of view) prophets, including Abraham, Moses, and Jesus. Like Judaism and Christianity, Islam is a monotheistic religion. The *shahada*, the Muslim creed, declares that "There is no god but God" and is routinely followed by a second creed setting Islam off from the earlier two religions: "and Muhammad was his messenger." The shahada is considered the first pillar of Islam, followed by four more: prayer, alms, fasting, and the pilgrimage (see Chapter 19).

Notice the splintering that took place within the early caliphate among Ali and the other caliphs. As with all struggles for succession, hard feelings between winners and losers affected not only the individuals immediately involved, but also family members and followers who were caught up in the conflict, even later generations. A series of power struggles ensued, and as you may imagine, the descendants and followers of Ali — later known as Shiites (or Shia) — weren't pleased with the way developments were taking shape. Future events later drove a wedge between these two factions, the Shiites, and the followers of the other three caliphs, the Sunnis (see Chapter 19 for more on Islam).

Ali moved the capital from Medina in Arabia to Kufa, a garrison city in Mesopotamia, where he had more political and military support. Muawiya, a nephew of Uthman and governor of Damascus, contested Ali's authority but couldn't unseat the caliph. In 661, Ali, the last of the four Rightly Guided Caliphs, was murdered by a splinter group of Muslims.

Beginning the Arab conquests

Amid the internal turmoil, the Arab tribes managed to forge a unified military force to be reckoned with. They first consolidated power on the Arabian Peninsula and then set their sights on the rest of the Middle East. In 637, when they pressed the frontier of the Sasanian Empire, the Iranian army was defeated. The Arabs then seized the capital of Ctesiphon (now Baghdad), and Emperor Yazdagird fled eastward. At every stop, the invading tribes seemed to meet with success. Syria, Palestine, Iran, Egypt, and Tripoli (Libya) all fell to the Arabs during the reign of the Rightly Guided Caliphs.

A new caliph in town: The Umayyads

Muawiya was only too happy to step into the power void left by Ali's death and to establish the Umayyad caliphate at Damascus, Syria. Although Sunni Muslims recognized the legitimacy of the Umayyads, the new caliphs didn't hold the same religious authority as did the first four, who as companions of the Prophet, were all endowed with special spiritual insight, an almost infallibility in religious matters.

The Umayyad rulers continued expanding their power (see Figure 5-2) so that within about 100 years of Muhammad's death, the Arabs had conquered territory from Spain and Morocco in the west to the frontiers of India and Central Asia in the east. Not since Alexander the Great had the Middle East seen such a wave of invaders (see Chapter 4 for more on Alexander the Great).

Like rulers before them, the Arabs didn't reinvent the wheel or discover fire. They merely utilized the existing administrative mechanisms that were already in place for ruling, collecting taxes, and running the empire.

Yazid and the slaughter of Husayn at Karbala

After Muawiya's death in 680, his son Yazid came to power. A number of disgruntled Muslims residing in Kufa petitioned Ali's son Husayn at Medina in Arabia to join them and assume leadership. Yazid's army intercepted Husayn's party of 50 armed men and a number of women and children at Karbala in Iraq. Outnumbering Husayn's tiny band many times over, Yazid's soldiers surrounded their opponents, denying them access to water. After eight days under the scorching Iraqi sun, thirst brought Husayn's people to the brink of death. As a last resort, his men rushed for the water but were brutally slaughtered. The soldiers took the women and children into captivity and delivered them, along with Husayn's decapitated head, to Yazid.

The slaughter at Karbala is still an open wound between Sunnis and Shiites. Even today during the annual Muharram celebration commemorating this tragedy, in places like Pakistan, bloody violence often breaks out between Sunnis and Shiites. The followers of Ali and Husayn became known as Shiites. They established a separate religious identity from mainstream Muslims, or Sunnis. Shiites didn't recognize the authority of the Sunni caliphs, and instead followed a series of spiritual leaders, called imams. Throughout the Medieval period, Shiites continued to pose a constant threat to Sunni political leadership. (See Chapter 19 for more information.)

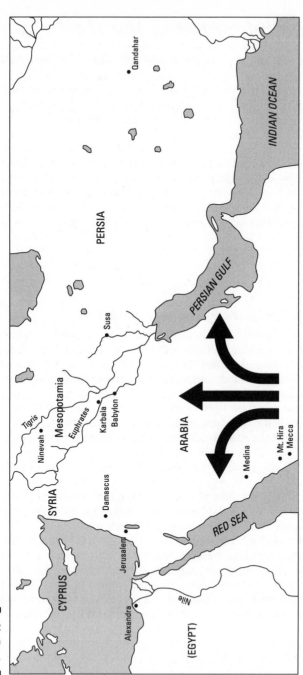

Figure 5-2:
The Arab
expansion.

Not happy with Arab superiority

The old notion that the Arabs spread Islam with the sword is a fallacy. On the contrary, the Umayyads actually discouraged conversion for several reasons:

- ✔ Quranic injunction: there is no compulsion in religion (Quran: 2:256).
- ✔ Muslims considered being Muslim an honor, not just for anyone.
- ✔ Taxes yielded higher revenue on non-Muslims.

Not only were Shiites dissatisfied with Umayyad rule, but non-Arab Muslims and non-Muslims were becoming increasingly disillusioned as well. The perception that their Arab rulers were arrogant only added to a growing discontent among the conquered masses. The Umayyads treated the non-Arab Muslims as second-class citizens. Besides paying higher taxes, some non-Muslim subjects faced even stiffer penalties for conversion to Islam.

Introducing the Abbasids

Led by a Persian convert named Abu Muslim, revolutionary forces from Khurasan in eastern Iran defeated the Umayyads in 750. Caliph Marwan II fled to Egypt, where he was later executed. Other Umayyads made it north to Africa and ruled there with Berber help. The new Abbasid rulers were no longer strictly Arab although Arabic remained the official language of the court. The caliphate was now more egalitarian: Arab and non-Arab Muslims theoretically now enjoyed equal stature. As was customary, the new caliphs utilized the existing administrative structure, and their system of rule resembled that of the Sasanian shahs (see Chapter 4 for more on the Sasanians).

The Abbasids moved the capital to Baghdad, which under Caliph Harun al-Rashid (786–809) became a great cosmopolitan center of high arts, sciences, and learning. While the heart of the Abbasid caliphate functioned in Arabic, the population of the Iranian Plateau continued speaking Persian. By the tenth century, a literary renaissance blossomed in eastern Iran. The Persian language mixed with Arabic words was written in the Arabic script and became the medium of expression. Khurasan and Bukhara (now in Uzbekistan) were religious and cultural centers in their own right.

The Abbasid political grip already started to weaken by the end of Harun's reign and the *amir*s (governors) often became semi-independent rulers with armies and administrative systems of their own. They represented the Abbasid caliph, ostensibly collecting taxes and forwarding revenue to Baghdad. Many petty amirs decided that keeping the taxes was a more lucrative strategy, so they established semi-independent sultanates of their own.

Mixing religion with politics: Just the right amount

Conversion to Islam in Iran came slow. The urban centers generally converted more rapidly than the rural areas, often over a period of centuries. A number of reasons contributed to the decision to convert:

- ✔ **Forced conversion:** rare, but it happened. On occasion a conquering army moved into a city and demanded that the ruler, noble families, and/or the population convert and pay tribute to the caliphate. After the army marched out, entire kingdoms sometimes reneged on both.

- ✔ **Rewards and incentives:** Laws and practices sometimes encouraged conversion to Islam by promising, for example, all a sibling's property to the convert. Other monetary, commercial, or political rewards and incentives persuaded others to convert.

- ✔ **Simplicity:** Compared to complex Zoroastrian purification rituals, for instance, Islam's simplicity was a positive factor for conversion.

- ✔ **Spiritual sincerity:** Converts were attracted to Islam's morality and spirituality.

- ✔ **Tax break:** Muslims paid lower taxes.

The Shiite followers of Ali and Husayn continued their dissatisfaction with the Abbasid caliphate's political and religious policies. Shiite uprisings posed a constant threat to the Sunni caliphate. One Shiite family known as the Buyids actually succeeded in seizing control of the caliphate from 945 to 1055, using the Abbasid caliph as a puppet ruler. When the Buyid Empire collapsed, the Abbasid caliph remained in power, although the position never matched the political control of the early caliphs.

Moving to the Fatamids and the Mamluks

Although the Abbasids hung on in the east, another group of Shiites came to power in the west. The Fatamids thrust aside traditional gender biases for the sake of establishing religious legitimacy by claiming descent from Fatima, the daughter of the Prophet and wife of Ali.

After escaping from prison in Tripoli in 909, Said bin Husayn established the Fatamid dynasty in Tunisia. He changed his name to Ubaidullah and set himself up as caliph of a Shiite caliphate. By 969, the Fatamids controlled Egypt and most of North Africa, making Cairo their capital, and expanding into Syria and Iraq. Ironically, the Shiite Buyids protected the Sunni Abbasid caliph against the Shiite Fatamid intruders.

Assassins: Medieval terrorists

In the late 11th century, one particularly dangerous sect of Shiites developed into a secret order known in the west as the Assassins. The Assassins obediently followed their own Shiite caliph, Nizar ibn al-Mustansir, and operated out of strongholds in the mountains near the Caspian Sea, conducting stealthy suicide missions to assassinate political and religious opponents. Like medieval terrorists hoping to achieve martyrdom, the assassins spread fear and panic across Iran, Mesopotamia, and the Levant until the arrival of the Mongols. In 1256, the Mongols destroyed the Persian order, and the Mamluks wiped out the Syrian order in 1272.

Tales of the assassins made their way to Europe from returning Crusaders and from the writings of Marco Polo, who passed through the region in 1271 and 1272. The European word *assassin* actually originates from a corruption of the Arabic word *hashishun,* which means *hashish user,* although stories of such use are unfounded. And because they killed Seljuk notables publicly, the term was applied to the manner of killing — hence assassination.

The 5th Fatamid caliph named Aziz employed foreign mercenaries from Sudan, Anatolia, and North Africa to sustain military dominance in the region. In 996, the 6th caliph, Hakim, undertook a path of religious intolerance — relatively rare among Muslim rulers — by persecuting Jews and Christians, and destroying synagogues and churches, including the Church of the Holy Sepulcher in Jerusalem. Hakim also claimed to be a reincarnation of God but was assassinated in 1021. The Druze of Lebanon and Syria are descendants of the original followers of Hakim (refer to Chapter 20 for more on The Druze).

Political and military infighting among the foreign mercenaries took its toll on the Fatamids. With the dynasty in decline, the famous Muslim hero Saladin assumed power in Damascus, Cairo, and Palestine in the late 12th century, when he held off a wave of Christian crusades. This Sunni commander became the sultan of Egypt and deposed the Fatamids.

After Saladin's death in 1193, Salih became sultan. He augmented his troops with increased numbers of Kurdish slave warriors, called Mamluks (see the sidebar, "Slave warriors: A different type of slave," in this chapter). Upon Sultan Salih's death, his Turkish concubine, Shajarat al-Durr, forged an alliance with the Mamluk generals and became the first and only *sultana* (female sultan). Shajarat later gave in to the social pressure arising from her unmarried status as a female ruler and married Aybek, who became the first Mamluk sultan.

The Mamluks suffered from internal turmoil but managed to defeat the following external foes:

✔ Christian Crusaders (see the section, "A Series of Crusades: Business as Usual, " later in this chapter)

✔ Assassins in 1272 (see the sidebar, "Assassins: Medieval terrorists" earlier in this chapter)

✔ Mongols in Syria

In 1517, the Ottomans (but not the Couches or Sofas) seized Cairo and defeated the Mamluks with superior artillery and with the help of the Janissaries, the Turkish version of slave warriors. (For more on the Ottomans, see "Unifying and Conquering: The Ottomans" later in this chapter.)

Making their mark: Seljuks strike Iran

About the time that the Shiite Fatamids were gaining steam in Egypt and North Africa, a Sunni whirlwind in the form of seminomadic people called Seljuks was sweeping over Iran. The Seljuks were Turks who invaded eastern Iran at the beginning of the 11th century and seized Baghdad in 1055 when their leader, Tughril Beg, proclaimed himself sultan. They conquered Syria and much of Christian Anatolia by defeating Byzantine Emperor Romanus IV at Manzikert. Although Constantinople didn't fall to the Seljuks at this time, Byzantine Emperor Alexius I appealed to his Christian counterparts in Europe for help against the invading Muslims in the 11th century.

Although originally Turkish-speaking people, the Seljuks became entirely Persianized. Like other Persian shahs, the Seljuks patronized art and literature. The famous Seljuk *vizier,* or minister, Nizam al-Mulk wrote a code of conduct for sultans called Mirror of Princes (see Chapter 22). He also established 300 *madrasa*s, or theological schools, that propagated Sunni ideology (see Chapter 8). In 1092, Shiite Assassins killed him.

Under attack from other Turkic forces, the Seljuk Empire fell in 1157, and the fragmented state of rule in Iran made an easy target for the Mongols who sacked Baghdad in 1258.

A Series of Crusades: Business as Usual

The Christian Crusades were a series of holy wars undertaken by European Christians to liberate the Holy Land from the grasp of the Muslims between the 11th and 13th centuries. You may be disappointed to discover that these crusades that played such an important role in European history weren't such a big deal in Muslim history for a number of reasons.

Slave warriors: A different type of slave

Slave warriors in an Islamic context often became elites and rulers themselves. Two examples are the Janissaries of Turkey and the Mamluks of Egypt. Muslims captured young non-Muslim boys at an early age, educated and converted them to Islam, and trained them to be warriors with their only allegiance to their owners. The slaves were then dispatched or sold off to Muslim rulers who relied on loyal warriors to defend their interests. Loyal service was highly rewarded with property, wealth, status, and power.

As you may suspect, wealthy, powerful slave officers, wielding long swords and commanding legions of loyal soldiers, discovered they really didn't need their owners and established varying degrees of independence. The Mamluks formed their own dynastic rule in Syrian and Egypt for two and a half centuries. In Turkey, the Janissaries became so independent and unruly, that Sultan Mahmud II ruthlessly massacred them.

- ✔ **Old hat.** People in the Middle East were accustomed to foreign invasions. So what were a few more invasions?

- ✔ **No major threat.** The Crusades weren't a united, focused effort, but rather a loosely knit series of nine unorganized, fleeting campaigns, spanning about 175 years.

- ✔ **Fizzled out.** The Crusades didn't leave their mark. They didn't last long, only about two to six years each, and the ground they gained was soon lost.

- ✔ **A no show.** During the 4th Crusade, the Crusaders never even made it to the Holy Land. They got distracted and ended up sacking Christian Constantinople in 1204 instead.

- ✔ **Slippery and ever-changing alliances.** Byzantine Emperor Isaac II, for instance, formed an alliance with Saladin during the 3rd Crusade.

- ✔ **Bigger fish to fry.** Compared with the Mongol hordes in the east, gobbling up land like locusts, the crusaders were minor nuisances.

The Fatamid caliph Hakim had persecuted Christians and destroyed the Church of the Holy Sepulcher. The Seljuks had seized much of the Byzantine territory, and the Byzantine emperor was screaming for help from Christian Europe.

Partly for these reasons, and partly for the promise of spoils, adventure, and a sense of religious duty, the European Crusaders took up the cross and set out to save the Holy Land from Muslims intruders. The nine crusades ran intermittently from 1095 to 1272.

Uninvited Guests: The Mongols

Uninvited guests are always a problem. When these "guests" are riding ponies, destroying cities, and building mounds of enemy skulls along the way, the hosts feel even less hospitable. In this case, the Middle Eastern inhabitants were the hosts, and the uninvited guests were the Mongols.

The Mongols were a seminomadic people originating from the region of modern day Mongolia. Chingiz (pronounced *ch,* not *g*) Khan established an empire that moved west, wreaking havoc on everything in its path with a vengeance, literally. As a deterrent to armed resistance, the Mongols brutally slaughtered inhabitants of cities that failed to submit. As the word of such massacres spread, the strategy apparently worked because entire populations submitted to the Mongol invaders.

With each victory, the Mongols assimilated the vanquished peoples into their military machine. In 1256, they sought vengeance against the Assassins whom they had encountered some 34 years earlier. In 1258, the Mongols sacked Baghdad and killed the caliph. Led by Sultan Baybars, the Mamluks stopped the Mongol onslaught in Syria in 1260. At the height of their power, the Mongols ruled from Mongolia and China in the east to Moscow and past Kiev in the northwest, and to the Persian Gulf and the Mediterranean in the west and southwest, as shown in Figure 5-3.

Never underestimate the economics of war

Just like the ABBA song, "Money, money, money!," everyone likes money. Governments, kingdoms, sultanates, even armies operate on revenue. So as a ground rule, you must never underestimate the value of economics to any political, military, or religious policy. The Mongols were no exception.

Early on, the Mongols secured the strategic Jungar Gate in Central Asia that led to China's treasures. They then established a mechanism of protection for the Central Asian leg of the Silk Route in order to maintain a constant flow of caravans, which meant revenue for whomever lent such protection. It was a simple business arrangement. A single event referred to as the Otrar Incident, stirred up the hornet's nest, by upsetting the business arrangement.

A local Central Asian ruler, named Khwarazmshah, plundered a caravan and slaughtered its Muslim traders and their Mongol protectors in 1218. An enraged Chingis Khan sent Mongol ambassadors demanding blood money, to which Khwarazmshah responded by killing the ambassadors.

The Mongols retaliated by sending waves of troops after their enemy. They laid waste to resistant populations and chased their fleeing enemy from Central Asia through eastern Iran and northern India, and into the Caspian region, where they first encountered the Assassins. When the campaign was over in 1225, Chingiz left Central Asia in the hands of his son Chaghatai and returned to Mongolia.

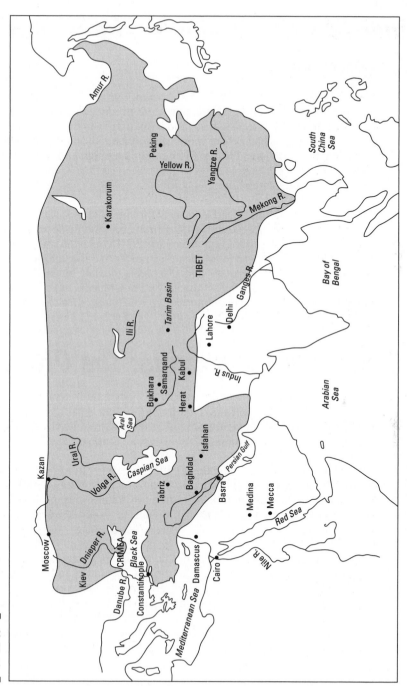

Figure 5-3:
The Mongol
conquest.

Succeeding the Mongols: The Ilkhanids and Timurids

For the next 75 years, the Mongol successors on the Iranian Plateau, the Ilkhanids, sought to undo the damage their predecessors had done. Mahmud Ghazan rebuilt cities, agriculture, and irrigation systems, and reestablished trade. Unlike the Arabs before them, the Mongols didn't make lasting linguistic or religious changes. Rather, the Persian language and Middle Eastern culture absorbed the Mongols even as they converted to Islam. The Ilkhanids used the existing Seljuk administration.

Quickly the dynasty dissolved into small provincial states. Another descendant of the Mongols, Timur, seized the opportunity to unite these states into an empire in 1370. From his capital at Samarkand (Uzbekistan), he succeeded in conquering Iran, northern India, Anatolia, northern Syria, and parts of Russia. He had a reputation for cruelty, and although a Muslim, he used Islam as a weapon to subdue his enemies, Muslim and non-Muslim alike. He died in 1405, but his Timurid descendents continued to rule parts of Iran for the next century.

Unifying and Conquering: The Ottomans

Long after the power of Seljuks dissolved in Iran, their seminomadic Turkish "cousins" in Anatolia continued jostling for power until 1280 when they finally unified under the leadership of Osman, a great warrior prince who was kind enough to lend his name to the Ottoman Empire. (See Figure 5-4.)

The Seljuks were Turkish-speaking tribes that overran Iran in the 11th century. They wrestled much of Anatolia from the Byzantines at this time, but couldn't seize Constantinople. Although the Seljuks in Iran picked up Persian and promptly forgot Turkish, their "cousins" in Anatolia never gave up their native language.

In the 14th century, the Ottoman military machine consolidated power all around Constantinople, the last bastion of Christianity in the Near East. These Turks gained territory in northern Greece, Macedonia, and Bulgaria. They seized Kosovo in 1389 and once again set their sights on the illusive Constantinople, but in 1402 Timur delivered the Ottomans a huge setback. He defeated them and captured Beyazid, their sultan. The Ottomans had to wait 51 years to claim Constantinople as their prize.

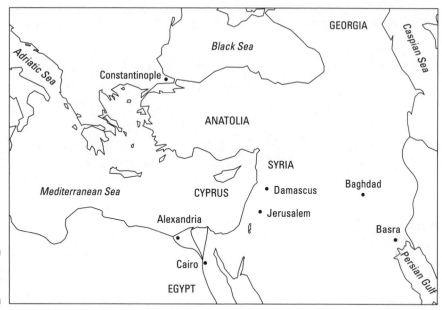

Figure 5-4:
Anatolia.

The fall of Constantinople

Weakened by internal and external crises, including assaults from Christian military contingents, the Byzantine Empire struggled to survive the 14th century. The empire had long ago lost its military recruiting grounds and rich agricultural revenue base in the plains of Anatolia to the Ottomans. The empire clung to power by importing foreign mercenaries who in turn had to be paid. The financial, political, and military strain eventually reduced the Byzantine Empire to a mere shadow of former greatness. After decades of circling the crippled Byzantines, the Ottomans finally swept in and finished off Constantinople in 1453.

The Ottomans on a roll

In the next century, the Ottoman military won numerous battles, extending the empire in all directions (see Figure 5-5). They absorbed parts of Hungary and Transylvania in the north, swept over Syria and Palestine, and expanded deep into Iran, Arabia, and Yemen in the south. They defeated the Mamluks in Egypt and pressed on to Algiers, Tunis, Tripoli, Malta, and Cyprus in the west.

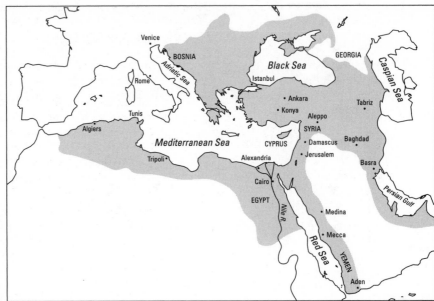

Figure 5-5:
The
Ottoman
Empire.

The Ottomans' military successes were due in no small part to the Janissaries, Christian slave warriors. A tax, called the *devshirme,* was levied against Christian populations in the Balkans. The royal court educated, groomed as Turkish gentlemen, and trained these children in modern warfare. Superior artillery and infantry strategies helped to make the Janissaries an elite military corps.

The Ottoman court's language was Turkish. Although the language is related to neither Semitic nor Indo-European families, Ottoman Turkish absorbed many Arabic and Persian words. Like many other Muslim rulers, the Ottoman sultan rulers patronized art, literature, and architecture.

Converting Safavids to Shiism

Ever since the beginning of written history in the Middle East, kings exploited religion for political gains (see Chapter 4). Few rulers have more adeptly seized religious opportunities to leverage political advantage than Shah Ismail, the founder of the Safavid dynasty in Iran.

With the remnants of the Timurid dynasty in shambles, Shah Ismail conquered Tabriz in Iran in 1501. He succeeded in garnering political and military support by demanding absolute obedience from religious adherents by claims of legitimacy as the following:

Five women worth remembering

As history advances, written records leave more and more information about women worth remembering. The following five women helped shape the Medieval Middle East.

✔ **Aisha** (seventh century): youngest wife of the Prophet and daughter of Abu Bakr, the 1st Rightly Guided Caliph. She participated in Muslim politics, went into battle, and transmitted more traditions of the Prophet than anyone and is highly regarded in Sunni Islam.

✔ **Fatima** (seventh century): daughter of the prophet, wife of Rightly Guided Caliph Ali, and mother of Husayn, who was martyred at Karbala. She is a central figure in Shiite Islam.

✔ **Rabia al-Adawiya** (eighth–ninth centuries): a freed slave girl who became a famous Iraqi Muslim saint. She purportedly stupefied pious Muslim men by performing miracles and rejecting offers of marriage because she had room in her heart for only the love of God.

✔ **Shajarat al-Durr** (12th–13th centuries): the only Egyptian *sultana* (female sultan). She forged an alliance with the Mamluk generals but eventually gave in to the social pressure arising from her unmarried status as a female ruler and married Aybek, who became the first Mamluk sultan.

✔ **Nur Jahan** (17th century): queen of the Mughal Empire in Muslim India (what is today India, Pakistan, and Afghanistan). She ruled the empire for the last years of her husband's reign.

Even in the highly patriarchal medieval societies of the Middle East, women found ways to exert political and religious influence. Women have continued to participate in various spheres of Middle Eastern society.

✔ The hidden imam, an infallible Shiite leader on earth (see Chapter 19 for more on Shiism)

✔ A reincarnation of Ali

✔ An epiphany of God

✔ The incarnation of Khidr, a legendary Sufi figure (for more on Sufism, see Chapter 20)

Ismail, however, faced two major obstacles to consolidation of power.

✔ The Sunni Ottoman Empire was quickly carving up Persian territory.

✔ The majority of Iranians were Sunnis.

In an effort to offset Ottoman political and religious authority, Shah Ismail, therefore, undertook a nationwide conversion from Sunnism to Shiism. He imported Shiite scholars, called mullas or ulema, from Kashmir, Syria, Lebanon, Iraq, Arabia, and Bahrain — hence the influence Iran still has in those regions through the descendents of those migrants. The shah set out to eliminate other forms of religion through persecution, massacres, violation of Sunni religious leaders' tombs, destroying Sufi (Islamic mystic) shrines, and insulting the first three Rightly Guided Caliphs. The pilgrimage to Karbala replaced the Hajj to Mecca (see Chapter 19). This religious persecution continued through the 17th century.

Iran's predominantly Shiite population today is a direct result of wheels of conversion that were set in motion by Safavid Shah Ismail in the early 16th century. (See Figure 5-6 for more on the Shiite world.) Modern conflicts between Sunnis and Shiites in Iraq, Iran, and Afghanistan can all be traced back to this forced conversion.

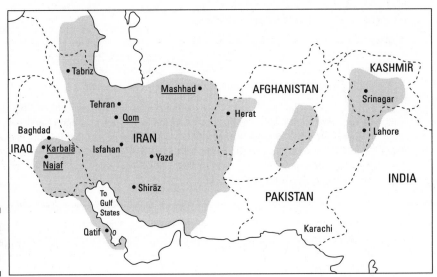

Figure 5-6: The Shiite world.

Chapter 6

The Modern Middle East

*W*hen you flip on your 24-hour news channel and see some foreign correspondent standing on Middle Eastern soil, describing an air attack against suspected terrorists, a suicide bombing, United Nations' resolutions affecting the region, or exclusive tapes released to an Arab TV network, you're witnessing the results of conscious and unconscious wheels set in motion much, much earlier.

To truly grasp the current situation, you need to understand some basic developments in the Middle East during the modern period. This period really marks the dynamic interaction between the West and the Near East. The relationship is kind of like a game of pool. When the cue ball strikes the racked balls, each one bangs into others, sending them all in unpredictable trajectories. Events in Nazi Germany, for example, forged animosities and sympathies that upset the balance of politics all across the Middle East that are still being felt. If you pay taxes, watch TV, or felt some stir of emotion caused by the events of September 11, 2001, and beyond, you're in some way influenced by a series of actions and reactions that are traceable to Hitler's Germany.

Unlike those pool balls though, in the field of politics, you can't re-rack and start over. No matter how hard political heavyweights tried to contain these events and minimize the damage of counter events, the violence and discord took on a life of their own. No matter how strategically new cue ball shots are planned, getting the balls back into the original racked form just doesn't happen. Incidents keep occurring, agendas and policies forge ahead, and political actions continue slamming into one another, creating counter reactions spinning off in unpredictable directions.

For the modern period, the events leading up to the Industrial Revolution in the 17th and 18th centuries served as a starting point, and this period continued through World War II. This chapter helps you trace the major events in the Middle East from their origins to the middle of the 20th century. I detail the histories of individual countries and the last 50 years or so in individual chapters on specific countries or regions.

A Love-Hate Relationship: The West in the Middle East

If you go to the Middle East, you're likely to experience unexpected hospitality tempered with measured suspicion. In the late 1980s, my family and I crossed over the Wagah border from India into Pakistan. In order to fill out a blank on an immigration form, an official asked me which hotel we would be staying in. When I told him I didn't know, he laid down his pen and looked at my family pensively. After a few moments, he said, "Okay, I've decided. You'll stay with me." Sure enough, my three children, my wife, her brother, and I then proceeded to his tiny flat in Lahore where we were treated like royalty. After a gracious meal and tour of the city, we retired to his house where we drank tea and discussed politics until early morning. I found myself in the awkward position of defending Western policy against informed and uninformed Pakistani criticisms. The next morning, after resisting sincere invitations to stay another night, his wife made us breakfast, drove us some distance to the bus stop, and bid us a warm farewell.

My point is that the degree to which much of the Muslim World *hates* the West is matched only by the love and admiration Muslims have for it. Likewise, the West has a similar set of reactions and attitudes toward the Middle East. To begin to understand this complex love-hate relationship, you have to look back across a couple of centuries of precarious interactions, a couple of world wars, military inequities, colonial legacies, allegiances, broken alliances, and mutual mistrust that truly began taking its current form in the modern period.

Western military superiority — guns, tanks, and bombs, oh my

The West has been sticking its nose into the Near East since at least the time of Alexander the Great, and the Middle Eastern powers have coveted European lands with equal tenacity. The invasions and counter measures of the Crusades, conflicts between the Iranians and Byzantines, and the Ottoman expansion into Europe created historical mutual distrust in the Medieval Period. Yet, memories on both sides are quite short. Today the emotions between the East and West are based primarily on modern events that developed over the last few centuries.

Europe's superiority in economic, military, and technological resources resulted in a growing tension and enmity between the West and the Middle East. Parties vying for power, therefore, forged new alliances, shifted strategies, and drew up new blueprints for fresh invasions and domination.

As is often the case, whoever controls the wealth, generally controls the military, and whoever controls the military, usually controls the wealth. Western domination of maritime trade routes and technological advances over the centuries led to a military superiority that shifted the balance of power to the West. These developments included

- ✔ **Superior European weaponry:** Europeans produced better guns in larger numbers.

- ✔ **Increased European wealth:** Discoveries of maritime trade routes led to new sources of wealth at the expense of Middle Eastern caravan routes. By the 16th century, most of the trade routes were in European hands.

- ✔ **European industrialization:** Trade, the influx of precious metals from the Americas, innovations in banking and credit, and the development of machines and factories by the 18th century fed the Industrial Revolution.

The Middle East reacted slowly to these Western successes. The only superpower in the region, the Ottoman Empire, was slowly losing its superiority. The Middle East, which for centuries had been home to some of the wealthiest, most luxurious, and advanced civilizations on earth, began diminishing in grandeur, strength, and influence.

Colonial legacy — tyrants and short-term memories

You can read the other side of the military and technological success story of the Europeans as exploitation of natural resources and human capital from the lesser-developed nations. The Western powers mined the precious metals recovered from the Americas with indigenous labor, took and maintained the trade routes by force, established uninvited colonies on foreign soil, stole riches from the most vulnerable, and maintained European supremacy, all under the accurate aim of a cannon barrel.

Hadn't the Assyrians, Hittites, Egyptians, Persians, Greeks, Romans, Arabs, Mongols, Ottomans, and every other dominant ruling force throughout Middle Eastern history exploited local populations? Well, yes, they had. But remember that people have short memories. What stands out in the mind of a vanquished and repressed people is the name of their *most recent* tyrant, not the one in the distant past. The fact that previous rulers exploited a nation didn't diminish the pain or cruelty of the current ruler. Human nature, and short memories, even allowed populations to look back on previous tyrants with nostalgia in the face of current tyranny.

Needing to modernize — not an easy step

Europeans ruled the seas on modern ships armed with modern weaponry. Dutch, Portuguese, Spanish, and British traders and merchants exploited the wealth of underdeveloped nations under the vigilant eye of modern armies. Although indigenous people stood by and watched helplessly, some Middle Eastern rulers realized that the only hope for independence lay in the modernization of their own nations. Updating their societies was no small endeavor; it meant

- ✔ **Modern armies:** Countries needed armies with updated skills training, weaponry, and transportation.

- ✔ **Modern education:** Someone had to build, manage, and operate the technology and factories; and someone had to read, translate, and interpret manuals, books, and documents.

- ✔ **Modern society:** Rulers revamped everything in society from roads to attitudes. This action meant challenging traditions, replacing old systems with new systems, and developing efficient bureaucracies, systems of taxation, and laws.

- ✔ **Modern technology:** Rulers focused on developing machinery and factories.

The rulers had a good idea, but two huge obstacles stood in the path of modernization: European resistance and internal Middle Eastern resistance. The European powers, England and France, knew a good thing when they saw one, and they had no intention of sharing technology and advances or giving up the lucrative inroads already made in the Near East. On the other hand, except for a few Middle Eastern visionaries, local populations looked upon efforts to modernize with suspicion, reluctance, and, at times, stiff resistance.

World War 1 — major changes for the region

Like most other parts of the globe, the Near East was drawn into World War I in a large way. The Ottoman Empire joined forces with Germany, in part, to regain territory lost to Russia in an earlier war. The Middle East experienced the effects of the following results in World War I:

- ✔ The European powers encouraged Arabs to seek independence from the Turks. Resistance to the Ottomans surfaced in the form of Arab Nationalism and other popular uprisings.

- ✔ The Ottoman Empire fell.

- ✔ *The Treaty of Sevre* enacted three changes after the war:

    - Dissolved the Ottoman Empire.

    - Gave Syria and Lebanon to France in the French Mandate (see Figure 6-1).

    - Awarded Palestine to Britain in the British Mandate (also in Figure 6-1).

- ✔ New states were formed: Saudi Arabia, Trans-Jordan, and Turkey.

When the smoke cleared, Britain emerged as the new powerhouse in the region and a force to be reckoned with.

World War 11 — even more dramatic changes for the region

During World War II, the Middle East (see Figure 6-2) became a major battle-field between the Allies and Axis, and served as garrison and supply center for Allied forces.

- ✔ **Libya, Eritrea, and Egypt:** The British fought the Italians in these three counties in 1940 and pushed back German General Rommel's reinforcements in Egypt in 1941. Rommel's defeat at Alamein in 1942 represented a major turning point in the war.

- ✔ **Syria and Lebanon:** After Hitler took France in 1940, these two countries fell under the control of the Vichy government (Nazi-controlled France). When German aircraft refueled in Syria in 1941 on their way to support the Iraqi prime minister, joint British and Free French troops launched an attack from Palestine and defeated the Vichy in six weeks.

✔ **Iraq:** Prime Minister Rashid Ali Gailani refused access to British troops. Joint Indian, Arab, and British troops ousted Gailani and replaced him with the more palatable Nuri al-Said.

Arabs, Jews, and Iranians (not to mention Indians) wanted their independence from European imperialism. The war's outbreak opened the way for two diametrically opposed Middle Eastern forces to attempt to secure independence. One approach was to fight along side the imperialists (Britain and Free France) in hopes that if victorious, their "masters" would make good on promises to grant independence. The following groups fought along side the Allies:

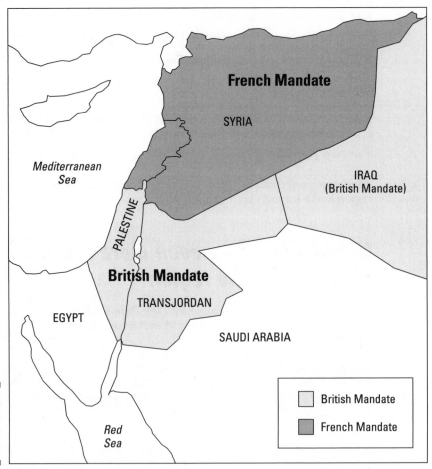

Figure 6-1:
The British
and French
Mandates.

✔ **Jews:** Approximately 27,000 Jewish troops from the Haganah (see side-bar "Haganah and other Jewish militants") fought on the side of the British in the Middle East. In time though, the Jews drove out the British.

✔ **Indians (soon to become Pakistanis *and* Indians):** The Fifth Indian Division fought against the Germans in Libya and Sudan, and supported the British in Iraq, while the Fourth Division served in North Africa, Palestine, and Syria.

✔ **Arabs:** Arab soldiers in Egypt, Iraq, Libya, and elsewhere served British interests.

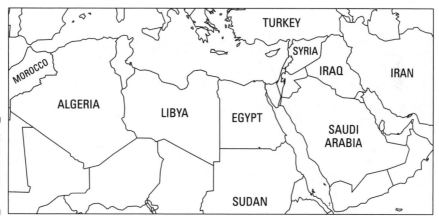

Figure 6-2: The Middle East during World War II.

Pro-Axis contingents in the Middle East sought to wrestle independence from their "masters" at their most vulnerable time by supporting Germany and Italy (the Axis). Notice the following examples:

✔ **Egypt:** Future president Anwar Sadat was arrested for collaborating with the Germans in 1942 but escaped two years later.

✔ **Iran:** Fed up with Soviet and British meddling, Reza Shah took a pro-Axis position. Iran's strategic geographical location and oil reserves meant that the Allies couldn't ignore Iran. Soviet and British military forces invaded Iran and forced pro-Axis Reza Shah to abdicate in favor of his son, Muhammad Reza Shah. The famous photograph of Roosevelt, Churchill, and Stalin was taken at the Tehran Conference in 1943.

✔ **Palestine:** The Stern Gang (or Lehi) and other Jewish militant organizations attacked the British, Arabs, and even other Jews in the Middle East and elsewhere. They even attempted to negotiate with Hitler whom they perceived as less threatening than the British.

The United States' entry into World War II had strong implications for the Middle East. After the war, British and French world supremacy waned, and the two countries were forced to relinquish their colonial rule in the region. The United States stepped in to take up the political slack. U.S. foreign policy had a huge impact on Egypt, Israel and Palestine, Iran, Iraq, and other countries in the region.

Clashing Ideologies: Zionism, Arab Nationalism, and the Islamic Revivalism

In the 19th and 20th centuries, three significant ideologies emerged that shaped the political landscape of the Middle East: Zionism, Arab Nationalism, and Islamic Revivalism.

Zionism

Zionism is basically another name for a type of Jewish nationalism that seeks to reestablish a homeland in their spiritual and historic center of Palestine. This movement gets its name from Mount Zion, the hill in ancient Jerusalem where King David's palace stood, and has come to mean the Jewish homeland. The doctrine took root in the 19th century under such Jewish thinkers as Austro-Hungarian Theodor Herzl.

Arab Nationalism

During World War I, the British and French sought to find support in the region against the Ottomans who had thrown their lot in with Germany. The European powers incited the Arabs to throw off the Ottoman yoke of supremacy and establish independence with Arab identity as a unifying factor. This movement that became known as Arab Nationalism sought to unify Arabs by appealing to a sense of common history, culture, and language. After Britain and France supplanted the Turks in the Middle East at the end of the war, Arab Nationalism continued to evolve, this time seeking to throw off the shackles of European colonialism. Sharing a common Arab heritage meant the inclusion of non-Muslim Arabs. Arab Christians, for instance, often played a prominent role in promoting Arab Nationalism because they had the most to lose under Islamic movements. Michael Aflaq, for instance, a Syrian Christian, helped to found the Arab Baath Party that would become dominant in Syria and Iraq.

Islamic Revivalism

Many Muslims, most notably the Islamic extremist group the Muslim Brotherhood (see Chapter 15), rejected the notion of nationalism that rang of a secular movement because it placed *Arab* before *Islam*. A number of political movements arose that utilized Islam, or specific interpretations of Islam, as unifying factors. The Wahhabi movement in Arabia, for instance, attempted to revive an Islam purified of foreign (non-Islamic) elements from accepted Muslim practices (see "The spread of Wahhabism," later in this chapter). In this sense, Muslim purists blamed the wretched state of affairs in the Middle East on the corruption, waste, and wicked practices of its rulers. The purists' ultimate goal was simple. They wanted to revert to the type of Islam practiced at the time of the Prophet. In order to do so, they sought to kick out the imperialists and corrupt Muslim rulers, purge society of non-Islamic elements, and implement a strict adherence to *sharia* (Islamic law).

Putting the "Saudi" in Saudi Arabia

Arabia was a backwater region in ancient times and even into the modern period. During their peak in the early 16th century, the Ottomans had swept over Palestine and Arabia, establishing rule over the Bedouin, or nomadic Arab, tribes (see Chapter 24).

The Ottomans had attempted to legitimize their foreign rule by constructing a pedigree that made the sultan both a Turk and a descendent of the Prophet. The sultan accepted the keys to the Kaba and sacred relics, including the sword of Caliph Omar, which the sultan carted off to Istanbul for safekeeping. With the sacred relics, military power, and forged lineage, the Turkish sultans assumed the unquestioned role as leaders of Sunni Islam. Part of the duty that accompanied this prestigious honor was to protect the two holy cities of Mecca and Medina, and to ensure the safety of pilgrims.

The spread of Wahhabism

The irony of foreign Turkish rulers holding authority over Arab lands and representing Islam, a religion defined by Arabic, wasn't lost on many native Bedouin tribes in Arabia. The appearance of Muhammad Ibn Abdul Wahhab, an 18th century Islamic reformer, challenged Ottoman authority in Arabia. The Wahhabi movement spread across the peninsula and succeeded in converting powerful Bedouin tribes, like the Saudis. Under the leadership of Abdul Ibn Saud, the tribe waged a *jihad* (religious war) on all other forms of Islam, and conquered most of Arabia in the process. In 1807, the Wahhabi army conquered Mecca and set about destroying and looting the holy city in the name of Islam. By 1811, the Saudis ruled all Arabia, except Yemen.

The Ottoman Empire strikes back

The Ottomans didn't take kindly to this indigenous Arab incursion into Turk territory, even if it was Arab land. The sultan was particularly peeved that the Wahhabis had sacked the holy cities under his protection. In 1813, the sultan unleashed the sons of Muhammad Ali (see "Muhammad Ali [no, not the boxer] fights back," later in this chapter), who retook the holy cities and massacred the Wahhabi army. In 1818, the Ottomans captured Abdul ibn Saud and sent him to Istanbul, where he was tried by the *ulema* (religious leaders) who conveniently found him guilty of heresy. Having secured the support of the ulema, the sultan was only too happy to behead Abdul publicly.

Forming (and fathering) the Saudi Kingdom

The Wahhabis were down, but not out. At the turn of the 20th century, a descendent of the earlier Saudi conquerors, a holy warrior named Ibn Saud, set about on a reconquest of Arabia, taking Riyadh in 1902. During World War I, the British, who themselves were upset at the Ottomans for siding with Germany and Austria, chose to support a different claimant to the Arabian Peninsula, the Hashemite clan. With British aid, the Hashemites launched a series of revolts against the Ottomans. When the dust cleared, the Saudis had wrestled the desert land from all their enemies, and had driven both the Turks and the Hashemites off the peninsula. In 1932, Ibn Saud established the Kingdom of Saudi Arabia, and four years later, the Arabian American Oil Company, better known as Aramco, discovered oil in the desert.

Stricken with disunity among the Arab tribes, Ibn Saud sought to unite the kingdom by undertaking an innovative strategy to bind the tribes through blood alliances. As permissible in Islam, the king set about marrying four wives at a time from various tribes. After the wives gave birth, he divorced them and married others. In this way, the Saudi blood that was flowing through the veins of diverse tribes served as a unifying factor. By siring 53 sons and 54 daughters, Ibn Saud succeeded in uniting the Arabs as even the Rightly Guided Caliphs had not.

Establishing the Hashemite Kingdom of Jordan

During World War I, the British had supported the Hashemite clan in Arabia against the Ottomans. Hashemite leader Abdullah bin Hussein had led a number of attacks against the Turks, but after the war, the Saudis sent Abdullah packing. As consolation prize, the British handed over a huge parcel of Palestinian land east of the Jordan River to their loyal ally Abdullah. In 1921, through the British Mandate, England formally awarded this region — known at the time as Trans-Jordan — to Abdullah (see "Dividing up Palestine — the British Mandate," later in this chapter). Over the next 25 years, the British took the following steps in the formation of Jordan:

- **1923:** Britain signs a treaty establishing the autonomy of Emirate of Trans-Jordan. Abdullah becomes the emir.

- **1923:** Britain helps Abdullah establish an army called the Arab Legion.

- **1928:** The constitutional monarchy secures hereditary Hashemite succession for Abdullah's descendents.

- **1946:** Britain gives the emirate its independence, and Abdullah and the nation undergo a name change: Abdullah crowns himself king and the country officially becomes the Hashemite Kingdom of Jordan.

In short, King Abdullah owed his kingdom, throne, army, and his children's future to the British.

Over the next 20 years, turbulent waters in far away Europe sent waves of chaotic proportion pounding the shores of Palestine and Trans-Jordan. When war erupted in 1948, King Abdullah sent military forces against Israel (see the sidebar, "The first of many battles: The First Arab-Israeli War," later in this chapter). The Arabs lost, but Trans-Jordan succeeded in annexing the West Bank. In July 1951, a Palestinian gunman assassinated King Abdullah after the king entered the al-Aqsa Mosque in Jerusalem with his grandson Hussein. A bullet bounced off a medal on young Hussein's uniform, and he escaped death to become king a few years later. This time wasn't the last occasion an assassin would make an attempt on Hussein's life.

Carving Israel from Palestine

Not all Arabs are Muslims. A small percentage is Christian. The Iraqi Foreign Minister who gained fame during the Gulf War, for instance, is Christian. Furthermore, before the formation of Israel, Arab Jews lived throughout the Middle East, including a number in Palestine. Not all Jews left Palestine after the Romans destroyed the second temple in 70 A.D. Many lived through the Crusades and other calamities of the Middle Ages, and over the centuries, Jews migrated back to Palestine from other countries so that by the early 20th century, Palestinian Jews, including Arabic-speak Jews, lived side by side with other Arabs in quite peaceful co-existence.

Sympathetic for the plight of the Jews, who had suffered persecution in Europe and elsewhere, Zionist currents (see "Zionism," earlier in this chapter) began sweeping across Europe impressing upon its rulers to resolve the issue of the Diaspora by establishing a homeland for Jews. As early as the 19th century, a handful of Jewish visionaries had proposed Jewish nationalism, and by the 1880s, the Zionist migration to the region had already begun.

Haganah and other Jewish militants

By 1920, Jews living in Palestine had already formed a secret, loosely organized band of militants known as the Haganah. With an original mission of self-defense, the Arab-Israeli clashes from 1929 to 1939 solidified the group into a unified military unit. Often with secret aid of the British, the Haganah:

✔ Produced and imported illegal weapons

✔ Established military training

✔ Supported illegal immigration

During World War II, 27,000 Haganah members volunteered to support the British against Hitler, forming the Jewish Brigade Group, which shared intelligence and participated in commando missions in the Near East. Other splinter militant squads like Irgun and the Stern Gang, carried out terrorist attacks against British, Arabs, and even other Jews. In November 1944, the Stern Gang executed British minister Lord Moyne in Cairo. In 1946, Irgun blew up the King David Hotel, killing 91 people, a number of them Jews. Many of these tactics earned the condemnation of more moderate Jews, but news sources later revealed that future prime ministers Yitzhak Shamir and Menachem Begin had commanded operations of this type.

After the war, three-way violence between the Arabs, Jews, and the British erupted in Palestine with unprecedented intensity. The Palmach wing of the Haganah cooperated with Irgun and the Stern Gang in destroying British infrastructure in Palestine: bridges, train tracks, and communications. By the First Arab-Israeli War in 1948, Haganah had more than 30,000 soldiers. Palmach, Irgun, and the Stern Gang carried out brutal attacks, including the Deir Yassin massacre of 254 Arab men, women, and children. After that war, Israel's first prime minister, David Ben-Gurion, merged all the military wings into the national military organization.

Dividing up Palestine — the British Mandate

British Foreign Secretary Lord Balfour originally thought that Uganda would be an ideal spot for the Jews to settle, but leading European Jews convinced him otherwise. On November 2, 1917, he wrote a letter to Lord Rothchild voicing the British commitment to establish a Jewish homeland within Palestine, which at the time was under the control of the Ottoman Empire. Demonstrating a single lack of imagination, historians have called Lord Balfour's letter the "Balfour Declaration."

After World War I had ended, the League of Nations provided its support for this strategy by granting England the British Mandate in July 1922 to govern the region of Palestine, roughly the area today of Israel, Palestine, and Jordan. Because this territory constituted spoils of the war gained from the Ottomans, no one bothered to ask the Palestinians what they thought. After all, the Turkish rulers had been foreigners, so what difference could one more set of foreign rulers make? The British gave the eastern half of Palestine to Abdullah for his loyalty in World War I. That land later became the Kingdom of Trans-Jordan. The other half was loosely slated as Jewish territory.

Migrating Jews — two by two

Even when the Ottomans ruled Palestine, Jews began trickling in. Often with donations raised among American Jews, migrants purchased land from Turkish landlords living in Istanbul and Beruit. One common Jewish practice involved establishing a rural commune called a *kibbutz,* in which workers drained marshes, planted trees, and revived wasteland into habitable, fertile fields.

The British Mandate only legitimized the migration, and the trickle became a steady stream of Jews who viewed their arrival, not as a migration, but as repatriation to the homeland they were forced to abandon nearly 2,000 years earlier, upon the destruction of the second temple. As you may imagine, the Palestinian Arabs didn't care much for foreigners moving in and settling on the land that they had often farmed for generations. Tempers flared. From 1929 to 1939, a series of violent struggles erupted that eased somewhat under a truce that lasted during World War II. In order to stem the stream of immigration and to appease Arab discontent, the British limited immigration and recognized the Arab Higher Committee (AHC) as a legal political body representing Palestinians through a declaration called the White Paper of May 1939.

Hitler's cue ball — ripple effects everywhere

If you imagine that Hitler's extermination of 6 million Jews in Europe as a cue ball sending pool balls scurrying about in unpredictable tangents, you get an appreciation for World War II's effect on the Middle East. The West's dismay at the Holocaust created a wave of sympathy for European Jewish survivors. Jews worldwide agreed that the only way to prevent a future holocaust was to create an independent Jewish state that protected its people and fulfilled the Zionist dream.

When the war ended in 1945, the steady steam of Jewish immigration to Palestine burst into a massive flow beyond British control. Violence between Arabs and Jews once again erupted. The British found themselves stuck in the middle, lacking means to stem the increasing cycle of violence. A Jewish militant group known as the Haganah (see sidebar "Haganah and other Jewish militants") seized the opportunity to support massive Jewish immigration at any cost.

Taking action: The Arab Higher Commission steps in

For their part, the Arabs didn't stand by idly watching events take place. Their frustration with continued developments led to a series of particularly violent revolts in the 1920s and 1930s. The discovery of a secret Jewish arms cache in 1935 forced an alliance between Arab factions, called the Arab Higher Commission (AHC) the following year. Heading the AHC, Hajj Muhammad Amin al Husseini rejected a British proposal for a joint legislative council of Arabs and Jews in 1936. The next year he also rejected the British Peel Commission's suggestion of a partition of Palestine. Eventually he fled Palestine to Lebanon and spent his time attempting to lead Arab opposition in exile.

Forming modern day Israel

Unable to contain the violence, the British decided to withdraw from Palestine. A series of key developments determined the formation of the modern state of Israel.

- **1947:** Through Resolution 181, the fledgling United Nations resolves to partition Palestine, giving roughly half to the Jews and half to the Arabs. The Jews accept, but the Arabs reject the resolution.

- ✔ **May 14, 1948:** The British Mandate ends as the last British high commissioner withdraws from Palestine.

- ✔ **May 14, 1948:** The Jewish National Council declares Israel an independent state.

- ✔ **May 1948 to January 1949:** Immediately, the First Arab-Israeli War erupts. As a result, Israel gains nearly half of the Palestinian share of the land. (See the sidebar, "The first of many battles: The First Arab-Israeli War," for more on the war.)

- ✔ **1949:** After the war, the Palestinians basically say, "Okay, we'll accept U.N. Resolution 181. Give us back our land."

- ✔ **1949:** The Jews more or less say, "No way! Too late! You had your chance." (Figure 6-3 shows the proposed 1947 borders and the borders after the end of the First Arab Israeli War.)

This development left 600,000 Israelis in charge of nearly ¾ of the land, and 1.2 million Arabs to eke out a living on the remaining ¼ although some 700,000 of those Palestinians became refugees, mostly in Trans-Jordan. The Israelis made two important decisions that further affected the population.

Figure 6-3:
Palestine before and after the First Arab-Israeli War.

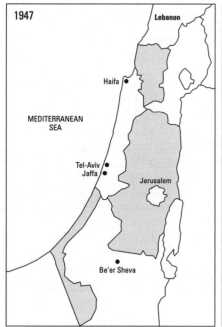
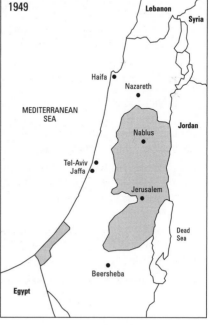

> ✔ They allowed the Arabs living within Israel's new borders to remain and eventually awarded them Israeli citizenship.
>
> ✔ The 1950 *Law of Return* encouraged the immigration of any Jew living anywhere in the world.

Jews of all shapes and sizes from all over the world, speaking a variety of languages, and practicing countless different customs, began migrating to Israel. In an effort to forge a new Israeli identity among disparate Jews, Israelis did something that had never been done in the history of humanity. They revived a dead language: Hebrew. (Read *Hebrew For Dummies,* by Jill Suzanne Jacobs [Wiley Publishing, Inc.] for more on the revival of Hebrew.)

The first of many battles: The First Arab-Israeli War

The First Arab-Israeli War has many names. Arabs call it the *Palestine War* while Israelis like to refer to it as the *War of Independence*. With the British on the retreat, and the Israelis declaring their sovereignty in May of 1948, Arabs quickly retaliated. Of the 40 million Arabs surrounding 600,000 Israelis, Trans-Jordan's King Abdullah barely mustered a force of 26,000. General Glubb and other senior British officers led the Trans-Jordanian troops, the only formally trained soldiers, into battle. The Egyptian, Iraqi, Lebanese, Palestinian, and Syrian troops comprised a mixture of irregulars, militia, and ill-equipped and poorly trained fighters.

Although within a month, the Arab numbers had swollen to 35,000, they were no match for the 60,000 well-trained Jewish forces. Israeli Haganah soldiers made up nearly half of the troops, and the experience they had gained in World War II paid off. The results of the war were the following:

✔ 18,500 Arabs died (including 16,000 Palestinians).

✔ 700,000 Arabs fled Israeli-controlled Palestinian territory during the conflict.

✔ 6,000 Jews died.

✔ Egypt gained the Gaza Strip.

✔ Jordan got the West Bank and East Jerusalem.

King Abdullah became the "King of all Palestine" although reports leaked that he had secretly negotiated with Israel. Two years later, a Palestinian gunman assassinated Abdullah in the most famous mosque in Jerusalem. Although the United Nations repeatedly demanded Israel allow the return of the refugees, Israel insisted that the issue could be settled at a later date. In a matter of months, half of Palestine's Arabs had become refugees.

Coming of Age: Egypt Grows Up

By the 18th century, Egypt's fertile agricultural lands produced coffee, wheat, and rice, and its strategic position linked Asia with Africa for both commercial and military reasons. In the eyes of the European powers, Egypt became a coveted prize: A prize worth fighting for.

Napoleon invades Egypt

At the age of 29, Napoleon invaded Egypt in 1798 in order to strike a blow to the British. The French conqueror defeated the Mamluk army at the Battle of the Pyramids. Napoleon tried to sell his invasion to the Egyptians as a Muslim mission. As a disciple of the Prophet, Napoleon claimed, he had defeated the pope and was now here to protect Egypt from Ottoman tyranny. In the meantime, his soldiers used the Sphinx as target practice — shooting off its nose and beard.

The British and Ottomans didn't take the imperialist invasion of Egypt lightly. Both foreign powers, with their own stake in Egypt, joined forces to oust Napoleon. In August 1798, Lord Nelson destroyed the French fleet in Abu Kir Bay in Alexandria. Meanwhile, the Turks dispatched an army led by an Albanian Muslim named Muhammad Ali. In an effort to head off the Ottoman forces, Napoleon met them in Syria. Unwilling to be bothered with 2,000 prisoners of war who had fallen into his hands, Napoleon executed them. Nonetheless, the following year, the remnants of the defeated French army escaped back to France.

Muhammad Ali (no, not the boxer) fights back

As head of the Albanian forces that defeated Napoleon in Syria, Muhammad Ali, who didn't speak Arabic, became the *pasha* (governor) in Egypt to represent the Turks after the French had gone. As you may imagine, the Mamluks, who'd been in charge for centuries, were none too happy about this development, and they resisted. In 1811, Muhammad Ali decided the best way to defeat them was to throw a *killer* party. The Mamluk local rulers accepted the pasha's invitation, and while entering through a corridor at the Citadel, they found themselves trapped, and Muhammad Ali's soldiers proceeded to slaughter the guests.

When Muhammad Ali wasn't defeating opponents, he was taking necessary steps to modernize Egypt. He instituted a number of sweeping changes:

- Introduced cotton and sugar into the agricultural sector
- Collected taxes and combated corruption with a heavy hand
- Invited French engineers to build dams and canals, which improved irrigation methods that expanded cultivation over a million new acres
- Built glass, textile, and weapons factories
- Upgraded the army with the help of French support and locally made weapons
- Improved education and health care
- Redistributed the land to increase productivity
- Increased tariffs on foreign goods to protect Egyptian-made products

His improved military was responsible for victories in Arabia, the Sudan, and Syria. Needless to say, the British didn't approve of the Egyptian independence because it threatened British commercial or military dominance. In 1840, the British overthrew the Egyptian army and dissolved the tariffs. As a result, the Egyptian economy collapsed.

A painful route canal (Suez, that is)

In antiquity, the value of a canal connecting the Red Sea with the Mediterranean wasn't lost on ancient rulers. Several kings had dug and maintained a canal from about 2000 B.C., but it fell into disrepair after the eighth century A.D. By the modern period, European powers were looking for shortcuts in the traditional route to India that went all the way around the tip of the Cape of Good Hope (South Africa). Competition between the European traders was fierce, and cutting the distance of each journey meant increasing profit. A canal through Egypt was a real possibility. It also carried political and military implications. The notion of a canal involved necessary funding, manual labor, and military protection.

The dream to revive the canal so that large ships could pass became an excruciating realization for Egypt in the 19th century. A French engineer named Ferdinand de Lesseps oversaw this monumental project funded with British loans and carried out by Egyptian forced labor, one painful shovelful of dirt at a time. Thousands of Egyptians lost their lives. When the Suez Canal was completed in 1869, Egypt was broke, but the canal fell under the joint French-British ownership of the Suez Canal Company overseen by British troops. The canal remained under British control for the next century until Gamal Abdul Nasser appeared on the scene.

Nasser rules

Throughout World War II, Egypt served as the center of British operations in the Near East. By 1949, Egyptian discontent with the West and Israel, and with their own leadership, had heightened. In light of the humiliating defeat during the First Arab-Israeli War, Gamal Abdul Nasser emerged as the leader of a band of talented military officers called the Free Officers who were determined to reestablish the honor of the Egyptian army. Operating in secrecy, the Free Officers seized power and sent King Farouk packing during the Egyptian Revolution of July 1952.

Nasser's regime was one of the most repressive in modern history. Its tactics included censorship, torture, imprisonment, and murder of political opponents. Communists and Islamic militants suffered as the most common targets. The charismatic Nasser, however, enjoyed extensive popularity by developing a sense of Egyptian national pride, in part, by standing up to the West.

Fearing Soviet influence in the region, the United States offered aid for the Aswan High Dam in 1956. When the United States refused to sell Egypt weapons, Nasser turned to the Soviets. Enraged U.S. President Dwight Eisenhower withdrew his support for the dam. One week later Nasser made a public speech that was broadcast on Cairo Radio on the anniversary of the Egyptian Revolution. The speech criticized the United States' withdrawal of support for the Aswan project. Using the code words *Ferdinand de Lesseps,* Nasser sent a covert message to his troops to seize the canal. After the dam was securely under his control, Nasser nationalized the Suez Canal, and expelled British oil and embassy officials.

The Second Arab-Israeli War (a.k.a. the Suez Crisis)

Needless to say, the European Powers were irked at Nasser. The British and French plotted with Israel to retake the canal. In October 1956, Israel invaded the Sinai. As agreed upon, the British and French demanded Israel and Egypt withdraw to a distance of 10 kilometers from the canal. When Egypt refused, Britain and France bombed Egyptian military targets for two days straight. In a rare spirit of cooperation at the time, the Soviet Union and the United States condemned the attacks on Egypt. Undaunted, British and French para-troopers landed at both ends of the canal. Israel seized the Gaza Strip. Finally, combined Soviet and American pressure convinced the invading forces to withdraw. The results of this war were the following:

- 1,650 Egyptians died.
- 190 Israelis died.
- 26 British and French died.
- Israel occupied Gaza but withdrew in March 1957.
- Most of Egypt's air force was destroyed.

In 1958, Nasser made an odd attempt at Pan-Arabism by merging Egypt and Syria into the United Arab Republic, of which Cairo was the capital and Nasser the president. Just three years later, Syria withdrew due to internal problems. Until his death in 1970, Nasser remained an Arab hero throughout the Arab World.

The Shah(s) of Iran

Like so many other rulers in the Middle East, Reza Shah Pahlavi came to power through military force. He overthrew the last Qajar king in 1925, with British support, had the parliament, or *majlis,* make him *shah* (king), and offi-cially changed the name of the country from Persia to Iran. The Shah insti-tuted many military and administrative reforms meant to modernize and secure independence. He built the Trans-Iranian railroad, strengthened indus-try, and established the University of Tehran before he fell out with the Allies in World War II and was forced to abdicate in favor of his son Muhammad Reza Shah in 1941 (see "World War II — even more dramatic changes for the region," earlier in this chapter).

When World War II was over, the United States began to play a larger role in Iranian politics. In 1947, the Truman Doctrine provided aid to Iran to help maintain relations with the West, to keep the pipelines of oil flowing, and to discourage cooperation with the Soviets. Like Nasser had in Egypt, a prime minister by the name of Mossadeq gained popularity by standing up to the British. He insisted on nationalizing the oil industry that the British had a his-tory of exploiting. Muhammad Reza Shah, known in the West as *The Shah of Iran,* tried and failed to replace Mossadeq. As a result, Muhammad Reza Shah was forced to flee for his life. At this point, the American CIA and British intelligence services stepped in, staged a coup against Mossadeq — in part by mobilizing the best street rabble money could buy — and restored the throne to the Shah six days later.

The Shah also attempted to force modernization through a number of reforms, including the promotion of literacy. Two reforms, however, earned him the contempt of the *mulla*s (religious leaders).

- ✔ Liberation of women
- ✔ Land reform that snatched land from the clergy

Among other support, the United States helped establish the feared SEVAK, a most brutal secret security force. As a result of the United States' collaborative efforts with the Shah, a wave of anti-Americanism washed over Iran in the late 1970s (see Chapter 18).

Talking Turkey

During their heyday, the Ottomans ruled over most of the Middle East. By the 19th century, the great Ottoman Empire became known as the Sick Man of Europe. The decline of the Ottoman Empire was due to many factors, including:

- ✔ Inability to keep pace with Europe
- ✔ Unwillingness (or inability) to modernize
- ✔ External wars
- ✔ Internal strife

Ethnic violence is one example of Ottoman internal strife. In 1915, a number of race riots emerged in Turkey. Sultan Abdul Hamid let loose his army to starve and slaughter some 600,000 Armenians (Christians).

Young Turks

In 1889, a secular Turkish nationalist group of intellectuals and military officers known as the Young Turks formed. In 1909,1908, they decided to take steps to revive ailing Turkey by deposing the current sultan and replaced him with Mehmet V in 1909. When World War I broke out, the Ottomans chose to side with Germany. Britain and France saw to it that Arabia, Palestine, and Iraq wriggled free of Ottoman control (see "World War I — major changes for the region," earlier in this chapter).

The Ottoman Empire ceased to exist in 1920 with the signing of the *Treaty of Sevre* between the sultan and the Allies. As in any war, the victors began divvying up the spoils. When the divvying up was over, Turkey was left with only a fraction of its former territory. A Young Turk general named Mustafa Kemal refused to accept and abide by the treaty. After the Turkish nationalists Ataturk signed a treaty of friendship with the Soviets, the Allies countered by encouraging the Greeks to attack the Turks. Ataturk's forces succeeded in driving the Greeks back in 1922 and deposing the sultan. In 1923 a new agreement, the Treaty of Lausanne, was drawn up to replace the earlier Sevre treaty. Ataturk established the modern state of Turkey the same year and became the new nation's first president.

Ataturk bites the bullet

Immediately after World War I, Greece invaded western Anatolia with a population of approximately one third ethnic Greeks, hoping to recover long lost territory. Turkish General Mustafa Kemal, who later adopted the name Ataturk "father of the Turks," raised an army in opposition to the sultan, who was at the time confined in Istanbul by Allied forces. Ataturk kicked the Greeks out of Anatolia in 1922, dissolved the sultanate, and proclaimed Turkey an independent state in 1923.

Realizing that the future of Turkey lay in modernization, he decided to create a modern secular state in Europe's image. He believed that the Ottoman Empire's failures were tied to fanatical obedience to Islam. He made the following reforms:

- Banned *sharia* (Islamic law), Muslim charities, and Sufi (mystic) orders
- Instituted a solar calendar
- Banned the fez (Turkish cap) and the veil
- Required Western clothing
- Established Western family law meaning no more polygamy
- Abolished the Arabic script, making everyone write Turkish in Latin script, which eliminated the basis for studying the Quran

Ataturk didn't stop there. He gave women the right to vote in 1934 (just a few years after their female counterparts in the United States and Britain earned the right) and required people to adopt last names, just like Europeans.

Claiming the Prize: Lebanon and Syria

France's regional prize for its role in defeating the Ottomans in World War I was Syria, the territory that covers Syria and Lebanon today.

Breaking up Lebanon and Syria

Lebanon's social makeup is that of various religious minorities living in separate communities: Maronites (Christian), Armenians, Sunnis, Shiites, and Druze (see Chapter 20). The Christian Maronite sector had maintained a relationship with France for centuries. During the Crusades, the Maronites provided cavalry to fight alongside the French. In the 17th century, Louis XIV developed an alliance with the Ottoman sultan as protector of the Maronites. When the Druze massacred the Maronite community in 1860, the French drove back the Druze and demanded the Ottomans take steps to protect the Maronites. After World War I, the French again stepped in to protect the Maronites and formed the state of Lebanon from the region with the highest density of Christians out of Syria that was predominately Muslim. Due to political problems, Lebanon didn't become an independent state until 1943. According to the constitution, governance was divided up in proportion to minorities as determined in a 1932 census. The traditional division is as follows:

- President is Maronite.
- Prime minister is Sunni.
- Speaker of the Chamber of Deputies is Shiite.

Half of the National Assembly is Christian and half Muslim, as well (see Chapter 16).

Getting serious about Syria

The Syrian Arab nationalists were none too happy about a European power, such as France, cutting off a slice of Syria and calling it Lebanon. They put up quite a fuss about it, in fact. In 1925, France had to quell a number of rebellions that ended with the French bombing Damascus. During World War II, a strong alignment with the Vichy government (under German control) caused the Free French and British to invade Syria and Lebanon. The Free French garrisoned a number of troops there for the remainder of the war. In 1946, Syria gained its independence.

Five women worth remembering

In the modern period, many women made contributions to the Near East. These five are worth remembering.

✔ **Golda Meir:** Russian Jewish immigrant to the United States. She moved to Palestine in 1921. She fought for Zionism until the formation of Israel. She became Israel's foreign minister from 1956 to 1966, and served as prime minister of Israel from 1969 to 1974.

✔ **Sattareh Farman Farmaian:** Iranian author, who as a daughter of one of the last Qajar princes, grew up in a small Persian harem. After an education in the United States, she returned to Iran and opened The Teheran School of Social Work, the first school of its kind for her country. Caught up in the whirlwind of the Iranian Revolution in 1979, she was arrested and nearly executed.

✔ **Nawal El Saadawi:** Egyptian physician, feminist, and author. From 1979 to 1980, she acted as an adviser for the United Nations in women's programs in Africa and the Near East. Seen as a political opponent, Anwar Sadat imprisoned her in 1980 although she was released shortly thereafter.

✔ **Hanan Ashrawi:** Palestinian Christian professor at Anglican University. She received her PhD in medieval literature at the University of Virginia. In 1988 during the first *intifada* (see Chapter 11), she became involved in Palestinian politics, and in 1991 Arafat named her the official spokesperson for the Palestinian Delegation to the Middle East Peace Process. In 1998, she resigned from the government citing widespread corruption.

✔ **Tansu Ciller:** economist from University of Istanbul who earned her PhD from the University of Connecticut. She proved to be an ambitious politician who became Turkey's first female prime minister in 1993, but was forced to step down three years later amid numerous scandals.

Part III

Politics, Islam, and Oil: Three Reasons Not to Ignore the Middle East

The 5th Wave   By Rich Tennant

ALONG WITH VAST AMOUNTS OF OIL, THE MIDDLE EAST ALSO CONTAINS 65% OF THE EARTH'S VINEGAR RESERVES.

In this part . . .

Part III outlines the central political, religious, and economic dynamics of the region that help to make the Middle East so important to the West today. This part discusses different attempts that countries in the region have made at establishing political systems that would work in a Middle Eastern context. This part also helps you to understand various dimensions and interpretations of Islamic militancy and reasons for the uneasy relationship between Islam and the rest of the world. Finally, this section explains how oil and other economic factors fit into the equation.

Chapter 7

Leadership: Kings, Presidents, and Dictators

*T*his chapter summarizes the development of various political systems in the Middle East beginning in the 20th century and ending with the current political environments.

This story picks up after World War I at the time of the fall of the Ottoman Empire, which had been the Middle East's powerhouse for centuries (see Chapter 6). Europe's colonial powers, which had already been dabbling in colonialist policies in North Africa, thought they'd try their hand at nation building in the Fertile Crescent. Britain established monarchies in Jordan and Iraq, while France clumsily drew up plans for governments in Syria and Lebanon.

Apart from a handful of exceptions, totalitarianism dominates the Middle East. Basic freedoms of speech, press, and assembly are hard to find. Opposition is routinely suppressed with torture, imprisonment, and intimidation. In some cases, murder, assassination, dismemberment, rape, forced marriages, and amputation are common political weapons and/or luxuries of the political elite. Government corruption is so common that average citizens no longer have faith in the system. In some places, people fear the police as much as the criminals. For these very reasons, many Muslims have turned to Islamic extremists who promise the establishment of an Islamic state and *sharia* (Islamic law). In the few cases where Islamic states have been established, their injustice and brutality have matched that of their secular counterparts.

Monarchy: Failures and Triumphs

The extent to which monarchies failed or triumphed in the region may be a matter of perspective, if not dispute. What is certain, however, is that some kingdoms collapsed in the 20th century while others clung to power. The following are notable monarchies that failed.

- ✔ **Afghanistan:** On July 17, 1973, King Zahir Shah's cousin, Prince Daoud, staged a coup that toppled the king, who went into exile in Italy. Daoud, who was already a military general, further appointed himself president, prime minister, foreign minister, and defense minister (see Chapter 13).

- ✔ **Egypt:** In light of the humiliating defeat at the hands of the Israelis during the First Arab-Israeli War, antimonarchist sentiments heightened in Egypt. The Free Officers seized power and sent King Farouk packing during the Egyptian Revolution of July 1952 (see Chapter 6). The Free Officers, under the leadership of Gamal Abdul Nasser, established a socialist dictatorship.

- ✔ **Iran:** Facing widespread rioting and violence in January 1979, the Shah and his queen boarded a royal Iranian Boeing 707 aircraft for vacation, and never looked back. The 78-year-old Shiite spiritual leader, Ayatollah Khomeini, returned from exile in France to establish the Islamic Republic of Iran (see Chapter 18).

- ✔ **Iraq:** On July 14, 1958, a group of Iraqi military professionals called the Free Officers led by Abdul Karim Qasim staged a military coup that brutally murdered and butchered prime minister Nuri al-Said and executed the king, slaughtering the entire royal family — women and children included — in the royal courtyard in the process. Qasim set up his own dictatorship (see Chapter 12).

The following are notable cases of kingdoms still clinging to power.

- ✔ **Jordan:** A success story, if there ever was one, in the Middle East is Jordan. With Britain's help, the Hashemite Kingdom of Jordan has endured wars, rebellions, and economic crises. King Abdullah bin Hussein inherited one of the most peaceful, crime-free, and educated nations on earth (see Chapter 16).

- ✔ **Saudi Arabia:** Despite a plethora of economic, military, political, and religious threats and obstacles, the Saudi royal family has endured, in no small part due to the largest proven oil reserves in the world (see Chapter 17).

What further twists and turns fate has in store for these two kingdoms — particularly in the light of Islamic militancy, globalization, the War on Terrorism, and other conflicts in the region — is anyone's guess.

Democracy: Failures and Triumphs

The default solution in the West for dictatorships, authoritarian regimes, and Islamic extremist governments is simple: democracy. Unfortunately, democracy in the Middle East has seldom meant to the people living there what democracy has meant in the West. For instance, the Algerians by the turn of the 20th century had already experienced a taste of French-style democracy, and they didn't like it. Democracy under French occupation meant rights and freedom for the French, and oppression and exclusion for the Arabs (see Chapter 15).

In the 21st century, the West may be able to point to two successful democracies in the Middle East: Israel, and, to a lesser extent, Turkey (see Chapter 9).

- ✔ **Israel:** Israel's parliamentary democracy is characterized by universal suffrage — including women, Arabs, Christians, and Druze (for more information on this religious group, see Chapter 20) — and free and open elections. The judicial branch is independent from the legislative branch. The 120-member Knesset (parliament) has a number of female and Arab members. Freedom of speech, press, and assembly are guaranteed for all Israeli citizens.

- ✔ **Turkey:** Turkey's government is a republican parliamentary democracy that also boasts universal suffrage. The constitution was ratified in 1982. The executive branch consists of the president, cabinet, and prime minister. The legislative branch is a 550-seat unicameral national assembly, and 22 members are women. Although the judicial branch is independent in theory, in practice, need for improvement is recognized. The military indirectly influences policy. Human rights abuses and restrictions on freedom of press, speech, and association still exist, particularly against Islamic extremists and Kurds.

Aside from farces in places like Iraq and Syria, where dictators have in the past won elections with more than 99 percent of the vote, the following examples serve as failures in democracy.

- ✔ **Algeria:** When the Islamic Salvation Front (FIS) party was on the verge of winning the parliamentary elections in 1992, the military suspended the final round of elections and banned the FIS (see Chapter 15).

- ✔ **Pakistan:** For many Pakistanis, democracy means corruption, repression, and human rights abuses. Each Pakistani stab at democracy seems to have been marred by accusations of corrupt leadership, followed by military coups (see Chapter 14).

The Muslim World has unfortunately been left with poor role models for democracy: Israel, considered the archenemy by many other Middle Eastern nations, a Turkish government that represses Islamic extremists and Kurds, and a series of failed attempts (see Chapter 9).

A failed U.S. model for democracy

Since the Eisenhower Doctrine of 1957, the United States has been promoting democracy in the Middle East. Democracy, however, never took off as expected for a number of reasons:

- Lack of democratic and civic values embedded in the population.

- Lack of regional role models.

- Internal resistance to secular, Western democracy. Many view anything secular or Western as un-Islamic.

- Success of brutal, authoritarian regimes in repressing democratic reform.

For much of the Middle East, U.S. commitments to democracy in the region seem empty, including:

- Support for Israel (seen as an oppressive regime).

- Support for repressive regimes that discourage democratic values, like Egypt, Iraq (in the 1980s), Iran (under the Shah), and Saudi Arabia.

The United States, as the champion of democracy, has lost further credibility in the Middle East since September 11, 2001. Much of the Muslim World perceives American designs in the region as neocolonial. The following two examples of U.S. actions in the region have validated Islamic extremist accusations in the eyes of many.

- **U.S. bid for democracy in the region is insincere:** Even though Yasser Arafat was the duly elected as president of the Palestinian Authority, the United States and Israel have been campaigning for a change of leadership, disregarding the will of the people.

- **U.S. desire to control Iraq's oil:** In March 2003, the Americans and the British invaded Iraq to control the oil in the region.

With a lack of models of democracy in the 21st century, optimists hold out hope that recent experiments in Afghanistan, Palestine, and Iraq may prove to be success stories in the region.

Theocracy: Failures and Triumphs

If Middle Eastern countries are lacking in successful models of democracy, they're equally lacking in successful models of *theocracy*, meaning a form of government governed by God or religion. Two stabs at establishing Islamic states have been made.

- **Islamic Emirate of Afghanistan:** The Taliban's theocracy ran Afghanistan from 1996 to 2001 until the United States and Northern Alliance forces overthrew it. The Taliban's human rights abuses became legendary (see Chapter 13).

✔ **Islamic Republic of Iran:** In 1979, Iran established an Islamic state based on Shiite doctrine, which soon proved to be as repressive as the former regime under the Shah. Many Iranian Islamic extremists argue that the model was a success, while many other Iranians see it as a patent failure (see Chapter 18).

Needless to say, the West viewed these experiments as total failures. Although both regimes have their supporters, much of the Muslim World also feels these efforts fell well short of the establishment of true Islamic states based on sharia.

Socialism

Some nations opted for a version of socialism in the mid-20th century including:

✔ **Egypt:** Although many Muslims may view Nasser's socialist experiment as the most successful, in part by standing up to the West, brutality and repression characterized his regime.

✔ **Iraq and Syria:** Baathist socialism as practiced in Iraq and Syria has been secular and authoritarian, and has brutally repressed opposition.

Today Egypt's social democracy run by President Hosni Mubarak is also authoritarian.

Communism

In the 20th century, communist members were persecuted all across the Middle East, including in Iran, Iraq, Egypt, and elsewhere. Two experiments with communism are worth mentioning.

✔ **Afghanistan:** Afghanistan's flirtation with communism in the 1970s led to a full-fledged Soviet invasion in 1979 and more than two decades of civil war (see Chapter 13).

✔ **Yemen:** In 1979, South Yemen signed a 20-year treaty with the Soviet Union and became the only Marxist state in the Arab World (see Chapter 17). With more pressing problems at home, the Soviets pulled out in May of 1990, leaving South Yemen to fend for itself (see Chapter 17).

The full effects of the Afghan experiment with communism are still being felt in the Middle East and elsewhere (see Chapter 13).

Disputed Areas

Disputed areas may be the greatest threat to stability in the Middle East and the world. Disputed areas are, well . . . disputed because, in order to secure peace in the here and now, warring parties decided to move forward and leave the resolution of the dispute for later generations to handle. As diplomatically astute as that approach may have been at the time of negotiations, some of these smoldering disputed areas have burst into flames at the turn of the 21st century, demanding attention. The following three regions are the most prominent.

Kashmir

In 1947, Hindu Maharaja Hari Singh refused to merge his kingdom of Kashmir with neither India nor Pakistan. Kashmiri Muslims revolted and violence spread. Fearing for his life, Hari threw in his lot with India and fled Kashmir on an Indian DC3. Fighting continued until January 1, 1949, when the United Nations brokered an agreement, temporarily providing half of Kashmir to Pakistan and half to India. India agreed to the U.N.'s call for a plebiscite, allowing Kashmiris to determine their own fate. In the meantime, Kashmir remained a disputed territory, divided along a Line of Control (LOC). The referendum has never taken place.

In the late 1990s, Islamic militants from Pakistan joined Kashmir extremists in attacks on Indian interests in Kashmir, hoping to force India to permit Kashmir's self-determination. In May 1998, India detonated five nuclear devices under the Rajastan Desert. Pakistan responded by conducting a series of underground nuclear tests in Baluchistan. Many Pakistanis, including religious extremists, praised the advent of Pakistan's nuclear might.

Tensions between the two countries increased into the next year. Hoping to pressure Delhi into a dialog over resolving the Kashmir issue, Pakistan unleashed Islamic militants against Indian interests in controlled Kashmir in the summer of 1999. Clashes in the region of Kargil brought the two nuclear powers to the brink of war. Again in December 2001, militant attacks on the Indian parliament caused the two nuclear powers to square off. We haven't heard the last of the Kashmiri crisis (see Chapter 14).

Kurdistan

When the Ottoman Empire broke up after World War I, the Treaty of Sevres in 1920 promised the Kurds a homeland. Because of political difficulties, the Kurdish state never took shape, and Kurds in the region have been struggling for independence off and on ever since. In Iran, Khomeini's Islamic Revolution allowed for brutal campaigns against the Kurds, as did Iraq's Saddam Hussein. After the Persian Gulf War ended in 1991, 1 million Kurdish refugees fled to Iran and another half million fled to the Turkish border, but Turkey's military did its best to keep them from entering. The United Nations adopted Resolution 688, establishing an autonomous region in northern Iraq.

Today some 25 million Kurds live in Syria, Turkey, Iraq, and Iran, the majority of whom hang out in Turkey. The Turkish forces have spent the past decade and a half brutally squashing Kurdish guerrilla uprisings. Although the Kurds are primarily Sunni Muslim, they joined forces with the Americans in the U.S.-led war against Saddam Hussein in 2003. The Turks have vowed to enter northern Iraq if the Kurds take the oil-rich Kirkuk region (see Chapter 18). The final chapter of Kurdistan has yet to be written.

Palestine

The Palestinian conflict is a complex affair dating back to at least 1948. With the culmination of the Oslo Accords in 1993, and subsequent peace process between Yasser Arafat and Ehud Barak in 1999, optimists began to see peace as imminent. The main obstacles — Palestinian autonomy and Israeli dismantling settlements and returning the Occupied Territories to the Palestinians — seemed to be a foregone conclusion. And then disaster!

When talks between Barak and Arafat stalled in 2000 over the fate of Jerusalem and other issues, violence erupted. New Likud leader Ariel Sharon visited al-Aqsa mosque (the Temple Mount for Jewish devotees), the most revered Muslim site in East Jerusalem. This visit ignited Palestinian outrage, and intensified riots erupted. The new wave of violence has been labeled the *al-Aqsa Intifada.*

A cycle of violence characterized by Palestinian suicide bombings and brutal Israeli retaliations had escalated to the extent that by January 2003 when Sharon had been reelected prime minister, most people had given up any hope for peace. Then, in April, 2003, Sharon admitted in an interview that in order to achieve peace, Israel would have to dismantle some of the settlements. In June 2003, Sharon, Palestinian prime minister Mahmoud Abbas, and George W. Bush participated in a peace summit in Jordan.

Chapter 8

Islamic Militancy in a Nutshell

In This Chapter

▶ Appreciating jihad's various shades of meaning

▶ Following extremist interpretations of Islam

▶ Discovering that Islamic militancy is sometimes taught in madrasas

Many summers ago, I sat in a room full of foreign students, many of whom were Japanese, in the International House at the University of Chicago. We were watching a film on World War II that illustrated the nuclear destruction wrought on Nagasaki and Hiroshima in 1945. The film justified President Harry S Truman's decision to destroy those Japanese cities. I felt increasingly unsettled as I glanced around the room wondering what the Japanese students truly felt about these events, about the Japanese military, and about the American government that carried out that destruction.

Cultural perspective almost certainly determines the heroes we hold dear. After the U.S. campaign began and ended in Afghanistan in 2001, I sat on a plane to Denver with a mother and her young son who was wearing a freshly purchased child's U.S. soldier's uniform. Sales of firefighters' hats and apparel soared after September 11, 2001, as well. In the United States at that time, American soldiers, firefighters, and police officers had suddenly become heroes.

Hold that thought! As you explore this chapter, understanding that every society identifies heroes and enemies according to predetermined cultural perspectives is important. Whether you label a militant a *terrorist* or *freedom fighter* depends on your point of view.

The Holy Warrior: Terrorist or Freedom Fighter?

Although Islamic militancy currently snatches the lion's share of headlines, most of the world's 1.2 billion Muslims have never participated in any act of violence, picked up a firearm, or seen an explosive devise. Most have never conspired against any nation, burned effigies of a U.S. president, or shouted "Death to America." By and large, Muslims are among the kindest, most tolerant, most hospitable people on earth. Although the vast majority of Muslims have no direct (or indirect) contact with Islamic militancy, they still may harbor ill will against the West or sympathize with suicide bombers or people the West labels as *terrorists*. But what is a terrorist, who gets to decide, and what is the difference between a *terrorist* and *freedom fighter*?

If you want to conduct a simple examination of perspectives on terrorism, read a few articles from Pakistani newspapers on violence in Kashmir, and then read a handful on the same events in Indian newspapers. Pakistani articles routinely use the term *freedom fighters* or *mujahideen* (holy warriors) while Indians call the same Islamic militants *terrorists*. How you interpret the story really depends on what side of the fence you're sitting. If you're a Kashmiri Muslim who's suffered misery at the hands of the Indian military or government, you probably see the Muslim insurgents as a liberating force and think of them in terms of *freedom fighters* or *mujahideen*. If, on the other hand, you're a poor Hindu or Sikh villager in Kashmir who has suffered violence at the hands of Muslim extremists, you're likely going to consider them *terrorists*.

For this reason, the labels *terrorist* or *freedom fighter* serve more as value judgments that betray one's cultural perspective. In order to understand Islamic militancy, you must avoid value judgments altogether. However, the very term *militants* refers to an irregular military force of fighters, and the term *Islamic militants* carries the connotation of irregular forces (perhaps with long beards and turbans) fighting for a cause they perceive as Islamic. *Mujahideen* in this context means *holy warriors,* or people fighting a *jihad* (holy war). To get at the root of Islamic militancy, we must then explore *jihad* and its multiple meanings.

Jihad: Holy War or Struggle?

Jihad has many meanings. So when you hear a Muslim stand up at some press conference and say jihad doesn't involve violence against innocent civilians, and ten minutes later you flip the channel to see Osama bin Laden call on all Muslims to take up jihad against all Americans, the confusion is understandable. Just like the terms *crusade* or *war* can mean many things — "crusade against breast cancer" or "war on drugs," for example — jihad has multiple meanings, and the debate over jihad is one of the hottest topics today.

Many American Muslims argue that jihad is nothing more than a personal struggle to overcome one's evil inclinations. Muslims who have grown up in insulated Islamic cultures, either in the United States or elsewhere, commonly understand jihad in such innocuous terms. For this reason, many Muslims routinely object to the media's use of jihad as "holy war against the infidel," or, worse yet, against innocent civilians. Literally, to them, jihad simply means *struggle*. Jihad can take on a variety of meanings, depending on its context, such as:

- ✔ **Armed defense:** Muslims justifiably wage jihad against an invading or oppressive force.

- ✔ **Good deeds:** Jihad can include good deeds conducted for the sake of Islam, like trying to spread Islam or improve society's morals through peaceful means.

- ✔ **Holy war:** Islamic law has traditionally defined jihad as an armed struggle for Islam. This struggle doesn't need to be self-defense. In this context, mujahideen means *holy warriors*.

- ✔ **Personal struggle:** Jihad can be a personal struggle to overcome one's evil inclinations. Attending the mosque or praying five times a day, for example, can constitute jihad.

When jihad involves a nonviolent struggle, Muslims traditionally refer to it as *greater jihad* as opposed to the *lesser jihad,* or violent struggle. Extremist interpretations, however, turn traditional understandings of jihad on their ears.

Extremist interpretations of jihad

Today's Islamic militants, however, have carefully mixed connotations of armed defense and holy war to reach a radical alteration of the meaning of jihad that suits their politico-religious agenda including:

- ✔ **Extermination of civilians:** Many Islamic militants argue that jihad allows, or obligates, the murder of civilians who oppose Islam.

- ✔ **Suicide bombings:** Some Islamic extremists have justified suicide bombings as martyrdom and as an act of jihad against Islam's enemies.

Sheikh Omar Abdul Ahmad Rahman, the blind sheikh, who helped plot the assassination of Egyptian President Anwar Sadat in 1981 and who was imprisoned in the United States for his role in the 1993 World Trade Center bombing, wrote that any Muslim who claims that jihad means attending the mosque or praying five times a day (greater jihad) is distorting the word's true meaning. True jihad, the blind sheikh argued, means fighting God's enemy with weapons equal to those of the Soviets, alluding to the Afghan jihad against the Soviet Union.

More than a river in Egypt: The Arab World in "denial" after September 11

In the West, conspiracy theories circulate like bad jokes. Did you hear the one about the president who attacked a nation to distract the public from his personal affair with a young intern? Or what about the one where a president starts a war in the Middle East because he wants to avenge an assassination plot that targeted his father? Conspiracy theories in the Middle East, on the other hand, are even more common, and are thick with intrigue and twists that all seem to highlight the underlying thesis: an Israeli plot. The whole reason that the United States supports Israel is because the American public has been brainwashed by wealthy Arab-hating Jews who run the media, control the purse strings of Congress, and manipulate all the presidents.

According to many Arabs, everything from litter on Arab streets to dogs that roam the West Bank are all part of a Jewish plot to humiliate the Palestinians. An educated Syrian woman asked me one day in the Amsterdam airport if it was true that the Monica Lewinsky scandal was nothing more than a Jewish plot to frame President Bill Clinton, the friend of the Arabs. (After all, she asked, Lewinsky *is* Jewish, right?)

Two Afghan doctors who'd studied in the United States told a roomful of Afghan educators (and myself) that the United States didn't have any Muslim doctors because Jews controlled all the hospitals and medical licensing boards. Try as I may, I couldn't convince them otherwise.

The ultimate conspiracy theory surfaced in the Muslim World after September 11, 2001: Arabs indeed *weren't* involved in the four hijackings and subsequent attacks on the World Trade Center and the Pentagon. Rather, these attacks were a Jewish plot carried out by Mossad (Israeli intelligence) and the CIA to discredit Arabs and to serve as a pretext to attack innocent Muslims in Afghanistan and elsewhere. In universities across North America, educated Muslims refused to believe that Arabs had taken any part in the attacks. As evidence continued to build that 19 Arabs had hijacked the planes and that Osama bin Laden and Al-Qaeda had planned the operations, huge numbers of Muslims were in denial. When subsequent tapes of bin Laden and other Al-Qaeda operatives took credit for the attacks, Muslims worldwide resisted: Hollywood, with access to all their special effects, had produced those tapes.

Extremist interpretations of the enemy

Most Muslims agree that oppressive forces attempting to wipe out Islam or exterminate innocent Muslims justify jihad — a violent rebellion or revolt against such oppression. (Many Westerners agree.) The Soviet invasion of Afghanistan serves as a clear-cut justification for jihad against an infidel army, the *enemy of God.* In fact, the U.S. government perceived the invasion in similar, albeit secular, terms, and provided the Afghan resistance with considerable military aid. The jihad's success in Afghanistan acted as a springboard for extremist operations elsewhere: Kashmir, Somalia, Chechnya, Yemen, and the United States, for instance. Ironically, Islamic militants used these extremist interpretations of jihad as ideological weapons against Western "infidel" forces — most notably, the very Americans who supported the Afghan Mujahideen in the war against the Soviets (see Chapter 13).

Islamic extremists continue to drape their language in the context of *enemies of God* and *enemies of Islam* to pack a more powerful punch for their cause. If extremists succeed in convincing larger numbers of Muslims that their targets are *enemies of God* or *enemies of Islam*, they'll recruit more mujahideen for their jihad against the West en masse. Although only since September 11, 2001, have these extremist interpretations become well known in the West, they actually have a long history in Islamic tradition.

Examining briefly the history of extremist interpretation

Bin Laden and other extremists didn't just invent their interpretations of Islam, jihad, and enemy out of thin air. Rather, they absorbed and built on a rich tradition of Islamic extremism dating back to the 13th century. Consider the following history of extremist thought.

- **Ibn Taymiyya (d. 1328):** To Ibn Taymiyya, jihad was a holy war that must be at the center of a Muslim's life, equally as important as the five pillars of Islam (see Chapter 19). He argued that the state had an obligation to enforce Islamic law (according to extremist interpretations), and Muslims had an obligation to wage jihad against any ruler who didn't do so. Any Muslim or non-Muslim who opposed jihad, therefore, was an *enemy of God.*

- **Ibn Abdul Wahhab (d. 1792):** The 18th-century reformist, Ibn Abdul Wahhab, was influenced by the teachings of Ibn Taymiyya. Wahhab launched a reform movement that redefined the practice of Islam on the Arabian Peninsula according to rigid, puritanical guidelines that sought to rid Islam of non-Islamic influences and sanctioned the sword to assure enforcement. With the support of the Saudi family, Wahhabism took root and spread throughout the Middle East (see Chapter 5).

- **Rashid Rida (d. 1935):** According to Rashid Rida, a leading Syrian intellectual living in Cairo, Muslims could trace the political and military failures in the Middle East to the introduction of Western law. Rida sought to purge Islam of all Western influences and reinstitute penalties of amputation and stoning under Islamic law. Muslim rulers who didn't enforce Rida's interpretation of Islam were deemed infidels.

- **Hassan Al-Banna (d. 1949):** Hassan Al-Banna founded the Egyptian Muslim Brotherhood, an extremist movement that reinforced many of the very same lessons of political Islam, as had his predecessors.

Al-Banna staunchly opposed Western-style democracy that separated religion from the state (see Chapter 15). Al-Banna insisted that Muslims were obligated to enforce strict interpretations of Islam with violent force if necessary. The Egyptian government executed him in 1949.

✔ **Sayyid Qutb (d. 1966):** All the preceding strands of Islamic extremism and militancy, including the use of violence to secure a political regime to support a narrow interpretation of Islam, converged in the teachings of Egyptian Muslim Brother Sayyid Qutb. Modern Muslim governments were illegitimate, and, therefore, all Muslims had a duty to wage jihad against them, execute those Muslim rulers, and establish true Islamic leadership (according to the Muslim Brotherhood's standards). His writings also contained vehement attacks against the West, which, according to Qutb, sought to conquer Islam's domain. The Egyptian government executed him in 1966.

The politicalization of Islam as propagated by these Muslim extremists paved the way for modern Islamic militants, like bin Laden, to reinterpret Islam and the duty of Muslims to achieve their goals through violent means: suicide bombing, extermination of civilians, and mass murder in the name of Islam.

Grinding their swords

So what do these Islamic militants want? Good question! Many of their demands are targeted at the United States.

✔ **Cease political activities in the Middle East.** Before the U.S.-led war against Iraq in 2003, this demand involved the United States lifting sanctions and other restrictions (and activities) against Iraq, or as they saw it, against the Iraqi people. Militants also demand that the United States withdraw support for Egypt, Jordan, and Saudi Arabia among other nations, which the extremists see as corrupt regimes, pliable to U.S. interests.

✔ **Cease support for Israel.** Muslims often call Israel the 51st American state. All support for Israel must cease.

✔ **Withdraw American troops.** All the American troops must leave sacred Saudi soil (see Chapter 17). Also U.S. forces would have to pull out of Kuwait and other Middle Eastern locations.

Extremists have found the United States a convenient target for venting anger and frustration pent up for generations. They tend to blame all the Middle East's failures and ills on U.S. and Western influence. Securing the withdrawal of Western political activities, however, would be just half the battle. Islamic militants further seek to do the following:

✔ **Establish a pure Islamic state (or Pan-Islamic state).** Most Islamic extremists today seek to return Muslim society to the purity of the original community of the Prophet. Because the prophet is no longer there to guide the community, extremists feel they can accomplish this purity only by enforcing Islamic law through the establishment of an Islamic state. For many Sunni extremists, the Taliban regime in Afghanistan served as an ideal model, and Shiite extremists see Khomeini's Islamic Republic of Iran as a model worth emulating. Others, naturally, feel that both models fell well short of the mark, and have plans of their own.

✔ **Purge Western influence.** One natural corollary to an Islamic state is to purge all non-Islamic influences, including Western-style democracy, many freedoms (including women's rights), secular education, some medical care and social services, music, clothes, and thought.

Extremist ideology has succeeded in convincing large numbers of Muslims that U.S. policy in the Middle East is an *enemy of Islam.* The extremists have yet to convince them that the American people are the enemy, although they try, with signs like the one in Figure 8-1. Nonetheless, matched with a fertile field of conspiracy theories and extremist education, the extremists are gaining ground.

Figure 8-1:
This sign was in a village near Hunza in the mountains of Pakistan in 1999.

Photo courtesy of Craig Davis.

Manipulating Madrasas: When Schools Teach Islamic Militancy

The promotion of values in education has a great deal to do with one's cultural perspective. The vast majority of schools and textbooks in the Muslim World promote innocuous topics and social values, whether through Islamic instruction or secular pedagogy.

Nonetheless, Islamic extremism has managed to flourish in some areas. Since September 11, 2001, many articles have surfaced on the role of *madrasas* (theological schools) on Islamic militancy. Before the Soviet invasion, only a few hundred madrasas existed in Pakistan and Afghanistan. These schools taught Islamic subjects, Arabic, religious texts, and basic math. After the invasion, donations from Saudi Arabia and other Gulf States poured in and madrasas cropped up all across Pakistan (see Chapter 13).

"Famous" graduates

Today, estimates indicate that only 10 to 15 of Pakistan's 45,000 madrasas teach Islamic extremism or militancy. The most popular products of the madrasa system are the Taliban. After the Taliban rose to power in the mid-1990s, they continued to recruit youngsters from the madrasas to serve as combatants against the Northern Alliance. Militant organizations linked to Al-Qaeda also recruited from madrasas in Pakistan to participate in jihad in Kashmir and elsewhere (see Chapter 25). Many of the Shiite Hezbollah leaders are graduates of Shiite madrasas in southern Iraq, where Ayatollah Khomeini once taught in one (see Chapter 16).

A lesson in militancy

Secular education has also played a role in Islamic extremism and militancy. In the 1980s, Afghan Mujahideen leaders developed a series of textbooks that taught math facts in terms of the numbers of weapons captured or Russian or communist soldiers killed. Consider the following:

> If a holy warrior aims his Kalashnikov rifle at a Russian soldier standing 2,400 meters away, and the shell travels at 800 meters per second, how long will it take the holy warrior to shoot the Russian soldier in the forehead?

After the war, the Mujahideen and Taliban used these same textbooks (see Chapter 13). In addition, Saudi, Palestinian, and Syrian textbooks have come under fire for promoting values of martyrdom, jihad, and hatred of Jews and Christians.

Chapter 9

Islam and the West

• •

In This Chapter

▶ Sizing up the clash of civilizations

▶ Recognizing the dynamics of a clash of values

▶ Figuring out uneasy friendships and mutual distrust

▶ Understanding apparent contradictions in the simultaneous rejection and embrace of the West

• •

Given the past history of the West in the Middle East, Muslims have every reason to look upon the West with suspicion. By the same token, with the recent rash of Islamic militancy, the West now regards Islamic extremists and those who support them as potential threats. This chapter explains some of the reasons for the uneasy relationship between Islam and the West.

The Clash of Civilizations

Some analysts, and most recently Islamic extremists, have tried to explain the conflict between the Middle East and the West as a *clash of civilizations*. This clash pits the West against the Muslim World; however, it's not quite that simple. Although this generalized motif may be helpful in understanding the differences between the Muslim World and the West to a degree, it fails to appreciate the complexities of these two civilizations. The following are a few of the manifestations of these complexities — examples that don't fit into that model.

> ✔ Secular Christians (and at times, atheists, one may imagine) demonstrated on U.S. and European streets against the 2003 war on Iraq, or acted as human shields against the bombing.

> ✔ Iranian students have pressed for democratic reforms, closer ties with the West, and criticized the unbalanced attention the Muslim World devotes to Palestine at the cost of support for their cause against hardline Iranian clerics.

✔ Iraqi exiles living in the West and Iraqi Kurds in the autonomous region welcomed the U.S.-led coalition invasion of Iraq (see Chapter 12).

✔ Some retired Israeli military generals see withdrawing from the West Bank and dismantling the existing settlements as the only hope for peace with the Palestinians, while others insist on military incursions to solve the problem (see Chapter 11).

✔ Many Middle Easterners seek political reforms in their own countries.

✔ The U.S.-led coalition in Afghanistan enjoys widespread Afghan support for continued Western military presence in order to stabilize their country while extremists seek to oust the foreigners.

All parties involved in any conflict or issue have vested interests, different competing goals, and diverse values. I prefer to see the problems less as a clash of civilizations and more as a *clash of values* at every level of society in each civilization.

The Clash of Values

In any large group, reaching a consensus on just about anything is difficult. Obtaining a consensus certainly gets no easier within a larger community, region, ethnic group, or nation (if you don't believe me, just flip the channel to the next debate in Congress). The Middle East comprises an assortment of religions, ethnicities, social groups, and tribes of varying educational and experiential backgrounds. Each component of any enclave brandishes a variety of political, social, and religious perspectives that contribute to clusters of individual values. Values naturally clash at every level of Middle Eastern (and Western) society. Two examples of clashes within Islamic societies include

✔ **Kurds:** The Kurds in northern Iraq supported and fought alongside coalition forces against Saddam's military in the 2003 U.S.-led invasion of Iraq. The Kurds value an autonomy that the Iraqi (or Turkish for that matter) regime wasn't willing to allow.

✔ **Palestine:** Yasser Arafat's Palestinian Authority seeks to establish secular autonomy, while Hamas and Islamic Jihad, two militant groups, envision Islamic states.

Compare countless clashes taking place inside Islamic societies with similar clashes occurring simultaneously in the West, and you have a significant variety of religious, social, and political values within, among, and against each civilization. In order to understand the development of these various values, you must look into the past experiences of Islam and the West.

Breaking up is hard to do

In the modern period, the history of Islam and the West is founded on complex relationships of colonialism, politics, and mutual economic and military dependency. For better or for worse, European powers were wed with much of the Muslim World until after World War II when the two parties began the painful breakup process.

The colonial legacy

To many Americans during the 2003 war with Iraq, the frequent Muslim accusation that the United States has designs on Iraq and a thirst for dominance of the Middle East and its oil seemed absurd. Nonetheless, given the history of colonialism in the region, the Middle East has every reason to be suspicious of Western intentions (see Chapter 6). Espionage, oppression, nation building, staged coups, wars, occupation, economic exploitation, colonization, murder, and torture were among the ugliest contributions the West had to offer the Middle East.

After World War II, the British, French, Italians, and others by and large pulled out of the region. Even as the scions of original European interlopers were withdrawing, new Jewish migrants were taking up residence in Palestine (see Chapter 6). Although most Middle Easterners were only too happy to see their old rulers pack up and leave, awareness was growing that the region's destiny relied on intercourse with the West.

The struggle to modernize

Certain Middle Eastern visionaries argued for generations that the Middle East would have to modernize to compete with the West (see Chapter 6). With the Europeans gone, the Middle East — like a liberated slave — was left without direction. Fledgling nations turned to the two emerging superpowers (the United States and the Soviet Union) for guidance and support. These nascent Middle Eastern countries sought expertise in four important areas.

- ✔ **Defense:** Saudi Arabia, Israel, and Iran relied on the United States for defense. Jordan turned to Britain, while Syria and Egypt felt more comfortable with Soviet military aid.

- ✔ **Economic aid:** Under the Eisenhower Doctrine of 1957, Saudi Arabia, Iraq, and Lebanon aligned themselves with the United States, and Syria, Egypt (see Chapter 11), and eventually Afghanistan opted to try their luck with the Soviets (see Chapter 13). Some countries, like Afghanistan and Egypt, flipped back and forth, or played one superpower off against the other.

✔ **Oil:** Countries like Saudi Arabia and Iran had plenty of oil under the sand but were ill equipped to bring it to the surface or refine it. In addition, Western markets were paying handsomely for petroleum products after they were refined.

✔ **Politics:** A political vacuum left many nations seeking role models for their own political systems. Saudi Arabia and Jordan decided to hang on to their kings, while Egypt, Iraq, Iran, and Afghanistan felt it best to dispose of theirs.

By aligning themselves in this way, Middle Eastern countries were experimenting in the dangerous world of politics.

Legal systems

One common theme in the establishment of an Islamic state is Islamic law. Most existing legal systems are based on some combination of Islamic law, tribal law, and/or Western law.

Sharia (Islamic law)

In the history of Islamic society, Muslim reformers have always argued for the establishment of Islamic law as a necessary step to setting the Muslim community straight. The underlying thesis is that by following Islamic law the contemporary Muslim community can reconcile itself with the earliest Muslim community of the Prophet Muhammad. Today many extremists seek to achieve the same goal: institute Islamic law. The first problem in establishing Islamic law, however, is how to determine what constitutes Islamic law. The second problem is deciding who gets to determine the correct interpretation of Islamic law. Read the following two examples of the debates regarding those interpretations.

✔ **Gender:** Saudi Arabia, Iran, and Afghanistan under the Taliban — three of the most conservative Muslim countries — have had different laws on women's participation in society. In fact, the debate within each society rages on as values clash and interpretations vary (see Chapter 21).

✔ **Penalties:** Some Islamic scholars explain that penalties, like amputation for theft (as common under Taliban rule) can't be instituted until a true Islamic state has eliminated the need to steal: poverty and hunger. Others argue that Iranian and Taliban models didn't institute authentic Islamic law.

Western values, more moderate Muslim values, and those of varying extremist interpretations vie for a stake in the determination of law.

Tribal law

In Afghanistan, Pakistan, Yemen, and elsewhere, tribal law and customs play an important role in society. Typical Muslims are often unable to distinguish between tribal and Islamic law. Tribal traditions to many Pashtuns, for example, *are* Islamic. Attempts to extricate tribal law and tradition from future legal systems will likely be met with stiff resistance. For example, the custom of marrying off one's infant, or signing a contract committing one's infant child to marriage, is still practiced in Afghanistan. (In fact an Afghan smuggler tried to marry his 1-year-old daughter to my 9-month-old son in 1988, but I told him I didn't let my son date older women.)

Western law

Western law, sometimes called Roman law, has been the basis for legal systems through most of the Middle East. Islamic extremists have attacked it, calling any secular legal system un-Islamic. Islamic extremists have attacked Western family law, for example, that regulates such social issues as polygamy, divorce, and inheritance. To extremists, Islamic law must govern these issues. Experiences with extremist interpretations of Islamic law in Afghanistan, Iran, Saudi Arabia, and elsewhere have convinced human rights groups, politicians, and activists that only Western, secular law can provide the universal human rights needed for 21st-century civil society.

Social values

The clash of social values is really wrapped up in religious and legal values but deserves separate treatment. As elsewhere in the world, Middle Easterners constantly debate social issues, often heatedly. A few elements worth mentioning include

- **Ethnicity, race, and tribe:** Ethnic, racial, and tribal identity are multifaceted issues. American black Muslims traveling on the Hajj (annual pilgrimage to Mecca) in the 1960s found that racial barriers disintegrate in the brotherhood of Muslim equality. Still a number of ethnic and tribal problems thrive in the Middle East.

- **Gender:** Gender issues are a huge concern among Muslims. Under the Taliban's restrictions on girls' education, many Afghan parents, who had weathered nearly two decades of civil war, migrated to Pakistan to educate their daughters. Inside Afghanistan, many Taliban parents managed to send their own daughters to school in Gardez and other regions (see Chapter 21).

> ✔ **Humanitarian:** Contrary to the common perception, some conservative Muslims can be the staunchest human rights activists, fighting against injustices against women, foreigners, and the poor. Islamic militant groups, like Hamas and Hezbollah, have established extensive social service networks of mosques, schools, and health clinics.

Remaining Aware of Uneasy Friendships and Mutual Distrust

Given the colonial past and subsequent invasions, wars, alliances, and aid, a complex, uneasy, and uncertain relationship has developed between the Muslim World and the West. Some examples to highlight these uneasy friendships include

> ✔ **Afghanistan:** Due to changing political events in Afghanistan, the United States supported Islamic militants against the Soviets in the 1980s, and led a military campaign to oust Islamic militants in 2001 (see Chapter 13).

> ✔ **Egypt and Jordan:** In the remote past, relations between Egypt, Jordan, and Western nations that supported Israel were strained to say the least. More recently, the United States has supported Israel, Jordan, and Egypt with military and economic aid. Although many Egyptians and Jordanians still consider Israel the archenemy, the United States has relied on these two Muslim nations to bring stability and peace to the region.

> ✔ **Iraq:** During the Iran-Iraq War in the 1980s, the United States and Saudi Arabia supported Saddam Hussein's regime in Iraq. In two subsequent wars — the 1991 Gulf War and the 2003 U.S.-led invasion of Iraq — the United States fought against, and defeated, Saddam with some degree of Saudi cooperation (see Chapter 12).

> ✔ **Saudi Arabia:** This country that may be the most conservative Sunni nation in the Muslim World has enjoyed a long, and at times rocky, relationship with the United States, including partnerships in two wars against Iraq. After news surfaced that 15 of the 19 hijackers from the September 11, 2001 attacks were Saudi, new suspicions and a mutual distrust has developed (see Chapter 17).

You may look at all parties involved and say, "Hey! This doesn't make sense." At a political level, the realities of shifting alliances, changing interests, perspectives, goals, and leadership all contribute to what may seem to be contradictions, but it doesn't have to make sense because it's politics.

Hating the West: Can you get me a visa?

If you travel to the Middle East, you may encounter hostility against the West, particularly against U.S. policy and Western morals. Given time, you notice a peculiar predicament: widespread criticism of certain Western values, on the one hand, and a loving embrace of other Western values, on the other. Individuals may approach you, launching diatribes against Western politics and morals in one breath, and seeking your help in getting an American visa in the next. The general assumption is if you carry a U.S. passport, you must have connections to the White House and the nearest U.S. embassy. (One Pakistani dentist once told me, "Hey, you are an American. You can get Clinton to resolve the crisis in Kashmir if you want.")

Deciphering the Contradiction: Western Culture and Technology

One of the most contentious issues in the Islamic World is *westernization,* the process of absorbing Western culture. Two key components of westernization are culture and technology. Although the degree to which Muslims embrace and reject products from the West may seem contradictory, this dynamic is merely another manifestation of values.

- ✔ **Western culture:** Although some elements of Islamic society reject Western culture (music, food, clothing, entertainment, and moral values, for starters), the demand in the Muslim World for Western culture seems to be growing.

- ✔ **Western technology:** Islamic extremists and militants selectively reject and embrace Western technology. They deplore Western TV, movies, and photographs, but adore Western weaponry, particularly nuclear arms. Meanwhile, countless Muslims see Western technology, like movies or photographs, as harmless, and nuclear arms as major threats to civilization.

The best way to reconcile these apparent contradictions is to look for common ground: shared values. Where shared values converge, you can find common ground for dialog; where values diverge, clashes ensue. The complex, multilayered relationship between Islam and the West should be understood as both a clash of values and common ground of shared values.

Chapter 10

It's All About the Oil: Economics in the Middle East

*O*ne huge misconception about the Middle East involves oil wealth. Not all Arabs are rich sheikhs who wear *hattas* (Arab headdress) and long white garments, ride camels or travel around in chauffeur-driven Rolls Royces, pausing only occasionally to fly to Las Vegas in their personal Lear Jets to drop millions of dollars at the baccarat tables.

Only a handful of Middle Eastern countries have large oil reserves. Those nations often have lopsided economies that rely heavily on oil exports. Many of the most populous countries in the area, like Egypt (70 million) and Pakistan (145 million), are home to the world's poorest people.

This chapter discusses the importance of oil in the economics and explains the role that oil and economics play in regional and international politics. The chapter also looks at some of the economic strategies undertaken in the Middle East, and how war and Islamic extremism have created obstacles to economic development in the region.

Struggling to Compete

In the 19th century, the Muslim World was struggling to modernize and to compete in a rapidly expanding international market dominated by the West (see Chapter 8). The Industrial Revolution had allowed Europe to produce goods at lower costs and export them abroad, often to the Middle East. Many Middle Eastern nations sought to keep up by turning to commercial agriculture that could produce goods for export: Silk from Lebanon, cotton from

Egypt, wine from Algeria, tobacco from Iran, and coffee from Yemen were among the most notable export commodities.

Although most Middle Eastern governments lacked modern mechanisms for competing in the international market, countries like Egypt and Turkey established new, centralized systems of taxation and secular education to increase the revenue and to provide workers and civil servants with the skills needed to compete. A few Middle Eastern visionaries imported Western technology to build railroads, irrigation systems, and water and power facilities. In order to fund such operations, the Middle East relied on European loans, and Western financial institutions popped up across the Muslim World. As debt increased, European lenders set up international commissions to oversee government spending, and for Morocco, Tunisia, and Egypt, these commissions often invited foreign occupation. Three events in the 20th century spelled changes in this world order.

- ✔ **World War I:** After World War I, the Ottoman Empire's fall allowed new nations in the Middle East to surface. The European superpowers, England and France, divvied up the spoils (see Chapter 6).

- ✔ **World War II:** At the end of World War II, the United States emerged as the new superpower on the block, as Britain and France relinquished their colonial claims on Middle Eastern countries one by one: Syria, Lebanon, Egypt, Palestine, Iraq, Iran, and Yemen among others.

- ✔ **Bubblin' crude:** The discovery of huge oil reserves in the region in the 19th century matched with the ever-increasing demand for oil in the industrialized nations in the 20th century changed the fate of oil-rich nations.

In the 1930s, the Arabian American Oil Company (Aramco) began producing oil for commercial export in Saudi Arabia. By the 1940s, oil exports from Muslim nations accounted for 8 percent of the world's consumption, but by the 1970s, more than 40 percent of the world's consumption came from this region. A new interdependency shaped relations between the West and the Middle East's oil-producing countries.

If It Runs, It Runs on Oil

Look around you! What items, luxuries, or comforts do you see that require oil? I bet there are more than you can imagine. Consider these products!

- ✔ **Food:** Apart from actually transporting food, every step of food production relies heavily on oil. For example, agricultural machinery, like tractors, trucks, and combines, runs on oil.

✔ **Heating:** During a frigid winter, residents in cooler regions feel the expensive effects of higher oil prices.

✔ **National security:** Military tanks, jets, helicopters, ships, jeeps, and transport vehicles run on oil. A military without a steady flow of oil can be rendered useless.

✔ **Petroleum-based products:** Plastics, asphalt for roads, perfumes, insecticides, synthetic rubbers, detergents, and chemical fertilizers are produced from oil.

✔ **Products:** Transportation costs affect every loaf of bread or gallon of milk as well. If semitractor trailer, train, and delivery truck operators pay more for fuel costs, they pass those expenses on to the consumer at supermarkets, malls, and furniture, electronics, and hardware stores. This increase also affects every business that relies on supplies: hospitals, construction companies, and restaurants, for starters.

✔ **Transportation:** Sure, cars, trucks, trains, buses, taxis, subways, and airplanes run on oil. So gas prices at the pump directly affect how we get to work, go shopping, and transport our children to school and events. Transportation accounts for 67 percent of U.S. oil consumption.

✔ **Travel and the entertainment industry:** Each fluctuation in oil prices affects airlines, hotels, restaurants, resorts, and other components of the travel and entertainment industry.

Okay, enough of this. You get the idea. If you live in the West, you benefit from lower fuel prices, and suffer from higher ones. About 40 percent of the energy used in the United States comes from petroleum products. So beginning in the 1930s, a new relationship between the West and the Middle East grew out of the need for oil: a co-reliance.

Co-reliance: Finding a delicate balance

Most oil-producing nations' economies rely as heavily on exporting oil just like the West's economy — particularly the United States' — depends on petroleum imports. This business relationship truly is a two-way street. In Saudi Arabia, for example, oil accounts for 90 percent of the desert kingdom's export profits and 45 percent of its gross domestic product (GDP). So when the oil industry gets a cold, Saudi Arabia sneezes. If, for example, oil prices suddenly drop, the desert kingdom feels it. The Saudi economy simply doesn't have any other component that can absorb a huge dip in oil revenue. Therefore, the relationship between a developing nation as oil producer and an industrialized nation as oil consumer is based on a delicately balanced co-reliance. This relationship involves a basic commercial interaction for the sake of profit and economy, on one hand, and competing political agendas, on the other.

Without oil dollars generated for the U.S. market — the largest consumer of oil — and other Western markets, the economies of oil-producing nations suffer. At times political agendas between all the players clash. One example is when oil-producing nations attempt to withhold oil from the United States in order to leverage political concessions.

Identifying OPEC's role

In 1949, Venezuela approached four oil-producing countries in the Middle East (Iran, Iraq, Kuwait, and Saudi Arabia) and suggested a coordination of efforts to maximize profits. Before long these countries decided that if they stuck together, they could assure themselves top dollar for their oil production. In September 1960, representatives of those five nations met in Baghdad and established the Organization of the Petroleum Exporting Countries (OPEC) to regulate oil production and stabilize prices. As Founder Members, these five countries located OPEC headquarters in Vienna, Austria. Soon Qatar, Indonesia, Libya, the United Arab Emirates (UAE), Algeria, and Nigeria joined as Full Members. Today these 11 developing nations making up OPEC's membership rely heavily on oil revenues.

Just as a spike in the price of a barrel of oil negatively affects economies in the West, a sharp decline in oil prices can damage the economy of these oil-producing countries. With the largest proven oil reserves in the world, Saudi Arabia has been a stabilizing force within OPEC.

Using oil as a weapon

All governments from time to time use the resources at their disposal to achieve political goals. In 2003, for instance, the United States offered Turkey more than $30 billion in loans, grants, and military and economic assistance to secure access to Turkish military bases for American troops on a military invasion of Iraq. So are you really surprised to discover that oil-producing nations at times attempt to use oil as a weapon to punish or leverage political concessions from the West? Some notable examples include

- **1973:** The Organization of Arab Petroleum Exporting Countries (OAPEC) imposes an oil embargo against the United States and other nations that supported Israel in the —'73 Arab-Israeli War (see Chapter 11). The price of oil quadrupled, causing a global oil crisis.

- **April 2002:** Iran's Ayatollah Ali Khamenei calls on Muslim nations to suspend oil exports to countries that support Israel. Iraq's Saddam Hussein goes one step further by cutting oil exports for 30 days in order to pressure Israel into suspending its military incursions on the West Bank. No sustained effort to withhold oil from the West takes place because most oil-producing nations couldn't afford the loss of revenue.

> ✓ **February 2003:** Malaysian Prime Minister Mahathir Muhammad, speaking at an informal meeting of the Organization of Islamic Conference (OIC), tells of a consensus of oil-producing nations to seek ways in which to withhold oil from the West to discourage an invasion of Iraq. (Fat chance!)

The OIC took no steps toward an embargo because the results could have had a global effect, destroying the economies of wealthy and poor countries alike. For its part, OPEC announced it wouldn't use oil as a weapon to prevent an invasion.

An ally: Saudi Arabia

Since the 1930s, the United States has nurtured a relationship based on "oil for protection" with Saudi Arabia. When Egypt threatened Saudi sovereignty in the 1950s and 60s, the United States provided military support. In 1979, as events in Iran and Afghanistan caused alarm in the Saudi kingdom, the Americans proved a solid ally. Then, again in 1990, when Saddam Hussein's incursion into Kuwait threatened peace in the region, the United States stood shoulder to shoulder with the Saudis to protect their oil fields (see Chapter 17).

Likewise, Saudi Arabia has proven a staunch U.S. ally in the region. With the exception of the 1973 oil embargo, the Saudis have historically taken steps to stabilize oil production and pricing, often raising or lowering production as needed, to keep the United States operating like a well-oiled machine. In return, until recently the United States has been more tolerant of Saudi extremism.

Economic Failures

The economies in countries like Iraq, Pakistan, Egypt, Saudi Arabia, Sudan, Somalia, and elsewhere are failing. The reasons for these failing economies in the region are manifold, varied, and complex. First, the region's vast majority of nations have little or no oil. So countries with huge populations, like Pakistan and Egypt, lack sufficient natural resources to offset extreme poverty. Even in the best of times, economic development in developing nations is difficult. A myriad of barriers, created through cultural or political inertia or human-vested interests, has curtailed efforts to improve economies. Among the barriers to economic development are the following:

> ✓ **Bureaucracy and corruption:** Huge, sluggish bureaucracies racked with corruption serve as effective barriers to development.

✔ **Failed strategies:** Oil-producing nations, like Saudi Arabia, have attempted to invest petrodollars subsidizing citizenry and improving social services. Because oil-rich countries have failed to diversify, their economies are hopelessly linked to oil exports. When the global oil market suffers, their economies suffer. Many Middle Eastern countries haven't developed market economies or stepped toward liberalization of economies and privatization because of stiff resistance.

✔ **Failure to modernize:** Most Middle Eastern countries have failed to modernize. Without modern secular education, modern technology, economic strategies, industry, tax structures, and infrastructure, nations can't compete.

✔ **Population:** Unfettered population growth may be the most alarming deterrent to economic development.

✔ **Unequal distribution of wealth and resources:** Among oil-producing nations, governments or a handful of the elite generally control the petrodollars, and therefore, the money doesn't trickle down. The wealthy landholding elite in many nations, at times bordering on feudalism, stands in the way of development.

Lack of political stability and inhospitable economic environments have discouraged foreign investment. In fact, many wealthy Middle Eastern entities have invested heavily in the West at the cost of investment in the Middle East. Without external investment, many of these nations' economies have little hope of improvement.

Linking Economics to Politics

You aren't shocked to know economics and politics are inextricably linked. I discuss the traditional connection between Middle Eastern oil and Western production earlier in this chapter. I now list other examples of how politics revolve around economics, and vice versa.

✔ Most insurgent groups attempt to cripple the government's economy in an effort to further rebels' agendas. The PPK Kurdish rebels in Turkey, for example, strategically targeted tourist sites in order to cripple the Turkish economy.

✔ In 2002, the United Nations determined that opium poppy cultivation was hopelessly tied to peace and stability in Afghanistan. The Taliban — as have others — profited handsomely from the drug trade. In 2000, Afghanistan was responsible for 70 percent of the global heroin production. In 2002, after the Taliban's fall, the situation hadn't improved. U.S. President George W. Bush waived penalties against Afghanistan (and

Haiti), citing national security interests. Political stability in Afghanistan can pave the way for Central Asian oil and gas exports through the war-torn nation to the Arabian Sea. Plans for pipelines have been on the drawing board since the 1990s. Pakistani and other foreign energy companies, including American-owned Unocol, are licking their chops to get at the 236 trillion cubic feet of natural gas reserves and 60 billion barrels of oil waiting to be tapped in Central Asia.

✔ The U.N. Oil for Food program allowed Iraq to sell two million barrels of oil a day and buy food, medicine, and other essentials although 30 percent of the revenue was slated for Kuwaiti war reparations (see Chapter 12). Iraq has the second largest proven oil reserves in the world at 112 billion barrels and potentially 110 trillion cubic feet of natural gas. According to many Arabs and other critics, U.S. policy against Iraq is focused on those reserves.

✔ In 1990, Iraq invaded Kuwait in order to get its hands on Kuwaiti oil fields.

Resisting economic reform — Islamic extremists oppose Western ideas

Economic decay and social and political ills throughout the Middle East have led many across the Muslim World to the conclusion that the problem lies with leadership based on Western-style democracy and economics. Corruption, waste, and other problems, some argue, can be cured by abandoning all attempts at modernization and westernization, and by implementing Islamic states based on Islamic law. Some of the stiffest resistance to economic reform, therefore, comes from Islamic extremists in the following ways:

✔ **Banking and interest:** Extremists view modern banking methods involving interest as un-Islamic although Islamic substitutions have been developed.

✔ **Gender equality:** Many Middle Eastern experts agree that countries can't possibly compete in the global market unless women enter the workforce. The first step is to educate women. Educated women have fewer children, contribute more to the family income, and are able to more effectively care for their families. Citing religious injunctions, extremists resist most elements of gender reform. The education of women, allowing women to drive automobiles, travel alone, earn economic independence, and have fewer children all fly in the face of extremist interpretations (see Chapter 21).

✔ **Insurance:** Islamic law has forbidden conventional insurance although Islamic substitutes have been developed.

✔ **Secular education:** Some Muslim extremist interpretations have rejected secular education as an un-Islamic influence from the West. All the skills necessary to function in an Islamic society — those valued by the original Muslim society at the time of the Prophet Muhammad — can be taught in *madrasas* (theological schools). Unfortunately, skills needed to compete in a modern society — computer skills, algebra, English, geography, history, and health, to name but a few — haven't been integrated into traditional madrasas. Therefore, madrasa graduates are ill prepared for the 21st-century global market.

✔ **Technology:** According to some interpretations, Western technology is seen as un-Islamic innovations. Photographs, drawings of animate beings, and television, are among the forbidden items. Other examples of technology, such as nuclear weapons, on the other hand, are perfectly acceptable.

The Muslim World has yet to reconcile dimensions of secular Western-style democracy and modernization needed to survive economically with the components of religious cultural heritage essential for spiritual satisfaction.

Crippled economies: War and poverty

As if the Middle East didn't have enough barriers to economic survival, war, violence, and political disturbances have crippled the economies of various countries in the region. Notice the following:

✔ **Afghanistan:** Twenty-five years of war in Afghanistan have devastated the economy. War has destroyed the infrastructure, caused the brain drain by forcing the trained and educated abroad, and saturated much of the farmland with land mines. Today land mines infest an estimated 344 million square meters of territory. More than 150 people a month, frequently children, fall victim to mines.

✔ **Iran and Iraq:** These countries are two of the original founding members of OPEC and were two of the richest states in the region in 1979. After an eight-year war between the two, their economies were brought to their knees. Saddam blamed his financial woes on Kuwait and invaded that oil-rich neighbor, drawing Iraq into the Persian Gulf War in 1991, from which it has never recovered (see Chapter 12).

✔ **Israel and Palestine:** Throughout the second *intifada,* or uprising (see Chapter 11), the Israeli and Palestinian economies have been hard hit. The tourist industry, for instance, has come to a screeching halt.

✔ **Jordan and Palestine:** Because Palestinians and Jordanians sympathized with Saddam in the Gulf War, the United States, Saudi Arabia, and Kuwait suspended economic aid to Jordan. The Gulf States also sent

700,000 Palestinian and Jordanian workers packing. These consequences were an enormous blow to Jordan and Palestine's economies which depended on the revenue generated by workers' remittances to their families back home (see Chapter 16).

✔ **Yemen:** After the USS Cole bombing in 2000, Yemen's already ailing economy has been reeling. After a spate of tribal kidnappings, bombings, and other violence, estimates list the loss of $7.6 million a month, which is substantial for a small developing nation of 18 million people.

By and large, war and violence, insecurity and doubt, and bloodshed and bullets aren't good for an economy.

Part IV
Regions in Turmoil

The 5th Wave   By Rich Tennant

"We knew traveling to the middle east could be dangerous, so we learned their customs, adopted their mode of dress, and kept close to the major cities, Hershey, Pittsburgh, and Philadelphia."

In this part . . .

Part IV peels back the various layers of complicated conflicts and gives you a look inside the dynamics involved. This part makes sense of the complexities of hot spots, including Israel and Palestine, Iraq, Afghanistan, and Pakistan.

Chapter 11

The Powder Keg: Israel and Palestine

As long as the descriptions of battles, wars, invasions, executions, and kidnappings occurred in the distant past of the Near East, the possibility of reopening fresh wounds was remote. In this chapter, we see how recent developments in the Middle East threaten to rub old scars or aggravate festering sores that haven't yet healed.

Think of the current political, religious, and social environments in the Middle East as a powder keg that was haphazardly created by a number of competing forces. It is, of course, convenient to blame this 21st-century threat on Hitler, who died more than 50 years ago. That answer is too simplistic. Other factors I discuss in Chapter 6, such as conflicting religious interpretations, competing ideologies, Western imperialism, personal ambition, greed, unequal resources, poor and corrupt leadership, and lack of modernization are all elements that went into the construction of that powder keg.

With this in mind, Chapter 11 lays out the steps of how Israel and Palestine got into this mess. You see how, not one, but countless fuses leading to the powder keg have already been ignited by the well intended and malicious alike, and how efforts to defuse these threats have often only hastened the burning.

Keeping the Mapmakers Busy

If you were a cartographer in the Middle East in the past century, you were probably never short of work. In Palestine alone during the first 50 years of the 20th century, the following major changes occurred:

✔ **Through 1917:** Ottomans control Palestine and Syria.

✔ **1922:** The League of Nations approves the British Mandate that carves up Palestine.

 • Half goes to Trans-Jordan.

 • Half is earmarked for future Zionists and Palestinian Arabs.

✔ **1947:** The United Nations partitions the remaining Palestinian territory.

 • Half goes to Israelis.

 • Half goes to Palestinian Arabs.

✔ **1949:** Results of the First Arab-Israeli War set new boundaries.

 • Israelis take three-quarters of the land.

 • Palestinian Arabs are left with the remaining one-quarter.

But these boundary changes were just the beginning. During the next 50 years, changes in the geopolitical landscape sent the mapmakers scurrying about with pencils and straightedges in hand trying to keep up.

Uncovering the Origins of Militancy

In the 1920s, many Jews living in Palestine found themselves stateless. As violence against their increased numbers arose, Jewish militants sought to fight for their right to form a state on their legendary and spiritual homeland of Palestine. They formed the militant group called the Haganah in order to defend themselves against Arab assaults and British intervention. Other militant spinoffs carried out terrorist activities against Arabs, British, and even other Jews (see Chapter 6). In times of intense political persecution and armed conflict, militant organizations typically emerge in order to resist the established political order.

Some background on the Palestinians

The United Nations' partition of Palestine in 1947 immediately left Palestinians on both sides of new Arab-Israeli borders. After the First Arab-Israeli war ended in 1949, many of those Arabs who stayed put found themselves across freshly drawn borders from their friends, families, schools, farms, and

businesses. The huge numbers of Palestinians who remained in the newly
formed state of Israel after the war became Israeli citizens.

Arab Israelis

From Israel's *Declaration of Independence* in 1948 forward, Arab Israelis have
played a formidable role in Israel. Although they naturally identify and sympathize with their Palestinian brothers and sisters, Arab Israelis are Israeli
citizens with the right to vote, hold political office, earn a government education, and access free health services. Some Arab Israelis even enter the Israeli
Defense Forces (IDF). Significant socioeconomic gaps still remain between
Israeli Jews and Arabs. Israeli Arabs presently constitute approximately 18
percent of the nation's population, and they hold 10 seats in the *Knesset*
(Israeli Parliament).

A new generation of militants

By the 1960s, the Jews were no longer stateless, but as Israeli citizens, they
found that they *were* the established political order, and Arab militant organizations of stateless Arabs began cropping up with much the same goals and
grievances that the stateless Jews once had.

Displaced Palestinian refugees

The First Arab-Israeli war sent hundreds of thousands of other Palestinians
seeking refuge in neighboring Arab lands, mostly in Jordan. Other displaced
Palestinians took up residence in refugee camps on the West Bank and Gaza.
The war in 1967 (see the "Firefighting with a Blowtorch: The Third Arab-
Israeli War" in this chapter) and its aftermath created new waves of refugees.
Today the United Nations estimates the total figure of Palestinian refugees at
3.8 million.

Jordanians

Just about 60 percent of Jordan's population is of Palestinian descent, including 1.6 million Palestinian refugees. Nowhere have Palestinians received the
open-arms welcome that they received from the Jordanian royal family.
Today Palestinians are interwoven into the Jordanian cultural fabric although
the road has often been rocky. In the early 1970s, King Hussein brutally
repressed Palestinian militant uprisings in Jordan (see Chapter 16).

Palestinians in Lebanon and Syria

Approximately 800,000 Palestinian refugees reside in Lebanon and Syria, and
less than half live in camps. The refugees have often felt neither welcome nor
accepted by their Arab hosts despite the fact that many were born there. The
Lebanese and Syrians have treated the Palestinians unfairly at times —
sometimes bordering on persecution — partially due to the instability that
Palestinian militants have caused, and in part due to ethnic biases.

The Palestinian Liberation Organization (PLO)

Foremost among Arab militant groups is the Palestine Liberation Organization (PLO). Some key developments in the history of the PLO include

- ✔ **1964:** At the first Arab summit, a number of smaller guerrilla forces form the PLO.
- ✔ **1968:** Yasser Arafat becomes leader of Al-Fatah, the largest guerrilla movement.
- ✔ **1969:** Arafat assumes chairmanship of the PLO.
- ✔ **1974:** The United Nations recognizes the PLO as the Palestinian government in exile.
- ✔ **1976:** The Arab League grants the PLO full membership.
- ✔ **1982:** Israeli troops led by General Ariel Sharon destroy all the PLO bases in Lebanon and corner the PLO in West Beirut. The United States brokers a deal to allow the PLO's evacuation and dispersion to other Arab countries. PLO headquarters move to Tunisia.

Early on, the PLO committed itself to the annihilation of Israel and undertook years of militant activities against Israeli civilian and military targets, including hijackings, kidnappings, and assassinations, promoting a one-state doctrine: Arab Palestine. One popular rhetorical line was *to drive the Israelis into the sea.* By the late 1980s, the PLO found a shift in strategy more politically astute.

- ✔ **1988:** The PLO proclaims an independent Palestinian state, renounces terrorism, and recognizes Israel's right to exist. This shift marks the change to a two-state policy: Palestine *and* Israel.
- ✔ **1993:** PLO reaches an accord with Israel that establishes limited self-rule in the West Bank and Gaza.
- ✔ **1994:** Arafat becomes president of the Palestinian (National) Authority (PA), which assumes PLO political authority.
- ✔ **1996:** An agreement with Israel extends self-rule to all the West Bank, and the Palestinians elect Yasser Arafat president.
- ✔ **1999:** Arafat and Israeli Prime Minister Ehud Barak sign an agreement to finalize borders.
- ✔ **2000:** Talks break down due to several reasons including the fate of Jerusalem, and violence erupts.

The PLO and Arafat didn't speak for all Arabs. Many Palestinian elements saw Arafat's conciliatory two-state policy as weakness. Competing militant groups, like Hamas and Islamic Jihad (see Chapter 25), remain determined to drive Israel into the sea.

Firefighting with a Blowtorch: The Third Arab-Israeli War

Those who are obsessed with dates also call the Third Arab-Israeli War the *'67 War* while the duration-minded like to refer to it as the *Six-Day War*. Apart from the Second Arab-Israeli War (see Chapter 6), which was really a European-contrived conflict over control of the Suez Canal, conflict between Israel and its Arab neighbors had been largely confined to border skirmishes, Palestinian guerrilla attacks, and Israeli retaliatory raids.

By the mid-1960s, discontented Arab populations became increasingly disenchanted with their leaders' inaction in the face of what they perceived as Zionist aggression and brutality. Israel and the surrounding Arab nations began posturing for war in the following ways:

- **1960s:** Syrian snipers attack Israeli fishermen in the Sea of Galilee and settlers from locations in Golan Heights.
- **1966:** Syria signs a defense pact with Egypt.
- **April 1967:** Israel mobilizes troops along the Syrian border.
- **May 1967:** Nasser requests the evacuation of U.N. forces that have been buffering the Sinai between the Israelis and Egyptians since the last war.
- **May 1967:** Nasser mobilizes Egyptian troops in their place.
- **May 1967:** Not to be outdone, Israel mobilizes troops to face the Egyptian forces in the Sinai.
- **May 1967:** Nasser closes the Gulf of Aqaba to Israelis, cutting off access to their port at Eilat.
- **May 1967:** Jordanian King Hussein signs a pact with Egypt, placing Jordanian troops under Nasser's command.

Realizing the advantage lies in a preemptive strike, Israel launched an air attack against Egypt on June 6, 1967. Within three days, the Israelis had destroyed Egypt's air force, captured the Sinai, and reached the Suez Canal. Half the war was over. The Israelis spent the next three days seizing Jerusalem, the West Bank, and Golan Heights.

The West Bank had originally been assigned to Palestine in U.N. Resolution 181 in 1947. During the First Arab-Israeli War, Trans-Jordan seized the West Bank in the name of Palestine. Jordan remained in control of the West Bank until 1967.

Packing the powder keg: The Arab dilemma

Don't think for a minute that all the conflicts in the Middle East revolve around the Arab dispute with Israel. Certainly, peace between Israel and its neighbors would put to rest many outstanding issues, but it wouldn't signal the end of conflict in the Arab World. The standing joke is *if you put three Arabs in one room, you'd get five different opinions.* (I've heard Jews apply the same joke to themselves, by the way.)

Diversity of opinion is only natural and healthy in a constitutional democracy where opposition is tolerated, if not encouraged. But true democracies in the Arab World are hard to come by, and political dissent isn't generally taken lightly. So this natural inclination toward diverging perspectives and vision within the context of 20th-century Middle Eastern politics created an unstable environment where politicians and military officers struggled for power. To complicate the problem, the region was still reeling from the following:

- Corruption and instability of Arab leadership

- Pressure of two emerging superpowers (the United States and the Soviet Union) attempting to fill their agendas

- Undercurrents of religious revivalism, socialism, Arab Nationalism, and ethnic and historical biases

- Vestiges of colonialism, two world wars, and a series of humiliating defeats at the hands of Israel

Set these factors all against the backdrop of the ongoing Palestinian-Israeli drama, and you have a recipe for chaos. At the end of the Suez Crisis, Gamal Abdul Nasser's popularity soared in the Arab World in the late 1950s. Yet he was just one force of many. An array of other powerful Arab leaders, struggling to fulfill their own political agendas, shaped the political map of the region in the late 1950s. Notice a four-year slice of the political dynamics in the Arab World from 1957 to 1961.

- **Eisenhower Doctrine (1957):** U.S. President Dwight Eisenhower proclaims communism the greatest threat to the Middle East, and commits aid to any country that aligns itself with the United States at the expense of the Soviets.

- Saudi Arabia, Iraq, and Lebanon are all takers.

- Syria and Egypt defer to the Soviet Union, who commits to building the Nile High Dam (or Aswan Dam).

- **Saudi Arabia (1958):** King Saud, who planned an assassination of Nasser, is forced to abdicate in favor of his brother Faisal.

- **Syria and Egypt (1958):** As socialism increases in popularity, the socialist Baathist party forces Syria into an alliance with Nasser by forming the United Arab Republic (UAR).

- **Jordan and Iraq (1958):** To counterbalance the UAR, Jordan and Iraq announce a union of their own.

- **Iraq (1958):** Brigadier Abdul Karim Kassem stages a coup and executes the royal family and the premier, and sets himself up as prime minister.

- **Lebanon (1958):** Civil war erupts. The United States sends 10,000 marines to support the tottering government.

- **Jordan (1958):** The federation with Iraq collapses, and currents of unrest sweep across Jordan. The British send troops to protect King Hussein's throne.

Opposition to the UAR from within Syria grew too strong to contain. In 1961, Syrian military officers arrested Egyptian Field Marshal Amer and sent him packing to Nasser, thereby dissolving the union.

The results of the war were as follows:

- 11,500 Egyptians died mostly of thirst in the Sinai.
- 2,000 Jordanians died.
- 700 Syrians died.
- 778 Israelis died.
- Israel gained control of the following areas (see Figure 11-1):
  - Golan Heights from Syria
  - West Bank from Jordan
  - Sinai and Gaza Strip from Egypt

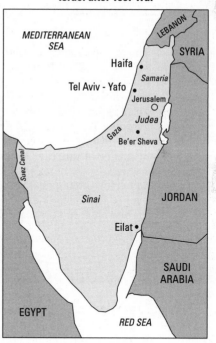

Figure 11-1:
Israel before and after the 1967 war.

A dark day in history: The Munich Olympics massacre

During the 1972 Summer Olympics in Munich, Germany, eight armed Arab terrorists took nine Israeli athletes hostage and killed two others in the process. The militants demanded the release of 234 Arab prisoners held in Israeli jails and two German guerrilla leaders held in Frankfurt. After a 17-hour standoff, German police snipers opened fire, killing five terrorists. The police were unable to save any of the Israeli athletes, who apparently died at the hands of the militants.

The Palestinian militants belonged to a movement called *Black September* (see Chapter 16). PLO leader Yasser Arafat denied any connection to Black September and the incident. A 1999 book written by one of the Black September leaders, Abu Daoud, confirmed Israeli suspicions that Arafat and the PLO were indeed involved in the attack.

The Israelis eventually annexed Golan Heights and East Jerusalem, and considered the West Bank, Sinai, and Gaza as *Disputed Territories.* On the other hand, Arabs referred to these lands as *Occupied Territories.* The Israelis maintained that the war demonstrated that the Arabs couldn't be trusted, and for reasons of self-defense, Israel must maintain a military presence in the *Disputed Territories* until Arab-Israeli relations improved. From this point forward, peace talks often centered around the return to *Pre-'67 Borders,* which means returning the *Occupied Territories* to Palestinian control.

So what's the big deal? How hard is it to turn the Occupied Territories back over to the Palestinians? Well, this return may not prove too difficult, except for one (big) obstacle: the Israeli settlements.

Adding More Fuel to the Fire: The Israeli Settlements

Increased Jewish immigration as a result of the *Law of Return* created an influx of immigrants, often poor, who had to live somewhere. The spoils of the Third Arab-Israeli War left Israel in control of plenty of extra lands in the West Bank, Gaza, and the Sinai. Some Israelis were only too anxious to begin building Jewish settlements on this newly acquired land. They set about settling on huge plots vacated by Arabs in earlier conflicts, land purchased from Palestinians, or on uninhabited spots outside Palestinian villages or cities.

Constructing the settlements involved running long arteries of water, electricity, sewage, and communications along fortified and protected highways that were restricted to Israeli use.

Of course, the Palestinians living in these areas frowned upon these settlements for the following reasons:

- The Arabs considered this land theirs whether they actually lived on it, or had deeds to it or not.

- The Israeli government regulated building and well-drilling permits. Arabs were routinely denied permits to build or dig wells on their own land while new Israeli expansion in the territories flourished.

- The construction of Israeli roads often entailed destroying, dividing, or absconding Arab fields and olive groves. Palestinian homes and other structures were also routinely destroyed.

- For security reasons, settlements controlled the surrounding land and were clustered together. Often Israelis appropriated the most fertile land when establishing settlements.

- Approximately 200,000 Israeli settlers controlled 40 percent of the remaining Palestinian land. As a result, the Arabs were severely restricted in travel, commerce, agriculture, and leisure on their own land.

In 1977, the Israeli Likud government stepped up construction of settlements, and in 1979 as part of peace agreement with Egypt, Israel dismantled the settlements in the Sinai and returned the land.

For 35 years, the settlements have been a point of contention between the Arabs and Israelis. On one hand, Arab militant attacks that have targeted settlers, including children, have earned the condemnation of some moderate Arabs. On the other hand, Israeli public opinion is divided over the settlements. Much to the dismay of many Israeli hard-liners, in 2000, Israeli Prime Minister Ehud Barak agreed to return 92 percent of the West Bank and all of Gaza, including the dismantling of settlements, but the negotiations fell apart.

Sending International "Firefighters" to the Rescue: The Fourth Arab-Israeli War

Like other wars in the region, the Fourth Arab-Israeli War has many aliases: Israelis often refer to it as *The Yom Kippur War,* Arabs call it *The Ramadan War,* while others cling to the term *The 1973 War.*

Egypt's performance in the last three showings against Israel had been a source of embarrassment. Egyptian President Anwar Sadat wanted the Sinai back. U.S. Secretary of State Henry Kissinger dismissed Sadat's request to negotiate the return of the Sinai to Egypt through diplomatic means.

The Egyptian president decided the only way to restore lost prestige and to win back the Sinai in the process was to attack Israel. So on October 6, 1973, the eve of the Jewish holiday Yom Kippur, Egypt attacked Israeli forces across the canal and pushed them back across the Sinai. At the same time, hoping to recover Golan Heights, Syria attacked from the north. The following series of events demonstrate that the incident almost brought the superpowers to blows. Caught off guard, Israel pleaded with the United States for immediate help.

- **October 8:** The Americans initiate a massive airlift of weapons to Israel.

- **October 9:** The Soviets counter with an airlift of weapons to Egypt and Syria.

- **October 21:** Kissinger flies to Moscow to defuse tensions between the two superpowers.

- **October 24:** Moscow prepares to support Egypt with seven airborne divisions.

- **October 25:** Washington raises its own military preparedness to *Defense Condition 3* (known as Def-Con 3 in the movies) status, poised to support Israel if the Soviets intervene.

- **October 25:** U.N. Security Council Resolution 340 establishes a cease-fire.

In addition to the superpowers, Iraq sent 30,000 troops to Syria, and forces from eight other Arab countries joined the Egyptian and Syrian side. When the smoke cleared, the results of the war were the following:

- 9,000 Egyptians died.

- 3,500 Syrians died.

- 2,552 Israelis died.

In the end, war had driven Israel to the bargaining table with Egypt. Sadat had wrestled concessions from Israel over the Sinai. Five years later, Israel pulled up stakes and left the Sinai, dismantling its settlements.

In September 1978, U.S. President Jimmy Carter brought Sadat and Israeli Prime Minister Menachem Begin to the negotiating table in Camp David, Maryland. The blueprint for peace included the following:

🖝 The Sinai would return to Egypt.

🖝 Security zones would be established in the Sinai.

🖝 Israeli forces would pull out.

🖝 The West Bank and Gaza were to gradually gain autonomy over a five-year-transition period.

🖝 Further talks would determine the final status of the Occupied Territories.

Egypt and Israel signed the final peace treaty on March 26, 1979. The United States committed billions of dollars of military and economic aid to both countries as an incentive for lasting peace. The two sides normalized relations, and Israel completed its withdrawal from the Sinai in 1982. With peace secured in the southwest, Israel now turned its attention to more pressing problems in the north: Lebanon.

Fanning the Flames in Lebanon

After the 1967 war, Palestinian guerrillas used southern Lebanon as a base to launch cross-border attacks against Israeli targets. As the guerrillas gained more autonomy, a number of incidents spiraled into a bloody war in Lebanon that spanned nearly two decades and claimed more than 100,000 lives, more than all the Arab-Israeli wars combined. This conflict involved forces from Israel, Palestine, Syria, the United States, Britain, France, and Italy (see Chapter 16). Israel's contribution to the conflict follows:

Dual lessons: Violence pays and violence costs

Although costly and dangerous, violence pays. Since 1947, Israel has discovered that armed forces pay big dividends. In each subsequent war, Israel military successes have translated into more political power and more land, and even on a limited scale, more security. The Arabs noticed this lesson, too. Until Egypt's surprise attack in 1973, Arabs had been mostly on the losing end of battles. Strategically flexed military muscle had forced the superpowers to intervene and Israel to visit the bargaining table.

Egypt also figured out that violence costs. Sadat realized that war alone wouldn't solve the Arabs' problems. Although violence could force Israel to the bargaining table and drive the superpowers to get involved, only mutual cooperation would lead to a peaceful coexistence. Other players in the game of Middle Eastern politics watched, planned, and studied the lessons of violence. Arabs and Jews alike have pursued a path of violence to drive their opponents into submission. Others, like Arafat, Peres, Rabin, and Barak sought alternative strategic uses of violence as a means to achieve peace.

- ✔ **1968:** Israeli army initiates a number of raids of Palestinian guerrilla camps in southern Lebanon in retaliation for cross-border attacks.

- ✔ **1973:** Lebanon doesn't play a role in the 1973 Arab-Israeli War.

- ✔ **1978:** Israeli forces cross into southern Lebanon to counter the PLO strikes in March but withdraw in June.

- ✔ **Early 1980s:** Israel routinely bombs Beirut where Palestinian militants have taken refuge.

- ✔ **1982:** During the *Peace for Galilee* operation, Israeli forces invade Lebanon to wipe out PLO camps, and trap 7,000 PLO guerrillas in Beirut. The United States brokers a deal for the evacuation of the militants to other Arab countries.

- ✔ **1982:** Christian militants massacre 1,000 Palestinians in Sabra and Shatila refugee camps under Israeli-controlled Lebanon, all under the watchful eye of the Israelis.

In 1985, Israel completed its own evacuation of the costly campaign in Lebanon, but left behind a number of soldiers to help the Christian Southern Lebanese Army (SLA) patrol a buffer zone. PLO activities continued.

A relative peace came to Lebanon in 1990 although Syria retained political and military control. Fresh violence erupted in southern Lebanon in the early 1990s.

- ✔ **Early 1990s:** PLO and Israel fighting in southern Lebanon continues.

- ✔ **Throughout the 1990s:** Iranian-backed Shiite Hezbollah militants (see Chapter 25) shell Israeli targets, and Israel returns the favor by firing rockets and bombing Hezbollah targets.

- ✔ **1990:** Most rival militias reach a cease-fire, but Israeli soldiers remain for security reasons.

- ✔ **1999:** Fulfilling a campaign promise, Israeli Prime Minister Ehud Barak announces a withdrawal of Israeli forces from Lebanon.

- ✔ **May 2000:** Israel completes its withdrawal, ending an expensive quagmire that lasted more than 20 years, and the U.N. establishes a Blue Line (border) between Lebanon and Israel. (See Figure 11-2.)

Five months later, Hezbollah launched fresh attacks against Israel (see Chapter 16).

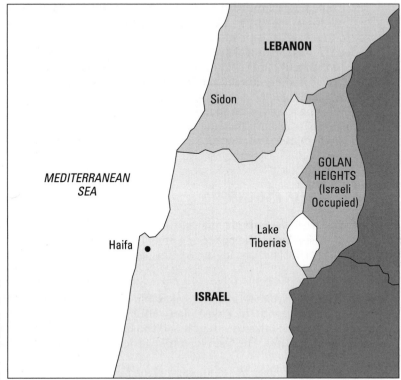

Figure 11-2:
S. Lebanon
and Israel
as of May
2000.

Lighting the Fuses: The First Intifada

In Arabic, *intifada* means "shaking off" but it now also refers to a political uprising in Palestine that began in December 1987. An Israeli was stabbed to death in Gaza while shopping. The next day four Palestinians died in an automobile accident in Gaza. Rumor spread that Israel had taken revenge for the earlier murder. Rioting erupted in Gaza and soon spread to the West Bank. Youngsters and adults threw rocks and Molotov cocktails, burned tires, and blocked roads. Israeli soldiers fired rubber bullets, live ammunition and tear gas, and demolished homes in an effort to try to stem the violence. More than 1,400 Palestinians died in the uprising, including children and teenagers.

Three militant groups, PLO, Hamas, and Islamic Jihad, seized the opportunity to press for a Palestinian state. International media coverage earned sympathy for the Palestinian cause. As a result, the 1993 Oslo Accords conveniently ended the *intifada* and set up a mechanism for a Palestinian ruling body. Israelis claimed that the Palestinians used grenades, explosives, and automatic rifles in their attacks and that by 1993 when the Oslo Accords were signed, more than 90 Israelis had died. They further charged the U.S. media with refusing to cover these more violent attacks and slanting coverage against the Israelis by showing only Palestinian rock throwing and funerals and Israeli military retaliation.

The Oslo Accords

Just as wars have multiple names, so can peace agreements. The *Oslo Accords*, referring to the peace agreements reached by Palestinian and Israeli leaders in Oslo, Norway, in August 1993, are also known as the *Declaration of Principles*.

In 1992, Israeli Prime Minister Yitzak Rabin assumed power on the promise to negotiate peace with the Palestinians. Foreign Minister Shimon Peres initiated a series of secret talks with Arafat and the PLO that culminated in the Oslo agreements in 1993. The Oslo Accords' basic tenets are the following:

- ✔ Israel recognizes the legitimacy of the PLO.
- ✔ The PLO recognizes Israel's right to exist.
- ✔ Israel extends a degree of autonomy to the West Bank.
- ✔ Israel was to withdraw from Gaza and Jericho within five years.
- ✔ Israel and the PLO continue future talks to resolve Palestinian statehood, the status of Jerusalem, and other issues.

By avoiding this last issue, temporary peace was achieved, but the unresolved issues came back to haunt both parties in 2000. As a result of the historic peace accords, Arafat, Rabin, and Peres received the Nobel Peace Prize in 1994. Many Jewish extremists saw Rabin as a traitor. In November 1995, one such extremist assassinated Rabin for his part in the accords.

The Palestinian Authority

The Oslo Accords brought a change in strategy from both the PLO and the Israeli government. The accords also lent legitimacy to the Palestinian

Authority (PA) as a ruling body. The militant PLO group that had survived on the political fringes, attacking and terrorizing Israel for nearly three decades, had transformed into a recognized government overnight, much the way that the Jewish Haganah and other fringe militant groups had mainstreamed almost 50 years earlier.

Head of the PLO, Yasser Arafat, became chairman of the PA in 1994. Two years later, self-rule extended to all the West Bank, and the Palestinians elected Arafat president. In 1999, Arafat and Israeli Prime Minister Ehud Barak signed an agreement to finalize borders. However, Arafat and the PA didn't speak for all Palestinians. As a result, many Palestinians shifted their allegiance from the PLO to Hamas (see Chapter 25) and other more radical militant movements that saw Arafat's negotiation with Israel for a two-state resolution as a betrayal of the Palestinian people. Disenchanted Arabs (and Israelis, for that matter) who sought to derail the new peace process, received their greatest opportunity in 2000 when Likud leader Ariel Sharon visited al-Aqsa mosque (the Temple Mount for Jewish devotees), the most revered Muslim site in East Jerusalem (see Chapter 19). This visit ignited Palestinian outrage and intensified riots erupted.

Trying to Stomp Out the Fuses: Ehud Barak

Like other Israeli prime ministers, Ehud Barak first excelled in the military. He earned a reputation for courage, leading two commando assaults against Arab extremists in the 1970s. By 1982, he became a major general. After retiring, he decided to try his hand at politics. Having served ministerial posts under Rabin and Peres in 1995 and 1996, Barak became the Labor party leader in 1997.

Like his mentors, Barak believed that Israel couldn't force lasting security and peace on the Palestinians, but rather the two sides had to reach mutual consensus on shared goals. Impressed with this approach, Israeli voters elected Barak's Labor party into power. Barak became prime minister in May of 1999 over the existing prime minister, Likud party leader Benjamin Netanyahu. Barak formed a fragile seven-party coalition within the Knesset and proceeded to make peace with the Arabs. First, he withdrew Israeli troops from southern Lebanon (see Chapter 16). With the mediation of U.S. President Bill Clinton, Barak and Arafat appeared to be making strides in the peace process over the next year. Barak's internal popularity began to wane as he demonstrated a commitment of dismantling the settlements and returning the Occupied Territories to the Palestinians.

East Jerusalem, almost exclusively Arab, had been under the control of Jordan until the 1967 war when Israel annexed it. Muslim, Jewish, and Christian spiritual sites are interwoven in the old city of Jerusalem.

The Oslo Accords in 1993 had deliberately left Jerusalem off the agenda because of the improbability of reaching an agreement. Both Jews and Muslims claim the holy city and demand free access to it. For security reasons, Israel has refused to allow the return of East Jerusalem to Arab control.

The talks between Barak and Arafat stalled on the fate of Jerusalem and other issues in 2000, and violence erupted. New Likud leader Ariel Sharon visited al-Aqsa mosque (the Temple Mount for Jewish devotees), the most revered Muslim site in East Jerusalem (see Chapter 19). This visit ignited Palestinian outrage and intensified riots erupted. The new wave of violence has been labeled the *al-Aqsa Intifada*.

Watching the fuses burn: The Second Intifada (Al-Aqsa Intifada)

Sharon's visit to the al-Aqsa Mosque (Temple Mount for Jews) in 2000 sparked a set of Palestinian riots called the *al-Aqsa Intifada*, or the *Second Intifada* for those of you keeping score at home. Other factors also played a part in this uprising.

- ✔ Palestinians were frustrated with the stalled peace talks.

- ✔ As had proved successful in the previous intifada, limited use of violence and civil unrest could strategically garner international sympathy and force Israel to the bargaining table.

- ✔ Palestinian opponents to the peace process, like Hamas and Islamic Jihad (see Chapter 25), seized the opportunity to rally support for their cause.

- ✔ Israeli discontents exploited the uprising as a political weapon against Barak's failed approach. In their view, Barak's concessions could resolve nothing.

Rock throwing and tire burning escalated into violent struggles as Palestinian militants stepped up armed attacks, and the Israeli military tried to crack down on the revolts with live ammunition. In the face of the increasing unrest, Barak's coalition government fell apart, and his Labor party lost in the 2001 elections to the hard-line Sharon (Likud) who promised to subdue the violence with a heavy hand.

Why can't we all just get along?

For many of us living in the West, the answer to the conflict in the Middle East is simple: Just lay down the weapons, respect the lives and opinions of others, and live in harmony. Well, believe me, an awful lot of skilled diplomats over the years have assumed the role of peace brokers and failed: Henry Kissinger, Richard Nixon, Jimmy Carter, and Bill Clinton, to name but a few.

Part of the reason for these failures lies in the complexity of the issues, many of which I discuss earlier in this chapter and throughout this book: migration, settlements, the Occupied Territories, religious intolerance, bigotry, and historical hatred among a whole range of others. The most difficult factor to overcome may be painful memories. Keep in mind that even today in the United States, many of the World War II generation find it impossible to forgive the Germans and the Japanese. Even though the geographical distance between the United States and Germany and Japan is so great, and all parties have since established superb political relationships, and the war ended more than a half a century ago, some Americans who fought or lost loved ones in the war refuse to buy Japanese and German cars.

Now imagine that you're a Palestinian or an Israeli. And the war didn't end five decades ago but is still raging on. And imagine that the enemy isn't halfway around the world but across the valley, living next door, or riding the same bus.

Perhaps your son was shot and killed while throwing rocks at the police. Or maybe your children died as collateral damage in an Israeli rocket attack on a suspected militant leader. Or your wife and sister may have died as an Arab teenage suicide bomber stepped onto a bus they were riding to work. Or maybe your nephew was shot and killed when Palestinian gunmen ambushed his school bus. Perhaps your niece was murdered while hiding under the bed during a raid on a settlement. Fresh wounds! Unforgivable crimes! All too commonplace in Palestine and Israel!

Every summer since 1993, international delegations of Arab and Israeli teenagers arrive at the *Seeds of Peace* camp in Maine. Arabs and Israelis bunk, eat, play, and debate politics together. These camps have been successful at creating an atmosphere of trust and understanding while instilling a sense of tolerance and peaceful coexistence. Before returning to their native countries, Arab and Israeli kids often pledge sincere friendship and enduring peace to one another. When these kids arrive home, the carnage and suffering they experience often propel them back into a violent reality that breeds animosity and hatred. Fresh wounds! Unforgivable crimes! It is no longer a matter of simply *getting along*; it's a matter of survival against an enemy who seems to be out to get you.

The Mitchell Report

In October 2000 at Sharm al-Sheikh, Egypt, a peace conference convened with the hopes of kick-starting the stalled negotiations. U.S. President Bill Clinton committed the United States to conducting a fact-finding mission to investigate the cause of recent violence in the Occupied Territories. The following month U.S. Senator and Majority Leader George Mitchell chaired the *Sharm al-Sheikh Fact Finding Commission*. Six months later, the commission presented the president with the mission's findings in a document known as *The Mitchell Report*. Apart from calling for an immediate end to the violence, the report suggested the following:

✔ Israel to freeze the construction of settlements in the Occupied Territories

✔ Israel to lift economic sanctions on Palestinian territories

✔ The Palestinian Authority to take steps to eliminate terrorism by 100 percent

By the time the report was made public, warning that the fragile framework for peace that had taken nearly a decade to build could be destroyed rapidly if the violence didn't cease, approximately 500 had died. Since the report's release, the cycle of violence has escalated. By May 2003, the conflict had claimed about 760 Israeli and 2300 Palestinian lives. And the meter is running.

Burning Still: The Cycle of Violence Continues

Most observers of the recent bloodshed in Palestine and Israel categorize the violence in one of three ways.

✔ Israeli aggression against Palestinian victims, who must defend themselves

✔ Palestinian terrorism against Israeli victims, who must defend themselves

✔ Cycle of violence, encompassing all the above

American media often present the last model because it seems a tit-for-tat pattern that best describes the violence. One side strikes. The other retaliates. The first takes revenge. The second evens the score and on and on. But this game has no winners, only losers.

The Jenin campaign

The Jenin campaign provides a snapshot of how a tit-for-tat armed conflict can escalate into violent combat where civilians suffer the most. Although the campaign actually started in March 2002, the events leading up to it are

Facade of security

In the summer of 1999, while my family and I were traveling through Israel and the West Bank, we witnessed an odd sight at the checkpoint between Bethlehem and Jerusalem. Around 7 a.m. we disembarked a local bus to pass through security. I noticed two lines. One funneled us through the front of the checkpoint, where Israeli soldiers checked our documents and bags, if they were so inclined, and a second line behind the building where hundreds of Palestinian men were walking with black plastic bags carrying their lunches. Their line easily was twice the size of ours. I assumed that the line in the back passed through a security check to screen laborers who carried some type of special permission or ID cards.

When we reached the other side, we obediently followed the crowd to a row of buses. The Palestinian laborers, however, shuffled down an incline and into a vacant field reaching the road some 100 yards ahead. One Israeli soldier appeared to observe the laborers with measured boredom until a brave, elderly Arab man tried to climb the bank to reach our buses. The Israeli soldier shouted something I couldn't make out, and the Arab turned and darted off in the direction of the distant buses soon disappearing into the throng of black-bag-toting workers.

When I asked about what I had seen, an Arab explained to me that I'd witnessed *maskhara,* or a farce or joke. Because the Palestinian laborers didn't have permission to work in Israel, the soldiers turned their heads and allowed them to enter because the Israelis needed gardeners and caretakers. Certainly any one of those black bags could have contained a bomb, grenade, or handgun. The facade gave the Israelis a sense of security when there was none. Most of those Palestinian men, however, were more interested in earning a day's wage to bring home to their family than spreading political discontent. So goes life in the West Bank.

---

traceable to the origins of the *Second Intifada* in September 2000. Israel's crackdown on the armed uprising in the Occupied Territories led to more violent Palestinian counterattacks. Israeli Defense Forces (IDF) launched an offensive against an estimated 200 militants in Jenin refugee camp, which is home to 14,000 refugees. The campaign included the following components:

- ✔ **Suicide bombs:** With no army, Palestinians increase the use of the suicide bombing, the most effective weapon against the IDF, by striking the most vulnerable Israeli targets: defenseless civilians. From October 2000 to March 2002, an estimated 28 suicide attacks originated from Jenin.

- ✔ **March 29:** IDF launches Operation Defense Shield, a series of military incursions into the West Bank, in an effort to stop suicide bombings and other attacks against Israeli civilians.

- ✔ **April 3:** IDF surrounds Jenin refugee camp, where an estimated 200 militants from Islamic Jihad, Hamas, and al-Aqsa Martyrs Brigade (see Chapter 25) have taken refuge. IDF intends to destroy the militants and their infrastructure.

- Palestinian militants set countless booby traps in preparation for the inevitable Israeli incursion and strategically post armed gunmen at the camp's entrances. The Arabs offer a much stiffer resistance than the Israelis had anticipated.

- With tank and air gunship support, Israeli troops enter the camp and begin a slow, arduous house-to-house battle inching their way to the center of camp where the militants are retreating.

- To clear a path for tanks and armored vehicles, the Israelis bulldoze homes and other buildings in order to widen alleys and narrow streets.

- Israeli soldiers use Palestinian civilians as human shields and bore holes in the walls of adjoining houses in order to move safely from house to house.

- **April 6:** Fighting intensifies as Israeli helicopters fire missiles destroying civilian homes, and Israeli troops move closer to the camp's center.

- **April 9:** Palestinian militants ambush and kill nine Israeli soldiers in Hawashin district. The most intense fighting occurs in Hawashin district where armored bulldozers raze nearly every home.

By April 10, most of the heaviest fighting had subsided although IDF continued to mop up until it officially withdrew on April 21. The following were the costs of the operation:

- 52 Palestinians died, about half of whom were civilians.

- 23 Israeli soldiers died.

- 150 buildings were destroyed. Destroyed property was valued at $27 million.

- 450 families were left homeless.

The United Nations and human rights groups have criticized both sides for putting civilians in harm's way. The Palestinian strategy included utilizing a heavily populated area to leverage international sympathy when the Israelis attacked, while the Israelis took such measures as denying the wounded access to medical attention.

Suicide bombing: An effective weapon

Israel and Palestine are at war. The sooner the West accepts this war, the easier the West can understand the struggle. You can't let all this talk of peace efforts cloud the fact that all the players in this conflict recognize the value of using violence to achieve certain goals, even if the ultimate goal *is* peace.

For example, when Arafat and the Palestinian Authority were caught trying to smuggle arms into Palestine in January 2002, why was anyone surprised? Opposing forces arm themselves during war all the time. You may recall that the Haganah illegally smuggled arms into Palestine from the 1920s through the 1940s. But can Arabs ship large enough quantities of weapons often enough to defend themselves against Israel? Not in a practical manner. Israel has the technology, an advanced air force, and a whole array of modern weapons including air gunships, tanks, rocket launchers, armored vehicles, and well-trained soldiers dressed in IDF uniforms. Palestine has only armed militants and suicide bombers, dressed in everyday clothes.

As is the case in most any war, the general population supports the soldiers on the front line. Because Israelis feel a sense of satisfaction when the IDF scores a victory, is it any surprise that many Palestinians and other Arabs share a sense of satisfaction when suicide bombers strike a blow to the enemy? It's just human nature. Palestinian teachers, *imams* (mosque leaders), relatives, friends, and individuals from most every sector of society encourage young people to carry out these suicide missions. Israel has committed to destroying the survivors' dwellings.

Because Palestinians are restricted with limited funds and an inability to mobilize and train forces in the Occupied Territories, they have relied on suicide bombings as the weapon of choice. A single suicide bomber can easily strap his or her body with explosives, step onto a crowded bus or restaurant, and cause incredible loss of life that is broadcast worldwide in a matter of hours.

Because Islamic tradition lauds martyrdom, Palestinian militants have conveniently interpreted suicide bombings as part of jihad against the infidel Israelis. As a result, many Arabs have embraced the suicide bomber as a glorified martyr who will be whisked off to paradise upon death. Other Muslims have denounced the suicide element or the civilian casualties component (or both) of suicide bombings as inhumane or un-Islamic. But even these opponents cite the despair that led to this attack, and often quickly follow their denouncement with a blanket criticism of Israeli oppression (see Chapter 8).

Approaching the Fire with a Cool Head

Although violence, intolerance, and bloodshed claim the lion's share of the media coverage in the region, the last quarter of a century has witnessed some encouraging steps toward lasting peace. Although ostracized by most Arab nations over the years, Egypt normalized ties with Israel in 1979. Jordan followed suit in 1994, becoming the second Arab nation to establish peace. The 1990s and early 21st century continue to show other encouraging signs.

Israeli military doves

Some of the most conciliatory approaches to stabilizing the region in the past decade have come from Israeli military doves. With the term military doves, I mean Israeli prime ministers who have made the most progress in establishing peace with the Palestinians like Rabin and Barak, whom have had distinguished military careers in the Israeli Defense Forces (IDF). These ex-military officers and others have argued that the military alone can't resolve the deep-seated problems with Israel's Arab neighbors. They believe lasting peace between Israel and the Palestinians is only attainable by trying to reach mutual goals of security, peace, and economic improvement.

More recently, other military doves have shared this vision. Former IDF Lieutenant Colonel Gal Luft has argued that the suicide bomb is an almost indefensible weapon that can only be countered by removing Palestinian grievances through unilateral dismantling of the settlements. Haifa Mayor Amram Mitzna, an ex-general in the Israeli armed forces, was the Labor party's candidate for prime minister in the general elections in January 2003. Mitzna was committed to withdrawing from Gaza and evacuating Jewish settlements within the first year.

Mitzna's proposals didn't convince the majority of Israeli population. In May 2003, he resigned after leading his party to its worst defeat at the polls in 55 years.

The Saudi proposal

As the cycle of violence escalated in Palestine and Israel, Saudi Crown Prince Abdullah proposed an initiative for peace in February 2002. The components of the plan included the following:

- Israel returns to pre-'67 borders.
- Israel recognizes the state of Palestine with its capital of Jerusalem.
- Israel allows the return of all Palestinian refugees.
- Arab nations normalize relations with Israel.

One month later, the Arab League adopted the plan, but Israel and the United States were less enthusiastic. With the proposal, the Israelis and Americans felt Arabs laid the blame for the current crisis squarely on the Israeli occupation and aggression. Furthermore, Israel was far from handing over East Jerusalem to Arabs or allowing free migration to all Palestinian refugees for fear that would amount to opening the floodgates to *terrorists* at their back door. A few months later U.S. President George W. Bush released his own vision of peace that addressed the Saudi Proposal's perceived shortcomings.

The Bush proposal — a road map

In June 2002, President George W. Bush outlined his own vision of peace. The elements are as follows:

- Change of Palestinian leadership that doesn't promote terrorism.

- Formation of an independent Palestinian state within three years. Its borders to be determined at a later date.

- The United States, World Bank, and international donor community rebuild Palestine's economy.

- Israel stops expansion of settlements in the Occupied Territories.

- Future negotiations between Israel and Palestine return to pre-'67 borders at a later date.

- Issue of East Jerusalem to be settled at a later date.

- Issue of refugees to be settled at a later date.

Most listeners interpreted *change of Palestinian leadership* to mean Arafat had to go. Although Arafat's popularity had severely diminished in recent years amid allegations of corruption and poor leadership, Arabs and many Westerners rejected Bush's implications that the Palestinian Authority was primarily responsible for the conflict because its leadership sponsored terrorism to achieve political goals. Opponents further criticized the plan because the two major points of contention (the status of East Jerusalem and the return of the refugees) were shelved for future negotiations.

While visiting the oval office, Jordan's King Abdullah stressed to Bush the need for a *road map,* and Bush committed to delivering it. After the 2003 war with Iraq had ended in April, two important events took place almost simultaneously that had an impact on the peace process:

- Mahmoud Abbas, also known as Abu Mazen, is sworn in as new prime minister for the Palestinian Authority. He denounces terrorism and commits to dealing with militant groups. (Arafat remains in power.)

- President Bush fully unfolds his road map. The PA is to clamp down on militancy, and the Israelis must begin pulling out of the West Bank and removing the settlements.

If the road map is followed, the Palestinians could have an independent state as early as 2005. Violence from both sides, however, threatens to toss the road map out the window. No sooner had the road map been publicized than militants on the Palestinian side and IDF from the Israeli corner proved unable to read a map.

✔ Hamas and al-Aqsa Martyrs Brigade coauthor a suicide bombing at a beachside bar in Tel Aviv near the U.S. embassy that kills three Israelis and injures 40 others.

✔ IDF seize a house of an alleged bomb maker in Gaza Strip. In the ensuing gun battle, 13 Palestinians died, including three children. Israeli bulldozers proceed to demolish 16 houses to boot.

In June 2003, Sharon, Abbas, and Bush (along with their host, King Abdullah) met in Aqaba, Jordan to initiate first steps along the uncertain road to peace.

Chapter 12

Iraq

• •

In This Chapter

▶ Recalling Iraq's turbulent relationship with the West

▶ Watching Saddam Hussein nurture the internal security apparatus

▶ Witnessing the Iran-Iraq War

▶ Monitoring the storm in the desert

▶ Inspecting the weapons inspections

• •

*U*nless you've lived in a cave for the past decade, you've probably seen Saddam Hussein's beaming face flashed on the TV screen, pasted on the front page of newspapers, or posted on gag novelty items at your local convenience store. Iraqi defectors, including his own sons-in-law, have echoed Hussein's reputation in the West as a madman, despot, and mass murderer of his own people.

In August 1995, the Kamel brothers — eerily named Saddam and Hussein — who were married to Saddam's daughters, Raghda and Rana, fled with their wives to Jordan. At first, Hussein Kamel, who happened to run Saddam's weapons of mass destruction program, was quite popular with American and British intelligence, as well as with United Nations weapons inspectors. After Hussein Kamel described in detail Iraq's secret chemical weapons plants, VX nerve gas compounds, and nuclear program to his hosts, the novelty of the Iraqi defector wore off. The Americans and British neglected to make Kamel feel welcome, and Hussein started having second thoughts about his defection. Although confined to the Jordanian king's guesthouse in Amman, Jordan, both couples allowed themselves to be lured back to Baghdad, where they were immediately forced to divorce. Saddam Hussein's daughters and grandchildren were packed away for safekeeping. After a night of heavy drinking, Saddam sent Iraqi Special Forces to the Kamel villa outside Baghdad where the brothers and other family members were killed in a firefight.

Weathering Iraq's Stormy Romance with the West

With some imagination, you may view Jordan as a success story of European meddling. During World War I, the British instigated the Arab Hashemite Bedouin clan of the Arabian Peninsula to revolt and throw off the yoke of their Ottoman oppressors and fight for independence. When the war ended and the smoke cleared, the Ottomans had been kicked off the peninsula, but so had the Hashemites. The British rewarded one Hashemite brother, Abdullah, with the territory that today is known as Jordan. (For more on Jordan, see Chapter 16.) What follows is the story of the other brother who ended up in Iraq.

The other brother

So now comes the story of Iraq and the *other brother*: Faisal. Still in the giving spirit, the British rewarded Faisal with Iraq in 1921. Like his brother Abdullah in neighboring Jordan, Faisal became the first king of Iraq. (See Figure 12-1.) The formation of Iraq involved merging three distinct populations of distinct ethnic or religious backgrounds. The Kurds from the north, who had been promised a Kurdish homeland of their own, were suddenly lumped together with Arabs from the central and southern regions. Shiites making up about ⅔ of the new kingdom were mixed with Sunnis, comprising the final ⅓, and a small percentage of Christians and Jews thrown in for good measure.

The Turks educated King Faisal in Constantinople. Faisal later took a seat in parliament as deputy of Jedda (in Arabia) before World War I. He first fought on the side of the Ottomans at the outbreak of the conflict, but later switched sides and joined the Bedouin revolts. After the war, the Syrians wanted him as their king, but the French, having no part of it, sent him back to the British, who set up house for Faisal in Iraq. Faisal's Iraqi kingdom may have been doomed from the start. He proved to be a weak leader unable to resist British demands for military presence on Iraqi soil and incapable of providing the vision and leadership needed to establish a solid functioning government amid the three diverse populations. Power slipped from the monarchy to more capable and ambitious political and military figures.

Riding through some turbulent years

Restive Iraqis wanted the British out, but with the promise of lucrative oil fields and rumors of a second world war, the British had their own plans. The years leading up to World War II set the stage for future turbulence in Iraq.

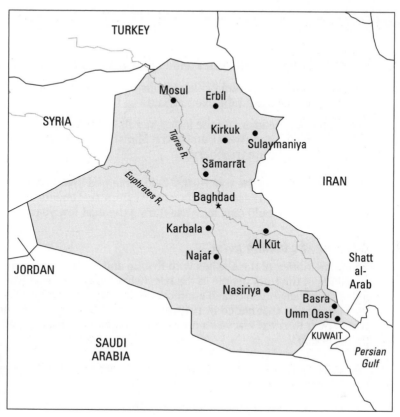

Figure 12-1:
Iraq.

- ✔ **1933:** Faisal dies. His son Ghazi succeeds him.

- ✔ **1933:** An Assyrian Christian revolt leads to a government crackdown and bloodshed — an ugly portent of minority struggles to come.

- ✔ **1934:** The first oil exports begin. Oil meant wealth, and promise of wealth meant that opposing forces would struggle for control of that oil.

- ✔ **1936 to 1941:** Seven military coups take place.

World War II brought a new generation of political conflicts. Iraq's strategic position in the Near East, matched with its rich oil fields, rendered it a perfect target for external forces wanting to establish themselves in the region. Internal Iraqi elements of discontent saw the window of opportunity open for rebellion against British military occupation. The two forces clashed in 1941:

- ✔ Prime Minister Rashid Ali Gailani sides with the Germans. With the support of the Golden Square (four military generals), he overthrows the pro-British emir Abdullah.

✔ Rashid Ali's forces attack a British Royal Air Force base outside Baghdad.

✔ Rashid Ali turns to the Germans for help, but the German preoccupation with events in North Africa and Europe delays their response.

✔ Joint Indian, Arab, and British troops oust Rashid Ali and replace him with the more palatable Nuri al-Said.

✔ Rashid Ali escapes, but the four generals are hanged. Their bodies are displayed on the street outside the Ministry of Defense in Baghdad to discourage future treachery.

For the remainder of the war, Nuri al-Said remained loyal to Britain and its allies. As a result of these conflicts, anti-Western sentiments started to rise — and the feelings would only increase during the next few years.

Reaching the boiling point

Painful memories of the clashes with Britain and its allies were still fresh in the minds of the Iraqi people in the late 1940s. No sooner had World War II ended than Palestinian-Israeli conflicts arose. After the Arabs' loss in the First Arab-Israeli War that ended in 1949, anti-Western bitterness abounded. Events over the next few years only compounded the problem and led to another coup.

✔ **1954:** Nuri al-Said dissolves all political parties and calls for new parliamentary elections.

✔ **1955:** The Soviet Union supports Kurdish nationalism in the north.

✔ **1955:** Iraq signs the Baghdad Pact, allying itself with Britain, Turkey, Pakistan, and Iran at the expense of the Soviet Union.

✔ **1956:** The United States begins providing military aid to Iraq.

✔ **1958:** Reacting to the union of Syria and Egypt (UAR), Nuri al-Said announces a merger of his own: The Arab Union, made up of Iraq and Jordan.

To certain military leaders and various political opponents, all these events meant that the time was ripe for another coup. On July 14, 1958, a group of military professionals called the *Free Officers,* led by Abdul Karim Qasim, staged a military coup that changed the face and direction of Iraqi politics.

✔ **Nuri al-Said eliminated.** Caught dressed as a woman and trying to escape, Nuri al-Said is killed. His killers drive over his corpse, bury it, dig it up, chop it into pieces, and parade the butchered chunks through the streets.

✔ **Monarchy abolished.** Qasim declares Iraq a republic, executes the king, and slaughters the entire royal family — including women and children — in the royal courtyard to drive home his point.

- ✔ **Arab Union dissolved.** Qasim dissolves the Arab Union of Iraq and Jordan that had been formed a few months earlier.

- ✔ **Baghdad Pact activities halted.** Qasim halts Iraq's activities in the Baghdad Pact, and in 1959 officially pulls Iraq out of the military agreement.

- ✔ **Relations with the Soviet Union restored.** Now that Iraq has withdrawn from the Baghdad Pack, it restores relations with the Soviets.

- ✔ **Sovereignty over Kuwait claimed.** Many Iraqis had coveted Kuwait because the region had fallen under the administrative rule of Basra before the British made Kuwait a protectorate in 1899 and because in 1938 oil was discovered in the Al-Burqan oil fields.

- ✔ **Claims to part of Iranian territory laid.** For more than 20 years there had been disputes over territory bordering Iran and Iraq, including the Shatt al-Arab waterway.

These changes ushered in a new era for Iraq. Not only did Iraqi policy on international affairs shift dramatically, but also the winds of internal political dissent began to signal an impending *Baath*.

Cleaning up Iraq with a Baath

The Baath political party originated in Syria (see Chapter 7). In 1954, the Iraqi Baath party had only 208 members. The party played a small role in Qasim's 1958 coup. Nonetheless, 12 of Qasim's 16 cabinet posts went to Baathist members. The Baathist movement at the time envisioned a pan-Arab union formed of various Arab nations, and sought to convince Qasim to join the UAR with Egypt and Syria. Although Qasim had originally entertained such notions, he later backed off the idea and threw his lot in with the communists instead. The years immediately following brought more internal intrigues, violence, and coups.

- ✔ **1958-9:** Arrests, trials, imprisonment, and persecution of opponents abound.

- ✔ **1959:** A coup fails against Qasim.

- ✔ **1959:** Qasim unleashes a violent communist backlash, resulting in rape, pillage, arrests, and persecution of noncommunist opponents.

- ✔ **October 1959:** An assassination attempt against Qasim fails. His chauffeur dies in the attack, but Qasim winds up in the hospital and later recovers.

This period's chaotic politics led to another coup in 1963 by a group of Baathist officers. More important for Iraqi history is the identity of one of the 1959 attempted assassins: one Saddam Hussein.

Saddam Hussein: A Killer Statesman

In his formative years, 6-foot-2-inch Saddam Hussein, (see Figure 12-2 for a photo later in life) earned a reputation as a thug. He actually bullied his way to prominence in the Baathist party by carrying out the most unscrupulous of tasks that no one else wanted. In the midst of Iraqi political chaos in the fall of 1958, 21-year old Saddam followed a certain Sadoun al-Tikriti home one evening and shot him in the back of the head at point blank. Al-Tikriti was a communist who had the bad judgment to cross Saddam's uncle. Young Hussein and his uncle spent six months in jail, but were released for lack of evidence.

When Qasim's policies took an anti-Baathist turn, the party looked to young, uneducated Saddam, among others, to carry out the assassination. Unable to contain his excitement, Saddam apparently botched the assassination attempt by firing prematurely at Qasim's car. In the subsequent mayhem, one of Saddam's colleagues shot him in the leg. Saddam fled Iraq and lived in the company of fellow Baathists in Syria and later in Egypt, where he finished his secondary education. The Baathist coup of 1963 opened the way for his return.

The 1963 coup and its aftermath

Saddam was in Egypt when the 1963 coup occurred. The Baathist victors executed Qasim and killed hundreds of his supporters. Immediately afterwards, Saddam flew home just in time for the carnage that followed. The National Guard terrorized suspected communists and leftists that rivaled the communist onslaught a few years earlier.

- ✔ Street clashes claimed 1,500 lives.

- ✔ The National Guard arrested, tortured, and executed suspected opponents and their sympathizers. The official number of executions stands at 149.

- ✔ Nadhim Kazzar made a name for himself as master torturer. He carried out personal interrogations at the Palace of the End, where he earned a reputation for putting his cigarettes out on his victims' eyeballs. Later, Kazzar rose to head of security under Saddam.

For his part in the activities, the party appointed Saddam to the intelligence committee, which was in charge of interrogating political opponents. President Arif, however, quickly ousted the Baathists who brought him to power. Three years later, President Arif and two cabinet members died in a helicopter accident, and the president's brother, Abdul Rahman, assumed power until 1968 when yet another coup displaced him.

Figure 12-2:
Saddam
Hussein.

One good coup deserves another (1968)

A close friend of Saddam, Major General Hasan al-Bakr, led the Baathist coup
in 1968 to oust President Abdul Rahman Arif. After al-Bakr had secured the
presidency, he began cleaning house: settling old scores, eliminating suspected opponents, and purging potential threats. The new president was able
to do so only with the help of his chief enforcer, his newly appointed head of
national security, Saddam Hussein.

Getting a grip

President Al-Bakr came to rely increasingly on Saddam to consolidate power.
Saddam spent the next decade getting a grip on power, fine-tuning his security mechanism, cracking down on dissent, and purging potential or imagined
enemies. By the mid-1970s, as oil prices rose sharply and Iraq's profits
increased, so did Saddam's grip on power. He constructed a brutal internal
security force.

Just "hangin' out" in Liberation Square

The Jewish community in Baghdad traced its origins back some 2,500 years to King Nebuchadnezzar's conquest of Israel in 586 B.C. when he brought thousands of ancient Israelite captives to Babylon. After Cyrus liberated Babylonia in 538 B.C., many Jews chose to stay in Mesopotamia.

Six months after the 1968 coup, President al-Bakr and Saddam Hussein, wanting to redress the Arab disgrace of the Six-Day War loss suffered at the hands of Israel, staged a public spy trial. Saddam's cohorts rounded up 14 men, and accused them of espionage; nine were Iraqi Jews. Under extreme duress, some admitted to being Israeli spies. The trial was televised and broadcast on the radio. The government pronounced January 27, 1969, a national holiday amidst a circus atmosphere at Liberation Square in downtown Baghdad. Tens of thousands of Iraqi spectators arrived, taking advantage of free bus and tram rides. Civilians picnicked on the flower beds. President Bakr and Saddam arrived in a limousine just in time for the festivities.

The Baathists hanged 14 men that day, including a 16-year-old boy. The bodies were left on exhibit for the public to see and the television cameras to film. Crowds cheered. Professional dancers danced under the gallows. The president gave a frenzied speech, denouncing Zionists, imperialists, Jews, and their sympathizers. More Baathist heavyweights gave speeches. This event launched a campaign that led to the arrest, torture, and execution of more than 50 Jews on espionage charges.

The last 45 miles of the Shatt al-Arab waterway leading into the Persian Gulf forms a natural border between Iraq and Iran. In 1974, conflicts with Iran over that waterway led to border skirmishes between the two countries. Iran countered by providing arms to Kurdish subversives in northern Iraq, who began demanding independence. Fighting broke out between the Kurds and Iraqi forces, and Iraq regularly bombed Kurdish villages inside Iranian territory. When Saddam signed the *Algiers Accord* in 1975 that settled the dispute between the two nations, Iran withdrew its support for the Kurds. But the conflict between Iran and Iraq was far from over. The winds of Islamic revolution swirling in Iran could be felt among Iraq's Shiite majority.

Spending the oil profits: The Iraqi economy prospers

The fact that Iraqi politicians and military leaders had staged coups, established regimes, and eliminated opponents during the past 50 years shouldn't detract from the progress the Baathists had made in other sectors of society. Profits from oil had made Iraq one of the wealthiest countries in the region. By the time Saddam assumed power in 1979, the economy was strong. Iraq had bankrolled $35 billion. Its military enjoyed sophisticated European hardware.

Education was free for all Iraqi children through the university level, and healthcare was available to all Iraqis at no cost. The standard of living was good and food cheap.

Shaking everything up Saddam-style

In 1979, Saddam discovered that Bakr was secretly negotiating with Syria's Hafiz al-Assad to speed up a union between the two countries — a merger that Saddam opposed. As a result, Saddam forced Bakr to resign. At the age of 42, Hussein stepped from the shadows into the spotlight. His first order of business was to deal with political dissidents (hard to believe any were left). One month after assuming office, Saddam put 68 top Baathist leaders on trial for conspiracy charges and executed 21. He then set about purging potential opponents in trade unions, the militia, local and provincial government offices, and anywhere else he could imagine. The largest threat, however, came from Shiite extremist elements inspired by Ayatollah Khomeini's Islamic Revolution next door in Iran. So Saddam decided the best way to deal with Shiite discontent at home was to launch an invasion of Iran. Figure 12-3 shows these neighboring countries.

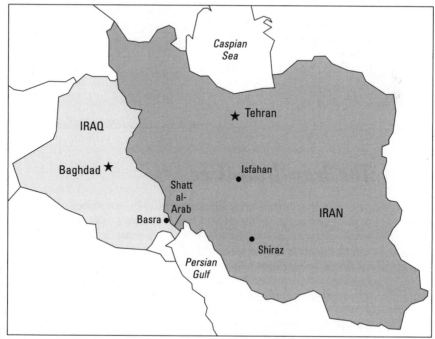

Figure 12-3:
Iraq and
Iran.

Playing dirty with chemical weapons

Most governments play by a set of written and unwritten ground rules established for military engagement. Sometimes, one side plays dirty by deliberately breaking those rules, including the rule: Never use chemical weapons. Iraq wasn't the first to use chemical weapons. The Germans first used chlorine in 1915 and mustard gas in 1917 against the Allies in Belgium during World War I. Although the Geneva Protocol banned the use of poisonous gases as a weapon in 1925, mustard gas has been used by the British in the Middle East, the Italians in Abyssinia, and the Japanese in China.

Saddam Hussein began playing dirty in 1984 when the United Nations reported that Iraq had used mustard gas and Tabun nerve agent against Iran to stave off massive waves of human suicide attackers. Iraq continued to use chemical weapons against its neighbors including the following:

✔ May 23 to 25, 1988: Iraqi forces launch an offensive in the north, central, and south using chemical weapons. They successfully recapture Shalamche.

✔ June 19 to 25, 1988: Iraq uses chemical weapons to regain Mehran in the central sector and Majnoon Islands in the south.

Iraq's most notorious chemical assault, however, wasn't against Iranians, but rather against Iraqi Kurds. Saddam's cousin, General Ali Hassan al-Majid, became known as Chemical Ali, an epithet he earned for his proclivity to launch chemical attacks against the enemy.

✔ 1987: Iraq launches chemical attacks against 24 villages in Kurdistan.

✔ 1988: The *Anfal* (spoils or booty) campaign kills 50,000 to 100,000 Kurds. On March 16, *Chemical Ali* massacres 5,000 inhabitants of the Kurdish city of Halabja with hydrogen cyanide and mustard gas. An estimated 10,000 men, women, and children are injured.

International specialists are still in the process of assessing the long-term medical aftereffects to survivors: cancer, neurological disorders, and congenital birth defects are the most common.

The Iran-Iraq War

After the Shah's defeat by Khomeini in 1979, a number of Iranian generals fled to Baghdad and convinced Saddam that Iran's military had been severely weakened and couldn't last against a full-scale attack more than a few days. Taking a page from the Israeli Six-Day War manual, the Iraqi air force launched an air assault against Iran with French Mirage jets on September 22, 1979, hoping to destroy the Iranian air force while still on the ground. Saddam had four goals in mind when he attacked Iran, including:

✔ Recovering lands of the Shatt al-Arab waterway that Saddam had conceded to Iran five years earlier in the Algiers Accord. At the time of signing the agreement, Iraq's military was inferior, but by 1979, Saddam felt Iraq had reached military superiority.

- ✔ Stemming the tide of Shiite extremist activity inside Iraq that gained its inspiration from Khomeini.

- ✔ Capturing the oil fields of Khuzestan in western Iran. (Nothing wrong with a little profit in war, right?)

- ✔ Inciting a revolt against the Iranian government among the Arab-speaking population of the Khuzestan region.

When self-proclaimed field marshal Saddam dispatched six mechanized divisions across the border in a ground invasion of Iran on the second day, everything was going as planned.

Momentum swings back and forth

Iraq enjoyed inroads into Iranian territory for the first two years. In 1982, however, Khomeini's forces pushed Iraq out of Iran. Other important developments during this period follow.

- ✔ **1981:** Israel bombs Iraq's Osirak nuclear reactor, alleging the reactor could be used to create nuclear weapons to be used against Israel.

- ✔ **1983:** Iraq bombs Iran's offshore oilfields of Nowruz, creating the largest oil spill in the Persian Gulf's history.

- ✔ **1984:** Iran captures the Iraqi oil fields of Majnoon Islands.

- ✔ **1985:** U.S. envoy Donald Rumsfeld visited Baghdad. As a result, the United States begins providing military and economic support to Iraq.

- ✔ **1986:** With Iran and Iraq enmeshed in war, Kuwait seizes the opportunity to sell its oil. In the process, Kuwait exceeds its OPEC quota, flooding the world market with oil, driving the cost of crude below $10 a barrel. This decrease of nearly 66 percent from a year earlier severely cuts into the revenues of both belligerent countries.

- ✔ **1987:** Iranian forces and Iraqi Kurdish allies seize terrain in Iraqi Kurdistan.

In July, a Kuwaiti oil tanker under the escort of U.S. naval ships struck an Iranian mine. This event spelled the beginning of the end for Iran's chances of winning the war.

Adding the West to the mix

Everyone wanted an end to the war. Because the West needed a stable flow of affordable oil, the United States had been protecting the Kuwaiti oil tanker when it struck the Iranian mine. This international incident was just the event that the West had been waiting for (or dreading; take your pick). The United States, Britain, and France sent 60 warships to the region. From this point forward, the United States began openly engaging Iranian forces in the Gulf.

- ✔ **1987 and 1988:** The United States sinks Iranian ships and destroys Iranian offshore oil platforms.

- ✔ **1987:** An Iraqi aircraft inadvertently fires two missiles and strikes the USS Stark, killing 37 crewmembers.

- ✔ **1988:** Iraq begins instituting the use of chemical weapons against Iranian forces.

- ✔ **July 3, 1988:** The United States shoots down an Iran Air passenger plane carrying 290 civilians, mistaking it for a military aircraft.

Most of the Arab countries supported Iraq, although the majority of their weapons came from the Soviet Union. The United States lent military support to Iraq while providing some covert munitions to Iran (see Chapter 18). In addition, Iran received aid from Syria and Libya, even though China and North Korea provided weapons.

In 1988, both sides accepted a U.N. cease-fire. In 1990, Iraq agreed to accept the terms of the 1975 Algiers Accord that had been signed 15 years earlier. The armed conflict that Saddam believed would last but a few days proved to drag on for eight years, bringing two of the Middle East's wealthiest nations to their knees, depleting the riches and progress that they had made with oil profits over the past quarter of a century. The eight-year struggle cost each country about $100 billion. In human life, the war cost approximately 500,000 human lives, much more than the Lebanese civil war and all the Arab-Israeli wars put together.

The Persian Gulf War

Although Saddam proved to be a brilliant architect of Iraq's repressive internal security system, and he knew how to interrogate, torture, and eliminate political opposition, he was no military tactician. Before the Iran-Iraq War, he had never led troops into battle or even taken part in a conventional armed conflict. He learned his lesson, though: Never pick on someone your own size.

Saddam used the Iran-Iraq War to build up his military machine. Apart from the valuable combat experience, his military grew from 250,000 soldiers before the war to 1.25 million troops in the early 1990s. Iraq now enjoyed the largest military apparatus in the region, bigger than even that of Egypt or Turkey. Now that the war was over, and the West on his side, Saddam began spending oil revenues to expand his military even more. European and U.S. businesses sought coveted Iraqi contracts. But by 1990, Saddam began to threaten stability in the region and to embarrass his Western supporters for the following reasons:

> ✔ He was caught trying to buy components to build nuclear weapons.
>
> ✔ He threatened to destroy Israel. Saddam claimed that Israelis were targeting Iraq's nuclear reactors just as they had done in 1981 when they destroyed Osirak.
>
> ✔ He picked a fight with Kuwait.

Former Western supporters of Saddam came to the realization that the Iraqi president was out of control and something had to be done to reign him in.

GROUND RULES

Fighting a common enemy

In recent times, the press and public opinion have been increasingly critical of those governments that provide a "friendly" nation with weapons during one struggle only to target that very same nation in a subsequent conflict. The common "the enemy of my enemy is my friend" cliché, although simplistically cute, lacks the historical perspective to appreciate the complexities of shifting political alliances. Think about it! The World War II Axis (Germany, Japan, and Italy) became allies with Britain, France, and the United States almost immediately after the war, and the former ally, the Soviet Union, assumed the role of archenemy throughout the Cold War. In the ancient and medieval Middle East, dethroned kings and rulers frequently sought exile in the land of their former enemy, often with the intent of raising an army and attacking opponents back home.

A better way to look at shifting political alliances is through the lenses of common interests. Heads of state join forces, even temporarily, with other nations to promote shared interests or to reach common goals. With the passage of time, many events happen to transform these alliances: leadership changes, interests diverge, or the goals are reached and new policies are outlined. Political marriages end in divorce because political leaders quite simply grow apart.

Take a look at the classic case: Saddam Hussein! The United States had just ended a hostage standoff with Iran that lasted from 1978 to 1981 (see Chapter 18). U.S. President Ronald Reagan feared that the Islamic revolution would spread to the oil-rich Gulf States and threaten global stability. So in 1985, when Reagan sent U.S. envoy Donald Rumsfeld to Baghdad to meet with Saddam Hussein, both countries shared a common interest: the defeat of the current Iranian regime of Islamic extremists. For the next three years, the United States supported Iraq's efforts to defeat Iran by providing intelligence, economic aid, and weapons. After the war was over in 1988, the United States and Iraq reevaluated the relationship. By 1990, they no longer shared common interests. Suffering from a devastating war that ended in stalemate and wrecked Iraq's economy, Saddam decided 1990 was as good a year as any to pick on someone much smaller than Iraq: the tiny, but oil-wealthy Kuwait. On the other hand, U.S. President George Bush now saw Iraq attempting what the United States had feared Iran might do a decade earlier: gobble up all the oil fields of the Middle East. So, as interests changed, so did alliances, and the world entered the Persian Gulf War.

Saddam on the war path again

After the Iran-Iraq War, an emboldened Saddam began making demands of his Arab neighbors. He expected them to write off $40 billion in war debt and stabilize the price of oil. Iraq claimed that it was losing $1 billion a year for every dollar dip in crude oil prices. On July 18, 1990, Saddam made three specific demands of Kuwait.

- Write off Iraq's outstanding loans from the Iran-Iraq War.

- Stabilize the price of oil. Kuwait had contributed to the glut of oil in the market and prices had dropped to $13 a barrel.

- Rebuild Iraq's infrastructure that had been devastated from the war.

Saddam seemed disappointed when the emir of Kuwait agreed to all three demands. The Iraqi president had other goals in mind including:

- **Annexation of Kuwait.** Baghdad had always laid claims to Kuwait because the British made Kuwait a separate entity in the 1920s and granted it independence in 1961.

- **Lucrative oil fields.** In the 1920s, Britain had paid little attention to Kuwaiti oil. By 1990, Baghdad was licking its chops at the thought of getting its hands on that source of revenue.

On July 21, ignoring the emir's agreement to Iraq's demands, Saddam mobilized 30,000 troops on the Kuwaiti border. You can see the Kuwait-Iraq border in Figure 12-4.

Green light, red light, or mixed signals?

With the Soviet Union in decline in 1990, the United States emerged as the sole superpower. Saddam, for all his faults as a diplomat and head of state, didn't want to invade Kuwait without the approval of the Americans. On July 25, just four days after the troop mobilization on the Kuwaiti border, the Iraqi president summoned American ambassador April Glaspie to the presidential palace. Whether wishful thinking, misunderstanding, or outright deceit, Baghdad has always claimed that Ambassador Glaspie gave Saddam the green light to carry out his invasion through these two messages.

- The United States wouldn't interfere in Iraq's domestic concerns.

- The United States considered the Kuwaiti border dispute an affair for Arab nations to settle.

Whatever the details of that meeting, Glaspie took the heat for sending mixed signals. After Iraq's invasion of Kuwait, Glaspie remarked that she didn't think that Saddam would seize *all* Kuwait.

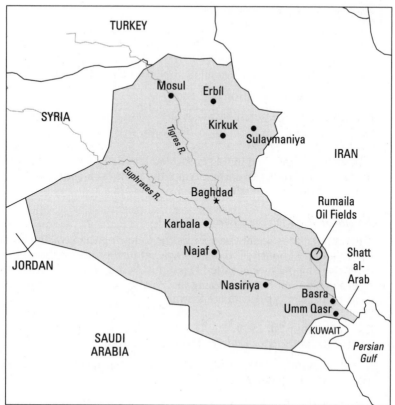

Figure 12-4:
Iraq and
Kuwait.

The invasion of Kuwait and the West's response

On August 2, 1990, approximately 100,000 Iraqi soldiers invaded Kuwait, whose 20,000 forces were no match for the Iraqis. Seven hours after the initial incursion, the battle was over. But the war had just begun.

- ✔ **August 2:** Iraqi troops begin a campaign of rape, torture, and pillage of Kuwaiti citizens and property.

- ✔ **August 6:** Saudi King Fahd, fearing he would be Iraq's next victim, turns to the United States for help. By January 1991, the West had stationed more than 600,000 troops on Saudi soil.

- ✔ **August 28:** Iraq officially announces the annexation of Kuwait, making it the 19th province of Iraq.

Saddam appointed his cousin, General Ali Hassan al-Majid, also known as Chemical Ali, governor of Kuwait in the fall.

Saddam's Middle East peace plan

As a "representative of international peace," Saddam proposed his own peace plan for the Middle East that included the following points:

- ✔ Israel to withdraw from all occupied lands: Palestine, Syria, and Lebanon

- ✔ Syria to withdraw from Lebanon

- ✔ Iraq to withdraw from Kuwait after all the other withdrawals were completed

Although the plan died in its tracks, Saddam had raised the Israeli issue to the forefront, hoping to garner sympathy from Arab countries. He got three significant takers: Palestine, Jordan, and Sudan.

A storm gathering in the desert

The United States spent the six months following the invasion amassing a coalition of 29 countries to defend against further Iraqi expansion. The U.S. defensive campaign was called *Operation Desert Shield*. At the same time, the coalition held out hopes of using diplomatic pressure and economic sanctions to force Iraq to evacuate Kuwait.

- ✔ **November 29, 1990:** The U.N. Security Council adopts Resolution 678, which authorizes military force against Iraq.

- ✔ **January 12, 1991:** The U.S. Congress votes in favor of military force to enforce U.N. Resolution 678.

- ✔ **January 14, 1991:** The Iraqi parliament votes to go to war instead of relinquish its stranglehold on Kuwait.

In January 1991, the defensive position of the coalition converted to an offensive campaign against the Iraqis called *Operation Desert Storm* that began January 16 and ended February 24, 1991.

Operation Desert Storm

The United States had forged a coalition of 29 United Nations members including forces from a number of Arab and Muslim nations: Bahrain, Bangladesh, Egypt, Oman, Pakistan, Qatar, Saudi Arabia, and Syria. The coalition amassed 600,000 Western troops and 220,00 Muslim forces against 545,000 Iraqi forces in Kuwait and southern Iraq. The major events of the war included the following:

- ✔ **January 16:** Coalition forces begin a bombing campaign of Baghdad using cruise missiles from U.S. warships in the Persian Gulf and with air sortie missions from Saudi Arabia, Turkey, and aircraft carriers in the gulf. The Iraqi military provides almost no resistance.

- ✔ **January 18:** Iraq responds by firing 18 Scud missiles at Israel.

> ✔ **January 22:** Iraq fires three Scuds at Israel, and approximately a dozen Israelis died of heart attacks and faulty gas masks.
>
> ✔ **February 24:** Coalition forces enter the ground campaign named *Desert Saber.* With allied forces steamrolling toward Baghdad, the Iraqi soldiers surrender en masse. Retreating Iraqi forces begin setting Kuwait's oil fields ablaze.

On February 28, Iraq accepted a truce, and a cease-fire went into effect. Coalition forces had flown 106,000 sorties in 42 days. As many as 45,000 Iraqis died in the conflict. Some 540 coalition forces lost their lives, including approximately 450 Americans. The war cost Iraq more than $200 billion and coalition forces nearly $82 billion.

Trudging through sanctions, weapons inspections, and beyond

U.N. Security Council Resolution 687 called for Iraq to destroy nonconventional weapons (or weapons of mass destruction): chemical, biological, and nuclear weapons as well as intermediate and long-range weaponry. The U.N.-imposed prewar economic sanctions, including the prohibition against selling Iraqi oil, remained in place. After the weaponry and capability to construct such weapons were destroyed, the United Nations was to lift the sanctions. The United Nations Special Commission on Disarmament (UNSCOM) began weapons inspections in May 1991.

Catch me if you can

Iraq's deputy prime minister, Tariq Aziz, became a trusted Saddam loyalist because of his fluency in English and his experience in diplomacy (and it didn't hurt any that he was an Arab Christian). Aziz oversaw an elaborate plan of concealment and deception that included mock inspections and training Iraqi officials on how to deal with U.N. inspection teams. Baghdad essentially went through the motions of cooperation while strategically concealing information and denying inspectors access to certain sites.

The initial inspections uncovered Iraqi programs to build chemical weapons and plans to produce nuclear materials for the construction of weapons. Some of the material was destroyed, but over the next seven years, Iraq successfully frustrated the UNSCOM weapons inspections. One exception was the 1995 defection of Saddam's son-in-law, Hussein Kamel, former head of Iraq's weapons procurement program. Because Kamel described the weapons program in detail, an infuriated Saddam was forced to disclose new information on biological weapons and efforts to acquire nuclear weapons.

As the years dragged on, U.N.-imposed sanctions took their toll on the Iraqi people. Tens of thousands of Iraqis lived in abject poverty and died of starvation and disease while Saddam sold oil on the black market and used the profits to build nonconventional weapons, increase the military's payroll, and raise the standard of living of the Iraqi elite. Saddam found success in a strategy that garnered international sympathy for the Iraqi people while thumbing his nose at the Western weapons police. The tide of international opinion began to turn against the United Nations and its two major supporters: the United States and Britain. Many people, including the same Arab countries most threatened by Iraq in the Gulf War, began to question the value and productivity of continued inspections and sanctions.

Oil for food

From the outset, the United Nations recognized the need to sell limited amounts of oil to provide sustenance to the Iraqi people. The United Nations, therefore, developed an Oil for Food program by which Iraq could sell oil and in turn purchase and import food, medicine, and other essentials, although 30 percent of the income was slated for Kuwaiti war reparations.

A problem arose because of the potential dual use of many items that Iraq wanted or needed to import. The United Nations denied the import of certain fertilizers, agricultural machinery, pesticides, and chemicals because Iraq could also find weapons applications for those same items. Many of the materials needed to reconstruct Iraq's destroyed infrastructure — electrical and water supply systems — were also off limits. To compound the problem, evidence mounted to suggest that all the supplies purchased with the oil money didn't reach the Iraqi people. The Iraqi army, for instance, often hoarded food and medicine, and the proceeds from supplies sold on the black market were used to line the pockets of Saddam's most loyal followers.

Cracks in the spyglass

The inspections were a highly visible and extremely political endeavor. The United Nations directed its efforts at achieving three goals through peaceful means:

- ✔ Disarming Iraq and neutralizing Saddam's ability to threaten stability in the region

- ✔ Securing enough economic stability within Iraq to stave off a wide-scale humanitarian emergency

- ✔ Supporting the interests of the United States and Britain, who as time wore on began to shift their goal from disarming Saddam to toppling him

Many opposing forces behind various events playing out from 1991 to 1998 made the achievement of any of those three goals less and less likely. Saddam's refusal to play by the rules by frustrating U.N. inspectors, selling oil on the black market, and building his military earned retaliatory efforts from American and British intelligence services. The following are some notable intrigues carried out during this period:

- ✔ The CIA sponsored Iraqi opposition groups in an effort to assassinate Saddam or overthrow his regime.

- ✔ Hussein foiled a number of assassination plots from within the Iraqi armed forces.

- ✔ The CIA had infiltrated UNSCOM and was gathering intelligence on the Iraqis.

This last charge came not from the Iraqis, but from a top UNSCOM inspector, Scott Ritter. This crack in the inspection apparatus helped to tarnish UNSCOM's reputation and cast further doubt on the effectiveness of the inspections and the validity of the accompanying sanctions.

When the Iraqis exploited the spy card to attempt to divert attention from their own underhanded dealings, no one paid much attention. But with accusations surfacing from Ritter, people took notice. Ritter's August 1998 resignation cited gross misconduct of UNSCOM. He accused Richard Butler, who led UNSCOM's mission to Iraq, of taking orders from Washington. Ritter further contended that a number of UNSCOM inspectors collected intelligence for the United States.

In his book *The Greatest Threat,* Butler defended UNSCOM's relationship with U.S. intelligence organizations as legitimate. In order to find out more about Saddam's hidden weapons program, Butler maintained, UNSCOM consulted with intelligence units of various governments. UNSCOM used a variety of techniques to gather information: questioned Iraqi defectors, utilized special sensory equipment, and examined U-2 photographs of weapons-related activities. Because the Iraqis had established their own intelligence mechanisms for spying on the weapons inspectors, Butler employed counterintelligence devices to cloak their own conversations while other devices picked up Iraqi communications. UNSCOM also collaborated with the United States to install technology for monitoring Iraqi messages although the equipment was later abandoned.

Taking it in stride

In the fall of 1998, Ritter's accusations highlighted the failures of the United Nations' efforts to disarm Saddam. After seven years of Baghdad's avoiding UNSCOM's inspection mechanism and rebuilding its military with revenues from smuggled oil, the U.N. weapons team pulled out. Seemingly at wits end, the United States and Britain launched *Operation Desert Fox* on December 17, 1998, an allied air campaign to destroy sites to which U.N. inspectors had been denied access. None of the 11 chemical and biological weapons facilities targeted was destroyed. Iraq refused to cooperate further with weapons inspections.

Saddam had successfully cultivated international sympathy. Although one would be hard pressed to find many supporters of the Iraqi dictator even in the Middle East, the futility of the sanctions and weapons inspections at the expense of the Iraqi people outweighed Saddam's potential threat. Aside from a plot to assassinate George Bush on a planned trip to Kuwait in April of 1993, more and more people believed that Iraq was incapable of lashing out against its neighbors.

At the end of 1998, Denis Halliday, who ran the U.N. Oil for Food program in Iraq, resigned his post, citing what he called the *genocidal* sanctions against the Iraqi people. He claimed that the sanctions were responsible for the deaths of 4,000 to 5,000 children a month. Countries linked with Iraq through common economic interests — countries such as Turkey, many Arab states, and Russia — felt it made more sense to lift the sanctions and stimulate Iraq's economy. As the year 1999 emerged, Saddam seemed to be winning the war of attrition and would be left to his own devices, conducting business as usual in the face of lax U.N. resistance. That is, until September 11, 2001.

A new sheriff in town (named Bush)

The terrorist attacks of September 11, 2001, changed everything. With George W. Bush in the Oval Office, the United States' War on Terrorism shifted its focus from an illusive, ill-defined enemy in Al-Qaeda that could disappear into the scenery of any Muslim community to a familiar, concreted enemy in Hussein. For British Prime Minister Tony Blair and President Bush, the Iraqi president with his weapons of mass destruction possessed the greatest threat to the United States and its allies. Three important factors contributed to the British and American determination that Saddam was a threat:

- ✔ **Track record.** Saddam had proven his willingness to build and launch chemical weapons against the enemy and against Iraqi Kurds.

- ✔ **On the record.** Saddam demonstrated outspoken hatred of Israel, the United States, and Britain.

- ✔ **Missing records.** No one knew what Saddam had been up to since the inspectors left in 1998. A number of Soviet nuclear scientists had turned up missing, some of whom may have been working in Iraqi laboratories.

Taking into account Al-Qaeda's willingness and ability to attack the United States and Saddam's propensity to develop weapons of mass destruction, Bush's greatest fear was that Saddam would provide Al-Qaeda with the means to deal the United States a catastrophic blow. In 2002, Blair and Bush initiated a campaign to mobilize the international community to disarm, or even better yet, to dethrone Saddam.

✔ **October 2002:** The U.S. Congress authorizes Bush to use force against Iraq if necessary.

✔ **November 2002:** Bush and Blair successfully negotiate with France and Russia the terms of the new U.N. Resolution 1441, designed to bring Iraq into compliance with earlier resolutions.

✔ **November 2002:** The Iraqi parliament rejects the resolution, but Saddam overrules parliament and agrees to give the U.N. weapons inspectors unfettered access to any site in Iraq.

✔ **November 2002:** U.N. inspectors return to Baghdad for the first time in four years and initiate inspections.

✔ **December 2002:** After studying the Iraqi arms declaration, the United States concludes that Iraq was in material breach.

With the whole world watching and braced for war, the inspections forged ahead.

✔ **January 2003:** UN weapons inspectors discover 12 warheads designed to contain chemical weapons.

✔ **February 2003:** U.S. Secretary of State Colin Powell presents evidence to the UN Security Council that suggests Iraq isn't disarming.

✔ **February 2003:** UN weapons inspectors discover Al-Samoud surface-to-surface missiles.

✔ **March 2003:** Iraq begins destroying the Al-Samoud missiles.

✔ **March 2003:** France, Germany, and Russia refuse to agree to a resolution authorizing military action against Iraq. Turkey refuses to allow U.S. troops on Turkish soil.

✔ **March 17, 2003:** U.S. President Bush gives Saddam 48 hours to leave Iraq.

✔ **March 19, 2003:** A U.S.-led coalition, comprised of Britain, Australia, and other nations launch attacks against Iraq. In a taped speech televised after the attacks on March 20, Saddam attempts to call Arabs to arms by saying, "Long live jihad and long live Palestine."

✔ **April 5, 2003:** Slightly more than three weeks after the attacks began, the U.S. Army's Third Division enters Baghdad.

✔ **April 9, 2003:** Thousands of Iraqis take to the streets to celebrate the fall of Saddam Hussein.

By mid-April, coalition forces controlled the entire country and began the arduous task of providing basic needs, like water, food, and electricity to a skeptical Iraqi population.

Chapter 13

Afghanistan

Author Ahmad Rashid wrote that Afghanistan (see Figure 13-1) and its people are among "the most extraordinary on earth." The Afghans epitomize contradiction. Although they have suffered indescribable misery over the past 25 years, many Afghans rank among the most loyal, hospitable, and gracious human beings on the planet. If you have ever had the chance to truly get to know them, they have likely stolen your heart. On the other hand, the treachery, intolerance, and bloodthirstiness practiced by other Afghans, more often than not against their own people, rival the worst behavior humankind has seen. Although the description refers to Afghans, I suppose you can apply this portrayal to any number of other civilizations. The sad story of the Afghan people is interwoven into the history of the British, Russians, Arabs, Pakistanis, and most recently, the Americans.

Just like the storm of Hitler's extermination of 6 million Jews that sent waves of turmoil slapping against the shores of the Middle East, the consequences of which are still being felt, you can trace the Islamic militancy prevalent in the 21st century to a single event: the Soviet invasion of Afghanistan in December 1979. The Afghans reacted by waging a *jihad* (holy war). The Muslim World and the West rushed to the aid of the Afghans, supplying them with weapons, humanitarian aid, and militant training. In the jihad milieu of Kalashnikovs (Soviet automatic weapons), hatred of the Soviets, and unprecedented Muslim sympathy, some *Mujahideen* (holy warriors) developed a stern form of Islamic militancy that was left unchecked. As the Americans, Saudis, Chinese, and others pumped resources to the Mujahideen through Pakistan, the jihad began to take on a life of its own. A sophisticated subculture of religious attitudes toward the *infidel* grew more bitter and intolerant.

After the Russians pulled out in 1989, this subculture comprised a network of Islamic extremists who promoted religious intolerance, and militancy had to find a new infidel to defeat. Some focused on the internal Afghan problems that abounded while others turned their sights on *liberating* Kashmir. Still others set about bringing other parts of the Middle East, like Sudan and Somalia, into compliance with their version of Islam.

But let's back up a second! Why Afghanistan? Why did the Soviets invade in the first place? And of all places, why Afghanistan? That tiny, landlocked country doesn't have oil or many natural resources worth exploiting. So what gives? In order to understand how Afghanistan got into this mess, we need to look back a century or two to see what was going on that brought about this tragedy. And you guessed it. A colonial power was involved: Britain.

By the way, many scholars don't consider Afghanistan to be a part of the Middle East, geographically speaking. But you can't deny Afghanistan's impact on the region, which is one of the reasons why I cover it in this book.

Figure 13-1:
Afghanistan.

Setting the Stage for the Soviet Invasion

Throughout history, foreign armies who happened to be in the neighborhood of Central Asia often stopped by Afghanistan for an invasion or two. The Greeks and Persians in ancient times and the Arabs and Mongols in the Medieval period set great precedents for modern incursions. Afghanistan's geography has always placed it in peril. Snuggled between Iran to the west, Russian-influenced Central Asia to the north, and British India (today Pakistan) to the south, Afghanistan in the 19th century became the perfect playing field for the "Greatest Game" on earth.

Playing the "Greatest Game"

The Great Game became the term to describe the 19th-century strategic struggle of espionage, treachery, and military incursions in Afghanistan between Russia and England. The Great Game represented a *cold war* of sorts, in which both imperial powers attempted to assert influence over Central Asia without actually coming to blows. Czarist Russia hoped to reach the warm water ports of the Indian Ocean, and the British — already in charge of Indian affairs — sought to foil those Russian designs by extending their own influence deep into the no man's land of Central Asia, and particularly into Afghanistan.

Obsessed with fears that Russia would encroach on Afghan territory, the British made a number of tactical blunders in their relationship with Afghanistan's rulers that led to three wars and racked up three defeats. The most famous of these wars was the first.

The first British-Afghan War

Emir Dost Muhammad assumed power in Afghanistan in 1826. In their superior wisdom, the British decided that Dost Muhammad wasn't the man for the job, and seeking instead to install someone more pliable, they chose to restore former-emir Shah Shuja. In order to switch leadership and make it stick, the British sent an army to Kabul. Approximately 20,000 British troops, with an entourage of 38,000 camp followers, set off for Afghanistan through the Bolan Pass. When the huge British contingent reached Kabul, Dost Muhammad fled, and the British installed Shuja on August 7, 1839. Shuja's forces and resources were much too small to support him, so the British stuck around hoping the situation would improve (sound familiar?).

By the winter of 1841, the situation on the surface indeed appeared to improve, and London employed a series of budget cuts that included reducing the number of troops in Kabul and lowering subsidies to the Ghilzai tribes who policed the road to Peshawar through the Khyber Pass. Without Ghilzai support, safe travel was impossible. British drinking in public and cavorting with local women in Kabul further increased the Muslim discontent with the British and their puppet regime. Frustration finally boiled over into violence.

- **November 2, 1841:** A mob attacks the home of British officer Alexander Burnes, where the treasury is kept. The mob kills Burnes and his brother.

- **November 22, 1841:** British forces sent to disband a group of Afghan insurgents surrounding the cantonment retreat under heavy fire.

- **December 23, 1841:** The insurgents decapitate British envoy William MacNaghten and hang his body for display at the entrance of the Kabul bazaar.

- **January 1842:** The Ghilzais, whose subsidies the British had slashed earlier, agree to provide safe passage to Jalalabad at the mouth of the Khyber Pass. Approximately 4,500 British troops and 12,000 camp followers set off for Jalalabad.

  - Many die of exposure to the cruel winter elements the first 24 hours. Eager for blood, the Ghilzais turn on the British and launch a series of attacks against the wayfarers on the second day. More than 3,000 die that day alone while others flee or defect.

  - Of the 16,5000 who started the journey, only one — Dr. William Brydon — succeeds in reaching Jalalabad.

The next year more than 100 British captives still held by the tribes were rescued, as well as more than 2,000 Indian soldiers and camp followers. Over time other stragglers made their way back to India.

Afghan tribes, ethnicity, and Pashtunistan

Before proceeding, you need to understand something about the tribal configuration of Afghanistan and Pakistan. Ever wonder why the dual phrase *Afghanistan and Pakistan* keeps popping up in the news and on TV? Well, news services often reference the two countries together because of the makeup and location of Pashtuns (Pashtu speakers). Pashtu is the first language for about 35 percent of Afghanistan's population. Pashtuns (who also call themselves Pathans) live in tribal areas on the Afghan side of the Pakistani border and spill over into the Pakistani provinces of the North West Frontier Province and Baluchistan (see Figure 13-2). Besides a common language, these Pashtuns share a common culture and, frequently, religious and political perspectives. Combined, the Pashtuns on both sides of the border constitute a force to be reckoned with.

The Tajiks, speakers of an Afghan dialect of Persian (or *Farsi* in Iran), called Dari, comprise about half of Afghanistan's population. Turkmen and Uzbeks speaking Turkic languages account for another 10 percent. Ethnic friction and violence has frequented Afghanistan in the past. Often one ethnic group sought to dominate the others. Whenever the British gave India its independence, India split into two parts: the northwestern chunk, calling itself Pakistan (see Chapter 14), and the remainder, calling itself India. In the 1950s, the Pashtuns in Pakistan and Pashtuns in Afghanistan decided they too wanted a separate nation called Pashtunistan. Their bid for an autonomous region was foiled in the 1960s and then again in the 1970s. Subsequent Pakistani and Afghan governments have been alert to Pashtun discontent that may spill over into secessionist violence.

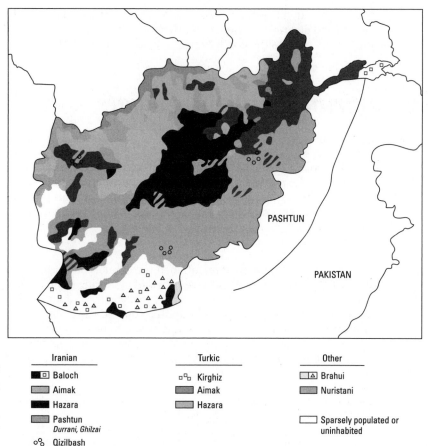

Figure 13-2: The ethnic divisions within Afghanistan.

Iranian	Turkic	Other
■▫ Baloch	▫ᵃ Kirghiz	▭△ Brahui
▨ Aimak	▨ Aimak	▨ Nuristani
■ Hazara	▨ Hazara	
▨ Pashtun *Durrani, Ghilzai*		▭ Sparsely populated or uninhabited
ᵒ Qizilbash		
▨ Tajik		

Although no official autonomous region for the Pashtuns exists, these tribes have traditionally operated with little interference from either government in the Pashtun belt resting along both sides of the border. This region, called the *tribal areas*, has for centuries remained an untamed frontier, hostile to outsiders. For this reason, beginning in the 19th century, the British army sent spies dressed as local tribesmen to gather intelligence on this region and beyond.

Today the Pakistani tribal areas are off limits to foreign travelers without special permission and escort from the Pakistani government. Often compared to 19th-century United States Wild West cowboys, the rugged, bearded Pashtun tribesmen tote weapons and exact revenge. Hostage taking and generation-long blood feuds among hostile clans are commonplace. Legal and civil disputes aren't settled in government courts but before tribal councils called *jirgas*. In the towns and villages, tribesmen produce and sell weapons in shops beside sweets and cigarettes. The fact that women are conspicuously absent from the streets reflects the conservative religious nature of the Pashtun culture.

Fraternizing with the Soviets

As elsewhere in the Middle East, the Afghan monarchy in the mid-20th century was in danger of losing its grip on power to other forces, such as democracy and communism. By the 1970s, the Americans had replaced the British influence in the region while the Soviets were still trying to expand their empire to the warm waters of the Indian Ocean. Amid this decade of communist undercurrents and Afghan nationalism, leaders entered the dangerous game of playing the Americans off the Soviets, a game that ended in the devastation on the Afghan people.

Afghan King Zahir Shah had maintained warm relations with the West and had taken some steps toward social reform and modernization, including some stabs at democracy, but his heart wasn't really in it. On July 17, 1973, the king's cousin, Prince Daoud, staged a coup that toppled the king, who was in Italy at the time. Daoud, who was already a military general, further appointed himself president, prime minister, foreign minister, and defense minister (putting all that on a business card must have been a printer's nightmare).

Flirting with communism

Daoud's republic initially had leftist leanings and relied heavily on Babrak Karmal, a leading figure in the communist *Parchimi* party and an agent for the Russian KGB. Daoud cracked down on Islamic extremists, including the arrest of the Muslim Brotherhood's leader, Muhammad Niazi. Many extremists fled to Pakistan, such as Gulbadeen Hekmatyar and Burhaddin Rabbani, both of whom later played leading roles in Afghanistan during the next three decades.

For many communists, Daoud's leftist lip service didn't fulfill their expectations. Like any truly good indulgence, one coup just wasn't enough. In 1978, Karmal's long-time associate, Nur Muhammad Taraki, head of *Khalq,* the other communist faction, seized power. Daoud and his family, along with 2,000 other Afghans, died in the fighting. Taraki set the nation back on the "left" track, closely aligning Afghanistan with the Soviets.

Taraki's regime was brutal, and a number of fateful events proved disastrous for the fledgling communist government.

✔ **February 1979:** Four left-wing extremists abduct and murder Adolph Dubs, U.S. ambassador to Afghanistan.

✔ **March 1979:** A major revolt in Herat erupts into the massacre of government officials, Soviet advisers, and their families. The rebels torture and kill approximately 100 Russian men, women, and children. The assailants mutilate the bodies and parade the chunks around the city like trophies. Frequent torture, arrests, and murder of dissidents (or of the rival Parchimis) even trouble Moscow.

But the Soviets had come too far to turn back. They simply couldn't run the risk of losing the ground they'd gained to the Americans.

In 1979 another communist leader, Hafizullah Amin, overthrew Taraki. However, Amin proved just as brutal as Taraki. Chaos ensued. Rebel attacks grew more frequent, army fighters defected, and assassination squads roamed the city knocking off communist rivals. And then everything got worse: The Soviet Union stepped in to keep the peace.

Invading Afghanistan: The Soviets seize the capital

On December 24, 1979, the Soviet 105th Guards Airborne Division began landing at Kabul airport. The next morning two divisions of Soviet troops crossed the Amu Darya River along the northern border and headed south. Within three days, the Soviets had secured the capital and killed Amin. They installed Babrak Karmal as the new Afghan president. Within a few weeks, more than 85,000 Soviet troops occupied Afghanistan, and at full strength grew to more than 100,000.

On the surface, communism appeared to have found another home. However, the Soviet leadership and policymakers must have been poor historians who didn't remember the British's experiences in Afghanistan. The Afghan tribes of the past had proven a foreign army wouldn't subdue them for long. In fact, the Soviet invasion served as a wake-up call to tens of thousands of Afghans who had until that time taken no interest in the politics of Kabul. Now hordes of Afghan men raced to the mountains and countryside to join the ranks of the Mujahideen.

Waging jihad: The Mujahideen retaliate

Jihad is an Arabic word that in the Afghan context of 1979 meant *holy war*. *Mujahid* is the person who conducts jihad, or *holy warrior*, and *mujahideen* is the plural form (see Chapter 8). When the Russians moved into Afghanistan, U.S. President Jimmy Carter committed the United States to helping the Afghan Mujahideen lest the Soviet Union steamroll over Afghanistan and on into the Persian Gulf region rich with oil fields.

- ✔ **January 1980:** Carter declares the *Carter Doctrine* clarifying the Persian Gulf region as central to U.S. interests and any incursion there would trigger American military action.

- ✔ **1981:** U.S. President Ronald Reagan commits $3.2 billion to Pakistani President General Zia ul-Haq, much of which is to be funneled to the resistance. Zia, who'd come to power through a coup and the execution of his predecessor Zulfikar Ali Bhutto (see Chapter 14), was only too happy to milk the Afghan crisis for all its worth.

The invasion sparked international condemnation against the Soviets, including the U.S. boycott of the 1980 Summer Olympics. In addition to the Americans, the Saudis and Chinese reacted by pumping resources to the Mujahideen through Pakistan, and to a lesser extent through Iran.

Forming the Seven-Party Alliance

Historically, the most significant problem among Afghanistan's tribes is the inability to function as a unified mechanism toward any common goal. Even when confronting the Soviet army, the Mujahideen suffered from divisiveness and factionalism that often led to intrigues, assassinations, and violence in Pakistan and Afghanistan. In 1980, Pakistan officially recognized seven Afghan parties of differing linguistic, ethnic, and religious backgrounds and each toting different political agendas. The Seven-Party Alliance set up shop in Peshawar, Pakistan, on the border of Afghanistan.

Two of the most prominent parties were Gulbadeen Hekmatyar's *Hisb-i Islami* and Burhanuddin Rabbani's *Jamiat-i Islami*. Hekmatyar was a controversial figure that many compared to Iran's Ayatollah Khomeini for his uncompromising Islamic extremist agenda. As a Ghilzai Pashtun, Hekmatyar earned a reputation for creating fierce and disciplined warriors on the battlefield and an unrelenting personal ambition that drove him to excesses, including trafficking drugs, intolerance, murder, and cruelty to his own people (see Figure 13-3). Rabbani's Mujahideen, on the other hand, were primarily Tajiks and other non-Pashtun tribes. Although Rabbani was a graduate of a *madrasa* (theological school), he created a more tolerant and less radical environment for resistance. His forces became known as the most effective in the field against the enemy.

Lion of the Panshir Valley

By far the most popular Afghan resistance commander was Ahmad Shah Massoud. Considered a tactical guerrilla genius who enjoyed years of success against the Soviet and Afghan communist forces in the Panshir Valley, north of Kabul, Massoud earned the epithet, *Lion of the Panshir*. In 1992, Massoud's forces captured Kabul from Nagibullah's communist holdouts. Four years later the Taliban (see the section "New Kids on the Block: The Taliban and Al-Qaeda" later in this chapter) drove Massoud's army from Kabul, and he and Rabbani formed a resistance force in the north known as the Northern Alliance. After Massoud's assassination by Arab extremists posing as journalists the day before the September 11, 2001, attacks in the United States, a cult emerged around Massoud's grave and his memory.

Figure 13-3:
Hekmatyar's Mujahideen sipping tea in December 1983.

Photo courtesy of Craig Davis.

SAM, I am: Surface-to-Air Missiles

The Afghan quagmire was costing the Soviets an estimated $10 billion a year. By 1985, the Soviets realized they were in a stalemate. The communists controlled the cities, but the rural areas belonged to the Mujahideen. Typically, the communist army could only achieve movement with large convoys, and even they were vulnerable to rebel ambush. The air superiority that the Soviets enjoyed, however, allowed them to resupply almost any city, town, or outpost by helicopter. For a number of years, the Mujahideen requested surface-to-air missiles (SAMs) from the United States and its allies. Fearing the SAMs would one day be used against Western targets, the West hesitated. A number of events in 1985 changed the war's complexion.

- **1985:** Mikhail Gorbachev's assumption of power brings about a shift in policy. He begins actively searching for a way out.

- **1985:** Reagan announces a directive to use "all available means" to drive the Soviets from Afghanistan.

In 1986, the Americans began providing U.S.-made Stinger SAMs and the British-made Blowpipe version to the Mujahideen, and the Soviet air superiority became a thing of the past.

Rebels without a cause: The interim government

Faced with severe economic and political problems at home, Gorbachev announced the withdrawal of Soviet troops from Afghanistan in 1988. By the following year, the Soviets had pulled out, leaving communist Najibullah as president. More than1 million Afghans had died during the Soviet occupation and 5 million had become refugees in neighboring countries. Lacking a foreign enemy on which to focus, the Afghan rebel leaders turned on themselves in bitter power struggles. The Mujahideen commanders were unable to seize Kabul until 1992, when Massoud outmaneuvered Hekmatyar for control of the capital. Najibullah and his brother took refuge in the United Nations compound, where they remained for four years.

The Mujahideen leadership established a fragile interim government, forming the Islamic Republic of Afghanistan. The government officials included

- **President:** Rabbani. The United Nations recognized him as the legitimate Afghan ruler even after the Taliban seized power.

- **Prime Minister:** Hekmatyar. At first, he refused the post and continued bombing Kabul. In 1993, he accepted the position but Massoud prevented

Hekmatyar from entering the capital. In 1996, Rabbani and Hekmatyar put aside their differences, and the latter finally assumed his post. His tenure was short lived because the Taliban came calling the same year.

✔ **Minister of Defense:** Massoud. (Of course.)

Lacking coherence, vision, and guidance, former commanders often became warlords in the countryside and set up tiny fiefdoms. Like gang warfare, competing Mujahideen forces became embroiled in petty conflicts over turf, and routinely raped, pillaged, and murdered civilians and opposing Mujahideen forces with impunity. Hekmatyar's indiscriminant and continuous shelling of Kabul destroyed entire neighborhoods and created more death and destruction in the capital than occurred during the entire Soviet occupation. More than 30,000 Afghans died in the subsequent fighting in Kabul. The Afghan people began to hope for a savior from the mayhem. Their prayers were answered in 1994 when the Taliban rose to establish order from chaos.

Importing and exporting jihad

The Mujahideen were poor in financial and military resources but wealthy in volunteers prepared to fight the communists. An estimated 1 million Afghan refugees migrated to Peshawar, Pakistan, in the 1980s. Afghan Mujahideen could be found everywhere in the city: in the streets, on the buses, or in the bazaars. On more than one occasion, I heard a variation of what one Mujahid told me, "We're not asking the Americans for soldiers. Just give us the weapons and we'll fight the Soviets." And *give weapons* and resources the Americans did. So did the Saudis, Chinese, Iranians, and many other countries. Arabs and Muslims from other countries volunteered to fight the Soviets as well.

The Mujahideen built a jihad mechanism that took on a life of its own. Saudi money established madrasas to educate Afghan and Pakistanis in Wahhabi-style Islam (see Chapter 8). The Pakistani Directorate of Inter-Services Intelligence funneled much of the CIA funds to form Islamic extremist indoctrination and militant training, but kept the Americans at arm's length from the training they were funding. Arabs, like Osama bin Laden, organized and trained Arab volunteers, known as Afghan Arab Mujahideen, many of whom later became the backbone of Al-Qaeda.

USAID supported a $50-million project for the development of children's textbooks. Much of the money went to The Education Center for Afghanistan, a Mujahideen entity that created violent images of Islamic militancy in elementary school books. As long as all these activities were meant to help the Afghan people oust the Soviets, no one in the West (including the press) seemed to mind. But the training, indoctrination, and education in Islamic militancy of the 1980s came back to sting the United States in the late 1990s and beyond. After the Soviets had gone, Islamic extremist elements used this jihad mechanism to export Islamic militancy elsewhere.

New Kids on the Block: The Taliban and Al-Qaeda

The plight of the Afghan people under the post-war Mujahideen was in some respects worse than during the Soviet occupation. The situation proved ripe for exploitation by a new force that could provide relief and stability. In 1994, the desired new order came in the form of the *Taliban* (students, in Pashtu), which was more than the Afghan people had bargained for.

Building the legend

Taliban legend has it that an incident sparked the rise of the Taliban in 1994. When a Mujahideen commander raped and killed three women in Kandahar, the victims' families and friends — desperate for justice and protection — turned to respected religious leader, Mulla Muhammad Omar. He raised a small militia of religious students, called Taliban, and executed the mujahid and scattered his followers. As word of this retribution spread, Omar's ranks of Pashtun students from madrasas in Pakistan grew.

Creating an Islamic state

Some evidence indicates that the creation of the Taliban may have been a more calculated endeavor by other countries and by the religious clerics themselves including:

- ✔ **Pakistan:** The Pakistanis wanted to stabilize Afghanistan and exert influence. The Pakistani government, always cognizant of and sympathetic to Pashtun causes, had ideological differences with the Tajik rulers in Kabul.
- ✔ **Saudi Arabia:** The Saudis, eager to create an Afghanistan in its own image, also played a role in the Taliban's rise, providing the Islamic extremists with funding.

The Taliban seized Kandahar in 1994 and continued to topple Mujahideen commanders wherever they found them. The Taliban inflicted heavy casualties on Kabuli civilians in a barrage of assaults against the capital. In 1996, the Taliban eventually seized it from Massoud. Taliban troops shot Najibullah and his brother and hung up their bodies for display near the presidential palace. After they firmly had control, the new rulers established the Islamic Emirate of Afghanistan.

Welcoming bin Laden and his followers

Like other Arabs volunteers, Osama bin Laden surfaced in the 1980s to fight against the Soviets alongside the Mujahideen. After the Soviet withdrawal, he returned home to Saudi Arabia just in time to witness Saddam Hussein's incursion into Kuwait. Bin Laden offered to raise a force of Islamic militants to defend Saudi Arabia against the Iraqis. When the Saudis passed him over and instead turned to the Americans, relations between bin Laden and the Saudis soured.

As a result of bin Laden's criticism of the Saudi royal family, he became a *persona non grata* in Saudi Arabia but found Sudan's Hassan al-Turabi only too willing to invite him (see Chapter 15). However, by 1996, his welcome in Sudan wore thin, and the Islamic Emirate of Afghanistan seemed like as good a place as any to set up camp.

Omar and other Taliban leaders, who were themselves products of the madrasa system that promoted Wahhabi-style Islam, saw bin Laden as an Arab spiritual leader with the wealth and expertise to secure jihad on the home front against the Northern Alliance, to export Islamic militancy to other points in the Muslim World, and to establish other Islamic nations where pure Islam could be practiced, just as it was in Afghanistan. Bin Laden's militant network, known as *Al-Qaeda* (military base, in Arabic), found refuge in Afghanistan where it taught extremist interpretations of Islam and trained militants to fight the Northern Alliance in northern Afghanistan and exported Islamic militancy to other parts of the world.

Implementing Islamic law

Initially the Afghan people enjoyed the security that the Taliban employed. The Taliban have never been given the credit they deserve. As part of their implementation of *sharia* (Islamic law), the Taliban disarmed the Mujahideen, reduced crime, dealt brutally with criminals, and for the first time in many years made the streets and roads safe to travel. All this was no small feat.

But as products of madrasas, the Taliban leadership knew (or cared) little about science, history, or the outside world. Many Muslim critics also argued that the Taliban weren't well-versed in Islamic law or Islamic history, and the Islamic extremist Arabs, like bin Laden, who had no religious credibility with which to issue Islamic injunctions (*fatwas*) in their own countries, served as poor advisers. As a result, the Taliban's version of Islamic law included human rights abuses that rivaled those of the Mujahideen before them including:

✔ **Violations of women's rights increased.** Most women in the cities weren't allowed to work or leave home alone. Education for girls was suspended in some areas while permitted through third grade in other areas (see Chapter 21). Many families fled Taliban territory to Pakistan so that educated women could find work or so that their daughters could receive an education.

✔ **Mutilation and murder of suspected criminals often took place in public without fair trials.** The soccer stadium, for example, in Kandahar served as a public forum for hangings and amputations.

✔ **Abuses and persecution against non-Pashtuns increased.** Huge numbers of Tajiks, Uzbeks, and other non-Pashtuns who'd survived 20 years of war in Kabul, now fled.

✔ **Prisoners of war were often slaughtered.** The Taliban, however, hadn't cornered the market on human rights abuses. Insurgents committed massacres of Taliban forces as well. In Mazar-i Sharif, for example, mass graves uncovered 2,000 bodies of massacred Taliban soldiers.

Floods of refugees fled political persecution to Pakistan. Ironically, by 2000, you could commonly find educated women and girls working in Islamabad, Pakistan, in order to bring home an income to support the male family members who had been unable to find employment.

Locating the last remnants of the Mujahideen: The Northern Alliance

In May 2000, one Afghan in Kabul jokingly told me that the Taliban had eliminated crime in Afghanistan. The criminals that the Taliban hadn't imprisoned or executed ran off to Peshawar, Pakistan. Certainly, 2001 looked good for Taliban and bleak for their opponents.

By and large the last vestiges of the Mujahideen that had defeated the mighty Soviet Red Army over a dozen years earlier were huddling in various corners of Afghanistan on their last leg. The most significant group was Rabbani's Northern Alliance. Commander of the Northern Alliance army, Massoud, had somehow clung onto 10 percent of Afghan territory in the northeast with Russian and Iranian support. The Northern Alliance was defeated and didn't know it. Then tragedy struck.

Massoud was assassinated.

Waging War on Terrorism: The United States Strikes Back

On September 11, 2001, 19 Middle Eastern men hijacked four American civilian airliners. They flew two of them into the World Trade Center and one into the Pentagon, while the fourth plane's passengers, likely destined for another target in Washington, D.C., allegedly rushed the cockpit and forced it to crash in a Pennsylvania field. (Not one of the hijackers was Afghan.) The United States determined the attacks to be the handiwork of bin Laden's Al-Qaeda network. In the first order of business after the attacks, U.S. President George W. Bush declared a War on Terrorism.

- ✔ **September 20, 2001:** Bush delivers the Taliban an ultimatum: "Turn over bin Laden or share in his fate."

- ✔ **September 21, 2001:** In broken English, Abdul Salam Zaeef, the Taliban's ambassador to Pakistan, holds a press conference in Islamabad and, in defiance of the American demand, states that Afghanistan won't turn over bin Laden.

- ✔ **October 4, 2001:** Bush promises $320 million in humanitarian aid for the Afghan people.

- ✔ **October 5, 2001:** Taliban foreign minister Wakil Ahmed Mutawakil offers to free the eight Western aid workers held on charges of Christian proselytizing if the United States promises to withdraw the threat of military retaliation. Bush says no. (After the Taliban flees Kabul, the aid workers are released on November 14.)

- ✔ **October 7, 2001:** The United States launches air strikes against the Taliban in Kabul, Kandahar, and Jalalabad.

Searching for bin Laden

Faced with an overwhelming humanitarian crisis due to a three-year-long drought, American military aircraft began dropping thousands of yellow plastic food packets to starving Afghans. Elsewhere in the Afghan skies, U.S. B-52s dropped so many bombs that in a matter of days the military had run out of targets. The incessant pounding proved too much for the Taliban who'd vowed to fight until "victory or death," and Kabul fell to the Northern Alliance with almost no resistance on November 12, 2001. Jalalabad, Herat, and Kandahar followed suit. Regardless of these successes, the Americans failed to find bin Laden or Mulla Omar.

Restoring order

Apart from short-lived, but vocal Pashtun demonstrations in Pakistan against the American overthrow of the Taliban and against Pakistan's supportive role in the war (see Chapter 14), the reaction to the Taliban's fall has been positive. At least on the surface, most Afghans have enjoyed their newly found freedom from Taliban religious restrictions.

- ✔ **December 2001:** The interim government is sworn in and Pashtun resistance leader Hamid Karzai becomes interim prime minister.

- ✔ **January 2002:** International donors meeting in Japan pledge $3 billion to help rebuild Afghanistan.

- ✔ **April 2002:** The 87-year-old king Zahir Shah returns to Kabul to lend legitimacy to the new government.

- ✔ **June 2002:** Loya Jirga (Grand Council) convenes and elects Karzai as prime minister of the transitional government. Karzai appoints Tajiks, Pashtuns, Uzbeks, and Hazaras (Shiites) to his cabinet.

Afghanistan's future is far from certain. Assassination attempts, both successful and failed, of government officials have plagued the fledgling administration. The rebuilding process rests precariously on the tenuous stability lent by the presence of international peacekeepers, including Americans, Germans, and Turks. Undercurrents of Islamic extremism, competing interests of warlords, ethnic distrust, anti-Western attitudes, and abject poverty threaten to destabilize Karzai's fragile government. Only time can tell whether the transition to democratic rule and a society free of violence shall endure, or if the leadership propped up by external forces will give way once more to chaos as in 1842.

Chapter 14

Pakistan

After returning from a year's research in Pakistan and Afghanistan in 2000, I attended a conference in Washington, D.C. Various times I showed a T-shirt I'd purchased at the bazaar in Peshawar, Pakistan. The T-shirt reads *World Hero: Osama bin Laden. The Great Mujahid* [Holy Warrior] *of Islam*. I wanted to explain how this message reflected the sentiments of a growing number of Pakistanis and other Muslims worldwide. I hoped to discuss the root causes of anti-Americanism in Muslim countries and the links between the Arab World and Pakistan. I tried to elaborate on the importance that education in these areas plays on anti-Western undercurrents.

No one was very interested in Pakistan or Afghanistan. I can't say that I blame them. Even Western policymakers seemed much more interested in criticizing General Pervez Musharraf's military coup the previous year and his reluctance to hold elections than various dimensions and root causes of Islamic militancy.

Less than a year later, the disastrous events of September 11, 2001, shook the world. Suddenly, everyone was interested in Pakistan, Afghanistan, and Islamic militancy. Musharraf, who'd been a pariah in the West just a year earlier, was now the United States' new best friend. The United States needed the Pakistani general's cooperation in order to conduct the War on Terrorism against the Taliban and Osama bin Laden in Afghanistan.

When the bombing of Afghanistan started, Pashtuns (the ethnic group comprising 90 percent of the Taliban's force) in Peshawar (the city where I'd purchased the T-shirt) and elsewhere began demonstrating, burning U.S. flags and effigies of President Bush, and calling for a *jihad* (holy war) against the United States. Pakistani school children interviewed on TV said that if Osama were killed, 100 new Osamas would take his place.

This chapter examines the history of Pakistan's political problems. Before starting, keep two points in mind. First, everything isn't as it always appears on TV. Although military coups, anti-Western sentiment, and Islamic militancy dominate headlines, most Pakistanis have never participated in violence of any kind. For the most part, Pakistanis are a kind, tolerant, and hospitable people who respect foreigners. Second, Pakistan's political, socioeconomic, and cultural problems have created a fertile environment for dissent that all too frequently has taken the form of violence, brutal repression, and Islamic militancy. This chapter examines the historical developments that created this milieu. And believe it or not, this story begins with British occupation.

As is the case with Afghanistan, many people don't consider Pakistan to be a part of the Middle East, but the history and politics of this country play an important role in the region, and I feel that it needs to be discussed in this book.

Partitioning India

Before 1947, Pakistan simply didn't exist.

The territory where 145 million Pakistani Muslims now live belonged to India prior to a blood-soaked partition. A relatively heterogeneous population comprising Muslims, Sikhs, Hindus, Christians, Jains, and others called this region home. The partition that created Pakistan (see Figure 14-1) uprooted 10 million Sikhs and Hindus, whose ancestors had lived there for generations or even centuries, and sent them scurrying to India for their lives. Likewise, millions of Muslims fled India into Pakistan, because they were no longer welcome in the land of their birth. The haphazard partition and subsequent migration pitted Muslims northwest of the border against Hindus and Sikhs on the other side. The mutual hatred and distrust between the two rivals has led to three wars and a race for nuclear weapons to obliterate the other side.

Muhammad Iqbal

In the early 20th century, a Muslim Indian poet and politician named Muhammad Iqbal first articulated the notion of a Muslim homeland on the Indian subcontinent. Educated in the West, Iqbal was an Indian nationalist who became president of the Muslim League in 1930. Iqbal envisioned Pakistan as a Muslim nation within the larger Indian federation. In 1933, Chaudhri Rahmat Ali, an Indian Muslim studying at Cambridge, came up with the name *Pakistan,* meaning *land of the pure* in Persian. But Pakistan remained merely an abstract notion in the minds of Muslims until Muhammad Ali Jinnah made it a reality at the end of World War II.

India before Partition

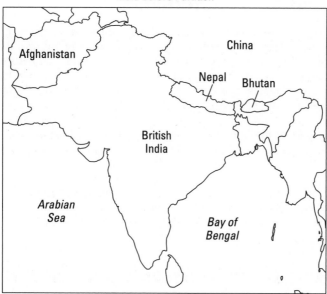

India and Pakistan after 1947

Figure 14-1:
The formation of Pakistan from British India.

Muhammad Ali Jinnah

The end of 200 years of British rule in India came after World War II. Faced with the overpowering Nazi threat, Britain was passing out promises of independence to the empire's colonial holdings, like a politician before election day. Britain promised to grant India its independence if it would fight alongside the British against the Axis. When the Allied victory finally came, Indian leaders held Britain to its promise.

The leading Muslim politician at the time, Muhammad Ali Jinnah, convinced everyone involved that while handing out independence, they may as well go ahead and cordon off a lump of India for the Muslims, who made up about 20 percent of India's population. As the last viceroy of India, Lord Mountbatten oversaw the partition. On August 14, 1947, Jinnah flew to Karachi, the new capital, and the Islamic Republic of Pakistan was born. The violence and carnage that followed, however, was more than anyone had bargained for.

The partition: Pakistan's painful birth

Partitioning India proved to be a monumental task due to logistic, humanitarian, religious, political, and linguistic complications.

✔ **Two Pakistans, not one:** Pakistan comprised two wings: West Pakistan (Pakistan) and East Pakistan (Bangladesh).

  • **Separation:** Nearly 1,000 miles separated the two wings. No roads (except through India) connected them.

  • **Languages:** The two countries didn't even share a common language.

  • **Culture:** Although both halves were Muslim, Bengali culture varied considerably from Pakistan's mixture of Sindhi, Baluchi, Pashtun, and Punjabi customs and traditions.

✔ **Government resources:** Civil services and the military were also divided. Railways, police and armed forces, revenue services, vehicles, supplies, and so on had to be divided and reallocated.

✔ **Mass exodus:** Approximately 10 million Sikhs and Hindus, not wanting to end up in Muslim Pakistan, moved south while 7 million Muslims, fearing a violent backlash in India, moved north across the newly formed border. This exodus created unimaginable hardship, loss of property and life, and terror. People were forced to leave their businesses, employment, schools, possessions, homes, fields, farm animals, and the only life they'd ever known.

As many as one million people died in the violence. Today stories of rape, pillage, robbery, butchery, and murder still abound on both sides of the border, told in vivid detail by the older generation, and continue to fan the flames of ethnic and religious hatred more than five decades later.

Dividing a nation with a pencil, straightedge, and a map

A few weeks before the partition, Mountbatten designated Sir Cyril Radcliffe, a British lawyer who had never stepped foot in India, as impartial cartographic surgeon of India. Almost single-handedly, Radcliffe determined the boundary lines between India and Pakistan based on density of Muslim and non-Muslim populations. This task would have been daunting in the best of worlds, but in 1947 in the province of the Punjab — the province most affected by the operation — Sikhs, Hindus, and Muslims were interwoven into the cultural fabric of society. On August 16, Radcliffe released the blueprint for the two nations. Needless to say, the blueprint had its share of controversy, including:

- **District of Gurdaspur.** Mountbatten encouraged Radcliffe to award this strategic strip of land — although predominately Muslim — to India, thus securing India's route to Jammu and Kashmir.

- **Lahore went to Pakistan.** Nearly 600,000 Muslims remained and 600,000 Hindus and Sikhs left their homes, businesses, and jobs behind and migrated to India.

- **Down the middle.** Radcliffe sliced villages, fields, and homes, often leaving communities or families on the wrong side of the tracks.

Without Gurdaspur, India would have been cut off from Kashmir. Mountbatten assumed that the award of Gurdaspur to India would avert future wars by allowing the Indian army access to Kashmir, maintaining a political balance. In fact, the opposite occurred.

Fighting three wars and facing unresolved issues

The announcement of boundaries led to increased violence. The province of Punjab erupted into nothing short of a holocaust. Violence on a lesser scale erupted in Delhi, the province of Bengal, and other parts.

Kashmir unresolved

Hindu Maharaja Hari Singh ruled over the predominately Muslim region of Kashmir. Hari refused to merge his kingdom with either India or Pakistan. Kashmiri Muslims revolted and violence spread.

- In October, hordes of Pashtun tribesmen (see Chapter 13) from Pakistan swept toward Srinagar, Kashmir's capital, eager to take the Muslim state by force.

✔ Fearing for his life, Hari threw in his lot with India and fled Kashmir on an Indian DC3.

✔ On October 27, Indian DC3s dropped 329 Sikhs soldiers from the First Sikh Regiment at Srinagar to secure the airport. Additional Indian troops arriving by air and ground reinforcements reaching Kashmir on Radcliffe's road through Gurdaspur drove back the Pakistani fighters.

Fighting continued until January 1, 1949, when the United Nations brokered an agreement, temporarily providing half of Kashmir to Pakistan and half to India. India agreed to the U.N.'s call for a plebiscite, allowing Kashmiris to determine their own fate. In the meantime, Kashmir remained a disputed territory, divided along a Line of Control (LOC). The referendum has never taken place. In the late 1990s, Islamic militants from Pakistan joined Kashmir extremists in attacks on Indian interests in Kashmir, hoping to force India to permit Kashmir's self-determination.

Starting off on rocky terms

Pakistan fought the first war with India over Kashmir, which ended in 1949. But the fledgling nation was embroiled in internal conflict. Pakistan's great leader (*Qaid-i Azam*), Muhammad Ali Jinnah, had emerged in the midst of the partition's turmoil as governor-general of Pakistan but died in 1948 of tuberculosis. Liaquat Ali Khan became prime minister, but an Afghan extremist assassinated him in 1951. Discontent arose in East Pakistan, which housed half of Pakistan's population and some 100,000 troops. In 1954, Karachi declared a state of emergency.

Facing political corruption, economic crises, and unresolved problems with India, General Muhammad Ayub Khan rose to power in a military coup in 1958. West Pakistan's capital shifted to Islamabad in the Punjab in 1959. A second war between India and Pakistan broke out in 1965, but the signing of the Tashkent Declaration in Uzbekistan the following year brought four years of peace.

Forming East Pakistan (Bangladesh)

The union of the two Pakistans (East and West) was doomed to failure from the start. The two halves, separated by 1,000 miles of India, had very little in common. Leaders in Dhaka (capital of East Pakistan) expressed increasing disenchantment with Islamabad's corruption and rule that treated East Pakistanis as second-class citizens. In 1966, Dhaka pressed for expanded autonomy. Riots ensued in 1968 and 1969, and Ayub Khan turned the government over to General Yahya Khan, who declared martial law. When it looked as if East Pakistani representatives would win a vote for independence in the National Assembly in 1971, Yahya Khan cancelled the elections and cracked down on the movement's leaders. East Pakistan announced a name change to Bangladesh and declared its independence. War erupted, and Bangladesh sought India's help. On December 3, 1971, India sent troops to Bangladesh, and two weeks later Pakistan surrendered. Hundreds of thousands of Bangladeshi civilians lost their lives in a matter of months.

Drawing a Blueprint for a Nuke

Zulfikar Ali Bhutto emerged from the rubble of the 1971 war as president and after the formation of the 1973 constitution, he became duly elected prime minister. Figure 14-2 shows the 1971 borders. Tensions increased as India forged ahead with the development of nuclear weapons. As early as 1965, Bhutto had vowed Pakistan would also have the bomb even if it meant Pakistanis would *eat grass* or *go hungry*. Now that Bhutto was calling the shots and after India tested its first weapons in 1974, the arms race was on. Allegedly with the help of the Chinese, Pakistan began developing its nuclear program. Although the Pakistani prime minister began pumping substantial resources into Pakistan's nuclear weapons program, he didn't live to see Pakistan's first test.

Figure 14-2:
Pakistan
after 1971.

The Afghan War

After Bhutto's reelection in 1977, nationwide riots erupted amid charges of election fraud. General Zia ul-Haq, Bhutto's chief of staff, had grown tired of the civilian leader. Zia staged a military coup, arrested the prime minister, and declared martial law in 1977. The following year Zia became president and declared the *Islamization of Pakistan,* instituting a number of religious reforms in an effort to appease the Islamic extremists, who had long been disenchanted with Bhutto's secular rule. A Pakistani court convicted Bhutto of the execution of a political opponent, and despite international pleas for Zia to grant clemency, Bhutto was hanged in 1979. Zia succeeded in securing his grip on power due to an event in December of that year: the Soviet invasion of Afghanistan.

Almost overnight Zia became an important ally for the West and a receptacle for billions of dollars of aid from Saudi Arabia, the United States, and China, all wanting to repel Soviet advances. In 1981, U.S. President Ronald Reagan committed $3.2 billion to Pakistan, much of which was funneled to the resistance (see Chapter 13). Zia milked the Afghan crisis for all its worth.

Experimenting with democracy

The United States pressed Zia for democratic reforms in the 1980s, and he promised to do so, but he died before he got around to it in a plane crash in August 1988 along with U.S. ambassador Arnold Raphel. The wheels of Pakistani democracy had already been set in motion.

- ✔ **1988:** Bhutto's daughter, Benazir, becomes the first female Pakistani prime minister only to be dismissed in 1990 amidst charges of corruption.

- ✔ **1990:** Nawaz Sharif becomes prime minister but is booted in 1993 by President Ishaq Khan for tampering with the president's power. The president is relieved of duty over the crisis as well.

- ✔ **1993:** Benazir makes a second stab at running the country but is removed again in 1996 for her involvement in a corruption scandal.

- ✔ **1997:** Sharif's second term as prime minister is as controversial as the first.

Widespread accusations of misconduct surrounded Sharif's term in office, which he didn't complete due to "general" difficulties.

Kargil: Kashmir in the crosshairs

In May 1998, India detonated five nuclear devices under the Rajastan Desert. Pakistan responded by conducting a series of underground nuclear tests in Baluchistan. Many Pakistanis, including religious extremists, praised the advent of Pakistan's nuclear might. U.S. President Bill Clinton responded by socking both countries with economic sanctions.

Tensions between the two countries increased. Hoping to pressure Delhi into a dialog over resolving the Kashmir issue, Pakistan unleashed Islamic militants against Indian interests in controlled Kashmir in the summer of 1999. Clashes in the region of Kargil brought the two nuclear powers to the brink of war. Amid international pressure, tensions eased in July, and Pakistan withdrew its forces and pulled the militants back across the Line of Control (LOC).

Staging a military coup

In October 1999, internal conflicts turned deadly. Prime Minister Sharif ordered that the airliner, on which General Pervez Musharraf was returning from Sri Lanka, be denied permission to land. Running short of fuel, the plane faced the danger of crashing. General Musharraf contacted loyal ground units to seize the airport, allowing the plane to land. Musharraf proceeded to seize power through a military coup and arrested Sharif.

Throngs of happy civilians celebrated in the streets and passed out sweets as a sign of good fortune. For many Pakistanis, an end to Pakistani-style democracy meant an end of corruption. The general assumed control of the country with the title chief executive, suspending the constitution, instituting martial law, and loosening restrictions on the press. He announced a unilateral withdrawal of the remaining troops from the Indian border in a demonstration of good faith.

Helping the United States Fight the War on Terrorism

I'm not exaggerating when I say that all the contentions, intrigues, crises, and unresolved issues came to a head after September 11, 2001. Disputes in Kashmir, nuclear escalation, military coups, failed democracy, promotion of militancy and cross-border attacks in Kashmir, support for the Afghan

Mujahideen, backing the Taliban, crippled economy, Pashtun unrest, political upheaval, and all the rest came back to haunt Musharraf in the face of America's War on Terrorism.

After the September 11 attacks, the United States determined the attacks to be the handiwork of Osama bin Laden's Al-Qaeda network (see Chapter 13). Despite Musharraf's requests, the Taliban, Afghanistan's leaders (see Chapter 13 for more on the Taliban), refused to hand over bin Laden, and U.S. President George W. Bush vowed that the Taliban would share in Al-Qaeda's fate. In order to carry out his military plans, Bush needed Pakistan's cooperation: use of its air space and military bases for starters. Bush reached out to Musharraf, and the Pakistani leader had a tough decision to make. There was no middle ground. Bush had made it clear to the world's leaders: "You're either with us, or you're with the terrorists."

Cooperating with Uncle Sam

Musharraf wasted no time in pledging his country's support for the American cause although his precarious military regime and stability was on the line. Any number of factors could topple Musharraf's government.

- ✔ **India:** Conflict with India hadn't gone away. Pakistan couldn't afford to let the War on Terrorism distract it from the looming threat of a conventional and/or nuclear war with India.

- ✔ **Islamic extremists:** Categorized as the vocal minority, the Taliban's many supporters within Pakistan's borders, including large numbers of Pashtuns in the tribal areas, threatened stability. The Taliban were Pashtuns, and Pakistani *volunteers* from the tribal areas (see Chapter 13) and the madrasas permeated the ranks of the Taliban armed forces.

- ✔ **Kashmir:** The Kashmir dispute was left unresolved. Islamic militants, many supported by Al-Qaeda, remained dedicated to freeing Kashmir through violence. Apart from extremists, huge numbers of Pakistanis were convinced that Indian abuses in Kashmir warranted military, or even nuclear, force by Pakistan.

- ✔ **Military:** Closer to home yet, Taliban sympathizers throughout the military wanted to see Islamic militancy succeed. Leading Inter-Service Intelligence (ISI) and military officials could stage a coup against Musharraf.

- ✔ **Nuclear:** The nuclear threat raised the stakes of any conflict considerably. Some Pakistani officials had warned of the government's willingness to strike first against India. More troubling was the concern that Islamic militants or renegade military officers may gain access to Pakistan's nuclear arsenal and trigger a nuclear war.

Musharraf's support of the U.S. campaign in Afghanistan created upheaval in the tribal areas. But the Pakistani protests and American flag burning died after the fall of the Taliban in late 2001 emitted widespread jubilation among the Afghan people. Still none of the previously listed issues have been resolved. The final chapter to the story of Pakistan's involvement in the War on Terrorism has yet to be written.

Paying the price: Islamic militancy

After the defeat of the Taliban in Afghanistan, many remnants of their forces and of Al-Qaeda dispersed into the tribal areas and elsewhere in Pakistan. Al-Qaeda's fingerprints seem to be all over a flurry of Islamic militant activity in Pakistan in 2002 and 2003.

- ✔ **January, 2002:** Daniel Pearl, a reporter for the *Wall Street Journal,* is kidnapped and savagely murdered.

- ✔ **March, 2002:** A plot on a Christian church in Islamabad kills five, including two Americans.

- ✔ **April, 2002:** An attempt to assassinate Musharraf during a motorcade in Karachi fails. Elements in Musharraf's own government are apparently involved, including Wasim Akhtar, an inspector for the paramilitary Pakistan Rangers, who provided Musharraf's itinerary.

- ✔ **May, 2002:** A bomb outside the Sheraton Hotel kills 14 people, including 11 French engineers.

- ✔ **June, 2002:** A car bomb explodes killing 12 Pakistanis outside the U.S. consulate in Karachi.

- ✔ **August, 2002:** Militants kill 11 in two separate attacks at a Christian hospital in Taxila and a Christian missionary school in Murree.

- ✔ **September, 2002:** Ramzi bin Al-Shibh, a leading figure in the September 11 attacks, is arrested in Karachi, Pakistan, after an Al-Jazeera broadcast, in which he praised recent militant activities.

- ✔ **September, 2002:** At the Institute of Peace and Justice, a Christian charity in Karachi, seven Christian workers are killed. Gunmen tape the victims' hands and mouths before executing them.

- ✔ **March 2003:** Pakistani officials arrest Khalid Sheikh Muhammad, a high-ranking Al-Qaeda officer believed to be the key planner of the September 11 attacks, in Rawalpindi, Pakistan, and hand him over to U.S. officials.

The price to be paid for aligning himself with America has yet to be determined. Musharraf hasn't heard the last of Islamic militants.

Part V
Regions in Repair

The 5th Wave   By Rich Tennant

"Good news! Sanctions have been lifted, they're ending the curfew, and we're getting 'Jazzercize' classes at the end of this month."

In this part . . .

The regions in repair were formerly regions in turmoil but now are struggling to rebound. Although these regions aren't out of the woods yet, this part traces the steps these various countries have taken through political, economic, and social minefields to arrive at their current state of repair.

Chapter 15

North Africa

As you may understand, try as they may, the European powers just couldn't keep their fingers out of the Middle Eastern cookie jars. The potential for the exploitation of resources and strategic locations of certain countries in the region proved to be too great a temptation to resist. Because in the Europeans' minds the Near East hadn't modernized and remained backward, the Europeans looked at the region like a plump fruit hangin' on the vine ready for the pickin'.

Settlers from France, Spain, Italy, and Malta, for instance, saw Algeria as uncharted territory begging for European know-how to spruce it up. So they moved in and set up house. The fact that "uncivilized" Algerians were already living there didn't seem to bother the European colonists until the Algerians started shooting, bombing, and demanding the invaders go back whence they came.

Don't misunderstand me! European colonization and interference by no means tells the whole story. North Africa had a whole host of other problems even before Europe started meddling in local affairs. For example, the foreign Turkish rulers and local ethnic unrest had been a source of continued friction. The fact that the Barbary States' Muslim rulers had a long history of cleaning up the piracy racket against Western merchant vessels actually invited American and European retaliation in the 19th century. In this chapter, you see that Algeria, Egypt, Libya, and Sudan suffered from various forms of violent struggles in the past and are now regions in the process of licking their wounds and attempting to rebound.

Algeria

The 19th century brought Algeria (see Figure 15-1) an uneasy relationship with the West. Algeria traded wheat, fruit, and woven goods to Europe. The Algerian *dey* (ruler) supplemented his income through kickbacks received from local pirates operating out of Algerian ports in the Mediterranean Sea (see the section, "Terrorizing merchant ships" in this chapter). Because Europeans often ended up the victims of these pirates, the British fleet bombed Algiers in 1816 to discourage such activities.

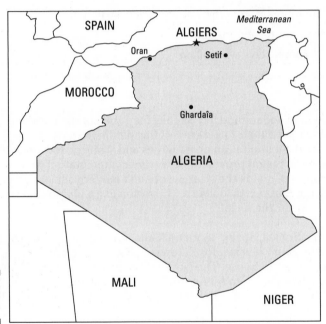

Figure 15-1:
Algeria.

Reacting to a perceived personal affront, the Algerian dey slapped French King Charles X with a flywhisk in 1827. Three years later, suffering from sagging popularity, Charles X decided an invasion could bolster his public image. In June 1830, France invaded Algeria to avenge the insult against the king three years earlier. The attack didn't work though. In July, a revolt back in France sent the king packing to England.

Making the French connection

European military success in the Middle East at times preceded political and economic exploitation of the indigenous populations. By 1837, the French had secured their hold on Algeria. They signed a treaty with Abdul Qadir, a local Berber leader who had fought for the Ottomans with varying degrees of success. Over the next two years Abdul Qadir consolidated his authority over the disparate ethnic factions in northern Algeria. Leaving his past of wine and women behind, he emerged as a religious leader prepared to deal with the French.

- **1839:** Abdul Qadir declares *jihad* (holy war) against the French. The Algerian rebels employ guerrilla tactics.

- **1841:** French general Thomas Robert Bugeaud de la Piconnerie uses antiguerrilla tactics against the rebels. This strategy involves destroying the enemy's economic base — burning crops and slaughtering civilians and livestock.

- **1843:** Bugeaud drives Abdul Qadir's troops into Morocco, where they receive military support from the Moroccan king.

- **1844:** The French defeat Morocco at the Battle of Isly. Abdul Qadir loses his Moroccan support.

- **1847:** Bugeaud defeats Abdul Qadir, and the Algerian resistance dies. Abdul Qadir spends the next five years in a French prison.

Victory over the Algerians came to the French on the battlefield, but Abdul Qadir had conquered the hearts and minds of the Algerian people. Stories of his heroic resistance against foreign invaders earned him almost legendary status. On the other hand, Bugeaud came to represent the worst the West had to offer, setting the stage for future rebellions. Aside from his brutal antiguerrilla tactics, Bugeaud's post-war policies included driving Algerians off the best land and giving it to French colonists.

Ruling European-style

Over the course of the next few years, thousands of Algerian farmers migrated from the rich coastal land to the rocky mountainous region where cultivation proved next to impossible. In 1848, France annexed Algeria. By the turn of the 20th century, the results of the French connection were as follows:

✔ **Massive European colonization:** Colonists from France, Spain, Italy, and Malta arrived. A system of dual status emerged. Colonists became French citizens with the right to vote, while Algerians remained second-class subjects with no such right.

✔ **European rule:** A European governor general, advised by a panel of primarily European advisers, governed Algeria.

✔ **European infrastructure:** The colonists modernized the cities; they built roads, railroads, hospitals, and schools for themselves.

✔ **European business booms:** Utilizing the richest farmland, the colonists capitalized on large-scale agriculture. They also built industrial enterprises, producing among other products wine and tobacco. Large-scale wine production in a Muslim country didn't sit well with the Muslim majority.

Rather than benefit from the progress the colonists had made, the Algerians paid the price for European success in several ways, including:

✔ The Algerian standard of living dropped significantly.

✔ Estimates suggest as many as ⅓ of the Algerian population died.

✔ Left with an economic base in ruins, Algerian society languished in overwhelming poverty.

✔ Large numbers of Quran schools were destroyed, and with them the capacity to teach Arabic.

✔ In the French-style of democracy, Algerians enjoyed very few rights.

Europeans and their culture dominated the cities while Algerians lived in the countryside, with very little interaction between them.

Dealing with World War II and its aftermath

By the beginning of World War II, the population in Algeria had risen dramatically. Approximately 1 million colonists ruled over 9 million Muslims. This rise in population spelled higher unemployment and increased poverty for Algerian Muslims. Algerian nationalism became an Islamic movement. Two trends emerged among Muslim Algerians.

✔ Complete Algerian independence, meaning Muslims would run the show

✔ Complete Algerian assimilation, meaning Muslims would gain equal footing with the colonists and share in governing Algeria

Ferhat Abbas originally pushed for the assimilation strategy, but the French wanted no part of it. Disheartened, Abbas switched sides and fought for full independence. During World War II, Algeria first came under Vichy control, but in 1942, the Allies established their headquarters there.

Slaughtering Algerians at Setif: The last straw

If any fantasies about assimilation and peaceful coexistence with the colonists remained in the minds of Algerian Muslims after World War II, the events sparked at Setif in 1945 brought home the reality of French-imposed double standards.

While celebrating the Allied victory, Algerian nationalists displayed the Algerian flag at the city of Setif. The French police confiscated the flag, resulting in clashes in which Algerian Muslims massacred 90 colonists. The French army retaliated by bombing villages and brutally slaughtering at least 1,500 civilians. The Algerians came to the realization that the colonists must go.

Flirting with democracy

French democracy had meant more and more freedom for the colonists, and less and less freedom for the Algerians. Democracy meant land reform: taking the most fertile farmland from the Muslims and giving it to the colonists. Democracy meant modernization: better roads, schools, and hospitals — for the colonists. Democracy meant representation, laws, and rights — for the colonists.

In an effort to appease Muslim discontents, France afforded the Algerians the right to vote on a dual national house of representatives. Corruption and fraud overshadowed the elections. The combination of these factors convinced most Algerian Muslims that democracy was a farce, a mechanism with which the foreign invaders could dominate their Algerian hosts. Democracy never meant to Algerian Muslims what it meant to French citizens.

Fighting the French-Algerian War: France's Vietnam

The French language has a different way of arranging acronyms. FLN, for instance, means the National Liberation Front. The FLN was a political movement of resistance against the French formed in 1954 of about 20 original members. The FLN's popularity grew, as did its attacks on the French.

- ✔ **November, 1954:** The FLN targets police and government headquarters.
- ✔ **1955:** FLN numbers grow to 2,000.

- ✔ **August, 1955:** In Phillipville, Algerian Muslims massacre 123 civilians, including women and children, in revolt. The French react by killing thousands of Algerians.

- ✔ **1956:** Eager to capture FLN militants, the French arrest known nationalists and routinely torture their victims to wring out intelligence.

Such measures only succeeded in driving hordes of moderate Algerians to join the FLN ranks. By 1956 and 1957, the FLN numbers had grown to approximately 25,000 operating inside Algeria. The year 1956 saw an escalation in the cycle of violence.

- ✔ **August 10, 1956:** The French bomb a bomb factory at 3 Theves Street, but 80 Algerian civilians die in the process. Until this point, both sides had attacked only military targets.

- ✔ **September 30, 1956:** The FLN retaliates by detonating three bombs against civilian targets. Civilian casualties on both sides become increasingly common. FLN attacks in cities, particularly Algiers, increase.

- ✔ **1956:** Morocco and Tunisia serve as refuge and bases for FLN militants. The French construct electric fences along their borders to stem the flow of weapons and guerrillas.

Ben Bella: Memoirs of an Algerian hero

According to his biographer Robert Merle, Ahmed Ben Bella was a righter of wrongs. As a simple peasant boy from Marnia, he never failed to stand up to the oppressor in defense of the victim. In school, he defended Islam against his teachers' verbal assaults and later resisted repeated Vichy pressure to remove a Jew from his soccer team. Whoever the wrongdoer may be, rest assured that Ben Bella would retaliate. When the Germans threatened the Free World, Ben Bella fought alongside the French in Italy. Upon his return from Italy, the Algerian war hero became increasingly disenchanted with French rule. Ben Bella succored starving thousands by illegally signing ration cards. Ben Bella helped form the FLN and carried out guerrilla activities against the French oppressors. He smuggled in weapons from Egypt and even attacked a post office. After having spent six years in prison, he was released when Algeria received its independence.

After independence in 1962, Ben Bella replaced Ben Yusuf Ben Khedda as prime minister. In 1963, Ben Bella was elected president. Like an Algerian Robin Hood, he set out on a campaign of nationalization and land redistribution. A coup in 1965 led by Houari Boumedienne, his defense minister, landed Ben Bella in house arrest until 1980 when he left the country. He returned in 1990 but steered clear of politics.

Looking through a French lieutenant's eyes in Algeria: The good, the bad, and the ugly

As a French lieutenant in Algeria, Jean Jacques Servan-Schreiber witnessed atrocities of the French-Algerian War. In his book *Lieutenant in Algeria,* Servan-Schreiber described the conflict as a complex one, in which both sides were at times good and evil. For Servan-Schreiber, no one was inherently evil, but rather unusual circumstances could awaken the beast inside.

The Good: Private Geronimo made friends with Arabs and played with Arab children, taking every opportunity to make them laugh with funny faces. Marcus was a French military officer who reached out to Algerian Muslims, fought against injustice from any source, be it Arab or French, and included 80 Muslims in his military unit. Colonel Galland led the *Black Commandos*, a combination police force and humanitarian organization for Arabs in the rural areas. On one occasion, the *Black Commandos* saved the life of an Arab youth unjustly arrested and destined for execution.

The Bad: That same Private Geronimo shot and killed Larbi, an old Arab man, who'd been trying to make peace between a gang of Arab youths and French soldiers. Ironically, Larbi, an ex-serviceman, had risked his life a week earlier by supporting the French. Anxious to prove to the men in his company that he could handle himself in combat, Sergeant Maure half-wittedly ordered the slaughter of a truckload of innocent Arab mineworkers, who had curiously enough risked the wrath of the Algerian insurgents by breaching the rebel's prohibition against working at the Albarache mine. To compound the problem, the French army leadership covered up both incidents. Without so much as flexing a trigger finger, the Arab insurgents had scored a huge victory.

The Ugly: The Arab militants also attacked their victims with equal brutality. Servan-Schreiber wrote of an Arab in Marcus's unit who slaughtered his fellow soldiers while they were trapped in a rebel ambush. When an Arab athlete, masquerading as a beggar, attacked an Arab peasant, the peasant's two fellow laborers dropped their tools and joined in the murder.

In 1957, the 500,000 French troops succeeded in putting down the rebellion in the cities and driving the FLN into the countryside, but the damage was done.

In 1958, news of the French torture tactics and abuses created a huge antiwar movement in France, which was in the midst of its own problems at home. Charles de Gaulle, who'd returned as head of the Fifth Republic, negotiated an end to French rule in March 1962. Fearing Muslim reprisals, most of the one million colonists, many of whom were born in Algeria, fled the country. Local Algerian hero Ahmed Ben Bella became the prime minister of newly independent Algeria in 1962 and assumed the presidency in 1963.

Battling civil wars and still hoping for peace

As you may have predicted, Algeria's problems didn't end when the French pulled out. In 1965, Houari Boumedienne ousted Ben Bella in a bloodless military coup just three years after independence. Like other Middle Eastern countries, the high prices for oil and natural gas of the 1970s translated into large profits for Algeria. But the plummeting oil prices in the mid-1980s spelled disaster for the country's economy. The following events plunged the country into civil war that lasted from 1992 until 1999.

- ✔ **1991:** Islamic Salvation Front (FIS), an Islamic extremist movement, wins in the first round of general and presidential elections. The FIS wins 188 of the 231 parliamentary seats. The ruling FLN captures only 15.

- ✔ **1992:** On the brink of losing to the Islamic extremist FIS, the FLN decides to pick up their toys and go home. The military cancels the subsequent elections, bans the FIS, and arrests FIS members. Violence breaks out between the military and Islamic extremists.

- ✔ **1992:** The military names Mohammed Boudiaf president, but the Islamic extremists immediately assassinate him.

- ✔ **1999:** The government grants an amnesty to members of the Islamic Salvation Army, the armed wing of the FIS, and other militant groups. The majority of FIS members surrender, as do other militias.

The civil war has cost more than 100,000 lives to date. Although the bulk of the fighting is finished, extremist violence continues, claiming 100 lives every month. Algeria suffers from widespread corruption, Berber unrest, massive unemployment, and the lack of diversity of an economy based primarily on petroleum. Although Algeria has a legacy of civil war, it still holds out for the promise of peace.

A Rebounding Egypt

In September 1978, U.S. President Jimmy Carter brought Egyptian President Anwar Sadat and Israeli Prime Minister Menachem Begin to the negotiating table in Camp David, Maryland (see Chapter 11). The following year, the two former enemies signed a peace treaty that laid to rest more than three decades of hostility. Sadat had hoped that by ending enmity with Israel, he could move Egypt (see Figure 15-2) into a new era of peace and prosperity, but forces that he'd helped to create wouldn't let him.

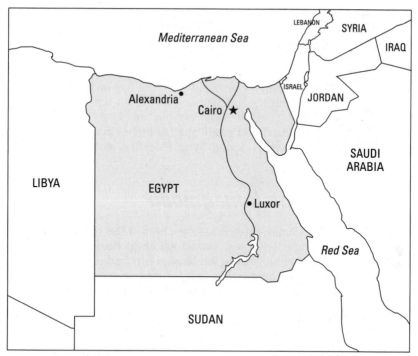

Figure 15-2:
Egypt.

The peace agreement with Israel drove a wedge between Egypt and other Arab countries, and the Arab League suspended Egypt's membership. Internal secular and religious uprisings abounded. Sadat's courting of the Muslim Brotherhood in the 1950s returned to haunt him in 1981 when Islamic militants assassinated him during a military parade.

The Muslim Brotherhood

Hassan al-Banna originally formed the Muslim Brotherhood in 1928 as a youth group to improve the morals of Muslim youngsters in Egypt. By 1939, in the face of a number of political developments in neighboring Palestine and elsewhere, al-Banna transformed the Muslim Brotherhood into a politico-religious movement. The Brotherhood had more than 500 branches by 1940, and each branch had its own center, mosque, school, and club.

During World War II, the ranks swelled and perpetuated anti-British propaganda. By 1946, the Brotherhood boasted half a million members. Within the next two years, the Brotherhood's militant activities against the Egyptians caused the government to declare martial law and ban the group in 1948. The Brotherhood responded by assassinating premier Mahmud Fahmi Nokrashi two weeks later. The Egyptian secret service retaliated with the assassination of al-Banna.

In 1950, the Egyptian government lifted the ban on the Brotherhood with the understanding that the Brotherhood would act strictly as a religious entity. In the subsequent period, Sadat established close ties to the Brotherhood. The Muslim Brotherhood established branches in a number of Arab countries, including Saudi Arabia, Sudan, Syria, Palestine, and Jordan.

Ending the honeymoon

In addition to Sadat, three other members of the 18-member Revolutionary Command Council that whisked Gamal Abdul Nasser to power in July 1952 (see Chapter 6) had links to the Muslim Brotherhood. The relationship between Nasser's new regime that focused on secular goals and the Muslim Brotherhood that wanted to implement *sharia* (Islamic law) soon soured.

- ✔ **1954:** Nasser bans the Muslim Brotherhood again.
- ✔ **1954:** A few months later, the Brotherhood attempts to assassinate Nasser.
- ✔ **1954:** The government retaliates by executing four of the would-be assassins and arresting 4,000 more.

Thousands of Brotherhood activists fled to Jordan, Lebanon, Saudi Arabia, and Syria. This crackdown and subsequent flight of Muslim Brotherhood militants to Arab countries, like Saudi Arabia, spread militant ideology that heavily influenced like-minded extremists, such as the Wahhabis, and would give rise to militant groups like Hamas and Islamic Jihad. In the case of Saudi Arabia, the refuge that the Saudis extended to these extremists and leniency they afforded them created a hotbed of Islamic extremists that nearly spiraled out of control (See Chapter 17).

- ✔ **1964 to 1966:** The Brotherhood attempts to assassinate Nasser three times.
- ✔ **1966:** Egypt tries 365 Brotherhood activists and executes a number of their top leaders.

Changes in popular sentiment after Egypt's defeat in the '67 War with Israel encouraged Nasser to release more than 1,000 Muslim Brotherhood members from prison in 1968. After Sadat became president in 1970, he released the remaining Brotherhood members, who in turn renounced violence. Many of the exiled extremists returned buoyant about Sadat's promise to govern by sharia. When it became apparent that Sadat would play by his own rules, the Brotherhood turned against him. Many extremists splintered off to form other even more violent organizations.

Living in the Sadat era (1970–1981)

Along with Nasser, whom he had met in the Royal Military Academy in the 1930s, Sadat was one of the original Free Officers. The Free Officers staged a coup in 1952 to seize power from King Farouk. General Muhammad Naguib led the new government, but Nasser held the real power with his control over the 18-member Revolutionary Command Committee, of which Sadat was a member. For the next 18 years, Sadat held a number of government posts, including the vice presidency to Nasser. When Nasser died in 1970, Sadat assumed the role of president.

Still reeling from Egypt's poor performance in the last three wars against Israel, Sadat decided the best way to restore Egypt's lost prestige and win back the Sinai would be to surprise Israel. On October 6, 1973, Egypt attacked Israeli forces across the Suez Canal and succeeded in pushing the Israeli forces back across the Sinai (see Chapter 11). In the end, having gained international recognition and wrestling concessions from Israel, Sadat set about a path of peace that allowed his country to focus on rebounding from 25 years of conflict with its neighbor.

Sadat's strategy of peace with Israel meant regaining the Sinai and concentrating resources on internal, economic, and political goals while receiving large monetary rewards from the United States. In November 1977, Sadat took the unprecedented step of addressing the Israeli Knesset (parliament) in Jerusalem. Along with Israeli Prime Minister Begin, Sadat received the Nobel Peace Prize in 1978 for his part in the Camp David Accords, facilitated by U.S. President Jimmy Carter. Sadat, Begin, and Carter are shown in Figure 15-3.

Figure 15-3:
Sadat,
Carter, and
Begin.

In the Arab world, Sadat's peace overtures weren't as popular as they were in the West. The Arab League's suspension of Egypt after the signing of the peace treaty with Israel caused increased isolation. In Egypt, Sadat took other unpopular steps to secure his power:

- **1979:** Sadat dissolves parliament.

- **1979:** He rigs the elections so that his NDP party can win with 83 percent of the votes.

- **1980:** He ousts his prime minister to make room for himself in that position.

- **1980:** He manipulates the constitution to allow himself to remain president beyond the six-year limitation.

- **1980:** He bans strikes.

- **1981:** He arrests 2,000 Islamic militants, most of whom are members of the same Muslim Brotherhood he'd courted in the early 1970s.

Doin' hard time

Egyptian Arab nationalists saw World War II as an opportunity to join forces with Britain's enemies. Hoping to oust the British, Anwar Sadat became a German agent during the war. The British arrested him in 1942, but he escaped prison two years later. In 1946, his militant activities against the British landed him in prison again. In his autobiography *In Search of Identity*, Sadat recalls the years of incarceration as therapeutic and as an opportunity to return to his roots, to the fundamentals of life, and to emerge with a clear vision of purpose. He finds the experience liberating because he regains an understanding of himself. Sadat discovers that he was a peasant inextricably linked to the land.

He also undergoes a type of mystical experience, whereby God becomes his best friend. His reliance on, and respect for, the Muslim Brotherhood increases. When Sadat's military colleagues had forgotten him, Brotherhood leader Hassan al-Banna provides Sadat's family ten Egyptian pounds every month. New horizons also open up for Sadat in the world of reading. He reads books, magazines, and newspapers in English and Arabic, and keeps a journal recording quotes from authors that influence him. He even takes advantage of this period to study German.

His political manuevers eventually caught up with him. In October 1981, Islamic militants exacted their revenge by assassinating Sadat during a military parade.

Giving it a go: Mubarak takes over

Egyptians didn't mourn Sadat's death as they had Nasser's. After Sadat's assassination by Islamic extremists in 1981, Hosni Mubarak became president. On the international scene, Mubarak embarked on a path to balance continued relations with the United States and Israel while improving interaction with Arab countries. During the Iran-Iraq War, Mubarak supported Saddam Hussein, and in 1984, the Egyptian president traveled to Jordan to reestablish diplomatic relations. After the Arab League shifted its strategy in 1988 and endorsed the PLO's efforts to negotiate peace with Israel, Egypt was reinstated as a league member the following year.

Like Sadat and Nasser before him, Mubarak faced serious domestic problems. One important order of business was to deal with the extremists in the Muslim Brotherhood and other Islamic militant groups. This task proved more than a handful for Mubarak.

✔ **From the late 1970s:** Because religious parties couldn't participate in elections, Muslim Brotherhood activists ally with legitimate political parties to gain seats in parliament.

✔ **1987:** Through the Labour Islamic Alliance, the Brotherhood wins 37 parliamentary seats. The Brotherhood demands the immediate implementation of sharia, suspension of ties with the United States, and a revocation of the peace treaty with Israel.

✔ **1990 to 1991:** The Brotherhood's support of Saddam Hussein's occupation of Kuwait proves an embarrassment for Mubarak, who condemns the invasion.

Egypt sent troops to participate in the U.S.-led coalition against Iraq in the Persian Gulf War (see Chapter 12). For its part in this war, the United States wrote off a $7-billion debt racked up by Egypt. Mubarak further played an important role in the peace process between Israel and the Palestinian Authority in 1993 (see Chapter 11). Like Sadat before him, Islamic extremists viewed Mubarak as a traitor to his religion and to all Muslims. A number of Islamic militant groups, including Islamic Jihad and Gamaat al-Islamiya, intensified antigovernment activities in the 1990s.

Lashing out: Extremists kill tourists in Temple Massacre

No achievement could please Islamic extremists more than a break with what they viewed as the Christian West. In an effort to create a rift, militant violence increased between 1992 and 1997, claiming more than 1,200 lives, mostly Egyptian Christians. Mubarak responded by cracking down on extremists by imprisoning an estimated 26,000 suspected Islamic militants and sentencing dozens to death. One offshoot of the Muslim Brotherhood, Gamaat al-Islamiya, ratcheted up militant activities in November 1997, setting the stage for international terrorist acts to come.

On November 17, 1997, six gunmen disguised as police officers descended the cliffs around the Temple of Queen Hatshepsut in Luxor and opened fired on unarmed tourists, most of whom were foreigners from Switzerland, Japan, Germany, Britain, Bulgaria, Colombia, and France, including a 5-year-old British girl. To make certain their victims had died, the gunmen approached the bodies and shot them in the head. One woman survived underneath the bodies of two dead tourists. More than 70 died in the attack, including 58 foreign tourists, Egyptian tourists, and police, and all six assassins, who turned the guns on themselves when they'd finished with their victims. Representatives for the Gamaat al-Islamiya promised more violence like the Temple Massacre.

Forging ahead along a rewarding and costly path

After the September 11, 2001, attacks, Mubarak vowed to join George W. Bush's War on Terrorism. Having chosen the path to align Egypt with the United States has been both a rewarding and a costly one. Egypt presently receives $2 billion in military and economic aid every year. By maintaining peace with Israel and garnering support among the Arab World for Western initiatives, resistance from within Egypt, including Islamic militancy, has taken its toll on the country. In fact, Mubarak's sympathy for American victims of the September 11 attacks stemmed in part from his own experiences at the hands of Islamic militants.

Libya: Trouble on the Shores of Tripoli

In the 16th century, the Ottomans cast their net over most of North Africa and ruled supreme, at least for a while. But the farther from Istanbul they went, the more difficult the Turks found long-distance rule to be. So the Ottomans didn't always maintain a secure grasp on far-off regions, like Tripoli and Algeria. In 1711, an Ottoman slave warrior (see Chapter 5) named Ahmad Karamanli murdered the old Ottoman governor and installed someone he liked much better: himself. This change of governorship established the Karamanli dynastic rule through 1835. The dey, like his Algerian counterpart, earned a considerable revenue from kickbacks by professional pirates on the Mediterranean Sea.

Terrorizing merchant ships

As long as merchants have been sailing the Mediterranean Sea, pirates have preyed on merchant ships. Pirates exploited Phoenician (see Chapter 4), Greek, and Roman vessels in ancient times. State-sponsored piracy, or privateering, served as a political weapon against one's enemies as well as a nice source of revenue. British pirates, for example, routinely preyed on Spanish vessels in the 17th and 18th centuries, all the while sharing their spoils with the crown.

The local Muslim rulers of three North Africa countries, known as the Barbary States (Tripolitania, Tunisia, and Algeria), earned revenue from such raids. Although the British and French fleets routinely bombed pirate hangouts, most merchants found it more prudent to pay protection fees (tribute) to the local Muslim rulers than to risk raids.

Tripolitan War

In 1801, the United States went to war with Tripoli over an unscheduled price hike in the protection fees arbitrarily imposed by the dey.

- ✔ **1801:** U.S. Commodore Richard Dale attempts a blockade of Tripoli.

- ✔ **1802:** President Thomas Jefferson sends envoy Richard Morris to Tripoli to negotiate a settlement with the dey, but the negotiations stall.

- ✔ **1803:** The *Philadelphia* runs aground in a storm. The captain and crew are captured.

- ✔ **1805:** William Eaton lands in Egypt and marches to the port of Derna, which he seizes.

In 1805, both sides reached a peace settlement, but the piracy continued. Combined U.S., French, British, and Turkish efforts over the next three decades successfully wiped out piracy in the region. By 1835, the Ottomans had once again established control over Tripoli.

Trying its hand at colonization: Italy conquers Libya

Seeing that the French and British had enjoyed success at ruling over North Africans, the Italians thought they would try their hand at colonization. After all, how hard could it be?

- ✔ **1911 to 1912:** During the Turko-Italian War, Italy seizes North Tripoli. The Ottomans grant Libya independence. The Italians, who wouldn't hear of it, decide they will settle for nothing less than complete domination of Libya.

- ✔ **1914:** Italy had conquered much of Libya, but a brutal war rages on. The Italians resort to public hangings, concentration camps, poison gas, livestock decimation, and civilian target bombing to show the Libyans the error of their ways. Nearly half of Libya's population is killed, starved, or forced to seek exile between 1912 and 1943.

- ✔ **1933 to 1940:** As governor-general of Libya, Italian Fascist leader Italo Balbo builds roads, schools, and hospitals.

- ✔ **1930s:** Approximately 40,000 Italian colonists settle in Libya.

- ✔ **1939:** Libya becomes part of Italy.

- ✔ **1940:** Italy joins Hitler's Axis of power in World War II. Libya becomes a major battleground.

By 1943, the Allies chased the Axis forces from North Africa. Although the war was over, the suffering and foreign presence wasn't. Figure 15-4 shows a map of modern Libya.

Sticking its nose in Libya's business: The West makes its "overtures"

The last three decades of conflict had taken their toll on Libya. The brutal Italian war of conquest matched with intense bombardment and violence of World War II had left Libya's people and economy in shambles. Postwar Libya looked like this:

✔ The country was a poster child for abject poverty.

• A main source of income emanated from scavenging the desert battlefield for scrap metal left behind in the aftermath of tank battles.

• The infant mortality rate soared to 40 percent and illiteracy to 90 percent.

✔ Millions of land mines remained undetected under the sand.

✔ The British and French occupied the territory and routinely jailed activists who opposed the occupation.

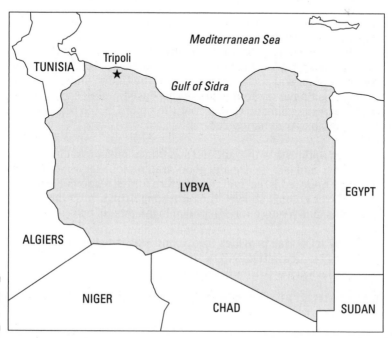

Figure 15-4:
Libya.

The United Nations granted Libya independence, which took effect in 1951. However, the West still played a key role in Libya.

- ✔ **1953:** The newly formed United Kingdom of Libya, led by British-backed King Idris, permits the British to establish military bases in the country in 1953 in exchange for economic subsidies.

- ✔ **1954:** The king makes a similar deal with the United States for a military base at Wheelus Field, renewing an agreement that began in 1943. The U.S. ambassador calls the base *Little America* on the Mediterranean's shores.

- ✔ **1957:** Libya adopts the Eisenhower Doctrine, aligning itself with the West at the expense of the Soviets. Anti-Western public opinion flourishes, particularly in light of Nasser's growing popularity.

The discovery of oil in 1958 greatly increased the country's revenue. As is often the case, the oil wealth enjoyed by the elite and corrupt government officials didn't make its way to the Libyan people, whose economic status hadn't improved. Arab nationalists and other Libyan discontents came to the conclusion that alignment with the West had failed. By 1964, the country no longer relied on foreign subsidies, and Libya kicked most of the British out, although some British and American forces remained in the country.

Meeting Qaddafi on the warpath

In the mid-20th century military coups were in vogue in the Near East. Following the stylish Free Officers in Egypt and the trendy Baathists in Syria and Iraq, the fashionable Colonel Muammar al-Qaddafi led a group of military officers to overthrow King Idris on September 1, 1969. If Qaddafi's unique blend of Islam and socialism concerned the United States, his staunch anti-Soviet position in the first years of rule eased American worries. With Syria and Egypt snuggling up to Moscow, the United States began to view Qaddafi as a tolerable Arab nationalist.

Western optimism with Qaddafi soon diminished amid clashes over oil, terrorism, and Israel. Like any good Arab nationalist worth his or her salt, Qaddafi opposed Israel and the Western forces responsible for its existence. In 1970, the colonel showed the remaining British and American forces to the door. His anti-Western foreign policy highlights follow.

- ✔ **1973:** Qaddafi provides troops and weapons, including aircraft, to the Arab forces in the 1973 Arab-Israeli War (see Chapter 11) and criticizes Sadat's cease-fire agreement with Israel.

> ✔ **1973:** After the war, Qaddafi campaigns to raise oil prices and reduce crude to Israel's supporters.

> ✔ **1981:** Two Libyan fighter jets launch an attack against American troops in the Gulf of Sidra. The Americans shoot down the fighters.

Although Libya seemed to be on a collision course with the West, in the eyes of the United States, Qaddafi's greatest offense was his sponsorship of terrorism.

Bankrolling terrorism

The major U.S. complaint against Qaddafi was his sponsorship of terrorism. In the 1980s, anti-Israeli and anti-Western militants found continued clandestine support from Libya. In 1986, U.S. President Ronald Reagan responded to Libya's support of terrorism — including the Abu Nidal terrorist attacks at the airports in Rome and Vienna a year earlier — with air strikes against Libyan targets designed to destroy terrorist sites and with hopes of killing Qaddafi and his family.

Nonetheless, Qaddafi's critics have given the Libyan dictator more credit than he deserves. The Munich Olympics Massacre in 1972 (see Chapter 11), for example, appears to have been conducted without Qaddafi's support, and evidence of support of the Abu Nidal terrorist organization in the mid-1980s points to Syria as the major sponsor, not Libya. But Qaddafi's involvement in other militant activities, including both the successful and failed assassination plots of Libyan exiles and of other Near Eastern leaders, has helped to create the terrorist mystique around the Libyan colonel. The most notorious act of terrorism linked to Libya was the bombing of a Pan Am airliner that killed 270 people in Lockerbie, Scotland in 1988.

Since the imposition of U.N. sanctions against Libya in 1992 and the international media attention focusing on his country after the Lockerbie bombing, few reports of Qaddafi's support for terrorist endeavors have emerged. Qaddafi has made overtures to repair his damaged relationship with the West. The colonel expelled a number of Palestinian militants and paid $25 million to the victims of a French airliner crash over Africa in 1989.

In April 2003, the Libyan Foreign Minister Abdul Rahman stated that his government accepted responsibility for the Lockerbie disaster because international law determines that a country is responsible for what its employees do. (Megrahi was a Libyan intelligence agent.) A $27-billion fund will be established to compensate the families of each victim approximately $10 million. In an earlier *Newsweek* interview, Qaddafi had said that if an average American needs $10 million compensation, then "Qaddafi's daughter" (referring to himself in the third person) must be worth billions, a reference to the death of his daughter in the U.S. air strikes in 1986.

Remembering Pan Am Flight 103

On December 22, 1988, a Boeing 747 with 259 passengers on its way to New York just a few days before Christmas exploded in midair. The plane disintegrated, instantly ripping apart. All 259 died. Burning chunks of the falling aircraft killed another 11 civilians on the ground. Flaming aircraft fragments landed in the Scottish village of Lockerbie, on the highway, across the fields, and in the forest. Rescuers found the bodies of the pilots and a flight attendant still inside the cockpit in a churchyard, where the flight attendant's pulse throbbed on for a few minutes before it stopped forever.

British and Scottish authorities determined an intentional explosive device (IED) to be the cause of the explosion. After nearly three years of investigation, the United States indicted two Libyan intelligence agents for the bombing: Abdul Baset Ali Muhammad Al-Megrahi and Al-Amin Khalifa Fhimah. Libya refused to extradite the two men. In 1992, the United Nations imposed sanctions on Libya. After drawn-out negotiations, Qaddafi turned the suspects over to authorities in April 1999. The prosecution determined that the bomb inside a suitcase was loaded in Malta. A court in the Netherlands found Al-Megrahi guilty of mass murder in January 2001 but acquitted Fhimah of all charges.

The Sudan: A Land of Civil War and Famine

The 19th and 20th century history of North Africa is one of waning and waxing foreign influence. The European colonial powers sought to pry loose the Ottomans' slippery political grasp of the region. Britain strove to exert influence in Egypt, the French took hold of Algeria, and the Italians wrestled Libya free from the Turks. Therefore, are you really surprised to find Britain and Egypt scheming to dominate the Sudan? See Figure 15-5 for a map of Sudan and its neighbors.

The colonial era

After kicking Napoleon and the French out of Egypt (see Chapter 6) at the turn of the 19th century and cleaning up against the Wahhabis in Arabia, Muhammad Ali turned his sights (and two armies loose) on Sudan in 1820. By 1823, he'd set up shop in northern Sudan with his headquarters at Khartoum and begun to deal in ivory and slaves. The British decided they wanted a piece of the action and forced themselves on Cairo in 1840 (see Chapter 6) and, with great difficulty, further extended Anglo-Egyptian influence into southern Sudan over the next 50 years.

Figure 15-5:
Sudan.

- ✔ **1881:** Muhammad Ahmad organizes a jihad against the British by claiming to be the Mahdi who has returned to purify Islam in the Sudan.

- ✔ **1885:** The Mahdi kills British General Charles Gordan and seizes Khartoum only to die six months later.

- ✔ **1896 to 1898:** The British and Egyptians seize control of the Sudan from the Mahdis (followers of the Madhi).

The Egyptians under a watchful British eye continued to run everything in the Sudan until the 1920s when a series of mutinies ended their control of the north. The British turned to a strategy of isolating southern Sudan from the north in hopes that it would merge with Kenya and Uganda, already under British control. In 1956, Sudan disappointed the British by declaring independence.

Waging the perpetual civil war

Shortly before independence, the southern non-Muslims, many of whom were Christians and followers of indigenous religions, revolted against the Muslim north. The revolt embroiled the country into a bloody civil war that lasted 17 years amid two military coups, government corruption, and brutal repression of southern dissidents. In 1969, General Gaafar Nimeiri staged a successful coup and immediately sought to end the civil war. In 1972, southern Sudan received a degree of autonomy, bringing the civil war to an end. The peace lasted ten years.

Nimeiri's institution of sharia in 1983 fanned the flames of southern discontent. The southern Sudan People's Liberation Army (SPLA), consisting primarily of non-Muslims, took up arms once again. Two years later a third military coup ousted Nimeiri. The elections in 1986 installed a civilian government that lasted just three years, when Lieutenant General Omar Ahmed al-Bashir seized power through a fourth military coup. He invited Hassan al-Turabi, the country's Muslim spiritual leader, to join forces in order to make Sudan an Islamic state.

Starving for a fight

Either natural causes or human device can cause famine. Sudan in the 1980s and 1990s suffered from both. The harsh climatic conditions contributed to the drought, while the resumption of the civil war in 1983 did its part to see that civilians died of starvation. Estimates place the death figures caused by civil war and famine at 2 million during the 1980s and 1990s. The politics of civil war played out like this:

- ✓ **1989:** Bashir reinforces sharia, bans opposition parties, and intensifies efforts to crush rebels in the south.

- ✓ **1989 to 1990:** The general employs starvation tactics against the famine-stricken south, by diverting international aid to the Muslim north.

- ✓ **1990:** The United States ceases humanitarian aid to Sudan.

- ✓ **1991:** Tribal and political differences in the SPLA erupt into violence, causing thousands of casualties.

- ✓ **1991:** The Persian Gulf War breaks out, and Sudan sides with Iraq.

The Gulf War was a defining period for Sudan's Sunni leadership. Whatever hesitation Turabi may have had about opposing the West, in which he'd been educated, melted away as he saw the United States and Great Britain lead

Muslim states into an invasion of another Muslim state. After the war, Turabi forged alliances with extremists in Iran and Islamic militants from all over the Muslim World, like Osama bin Laden. Turabi and Bashir also consolidated their power at home. As head of the National Islamic Front (a spinoff from the Muslim Brotherhood), Turabi became speaker of the National Assembly in 1996 while Bashir assumed the presidency in 1993.

After the bombing of the U.S. embassies in Tanzania and Kenya on August 7, 1998, that killed 224 people, U.S. President Bill Clinton ordered missile attacks of suspected terrorist camps in Afghanistan and a suspected chemical-weapons site in Khartoum. The Sudanese claimed that the plant produced pharmaceuticals, and international investigators failed to find evidence of chemical weapons.

In 1999, a struggle for power between Bashir and Turabi resulted in a state of emergency by which Bashir dismissed Turabi, dissolved the parliament, and suspended the constitution. And the civil war continues on.

A match made in paradise?

Hassan al-Turabi received a master's degree in law in Britain in 1957 and completed his doctorate in the Sorbonne in 1964. His ties with the Muslim Brotherhood and his writings on sharia over the next two decades made him a religious authority in Sudan. The results of the Gulf War convinced Turabi that he must take steps to cleanse the Muslim World of Western influence and U.S. puppet regimes, such as Saudi Arabia and Egypt. Sudan's Islamic dictatorship, run by Bashir and Turabi, became a natural refuge for Islamic militants in the early 1990s. With Iranian support, Turabi converted economically devastated and war-torn Sudan into an outpost for Islamic militancy in North Africa. Iran imported weapons and provided military training in addition to interrogation methods, not only for Khartoum's continued war in the south but also for future jihads elsewhere.

After meeting with Turabi, Osama bin Laden set up shop in Sudan and ran legitimate and militant front operations out of Sudan from 1991 until 1996. It was a match made in paradise. Or was it? Bin Laden supplied financial backing and connections while Turabi provided the Arab millionaire with a safe haven to conduct his militant affairs unfettered by government restrictions. Estimates suggest that bin Laden had funded 23 militant training camps in Sudan by 1996. But all good things must come to an end. As a result of increased pressure from Washington, Saudi Prince Sultan convinced Bashir (through a number of financial incentives) to expel bin Laden in 1996. At that point, bin Laden pulled up stakes and moved to Taliban-run Afghanistan, where bin Laden set up camp.

Chapter 16

Jordan, Lebanon, and Syria

A *Washington Post* correspondent wrote that King Abdullah bin Hussein — the current king of Jordan — has been known to state that Jordan is "caught been Iraq and a hard place — Israel." Whether or not King Abdullah ever voiced these words doesn't detract from the fact that Jordan indeed is in a very tight spot and has been for half a century.

A number of reasons account for Jordan's tight spot in the Middle East. This country of a little more than 4 million people is flanked on the east by Iraq, with whom it's linked economically, religiously, culturally, and politically. Iraq has provided Jordan with a cheap oil supply. Presently, Jordan is home to 250,000 Iraqis, many of whom are refugees, and the tiny kingdom is struggling to cope with the burden these immigrants place on an already strained economy.

On the west, Jordan shares the longest common border with Israel — the largest of any Arab nation — which places it in a particularly precarious spot (see Figure 16-1). Approximately 60 percent of Jordan's citizens are of Palestinian descent, and 1.6 million refugees living in Jordan are Palestinian. After the 1991 Persian Gulf War, 700,000 out-of-work Jordanian and Palestinian workers returned home from the Gulf States, placing even greater stress on the country's economy (see "Carrying a grudge about the Gulf War" in this chapter). Because Jordan has no oil and few natural resources, the kingdom relies on tourism to help bolster the economy. In other words, Jordan has as much to lose as anyone in the region by instability in Israel, Palestine, or Iraq.

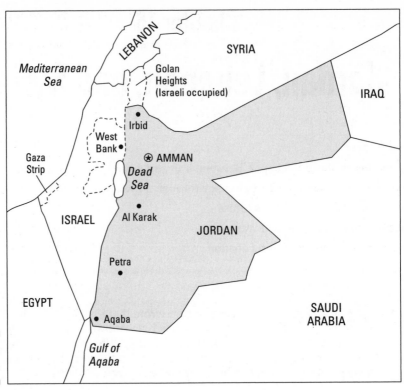

Figure 16-1:
Jordan.

This chapter discusses the political developments in the past generation or so in the nations surrounding Israel and Palestine: Jordan, Lebanon, and Syria. (See Chapter 11 for more on Israel and Palestine.) These developments have played a crucial role in the current level of instability or stability in the region.

Juggling Diplomacy: How Current Politics Took Their Shape

Maybe all truly good statespersons are good jugglers. The Hashemite kings of Jordan (see Chapter 6) have been exceptionally skillful jugglers of diplomacy. Jordan's current tough spot is only the most recent in a series of difficult positions. For nearly half a century, the late King Hussein adeptly played the game of regional politics. The king's ability to survive the volatile political and military environment in the Middle East for nearly 50 years is a testament to his skill as master juggler.

King Hussein and the West

In July 1951, sixteen-year-old Hussein was in the company of his grandfather King Abdullah in Jerusalem. As they entered al-Aqsa mosque, a Palestinian nationalist opened fire. Abdullah was killed, but a bullet bounced off a medal on young Hussein's uniform. Two years later, Hussein became king by replacing his father, Talal, who proved mentally unfit to rule.

Although the majority of Jordanians are Palestinian, the royal family and the rest of the kingdom are Bedouins (see Chapter 24) from the Arabian Peninsula. The royal family traces its lineage back to the prophet Muhammad. Yet, the Hashemite Kingdom of Jordan doesn't owe its existence to Arabs in Saudi Arabia, Iraq, or Egypt. Jordan's royal family owes its existence to the British who placed Abdullah on the throne and helped him establish the kingdom after World War I.

King Hussein was educated in England and, like his grandfather, cultivated a friendly relationship with the British and the West. Hussein's second queen was British and his last wife, Queen Nur, is an Arab-American, who graduated from Princeton University. However, under a rolling wave of Arab nationalism in the 1950s and dissatisfaction with the West's support for Israel, King Hussein severed many of his ties with the West, including economic aid from Britain. Promises of support from Saudi Arabia, Egypt, and Syria in the late 1950s were meant to offset the lost aid. Unfortunately, Egypt and Syria never made good on these promises.

Dealing with significant losses after conflict with Israel

In the 1960s, tensions between much of the Arab World and Israel heightened (see Chapter 11) and surrounding Arab nations began to unite in opposition to Israel. Posturing for an attack against Israel in 1967, Jordan and Egypt signed a defense pact, which placed Jordanian forces under the command of

Egyptian President Gamal Abdul Nasser, but Israel beat them to the punch. On June 5, Israel's preemptive strike devastated the Arab air forces in Egypt, Syria, and Jordan. Israel seized the Sinai, Sharm al-Sheikh, and the Gaza Strip (see Chapter 6) from Egypt; the West Bank and Jerusalem from Jordan; and the Golan Heights from Syria. About 250,000 Palestinians from these seized regions sought refuge in Jordan, where King Hussein welcomed them. Figure 16-2 compares Israel's boundaries before and after the 1967 War.

Facing an internal Palestinian threat

Although a U.N. Security Council resolution on November 22, 1967, called for Israel to withdraw from the Occupied Territories (see Chapter 11), King Hussein soon realized that the Israelis had no intention of leaving. Faced with the recent failure of conventional military forces, the king adopted a new strategy: supporting Palestinian guerrilla organizations that would force the Israelis off the land.

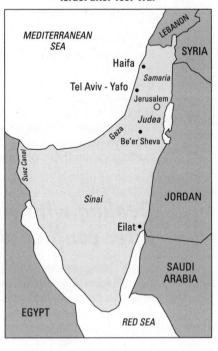

Figure 16-2: Israel seized Jerusalem and the West Bank from Jordan in 1967.

The continued support of such groups over the next few years began to take its toll on Jordan as much as it did Israel. The guerrilla groups operating from inside Jordan demonstrated contempt for Hussein whom they claimed hadn't done enough to oust the Israelis. They established their own goals, including the establishment of an independent Palestine, something King Hussein and Jordan wouldn't support. Skirmishes between the Palestinian militants and Hussein's forces erupted.

The violence continued to escalate and finally culminated in a ten-day civil war in September 1970, known as *Black September*. (See the sidebar, "The month the lights went out in Jordan: Black September" in this chapter.) According to some accounts, thousands of people died, most of them Palestinian. By the following year, King Hussein's forces had wiped out the guerrilla forces inside Jordan (many fled to Syria and Lebanon).

The month the lights went out in Jordan: Black September

On September 6, 1970, the Popular Front for the Liberation of Palestine (PLFP) hijacked four air-liners. The terrorists flew the first two aircraft (TWA and Swissair) to Dawson's Field, an ex-Royal Air Force airfield in the Jordanian desert. A third aircraft (Pan Am) proved too big to land at Dawson's Field so the terrorists flew it to Cairo and blew it up after the 176 crew and pas-sengers made a three-minute forced evacua-tion. The two hijackers on the fourth plane (El Al) over London were overpowered by security staff. The male terrorist was killed, and the female, named Leila Khalid, was arrested and taken into British custody when the plane landed in London.

The remaining hijackers aboard the two aircraft in Jordan demanded Khalid's release along with a number of guerrilla members imprisoned in Germany, Switzerland, and Israel. A few days later, PLFP militants hijacked a fifth plane (BOAC) on flight from India to Lebanon and landed it in Jordan. In total the militants were holding some 360 hostages, 65 of whom were British. The hijackers gave the British govern-ment a 72-hour ultimatum. Because of the hostages and that Khalid was in their custody,

the British contradicted their own policy of never negotiating with terrorists. The militants extended the deadline, but by September 12, their patience had run out. They blew up the three remaining planes. The act, meant to demonstrate their resolve, was televised.

Meanwhile the increased violence between King Hussein's forces and the Palestinian mili-tants became an international incident. Syria sent 200 tanks and other military support to the guerrillas and was prepared to intervene on behalf of the militants if necessary. King Hussein contacted both Britain and the United States requesting support and asking them to invite Israel to bomb Syrian troops. Although the Israeli attack never happened, Palestinians have since accused Jordan of accepting weapons from Israel during the ordeal.

The hostages were exchanged for Khalid and six other Palestinian militants. Hussein eventu-ally crushed the Palestinian uprising in his country. And although relations between the king and the Palestinians improved consider-ably over the next three decades and wounds have healed, the emotional scars are left as reminders of Black September.

Diminishing roles as conflict continues

In 1973, Jordan may have been as surprised as anyone (except for the Israelis) when Egypt and Syria attacked Israel on the eve of Yom Kippur, initiating the Fourth Arab-Israeli War (see Chapter 11). Although King Hussein was left out of the war-preparation plans, he sent a small contingent of soldiers to Syria. Jordan's role in the war, therefore, was minor. When the smoke cleared a few weeks later, Egyptian President Anwar Sadat had wrestled concessions on the Sinai from Israel, but Jordan's West Bank and Jerusalem (and Syria's Golan Heights) remained under Israeli occupation.

The following year, the king's hopes of regaining the West Bank were further dashed when he was forced to accept the Arab League's ruling that the Palestinian Liberation Organization (PLO) (see Chapter 11) would be the sole negotiating body for the Palestinians. When Henry Kissinger brought Egypt and Israel together to sign the Second Sinai Agreement in September 1975, creating more concessions for Egypt, Jordan and Syria felt increasingly alienated. The two Arab nations, therefore, forged closer ties hoping to salvage their diminished roles as political powers in the region.

Dividing the Arabs: The Camp David Accords

In September 1978, U.S. President Jimmy Carter brought Egyptian President Anwar Sadat and Israeli Prime Minister Menachem Begin to Camp David, Maryland, where they signed the historic Camp David Accords (see Chapter 11). The final peace agreement, which was signed in 1979, returned the Sinai to Egypt and normalized relations between the two countries. In the West, the peace accords have been hailed as a significant first step toward peace in the region. For the most part, the Arab World didn't see it that way.

Although the United States tried to include Jordan in the peace negotiations, King Hussein refused to take part in any agreement that left the West Bank under Israeli occupation (even though there was a provision for future plans to resolve this issue). In 1980, he traveled to Washington to try to convince Carter that the peace accords were actually counterproductive.

The agreement drove the Arabs into two camps. Oman, Sudan, and Somalia continued to support Egypt while Jordan and the rest of the Arab nations severed relations with Egypt. The Arab League suspended Egypt's membership from 1979 until 1989. For its part in the peace process, Egypt received substantial military and economic aid from the United States. Most Arab countries, therefore, saw Sadat as having sold out to American interests. Two years later, Islamic extremists assassinated Sadat.

In a league of their own: The Arab League

The Arab League, or the League of Arab States, was created in 1945 with Egypt, Iraq, Lebanon, Syria, Saudi Arabia, Trans-Jordan, and Yemen as member states. The Arab League represented a united body of Arab nations meant to coordinate and promote common political, legal, economic, and social goals and interests on the international front. The Palestinian Liberation Organization (PLO) became a full member in 1976, and most of the remaining Arab nations have since joined, including Algeria, Bahrain, Kuwait, Libya, Morocco, Oman, Qatar, Somalia, Sudan, Tunisia, and the United Arab Emirates.

The Arab League voted to attack Israel in 1948, and has since actively sought violent and peaceful means to achieve the liberation of Palestine. When Egyptian President Anwar Sadat normalized relations with Israel in 1979, the Arab League suspended Egypt's membership. In 1988, the Arab League shifted its strategy and endorsed the PLO's efforts to negotiate peace with Israel, and reinstated Egypt's membership the following year. The league predictably sided with Iraq (an Arab nation) during the *Iran-Iraq War* (Iran isn't an Arab nation) but remained divided on the issue of the *Persian Gulf War*.

Siding with another Hussein: The Iran-Iraq War

In the early 1980s, Jordan's economy was booming, thanks in large part to Iraq, which was a major market for Jordanian exports and Jordan's main source of cut-rate oil. In May 1981, when King Hussein agreed to purchase $200 million worth of weapons from the Soviet Union, Saddam Hussein promised to pick up the tab. No one was surprised then that King Hussein chose to support Saddam in the Iran-Iraq War (see Chapter 12) that ran from 1980 to 1988. By the end of the 1980s, when Iraq was strapped for cash and threatened not to repay its debts, Jordanian exporters suffered.

Supporting the Reagan plan: Warming up to the West

After Ronald Reagan moved into the White House in 1981, he proposed his own solution to the Palestinian crisis.

  ✔ The Israelis would retreat to pre-1967 borders (see Chapter 11).

  ✔ Arab nations would recognize Israel's right to exist.

Sound familiar? Notice the similarities between Reagan's plan in 1981 and the Saudi and Bush plans in 2002 (see Chapter 11) (except for the obvious lack of jellybean homage). Unlike previously proposed settlements, King Hussein did support this peace initiative because his primary interest was addressed: The West Bank would return to the Palestinians.

In 1982, the Israelis evacuated the Sinai, fulfilling the conditions of the 1979 treaty with Egypt. King Hussein, who was edging toward a settlement with Israel and warming relations with the West, called on the remaining Arab nations to normalize relations with Egypt. Jordan and the United States at the time had another common interest: They were both supporting Iraq against Iran (in the Iran-Iraq War).

Choosing sides in the Persian Gulf War

By 1990, Reagan had retired, and George Bush was in the Oval Office. The United States began to view King Hussein as a moderate Arab ally and stabilizing force in the region. As a result, Jordan saw an increase in economic aid from the United States. When the Persian Gulf War broke out in January 1991, Hussein had a tough decision to make. He had two options:

- ✔ Abandon Iraq, his neighbor and his largest trading partner and source of cut-rate oil, at the risk of enraging the vast majority of his Palestinian subjects, who sympathized with Iraq. Saddam had publicly declared his support for the Palestinians and openly vowed to destroy Israel.

- ✔ Face the wrath of the Americans, Western allies, and other Arab nations by siding with Saddam.

The Jordanian king's decision to remain loyal to Iraq was a costly one because Jordan suffered in various ways:

- ✔ The United States, Saudi Arabia, and Kuwait suspended economic aid to Jordan.

- ✔ The oil-rich Gulf States, like Kuwait and Saudi Arabia, sent 700,000 Palestinian and Jordanian workers packing, which was a enormous blow to Jordan's economy because Jordan depended on the revenue generated by the workers' remittance to their families back home. King Hussein met the first group of returnees at the airport with open arms (see sidebar "Carrying a grudge about the Gulf War" below).

✔ The U.N. sanctions against Iraq cut off Jordan from its largest trading partner and cheap source of oil.

✔ Unemployment reached 80 percent among returnees and 40 percent in the overall workforce.

The strain took its toll on Jordan's economy. The unemployment and financial plight of workers returning from the Gulf States meant frustration and anger that were vented in one of two directions: eastward against Saddam, or westward against the United States and Britain.

Making his peace

The Oslo Accords had established a framework for peace between the Palestinian Authority and Israel in 1993. The day after the accords had been reached, Israel and Jordan agreed on the Israel-Jordan Common Agenda outlining steps for a treaty of their own. On October 24, 1994, King Hussein (see Figure 16-3) and Israeli Prime Minister Yitzhak Rabin signed a peace agreement. The West increasingly looked to Hussein to defuse tensions and build stability in the region. In 1997, the king negotiated the Israeli withdrawal from Hebron. In February 1999, after surviving more than a dozen assassination attempts, World War II, four regional wars, and Black September, King Hussein bin Talal lost his final battle — to cancer.

Carrying a grudge about the Gulf War

Before the war, hundreds of thousands of well-trained and educated Palestinian and Jordanian workers lived in the oil-rich Gulf States — like Kuwait and Saudi Arabia — earning large salaries. They sent remittances to their families in Jordan to supplement incomes, construct homes, and build "nest eggs." One common financial strategy for Jordanians was to build a small two- or three-story concrete building. The owners lived on one floor and rented the other floors out as apartments. The rental income provided financial stability in the present and security for the future.

Because of Palestinian and Jordanian support for Saddam during the Gulf War, oil-rich Gulf States, like Saudi Arabia and Kuwait, sent 700,000 Jordanian and Palestinian workers packing. These workers returned to Jordan to face massive unemployment, low salaries, and frustration. In the late 1990s, you could commonly find the engineers, professors, or other professionals, who had once worked in the Gulf Sates, now driving taxis in Amman. Some blamed the United States and Britain for their ills, while others cursed Saddam. In 2001, Kuwait began to allow Jordanians to return.

Figure 16-3:
King
Hussein of
Jordan.

A hard act to follow: Abdullah's legacy

In King Hussein's last days, many in the international community grew anxious that a violent power struggle could erupt upon the king's death. His brother, Crown Prince Hassan, had been in the shadows patiently awaiting his turn for some 34 years. One month before his death, however, the king renounced his brother in favor of Abdullah, Hussein's son. The feared violent confrontation between Abdullah and Hassan never materialized, and the transfer of power from father to son occurred smoothly. The king's funeral was truly an historic event. On February 8, 1999, just one day after his death, 50 heads of state, including four U.S. presidents — former presidents Gerald Ford, Jimmy Carter, and George Bush, along with current president Bill Clinton — paid tribute to the late King Hussein in Amman.

Prior to assuming power, young Abdullah had studied in England and the United States. He attended the Royal Military Academy at Sandhurst in the United Kingdom and studied at Oxford before returning home to join the Jordanian armed forces, where he earned his qualification as a Cobra attack helicopter pilot. In 1994, he assumed command of the Royal Jordanian Special Forces.

In key ways, King Abdullah picked up where his father left off, pressing for a peaceful resolution to the region's turmoil. He has pressed for negotiation between Syria and Israel, a just and enduring settlement in Palestine, and productive measures to establish stability in Iraq. The West has seen the king as a stabilizing force in the region, and he has become a strong ally in George W. Bush's War on Terrorism.

Lebanon

In 1952, Camille Chamoun was elected president of Lebanon. As beneficiary of aid supplied under the Eisenhower Doctrine (see Chapter 11), Lebanon grew closer to the West. Not all Lebanese agreed that the country should be moving in that direction, and in 1958 anti-Western riots erupted in Beirut. With everything out of hand, Chamoun turned to the United States for military support. Approximately 10,000 American troops landed in July but left a month later when General Fouad Chehab was elected Chamoun's successor, and the troubles subsided.

The Switzerland of the Middle East

Lebanon's geographical location makes it the crossroads of east and west. Bordering on the Arab World and secular Turkey, linked ideologically and culturally to Europe through France, and its uniquely diverse ethnic and religious composition created a rare environment that was at once Arab and European, developing and developed, cosmopolitan yet communal. The French army had established a ski resort in the northern area of the Cedars in the 1930s. After World War II, Lebanon earned a reputation as *The Switzerland of the Middle East.* Foreign tourists enjoyed the skiing, reasonable prices, good entertainment and food, and Arab hospitality. In the late 1960s, regional and local politics finally took its toll on the country, and Lebanon's peaceful milieu degenerated into a bloody and complicated civil war that spanned nearly two decades, destroyed Lebanon's infrastructure, ruined the economy, decimated tourism, and claimed more than 100,000 Lebanese lives, more than all the Arab-Israeli wars combined.

Stirring up a civil war

Lebanon played a relatively minor role in the 1967 war with Israel. After the war, southern Lebanon became a major base for Palestinian guerrillas who ventured back and forth across the border, launching attacks against Israeli targets. As the guerrillas gained more autonomy, a number of violent incidents invited brutal reprisals, and measures meant to curb the violence led to countermeasures that spiraled into a bloody war in southern Lebanon.

- ✔ **1968:** The Israeli army retaliates against the PLO through a number of raids on Palestinian guerrilla camps in southern Lebanon.

- ✔ **1969:** An attempted Lebanese government crackdown on the Palestinian guerrillas leads to an armed conflict. Many Lebanese, particularly Christian populations, oppose the PLO's activities that spell almost certain consequences from Israel.

- ✔ **1970:** An influx of Palestinian refugees reaches Lebanon from Jordan, where King Hussein had brutally repressed similar guerrilla uprisings in his kingdom. The PLO sets up shop in Lebanon.

- ✔ **1972:** Heavy fighting resumes between Palestinians and Lebanese.

Ironically, Lebanon didn't play a role in the 1973 Arab-Israeli war. Lebanon also didn't learn the lessons from the experiences of Jordan's King Hussein when a few years earlier he kicked all the Palestinian militants out of Jordan. Many of those subversives ended up in southern Lebanon. Lebanon allowed the PLO to continue attacks against Israel, and the next few years the situation deteriorated.

- ✔ **1975:** A bloody civil war among Christians, Muslims, and Palestinians breaks out.

- ✔ **1976:** Syrian armed forces enter Lebanon on the side of Christians to stop the violence although the alliance is short-lived. The violence subsides, but Syria fails to disarm the countless militias.

- ✔ **Mid-1970s:** PLO cross-border attacks against Israel continue.

- ✔ **1978:** Israeli forces, allied with Lebanese Christians, cross into southern Lebanon to counter the PLO strikes in March but withdraw in June.

At this point, the United Nations decided to take action. It sent 6,000 peacekeeping forces to maintain security. A number of independent militias with their own agendas arose and waged war on one another, switched allegiances, and created fear and chaos in the streets. The U.N. security forces failed to keep peace. Then everything took a turn for the worse.

- ✔ **1981:** Fighting between Syrian forces and Christian militia groups escalates.

- ✔ **1981:** Israel routinely bombs Lebanon's capital, Beirut, a favorite Palestinian hideout.

- ✔ **1982:** Israeli forces invade Lebanon to wipe out PLO camps once and for all. They trap 7,000 PLO guerrillas in Beirut, but the United States brokers a deal for their evacuation to other Arab countries.

- ✔ **1982:** Christian President Bashir Gemayel is elected and assassinated three weeks later. His brother Amin Gemayel was elected president a few days later.

- ✔ **1982:** Christian militants retaliate by massacring 1,000 civilian Palestinians in Sabra and Shatila refugee camps in Israeli-controlled Lebanon, all under the watchful eye of Israeli forces.

- ✔ **1982:** Various militant groups begin taking hostages.

In an effort to stabilize Beirut, a multinational peacekeeping force from the United States, Britain, France, and Italy entered the city in 1982 and 1983. By this time, Hezbollah had begun to make its presence felt. The 1980s saw more complex layers added to the Lebanese conflict including:

- ✔ **1983:** Hezbollah detonates a suicide truck bomb that kills 241 U.S. Marines and 60 French soldiers.

- ✔ **1984:** The multinational peacekeeping force evacuates Lebanon.

- ✔ **1985:** Israel completes its own evacuation, leaving a number of soldiers to help the Christian Southern Lebanese Army (SLA) to patrol a ten-mile buffer zone between Lebanon and Israel (see Figure 16-4).

- ✔ **1987:** Approximately 7,500 Syrian troops once again enter Beirut to suppress the violence.

- ✔ **1988:** The Lebanese parliament can't agree on a president. Departing President Amin Gemayel appoints Maronite general Michel Aoun as prime minister, but the former Sunni prime minister refuses to step down.

- ✔ **1989:** Syrian-backed President Rene Maowad is assassinated.

- ✔ **1989:** The Arab League brokers the Taif Accord in Saudi Arabia, paving the way for peace and stability.

- ✔ **1990:** Shiite forces sign an agreement to end their struggle.

- ✔ **1991:** Lebanon signs a treaty with Syria, allowing Syria to run the show because the Syrian military by then has already consolidated its power throughout most of Lebanon.

Hezbollah released the last of the American hostages in 1992.

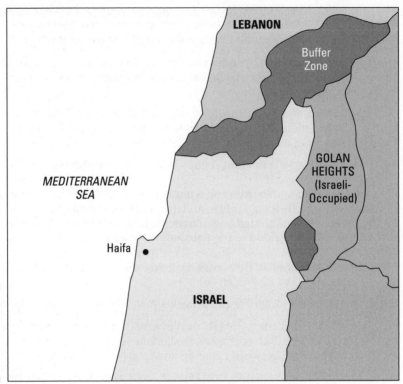

Figure 16-4:
Southern
Lebanon
and the
buffer zone.

Hezbollah (the party of God)

A Lebanese Shiite militant movement that called itself Hezbollah, or *The Party of God,* emerged as a major political force in Lebanon around 1982 in the midst of the civil war. A month after the Israeli forces invaded Lebanese territory to stomp out the PLO, Iran's Islamic revolutionary fervor spilled over into Lebanon when Syrian President Hafiz al-Assad agreed to allow 1,000 Pasadaran (Iranian revolutionary guards) to set up training camps in southeastern Lebanon's Beqaa Valley. The Pasadaran recruited young Shiite extremists from existing militant organizations, including Amal, and provided them with military training and the religious instruction promulgated by Ayatollah Khomeini (see Chapter 18). These teachings were well received by core Hezbollah students, many of whom had graduated from Shiite *madrasas* in southern Iraq — the Ayatollah's old stomping grounds (see Chapter 18). As a result, Hezbollah pledged an allegiance to Khomeini and vowed to replicate their benefactor's success in Lebanon through the establishment of an Islamic state.

Long before the Sunni Palestinians began to employ the suicide bomb as a weapon of choice against Israelis, Hezbollah and other Shiite groups experimented with suicide attacks against Western targets in Lebanon. In April 1983, Hezbollah detonated a suicide car bomb outside the U.S. embassy in Beirut, killing 63 people. Hezbollah carried out a suicide truck bombing at the Marine barracks in Beirut in October 1983, killing 241 U.S. Marines and 60 French soldiers. Hezbollah was also responsible for the 1985 hijacking of TWA flight 847, in which they tortured and killed American Navy SEAL Robert Stethem. Of all their violent methods, kidnapping proved to be their most effective weapon.

Kidnapping and hostage taking: How to get political concessions

Hezbollah wasn't the first group in Lebanon to take hostages. The Christian Phalange militia, for instance, kidnapped four Iranian diplomats and killed them all in 1982. During the civil war, various militant groups kidnapped more than 14,000 victims, killing about 10,000. However, the abduction of foreign hostages raised the profile of this political tactic and drew the desired international attention.

Khomeini's success at taking American hostages in Iran in 1979 encouraged his Lebanese protégés to try their hands at kidnapping. In the early 1980s, Iran was enmeshed in the Iran-Iraq War, and the United States had blocked arms sales to Iran while providing Iraq with weapons. Among other goals, Hezbollah hoped that by seizing Western captives they could do Khomeini's bidding by pressuring the United States and its allies to lift the arms embargo. Between 1982 and 1992, Hezbollah and other Shiite factions abducted about 50 Western hostages. The captives were often kept blindfolded and in chains for up to five years. Three of the highest profile kidnappings were the following:

- ✔ **1982:** Islamic Jihad kidnaps David Dodge, the president of the American University of Beirut. They release him a year later.

- ✔ **1984:** Hezbollah kidnaps and murders William Buckley, the U.S. Central Intelligence Agency station chief in Beirut.

- ✔ **1987:** Hezbollah abducts Terry Waite, the envoy for the British Archbishop of Canterbury, who had arrived in Lebanon to negotiate the release of other hostages. He had enjoyed success in securing the release of British captives in Iran in 1981 and Libya in 1985. Waite is released four years later.

Hezbollah abducted non-Westerners as well. Communists and socialists, including four kidnapped Soviet diplomats, became prime targets. Israel also saw the advantages to kidnapping. In 1989, Israel took Sheikh Abdul Karim Obeid captive to force concessions from Hezbollah.

Bargaining chips

Hostages proved to be valuable bargaining chips for the captors and their supporters. In November 1986, reports surfaced that the United States had been negotiating with Iran for the release of American hostages held by Shiite captors in Lebanon. The arms-for-hostages affair dubbed Irangate became an embarrassment for U.S. President Reagan, who had publicly taken a tough stance against Iran and against negotiating with terrorists. As Iran's influence over Hezbollah diminished due to Khomeini's death in 1989, and after the end of the Iran-Iraq War, concessions for Iran were less of a priority for Hezbollah. They pressed instead for Israel's release of Arab prisoners. In late 1991, the United States, Israel, and Hezbollah reached an agreement "brokered" by Syria. Israel released 450 Palestinian and Lebanese prisoners, and Hezbollah released seven Israeli soldiers (some already dead) and the remaining Western hostages. In 1992, Hezbollah released the last Western hostage. Although Hezbollah stopped targeting Western civilians, kidnappings of military targets continued, including the abduction of three Israeli soldiers in 2000.

Hezbollah's success in Lebanon in the 1980s precipitated other Islamic militant applications for suicide bombings, hostage taking, and hijackings two decades later. Like their Shiite counterparts, Sunni Palestinians implemented a campaign of suicide bombings during the *Second Intifada*. The Palestinians have since perfected the use of the suicide bomb as an inexpensive and effective weapon against Israeli civilians (see Chapter 11). Kidnappings of Western civilians in Yemen, the Philippines, and elsewhere in the Muslim World have become increasingly commonplace. And of course, Al-Qaeda's effective blending of hijacking and suicide bombing on September 11, 2001, set the stage for U.S. President George W. Bush's War on Terrorism.

The plot thickens

You may understand why Hezbollah targeted Israeli invaders or Western multinational peacekeeping forces in Lebanon, or Christian militias, like the South Lebanon Army (SLA) and their supporters, but politics in the Middle East are seldom so simple. Worse yet, political intrigues and shifting alliances and treachery in Lebanon in the 1980s were as common as kidnappings, massacres, and car bombings. Although Syrian President Hafiz al-Assad had supported Hezbollah as a militant organization to apply pressure on the Israeli forces, he shared neither the movement's dedication to Iran, nor its design to convert Lebanon into an Islamic state. Hezbollah soon became difficult to reign in. So Assad strategically pitted the secular Shiite Amal militant group against Hezbollah.

To complicate matters, Syria also had little sympathy for the PLO who Assad saw as a destabilizing force in Lebanon.

- **1985 to 1987:** Syria turns loose Amal on the Shatila Palestinian refugee camp in Beirut, and for the next two years, fighting between the forces — known as the *War of the Camps* — leaves more than 2,500 dead.

  As a strong supporter of the Palestinian cause and a provider of humanitarian aid in Shatila, Hezbollah denounces Syria and Amal, and even provides military assistance to the Palestinians at times.

- **1987:** Syrian forces enter West Beirut in support of Amal and kill 23 Hezbollah members, eight of which were women and children.

  Hezbollah's claim that the victims' hands were tied behind their backs leads to public outrage. A reported 50,000 mourners attend the funeral. A leading Iranian cleric labels the massacre the "Karbala of the 20th century."

- **1988:** Feeling the full support of the Syrian army, Amal confidently attacks Hezbollah strongholds in southern Beirut and southern Lebanon. With no end to the violence in sight, Syria steps in and imposes a cease-fire although battles, kidnappings, and assassinations continue off and on for the next two years.

In 1989, Khomeini, the spiritual leader of Hezbollah, died and with him Hezbollah's unquestioning allegiance to Iran. That same year the Arab League brokered a peace plan for Lebanon known as the *Taif Accord*, after the city in Saudi Arabia where the negotiations were held. Because the plan offered no special political concessions for Shiites, who were now Lebanon's largest minority, and because it dashed hopes for the establishment of an Islamic state, Hezbollah rejected it. Nonetheless, the *Party of God* came to terms with Syria's permanency in the region after its military consolidated control over most of Lebanon in 1991. Hezbollah agreed to play by Syria's rules.

Calling the shots: Significant Syrian influence

With Assad influencing the outcome of Lebanese politics, Hezbollah assumed its new role as unofficial military arm of Syrian intelligence that could reach where Syria couldn't — Israel. Hezbollah accepted this role because it allowed for restrained military campaigns against its primary enemies — the Israelis. For its part, Syria enjoyed the plausible deniability that Hezbollah afforded it as a third party. Syria strategically regulated Hezbollah's militant attacks against Israel in the hopes of regaining control of Golan Heights and other disputed territories.

As Syria set about disarming militias in Beirut, Hezbollah moved to the Beqaa Valley in southeastern Lebanon close to the buffer zone, routinely patrolled by Israel and the SLA. Vowing not to disarm until Israel withdrew, Hezbollah continued to launch assaults, and Israel continued to retaliate with artillery and air attacks off and on throughout most of the 1990s.

In May 2000, Israeli Prime Minister Barak pulled Israeli forces out of southern Lebanon, and the United Nations established a *Blue Line* border between Lebanon and Israel, where UN Interim Forces in Lebanon (UNIFIL) are stationed. Five months later Hezbollah launched fresh attacks against Israeli soldiers in Golan Heights. Syrian support of Hezbollah's continued aggression against Israel has created a degree of discontent within Lebanon. Many Lebanese who would prefer to see the government focus on building the economy and encouraging foreign investment view Hezbollah as a destabilizing force in the region that frustrates productive efforts for peace and progress.

More than militancy

Hezbollah's "fame" in the Western press as a militant organization has overshadowed other dimensions of the movement. The militant wing of Hezbollah is only part of a larger entity that operates a social-welfare network, holds legitimate seats in parliament, runs schools, and even has a soccer team. Hezbollah's reputation for austerity, anticorruption, protection of Palestinians, humanitarian aid, and undaunted aggression against Israel has earned it a strong following among the Lebanese Shiite community. These other dimensions of Hezbollah, often hidden to the Western public eye, go a long way toward explaining the popularity — among Muslims — of militant groups labeled *terrorists* in the West (see Chapter 8).

Picking up the pieces

Lebanese civilians are attempting to pick up the pieces of their existence that were shattered by the long, drawn out civil war. An estimated 100,000 Lebanese died, 250,000 were maimed or injured, and more than 1 million were forced to flee their homes. Although Syria continues to exert its influence in Lebanese political affairs, its role in disarming the militias, brokering peace, and setting the nation back on track for security can't be ignored.

Many Lebanese admit that through the 1980s they became accustomed to the violence, bloodshed, massacres, and kidnappings. In 1998, one Lebanese professor told me that after years of civil war ,when the people of Beirut heard of violence in their neighborhood, a neighbor's murder, or a local kidnapping, they simply shrugged their shoulders and carried on business as usual. Only by 1998 were they beginning to feel human again.

Although the Lebanese democratic political machine has resumed functioning, Syrian influence continues to overshadow the process. International observers noted irregularities in the 2000 parliamentary elections, yet it seemed to be an improvement over the process four years earlier. Syria has yet to fulfill its obligations under the Taif Accord, including the withdrawal of its 22,000 troops.

Despite countless problems, Lebanon is a country in repair. The government has made efforts to rebuild Lebanon's infrastructure: power plants, roads, communications, buildings, and offices. The economy has shown some signs of recovery. People's lives are returning to some sense of normalcy, focusing on work and education, planning weddings, and having children.

Syria

As the spoils of World War I, the French received Syria under the French Mandate. The French proceeded to split Syria into two nations: Lebanon and Syria (see Chapter 6). In September 1941, the French granted Syria independence, although French troops hung around until 1946 when it became official. Two years later, Syria joined the Arab League in attacking Israel as part of the First Arab-Israeli War.

Adding the "bubbles" to Syria's Baath

Syria suffered from serious internal conflicts that led to three military coups in 1949 alone. The next few tumultuous years saw the rise of the socialist Baath party in Syria (and Iraq). As Arab countries tried to deal with their new-found independence and searched for a stabilizing form of government at the national level, strong international currents began to draw these fledgling nations into one of two camps: that of Britain and the United States, or that of the Soviet Union. Lebanon drifted westward while Syria (and Egypt) chose to sign economic and military treaties with the Soviets. Syria's merger with Egypt into the United Arab Republic in 1958 proved unpopular with Syrians. In 1961, Syrian military officers arrested Egyptian Field Marshal Amer and sent him packing back to Egypt, thereby dissolving the union. The following year another coup took place, only to be followed by a 1963 coup that ushered the Baath party in to power. From that point up until today, Syria remains in a state of martial law. The new socialist government instituted a plan of nationalization and land redistribution to the peasants. But the staging of coups wasn't over. In 1966, radical elements of the Baath party overthrew the existing government and installed their own prime minister and president.

As if Syria didn't have enough internal strife, Syrians sought to actively raise tensions with Israel during this period by:

- Threatening to divert waters from the Jordan River
- Sniping Israeli fishermen in the Sea of Galilee
- Firing upon Israeli farmers from positions on the Golan Heights

These incidents contributed to Israel's decision to make a preemptive strike against Syria in 1967 (see Chapter 11). When the smoke cleared, Israel had seized the Golan Heights, and Syria would spend the next 35 years trying to get it back.

Hafez al-Assad stages the final coup

From 1966 to 1970, a general by the name of Hafez al-Assad had served Syria as minister of defense and commander of the armed forces. When political infighting broke out after the '67 War, the general staged the final coup that secured him the presidency for the next three decades. Hafez al-Assad's authoritarian rule brutally repressed opposition throughout his rule from 1971 until 2000. In 1973, he executed 42 military officers for plotting a coup against him. That same year Syrian forces attacked Israel from the northeast making advances into Golan Heights, but after the Israelis regrouped, they pushed Syria back (see Chapter 11). Although a peace treaty was signed in 1973, both armies kept fighting well into the next year. U.S. Secretary of State Henry Kissinger brought both parties to Geneva, where they signed a peace agreement that ended the military strife. Golan Heights became part of the security zone to be patrolled by international peacekeepers. (Israel later annexed the Golan Heights in 1982 and currently has many settlements there.)

When religion and politics clash

Because Baathist doctrine is largely secular and socialist, the Baathists often clashed with Islamic extremists (see Chapter 7). In Syria's case, another reason stands out. Assad belonged to a Shiite subgroup indigenous to Lebanon and Syria known as Alawis (for more on the Alawites, see Chapter 20). Assad made a number of token efforts to accommodate religious leaders in the first few years of his rule, but Islamic extremists, like The Muslim Brotherhood (Sunnis), remained unimpressed. Clashes arose.

- **1976:** Assad sends Syrian forces to Lebanon in support of a Christian militia. Islamic militants vow to overthrow the Syrian president. The extremists launch a campaign of terror against his government.

- **1980:** Riots break out in Aleppo and Hama that culminate with an assassination attempt against the Syrian president. Assad retaliates with brutal suppression of the extremists.

- **1982:** Islamic extremists revolt again in Hama, and the Syrian president squashes the uprising, resulting in thousands of deaths.

The next year Assad suffered a heart attack, and his brother Rifat attempted and failed to seize power for himself. By 1984, Assad had succeeded in again securing his political control.

Reasserting influence in Lebanon

Like many Syrians, Assad didn't care much for the fact that Lebanon had been carved out of Syria in the early part of the 20th century. When chaos broke out in Lebanon in the mid-1970s and as momentum of the civil war built, the reasons for Syria's intervention in Lebanon were many:

- ✔ Because the land originally belonged to Syria, Syria believed that it should have a say in Lebanon's politics.

- ✔ Israel and its Lebanese Christian allies wanted to establish a Christian ministate in southern Lebanon that would act as a buffer to Muslim extremists.

- ✔ Shiites in southern Lebanon formed the majority, and Assad sympathized with their cause.

- ✔ Syria believed any opportunity to aggravate Israel was worth taking.

- ✔ Israeli Prime Minister Menachem Begin annexed Golan Heights in 1982.

- ✔ Iraq, Syria's archenemy, tried to exert its own influence in Lebanon by supporting Christian and other militias.

- ✔ The presence of European and Israeli forces in Lebanon threatened Syria's sense of security.

Don't discount the fact that Assad truly wanted stability in the region. A civil war in Syria's backyard was bad for business. Apart from sending invading forces to Lebanon, Assad nurtured the Shiite extremist organizations like Amal and Hezbollah, which pursued Syrian military goals (see the section, "Hezbollah [the party of God]" in this chapter).

Shortly after the Taif Accord in 1989, Syria began to realize some success in quelling the chaos in Lebanon. By 1991, Syria extended its military authority over most of the country. In 1992, Hezbollah returned the last of the foreign hostages. Syria disarmed most militias but left Hezbollah intact as a reminder to Israel that all the scores hadn't been settled.

Syria and the West

For many years Syria had relied on the Soviet Union for support. But by 1990 with the Soviet Union in shambles, Assad shifted strategies, hoping to achieve his goals through improved relations with the West. That same year Iraq invaded Kuwait, and Syria was the first country to condemn the invasion. The following demonstrate Syria's drift toward the West.

- ✔ **1991:** Assad sends 20,000 troops to join the U.S.-led coalition in the Persian Gulf War.

- ✔ **1991:** Syria takes part in peace talks with Israel, along with the PLO and Jordan. Syria's persistence to get Golan Heights back in the process serves as stumbling block to Syria's participation in a settlement. Talks break down in 1996.

- ✔ **1999:** When Ehud Barak becomes Israeli's prime minister, Syria resumes peace talks, but they stall the following year.

- ✔ **2001:** Syria joins U.S. President George W. Bush's War on Terrorism, providing intelligence and making arrests of suspected terrorists.

Syria still wants Golan Heights back. Although Israel pulled out of Lebanon in 2000, Syria continues to permit Hezbollah to attack Israeli targets. Even though the United States has placed Hezbollah on its *Foreign List of Terrorist Organizations*, Syria maintains that it sees a difference between terrorism and freedom fighting. It considers Hezbollah a group of heroes fighting for Muslim freedom against Israeli tyranny (see Chapter 8).

Transferring power, father to son

Assad died on June 10, 2000, after three decades in power. Immediately parliament revised the constitution to reduce the minimum age of the presidency to 34 from 40. This revision permitted the Baath party to nominate Assad's 34-year-old son, Bashar al-Assad, party leader. The same day his father died, running unopposed, Bashar al-Assad, who studied optometry in London, was elected president with 97.29 percent of the vote. President Bashar has by and large picked up where his father left off — tough stance on Israel, support of Hezbollah, dominance of Lebanon, and authoritarian rule at home. Syria has remained in a state of martial law since 1963. The regime argues that military dominance over the Syrian civilian population is needed to protect against Israeli injustices and internal terrorist groups.

Chapter 17

The Arabian Peninsula

For Muslims, the Arabian Peninsula serves as the most hallowed ground on earth. According to Islamic tradition, centuries before the Prophet Muhammad's birth, Abraham delivered Hagar and their infant son Ishmael to Mecca and returned to Canaan on his magical horse Buraq. When Hagar's breast milk dried up and mother and son were on the verge of death, the Angel Gabriel appeared and rubbed his heal in the sand. Little Ishmael hopped up and imitated the angel by rubbing his own heal in the sand. Water gushed forward. So much water burst forth that Hagar had to seal the flow. Today this site is the famous well of Zamzam at the center of Mecca. When Ishmael grew up, he and his father built the Kaba, the square black structure around which millions of Muslims circumambulate during the annual Hajj, or pilgrimage (see Chapter 19). Mecca is off limits to non-Muslims. By extension, the territory of Arabia is sacred and non-Muslims must seek special permission before entering.

Fast forward to the Persian Gulf War in 1991. Many Muslims argue that American soldiers ("infidels," or nonbelievers, by the way) desecrated hallowed Saudi land. This offense is a major grievance of Islamic militants, like Osama bin Laden. The militants see the Saudi royal family as sellouts, who've bartered their faith to the oil-hungry Americans for military protection. More moderate Saudis are equally disenchanted with the royal family, alleging that the family refuses to open up society to democratic and liberal reforms, and brutally represses dissidents. The Saudi family itself is divided. Members of the royalty who sympathize with dissenters call into question Saudi Arabia's future.

This chapter looks at the history of the Arabian Peninsula's two major players in global politics: Saudi Arabia and Yemen. The pasts of these two countries have laid the groundwork for contradictory roles they currently play in Islamic militancy and the War on Terrorism. This chapter traces the developments that led to the current dilemma.

Saudi Arabia

The story of Saudi and U.S. relations is a peculiar one. The story focuses on a desert kingdom (see Figure 17-1), rich with oil, run by a single royal family of Bedouins descendants who have attempted to hold onto its power, wealth, and religious legitimacy. Contradictory links to the West with which the family shares few political, cultural, religious, or social values highlight the story. The common link has always been oil and protection. The Saudis wanted protection, and the Americans wanted oil. Both protection and oil have been their common strength and, most recently, their common undoing.

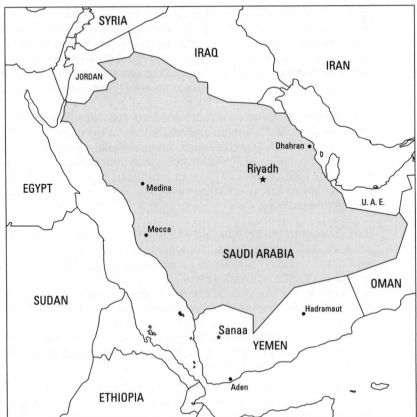

Figure 17-1:
Saudi
Arabia.

Facing threats from the neighborhood

Saudi Arabia's experience with the West had been quite different than, say, that of Egypt, Libya, or Algeria. The Colonial powers (Britain, Italy, and France, for example) hadn't really been influential in Saudi politics in the way they had in other Middle Eastern countries. In fact, in the 20th century, the greatest threats to the Saudi kingdom came from its Muslim neighbors and from within.

The Arabs living on the peninsula had long been under Turkish rule until the end of World War I (see Chapter 6). In the 1930s, Aramco (Arabian American Oil Company) began producing oil for commercial exportation. During World War II, the United States started construction of an airbase at Dhahran, and the U.S. military continued to operate it after the war. When Ibn Saud died in 1953, two of his sons, Saud and Faysal, began to argue over control of the oil-wealthy kingdom. Saud became king, and Faysal crown prince.

Confronting Egyptian and Yemeni threats

Throughout the late 1950s and 1960s, Egyptian President Gamal Abdul Nasser began to pose physical and ideological threats to Saudi Arabia in several ways. His promotion of secular, socialist, and pan-Arab values clashed with Saudi Arabia's aspirations as a leading Islamic nation. When Nasser cracked down on the extremist Muslim Brotherhood (see Chapter 15), Saudi Arabia provided them refuge. Nasser lost no opportunity to criticize the Saudis' contradictory relationship with the Americans. The feud was on.

- ✔ **1955:** King Saud finds out about a planned coup by Saudi officers trained in Egypt.

- ✔ **1957:** Saud travels to Washington, seeking American aid. He extends the American contract at Dhahran airbase through 1962, and the United States promises to supply weapons and training to the Saudis.

- ✔ **1958:** Saud hires a Syrian officer to assassinate Nasser, but the attempt fails.

- ✔ **1962:** Nasser begins meddling in Saudi Arabia's backyard by supporting the overthrow of the Yemeni monarch. The Egyptian president sends 20,000 Egyptian troops to Yemen. Nasser openly begins calling for Saud's overthrown.

- ✔ **1962:** Egypt attacks the Saudi border with Yemen. The United States counters with war planes flying sorties near the Yemeni border (although they don't engage the Egyptians), sets up an air defense system, dispatches warships to the region, and participates in joint military exercises with their Saudi counterparts.

- ✔ **1962:** King Saud, hoping not to be the next Arab king to get the boot, throws his weight behind Yemeni royalist forces and breaks off relations with Egypt.

Saud's strategy failed though. In 1964, Saud was overthrown, not by the Egyptians, but by his brother Faysal. (Saud went into exile and eventually died in Greece in 1969.) After Israel defeated Egypt in the 1967 War (see Chapter 11), Nasser could no longer afford a military presence in Yemen and pulled out. Newly crowned King Faysal buried the hatchet with the Egyptian president.

Tackling Iranian threats

A new wave of regional threats beginning in 1979 set Saudi Arabia again on a defensive posture. The first was Ayatollah Khomeini's Islamic Revolution in Iran that overthrew The Shah of Iran (see Chapter 18). As Khomeini sought to prove to the Muslim World that the newly formed Shiite Islamic Republic of Iran was the only legitimate Islamic state on earth, he seized every opportunity to launch criticisms of other Muslim regimes. Saudi Arabia's Sunni-based monarchy became a convenient target.

Iran condemned the royal family's corruption, treatment of Saudi Shiites, and of course, Saudi Arabia's contradictory relations with the United States. Iran's condemnations challenged Saudi Arabia's reputation and special status as keeper of the sacred cities of Mecca and Medina and as authority of Sunni Islam. More threatening yet was Iran's superior military machine inherited from the Shah. Instead of forcing a breach between the royal family and the West, Saudi leadership edged closer to the United States for protection. The Americans, who had their own problems with Khomeini, were only too happy to oblige (see Chapter 18).

Stopping Soviet threats

In 1979, the Soviet Union invaded Afghanistan (see Chapter 13). Fearing a Soviet expansion to the Persian Gulf and its oil fields, Saudi Arabia determined it better to isolate the Russian threat by pumping oil revenues to the Afghan resistance. The Saudis funneled aid through Pakistan and encouraged Saudi citizens to volunteer to train and fight the communists, whom most Muslims perceived as enemies of Islam. (This decision came back to bite the Saudis after the war had ended when extremist products of the war, like Osama bin Laden, became too hot to handle.) Americans shared the Saudi goal of dislodging the Soviets from the region, and the two allies committed considerable resources to do so.

Blocking the internal threats

Subsequent threats arising from within the Saudi community posed more immediate dangers. Two significant uprisings occurred in 1979.

✔ **Grand Mosque seizure:** A religious cleric and former captain in the national guard named Juhayman organized a siege of the mosque at the center of Mecca. Approximately 500 militants seized the mosque and took 6,000 pilgrims hostage and began preaching against the royal family's corruption, materialism, and unsavory relations with the American infidels. Swayed by Juhayman's message, many of the hostages took up weapons and joined the militant's cause. News of the seizure and Juhayman's sermons spread outside the compound, and sympathizers stormed local mosques and detonated explosives at targets sensitive to the royal family. The Saudi government contained the rebellion with the help of French paramilitary forces.

✔ **Shiite revolts:** Saudi Shiites had suffered persecution and treatment as second-class citizens and religious outcasts for generations. The dominant Wahhabi branch of Islam (see Chapter 19) discriminated against Shiites, whom they labeled as heretics. The Shiites lived in the eastern province, where many worked in the oil fields as unskilled laborers and survived in substandard social conditions compared with their Sunni counterparts in other regions. Shiite successes in Iran fueled the discontent in Saudi Arabia. Revolts in 1979 and 1980 led to nominal Saudi reforms.

These winds of discontent swirling through the desert kingdom were just precursory currents of an impending sandstorm.

Working like a well-oiled machine

As long as oil revenues were healthy — through the 1970s — the Saudi governing system worked like a well-oiled machine. Essentially, the Saudi royal family purchased success.

Internally the royal family garnered religious legitimacy from the Wahhabi *ulema* (religious scholars) by building Islamic universities and schools and by providing ministerial posts for the most loyal clerics. The Saudi leadership instituted reforms cautiously designed not to offend the ulema. For example, the king implemented female education only after convincing the ulema that the girls would be grounded in religious education. They also invested in infrastructure — roads, electricity, airports, and communications — and social services, such as hospitals and medical centers.

Although Saudi royalty members spent their oil profits extravagantly on themselves, they took special care to appease Saudi citizens. To keep tribal and political cohesion, Saudi society became increasingly dependent on royal handouts. The government sent advantaged Saudi students abroad to earn an education in foreign universities while providing other college students generous stipends for studying in Saudi institutions. Saudi college graduates found fat salaries awaiting them in the government after they graduated. The state was the largest employer in the kingdom. Saudi citizens didn't pay income taxes. With all the economic success and stability, the unequal access to wealth loomed in the shadows waiting for an opportunity to emerge to the forefront of Saudi politics. That opportunity came in the 1980s when oil profits plummeted.

Introducing disaster: The Iran-Iraq War

Although the Americans had been unable to save The Shah of Iran, the Saudis maintained faith that close ties with the United States would prevent direct external threats to Saudi oil fields. While the Saudis were still involved in supporting the Afghan resistance against the Soviets, tensions erupted in 1980 between Iran and Iraq that led to full-scale war threatening the stability of the entire region. Because the United States and Saudi Arabia shared a common enemy in the Islamic Republic of Iran, those governments threw their support behind Iraq in the eight-year struggle that cost around 500,000 lives.

In July 1986, oil plummeted to $8 a barrel, nearly a 66 percent decrease. The Saudi economy suffered drastically. The government dared not contemplate taxing a Saudi population that had lived for so many years on handouts. Weakened by decreased revenues, the state simply couldn't employ all the Saudi graduates aspiring for government jobs with fat salaries. The Saudi unemployed were likewise unwilling to do the menial labor supplied by millions of foreign nationals who supplied 71 percent of the Saudi workforce. As a result, the divide between the wealthy and the unemployed widened. Messages of the Saudi leadership's failures — materialism, wastefulness, and corruption — matched with their unholy alliance with American infidels began to find audiences more and more sympathetic.

Parting ways: The Persian Gulf War

As long as they shared a common enemy in Afghanistan — Soviets and communists — the Saudi royal family, Islamic extremists, and the Americans seemed to overlook ideological differences. After the Soviets withdrew from Afghanistan, Saudi *Afghans,* like Osama bin Laden (see Figure 17-2) who'd fought with the resistance, returned to their homeland triumphant.

Figure 17-2:
Osama bin
Laden.

When Saddam invaded Kuwait, bin Laden approached the Saudi leadership offering to raise an army of Islamic militants to protect the desert kingdom just as they'd done in Central Asia. The king's decision to turn to a more reliable military force, the Americans, was like a slap in the face for bin Laden. He began openly criticizing the Saudi royal family and soon found himself a *persona non grata* in Saudi Arabia. Sudanese spiritual leader Hassan al-Turabi was only too willing to invite bin Laden to Sudan in 1991 (see Chapter 15). His welcome in Sudan had worn thin by 1996, and the Islamic Emirate of Afghanistan under the leadership of the like-minded Taliban seemed like as good a place any to set up camp.

Meanwhile, in 1990, U.S. President George Bush sent 500,000 American troops to Saudi sacred territory under the guise of multinational forces along with token contingents of Egyptian, Syrian, Moroccan, and European troops in order to offset Islamic extremist opposition. In January 1991, the Saudi leadership secured a *fatwa* (Islamic injunction) permitting foreign troops to assist Muslims in a jihad against Saddam. These conciliatory measures did little to pacify the Islamic extremists, who argued against the Saudi policy. Islamic extremists commonly lodged the following complaints:

✔ The American infidels were desecrating sacred soil.

✔ Saudi royalty had squandered vast military resources, leaving the kingdom vulnerable to Iraqi attack.

✔ It was un-Islamic to ally with infidels to fight against Muslims.

✔ The West was a greater evil than fellow Muslim Saddam.

✔ The Americans wanted to dominate Saudi Arabia.

The consensus among extremists was that the corrupt Saudi monarchy had failed its Muslim subjects, and events could only be set right by purging the holy land of foreign influences and instituting *sharia* (Islamic law).

Providing refuge for the homeless Muslim Brotherhood

Egyptian President Gamal Abdul Nasser cracked down on the Egyptian Muslim Brotherhood in the 1950s and 1960s. In 1966, for instance, Nasser executed Sayed Qutb, a prominent Egyptian thinker and author who openly preached of jihad and militant Islam. During this same time, secular regimes in Syria and Iraq persecuted the militant members of the Muslim Brotherhood. Thousands of the Islamic extremists fleeing persecution from these countries found refuge in Saudi Arabia because the dominant Wahhabi doctrine coincided with the extremist values of the Brotherhood. The Saudis found spots for them as educators in schools and universities, as senior officials in the ministry of education, and as authors and designers of school textbooks and curricula.

Some became *imams* (leaders) in mosques and many published viewpoints that expressed extremist interpretations of Islam. Some analysts believe that until the arrival of the Brotherhood, the Wahhabi ulema had been an apolitical branch, more interested in puritanical Islam on a personal level. The Muslim Brotherhood's message that Islam could only be purified through political and militant force fell on sympathetic ears in Saudi Arabia. The Saudi leadership seemed to agree in the 1970s and 1980s and liberally used oil revenues to fund a campaign of Islamization across the Middle East. The Saudis built and supported thousands of mosques, religious schools, and cultural centers in the Muslim World. Because their agendas often coincided in regions like Pakistan and Afghanistan (see Chapters 13 and 14), the Saudi royal family, Islamic militants, and the Americans became the best of bedfellows, funding and supporting extremist Mujahideen efforts against the common enemy: The Soviets. Although signs of fragmentation could be seen in the late 1970s and 1980s, the moment of truth didn't come until 1991, when Saddam Hussein entered Kuwait, and the three agendas diverged.

Coping with the Gulf War's aftermath

The Gulf War ended on February 28, 1991, just about five weeks after it began. Although the combat was short lived, the damage between Islamic extremists and the Saudi leadership had been done. To exacerbate matters, elements within the Saudi military and even in the royal family sympathized with the extremists. To safeguard against future Iraqi mischief, the Americans left a military presence in Saudi Arabia.

Disenchanted youth

Frustration stemming from economic problems has played a crucial role in the growing disenchantment of Saudi youth. Saudi Arabia is home to 21 million people, 14 million of them Saudis and 7 million foreign workers. Spoiled by a economic system established when the *well-oiled machine* was producing posh positions with bright futures back in its heyday of the 1970s and early 1980s, many of today's young, educated, unemployed Saudis place conditions on the type of jobs they will accept. Often they demand to work close to home and only one shift; the job must be high paying and carry a certain prestige. With no job, prospects for marriage and raising a family are limited. Under puritan Wahhabi restrictions that forbid interactions between the sexes (no dating), alcoholic beverages, and a wide range of other activities taken for granted in the West, boredom and frustration mounts. Disenchanted Saudi young men become a fertile recruiting field for Islamic extremists. The Al-Qaeda recruiters exploited this "talent pool" to assemble a team of 15 Saudi hijackers for September 11, 2001, not only to conduct the attacks against the United States, but also to drive a wedge between Saudi Arabia and its American allies. Bin Laden hoped to end a bond that had lasted since the 1930s and to oust some 5,000 U.S. "infidel" troops from sacred Saudi soil in the process.

Dissenting voices

Various contingents of Saudi dissidents brandishing lists of economic, political, and religious grievances have attempted to influence Saudi policy.

- **Moderate:** This voice, also labeled *secular* by some, presses for civil society and democratic reform, modernization of the judicial system, egalitarian reforms (including on women's issues), and greater freedoms of speech all within the framework of sharia.

- **Extremist:** The extremist voice demands theocratic reforms strengthening the power of the ulema to implement sharia in almost every aspect of government, society, and private life. Under these reforms, sharia would take a larger role in guiding the Saudi media, which until now Western influences have "corrupted." Likewise, this voice calls for greater expenditures on social programs, the establishment of an Islamic army based on *jihad* (holy war), a commitment to support only Islamic causes, and foreign aid only to nations promoting Islamic teachings.

A mind is a "terror"ible thing to waste

Did you ever wonder why 15 of the 19 hijackers from the September 11, 2001, attacks were Saudis? Do a disproportionate number of Saudis have swords to grind with the Americans? Certainly Osama bin Laden could have found Chechens, Afghans, Palestinians, Pakistanis, or devotees from any number of other Muslim countries to carry out the task. But the impact wouldn't have been the same if, say, only two hijackers had been Saudi. Because this pool of Saudi "talent" laid untapped, bin Laden decided to exploit it in hopes of forcing Americans and Saudis to reassess their contradictory relationship and raise mutual suspicions. That much has worked. Bin Laden had hoped that the mutual suspicions would escalate into broken relations and an American withdrawal from Saudi territory.

Note: One of the young Saudis recruited by Al-Qaeda for the suicide mission was Hani Hanjour, a frustrated Saudi pilot who'd failed to achieve his goal of landing a job with the Saudi national airlines. Hanjour had studied in the United States in order to fulfill the requirement that all Saudi pilots become certified in a U.S. flight school. (For this reason, Saudis could easily obtain visas to attend flight schools in the United States.) He studied English in Arizona and Oakland, and took flight lessons in Arizona in 1997, 2000, and again in 2001. But even after Hanjour earned U.S. certification, he failed to land a job back home. His failure turned to bitterness tempered with the comfort provided by Wahhabi religious texts and militant sermons. Finally on September 11, he achieved his dream of flying a commercial airliner. Hanjour piloted American Airlines Flight 77 into the Pentagon.

These voices have challenged the Saudi royal family's legitimacy. The family's response has made attempts to appease or discredit opposition, when possible, and to stifle it when not. The tightened Saudi grip — often involving arrests and torture — on the most vociferous of dissent, however, has served to drive dissidents underground or abroad, often into the arms of the West they so bitterly reject.

If you can't beat the West, flee to it

Historically, many of those Muslim extremists most vocally opposed to the West, end up seeking refuge in the West. The pervasive freedoms of movement, speech, and press in Europe, for example, allow extremists (Islamic or otherwise) to criticize regimes through the media in a way that would often be unthinkable in Muslim countries. In 1964, Khomeini, for example, fled Iran in exile and took up residence in the Shiite communities of southern Iraq while Iran and Iraq weren't on speaking terms. In 1978, Saddam asked Khomeini to leave Iraq, and Khomeini shifted his exile to France (see Chapter 12).

Many Saudi dissidents follow similar paths to the West. The Committee for the Defense of Legitimate Rights (CDLR), for instance, formed in Riyadh in 1993. After the royal family realized the group's threat, the Saudi-controlled (or at least influenced) Council of Higher Ulema denounced the organization, while the government banned the CDLR, and imprisoned some of the ringleaders. The Islamic extremists relocated their headquarters to London where they commenced a media blitz against the Saudi leadership. They set up a Web site, sent faxes and e-mails, printed pamphlets and other publications, and established a network of communications to voice their opposition.

The CDLR compared the Saudi royal family to the Mafia and pressed for reform, criticized the Council of Higher Ulema as sellouts to the royal family, and called for theocratic reforms. The CDLR further disseminated evidence of the Saudi leadership's corruption and abuse of human rights, including torture and imprisonment of political opponents. Although the vocal opposition, such as the CDLR, in the West remained within the boundaries of free speech, some people felt that words weren't enough. These extremists took action.

Islamic militancy — when Islamic extremism turns violent

Islamic militants have conducted a series of violent attacks on Saudi soil in an effort to oust the 5,000 Americans from Saudi soil:

- **November 1995:** A car bomb explodes in Riyadh, killing five Americans.

- **June 1996:** A bombing at a military complex at Khobar Towers military housing complex in Dhahran kills 19 Americans. Many U.S. forces move to Prince Sultan Air Base near Riyadh after the attack. The base engulfs 230 square miles of open, easily defensible land.

- **November 2000:** Mistaken for an American, militants kill a British citizen in Riyadh.

- **May 2003:** Suicide bombings at three compounds in Riyadh housing Westerners kills over 30 people. Investigators linked the bombings to a raid on an al-Qaeda safe house a week earlier that uncovered stockpiles of weapons believed to have originated with the Saudi national guard.

After the world discovered that 15 of the 19 hijackers in the September 11, 2001, attacks were Saudi natives, Saudi Arabia has faced increased scrutiny in the West. The fact that bin Laden is also Saudi and that one of Al-Qaeda's stated goals is to expel American military troops from sacred Saudi soil has only intensified concerns. In August 2002, a briefing given to the White House by independent analyst, Laurent Murawiec, suggested the Saudis were involved in every facet of terrorism. In November 2002, the FBI launched an investigation into the possible Saudi financial links to two of the hijackers. In May 2003, a Saudi consular official was expelled from the United States for suspected terrorist links after being held for two days.

In April 2003 after the U.S.-led war in Iraq had ended, and Saddam Hussein no longer posed a threat in the region, U.S. President George W. Bush announced that he would withdraw almost all of the American troops from Saudi Arabia.

Distrust — a two-way street

Just as the West examines Saudi Arabia's intentions, voices of Saudi citizens are calling into question the United States' designs for the region, especially for Saudi soil. These voices criticize the Saudi rulers' relationship with the Americans and serve to reinforce the Islamic extremist rhetoric. In the middle is the Saudi royalty who has remained in power thus far by playing a dangerous game. On one hand, the royal family has staved off external Arab enemies by teaming up with the Americans when convenient. On the other hand, the royal family has appeased powerful internal religious clerics by giving them relatively free reign in governing social and family affairs in Saudi society. With one foot in each camp, the Saudis have created a fertile bed of hostility at home that indeed came back to haunt them (and others) on September 11.

Attempting to reconcile

Saudi Arabia rushed to demonstrate solidarity with the United States after September 11. Prince Al-Walid bin Talal bin Abdul Aziz, the sixth richest man in the world and King Fahd's nephew, flew to New York and visited Ground Zero with New York City Mayor Rudy Giuliani. Prince al-Walid called the attack a crime and gave Giuliani a check for $10 million.

In a separate statement, al-Walid stated that the United States should reexamine its policies in the Near East to show more balance with regard to Palestine. Still reeling from the attacks, an incensed Giuliani perceived the statement as justification for the attacks. The mayor announced that New York wouldn't accept the Saudi donation and that the prince's remarks were extremely "dangerous."

Looking into a crystal ball: An uncertain future

Saudi failures to institute democratic reforms highlight this peculiar relationship between the United States and Saudi Arabia. A deteriorating economy produces growing numbers of unemployed Saudi young people who turn sympathetic ears to Islamic militant voices of discontent. After the United States once again asked a reluctant Saudi Arabia for support in launching fresh attacks against Iraq in 2003, and increased American military presence in the region, American-Saudi relations turned a dangerous and uncertain corner.

Yemen

Before the bombing of the USS Cole in the port of Aden on October 12, 2000, you probably hadn't given Yemen a second thought. A map of Yemen is shown in Figure 17-3. Since this time, Yemen has come under suspicion as a haven for Al-Qaeda and other Islamic militant groups. After Al-Qaeda dispersed in Afghanistan in the winter of 2001, some analysts believed that many Al-Qaeda operatives, including Osama bin Laden, whose father was born in Yemen, may have taken up residence in Hadramaut, the eastern region of Yemen. Hadramaut has a reputation for harboring militants.

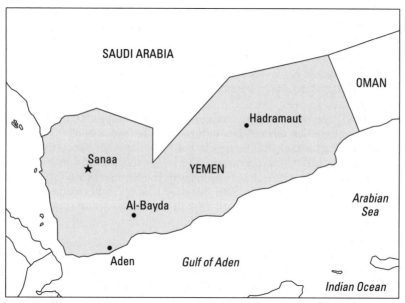

Figure 17-3: Yemen.

The tale of two Yemens

Before 1990, there were two Yemens: North Yemen and South Yemen. The recent history of both countries involves foreign intervention. Britain and the Soviet Union played roles in South Yemen's politics, while Saudi Arabia, Jordan, and Egypt had their fingers in the affairs of North Yemen.

South Yemen (People's Democratic Republic of Yemen)

The British seemed to be everywhere and involved in everyone else's business in the 19th century, didn't they? So why not Yemen? In 1839, they set up a colony in Aden. By 1963, the British colony of Aden merged six emirates, sultanates, and sheikhdoms to form the Federation of South Arabia. Opposition groups forced the British out in 1967 and formed South Yemen. In 1970, the country drew up a new constitution and changed its name to the People's Democratic Republic of Yemen. In 1979, the government signed a 20-year treaty with the Soviet Union and became the only Marxist state in the Arab World. The Soviets were only too happy to set up naval bases in Yemen.

North Yemen (Yemen Arab Republic)

Seeing Europe's colonial success, Egypt President Gamal Abdul Nasser decided to show the West that anything they could do, he could do better. Nasser began dabbling in Yemeni affairs when North Yemen first joined Egypt and Syria to form the United Arab States, a union that lasted from 1958 to 1961. Nasser backed a Yemeni military coup that ousted the *imam* (ruler) and sent 20,000 troops to support the republic's army in 1962.

Saudi Arabia and Jordan, on the other hand, supported the loyalist forces. When Egyptian aircraft began attacking the Saudi border, the Saudis feared a full-scale attack and turned to the Americans for protection. The United States flexed its military muscle to keep the Egyptians at bay. After the humiliating Egyptian defeat at the hands of the Israelis in 1967, Nasser pulled his troops out of Yemen. In 1970, Saudi Arabia brought peace to Yemen by ceasing to fund the royalists and formally recognizing the republican government.

Civil war and unification

Border skirmishes between North and South Yemen raged on from 1967 until an agreement was reached to unify the two nations in 1972. The merger never took hold and fighting led to a full-blown war between the North and South in 1979. The two Yemens became one Yemen on May 22, 1990. President Ali Abdullah Salih, the former leader of the North, ruled the newly formed nation with Sanaa as its capital. Tensions between the northern and southern militaries broke out into a nine-week civil war in 1994. The North and Salih emerged victorious.

The bombing of the USS Cole

On October 12, 2000, the guided missile destroyer USS Cole had docked in the Yemeni port to refuel. Two suicide bombers appeared to stand to attention and salute just before crashing their small boat packed with explosives into the American ship's hull. The subsequent explosion blew a 40-x-40-foot hole in the destroyer's hull, killing 17 sailors and injuring 39 more (see Figure 17-4). The U.S. government determined that bin Laden's Al-Qaeda network was responsible for the attack. In October 2002, Abdul Rahim al-Nashiri, a Saudi suspected of masterminding the Cole attack, was arrested and handed over to the United States.

Figure 17-4: Damage to the USS Cole after the October 12, 2000, bombing.

© AFP/CORBIS.

Making their point: Kidnapping foreigners

Arab tribes still control rural areas of Yemen. Tribes with special grievances against Ali Abdullah Salih's government have kidnapped foreigners, often tourists. On March 1, 2000, the Polish ambassador was kidnapped after the government's arrest of a local sheikh at the Sanaa airport the previous day. The ambassador was released three days later after the kidnappers had been given five cars, five knives, and five men to hold until the sheikh could be released. The tribes release most foreigners after they receive a "hospitality fee" from the hostage negotiator. In 1998, 33 of the approximately 100,000 foreign tourists that visited Yemen were kidnapped, and in 2001 only two. From 1996 through 2001, approximately 157 foreigners were kidnapped, nine of which were Americans. Five were killed, and the remainder was released safely.

Joining the War on Terrorism

After September 11, 2001, Yemen came under international scrutiny. Not wanting to become the target of U.S. action like Afghanistan, Salih went to great lengths to distance himself from Al-Qaeda and agreed to cooperate with America's War on Terrorism. After Al-Qaeda dispersed in Afghanistan later that year, many analysts feared Yemen would become a haven for terrorists. One of the biggest obstacles facing an effort to wipe out militants is that militants can hide in the Yemeni mountainous regions home to unruly Arab tribes, much as is the case in Afghanistan. Yemeni officials claim to have demonstrated their commitment by rounding up more than 100 suspected Islamic militants. Despite such efforts, Yemen has become a battlefield for the War on Terrorism.

- **December 2001:** As the Yemeni military attempts to flush out an Al-Qaeda cell from the tribal area, 13 Yemeni soldiers are killed.

- **October 2002:** A small, swift craft strikes the French Oil Tanker Limburg, resembling the attack on the USS Cole that took place two years earlier. One Bulgarian crew member dies.

- **November 2002:** An unmanned CIA Predator drone fires a Hellfire missile that strikes a car killing six suspected Islamic militants, including Abu Ali al-Harithi, a key Al-Qaeda operative linked to both the USS Cole attack and Limburg bombing.

- **December 2002:** A 30-year-old Islamic militant named Abdul Razzak Kamel rushes into a Southern Baptist missionary hospital and slaughters three U.S. aid workers and wounds a fourth.

Hadramaut province, comprising the eastern third of the country, remains largely beyond government control. Bin Laden's father originated from Hadramaut. This region has also been the home to many Al-Qaeda militants, including the suspected suicide bombers in the Limburg attack.

Chapter 18

Non-Arab Muslim States

Many of the problems that have plagued the Arab World in the past century have also affected non-Arab countries in the Middle East. Political, military, religious, and ethnic disturbances and violence are the most notable. Although the non-Arab countries have suffered from some of the same ills as many Arab nations, each situation is unique, deserving a special understanding of the history and circumstances. More important, the three non-Arab countries — Iran, Somalia, and Turkey — that I discuss in this chapter have contributed in special ways to the Middle East's complex and volatile environment.

Iran

Iran has two names: Iran and Persia (see Chapter 4). That's where the Persian Gulf gets its name. In fact, if you ask a dozen Iranian taxi drivers or gas station clerks living in the United States where they're from, you'll likely hear *Persia* more than half the time. They think it's safer to say *Persia* than *Iran*. Before the Iranian Revolution in 1979, few Americans had even heard of Iran. But after The Shah fled and a group of students scaled the U.S. embassy wall in Tehran and took 52 hostages — all under the watchful eye of their spiritual leader the Ayatollah Khomeini — and after a botched American helicopter rescue attempt, and after the hostages remained in captivity for almost two years, well, many Americans soured on Iran. Unfortunately for innocent Iranians living in the United States, many Americans harbor resentment about the hostage affair, and the mere mention of Iran dredges up all those old images. Fortunately for Iranians, however, most Americans are geographically challenged and don't have a clue where Persia is. Figure 18-1 can give you a clue.

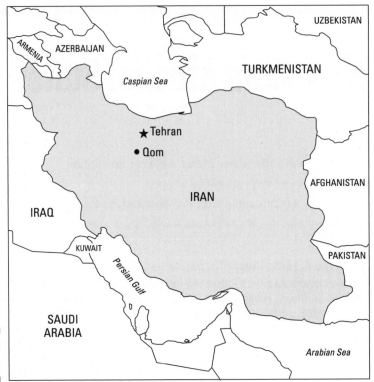

The Shah of Iran

After World War II, the United States began to take over Britain's role as leading foreign player in Iranian politics. Iran was rich with oil, and the West wanted to keep the pipelines flowing. The United States continued to support Muhammad Reza Shah, known in the West as *The Shah of Iran* or *The Shah* for short. In 1952, Prime Minister Muhammad Mossadeq tried to nationalize the oil industry and dethrone the Shah. The CIA mobilized the best street rabble money could buy, booted Mossadeq, and restored the throne to The Shah six days later. The grateful Shah cranked back open the valves and the oil once again flowed westward. (Iran actually awarded oil contracts to a European oil consortium of American, British, Dutch, and French companies.)

The White Revolution

Beginning in 1963, The Shah attempted some democratic and social reforms known as *The White Revolution* meant to modernize the country, including the promotion of literacy. Many of the reforms undermined the power of the *mullahs* (religious leaders), which was, of course, the idea. The following reforms earned The Shah the contempt of the clerics.

- ✔ **Women's rights.** The liberation of women included the right to vote. Women were also awarded more freedom in divorce and in attire. They were permitted to wear Western dress and abandon the veil.

- ✔ **Education.** Education became more modern and secular, therefore curtailing the clergy's influence in shaping Iranian youth.

- ✔ **Food.** Accusations that The Shah implemented his mother's home-cooked beef kabob as the official national food for all Iranians, and that McDonald's soon started carrying The Shah's McMama Kabobs in Tehran are unfounded.

- ✔ **Land reform.** The reform snatched some of the clergy's land holdings. (No one much supports land reform if they're on the giving side of reform. Those individuals on the receiving side, however, almost always consider themselves reformists.)

The mullahs also criticized The Shah's relationship with the West. The United States (and Israel) helped The Shah establish the feared SAVAK, a most brutal secret security force that employed torture and murder as deterrents against opposition. As a result of these collaborative efforts with The Shah, a wave of anti-Americanism washed over Iran, and the clerics exploited the situation to rally support from the poor on religious grounds and from the wealthy landowners and merchants for financial reasons. The Shah had a number of leading clerics arrested in Qom, their spiritual center. Riots erupted. A number of mullahs fled the country, including Ayatollah Khomeini who went into exile in neighboring Iraq in 1964.

The Shah's days are numbered

Despite The Shah's numerous reformist policies that helped to improve conditions for a middle class he helped to create, the standard of living for the poor improved very little. In the late 1970s, the king became extremely unpopular in his own kingdom. All the past political, social, religious, and economic problems seemed to resurface in the form of current dissent that came to a head. In September 1978, The Shah instituted martial law. A number of factors led to widespread unrest across Iran.

- ✔ Recession and inflation plagued the country.

- ✔ SAVAK continued to repress dissidents.

- ✔ The Shah lacked the resolve necessary to fight the unrest due to a losing bout with lymphatic cancer.

- ✔ A wave of anti-American sentiment was rolling across Iran.

✔ Shiite exile Ayatollah Khomeini (see in Figure 18-2) seized the opportunity to convince many Iranian dissidents that all the nation's ills could be traced to two sources of anti-Islamic contention:

- The Shah's secular practices and policies

- Influence of the "Great Satan" (The United States)

Khomeini's solution was simple: Get rid of The Shah, and give *me* the power! The increased demonstrations, protests, and riots convinced The Shah his days were numbered. In January 1979, The Shah and his queen boarded a royal Iranian Boeing 707 aircraft "for vacation," and never returned home.

Figure 18-2:
Ayatollah
Khomeini.

© Bettmann/CORBIS

Striving for an Islamic Revolution

With The Shah out of the picture, Khomeini flew from Paris to Tehran into the throng of his adoring fans, who lined the streets of the Iranian capital and swarmed his vehicle as if he were a rock star. The Iranians were exuberant at the return of the 78-year-old, robed patriarch and at his announcement that he would establish the Islamic Republic of Iran — the first truly Islamic state in modern history — and would reinstitute pure Islam as it was in the golden days of the Prophet Muhammad.

Ayatollah Khomeini: A legend in the making

In the 1970s and 1980s, the Ayatollah Khomeini represented to Muslims and the West pretty much what Osama bin Laden represents to each respective group today. Khomeini had voiced stinging criticism of The Shah's White Revolution and his relationship with the United States on January 22, 1963. The Shah's intimidation of Islamic clerics started just two days later as an armored unit entered Qom, the Shiite spiritual center. The Ayatollah intensified his criticism, citing violations of the constitution, moral corruption, tyranny, and submission to the United States and Israel. The Shah retaliated with a violent crackdown on the mullahs and their supporters. Khomeini was arrested and released the following year, but he continued his assault. On November 4, 1964, the military arrested Khomeini and put him on the next plane to Turkey. The surveillance and restrictions placed on Khomeini by Turkish authorities cramped his style, and he moved to neighboring Iraq, which had fallen out with Iran.

In Najaf, Iraq, Khomeini's teachings at the Sheikh Murtaza Ansari *madrasa* (theological school) left a lasting impression on Shiite extremists for decades to come. By 1978, Iran and Iraq had begun to mend fences, and Iraq decided Khomeini had to go. Khomeini tried to enter Kuwait, but Kuwait refused to have any part of his activities. So he moved his exile to France in 1978.

The legend lived on in the Shiite *madrasa*s of southern Iraq — Khomeini's old stomping grounds — where new militant leaders received training: Hezbollah. Although Khomeini preached against the West's evils, he discovered the freedom of speech in France conducive to his anti-Shah propaganda. Long before the Internet, Khomeini found Western technology a useful tool. He launched a campaign to oust the Shah from exile through the Western media and taped sermons that made their way back to Iran. The campaign succeeded in instigating widespread riots in 1978 and The Shah's flight in 1979.

Khomeini wanted to reproduce in Iran an ideal Islamic society based on the seventh-century model of the first Muslim community. Many movements in the Muslim World, even those remotely associated with Islam, attempt to gain their legitimacy from the Prophet Muhammad's earliest practices and messages. Women's rights activists or peace and conflict resolution campaigns, for instance, look to the first Muslim community as the ideal model, just as Islamic extremists do (see Chapter 8). Not many people disagree that "pure" Islam as practiced by the Prophet is a flawless model for human rights, governance, taxation, and all the other components of a functioning society. The disagreement arises over exactly what pure Islam is, and over interpretations of how (and why) it was practiced by that first community. No sweat for Iranians in 1979, though! Khomeini had it all figured out. The best interpretation was Khomeini's interpretation.

Establishing a theocracy

Khomeini set up a theocracy, the first modern Islamic state in history. The Iranian cleric made it clear that the rest of the regimes throughout the

Muslim World were corrupt, more often than not as a result of close ties with the "Great Satan" (the United States). But establishing an Islamic state was hard work. It involved cleaning up all un-Islamic elements of society through arrests, torture, and execution (the Shah's SAVAK was now at Khomeini's disposal). The purification of Iran came through the rigid enforcement of Iran's Shiite version of *sharia* (Islamic law), which translated into implementing the following measures:

- Purging Iran of all un-Islamic influences. Banking, for instance, was set on an Islamic model (interest is forbidden).

- Purging Iran of all Western influences (also seen as un-Islamic). Music and dancing were among the prohibitions.

- Enforcing the revolution's new Islamic regulations (the enforcers were squads of young men roaming the streets).

- Persecuting all non-Muslims, secular nationalists, and leftists.

- Imposing strict regulations on women, including the mandatory use of the veil in public, covering head to toe.

- Taking advantage of the ensuing chaos to settle old scores in the name of the revolution.

For Westerners, particularly Americans, these extremist practices mixed with future events earned Khomeini the reputation as an evil Islamic madman that wouldn't be matched until Osama bin Laden surfaced nearly two decades later. For much of the Muslim World, including extremists in neighboring Pakistan and Afghanistan, Khomeini's revolution meant a model for future emulation.

Concocting a volatile mix: A bearded cleric, Iranian students, and American hostages

Well on their way to cleaning up Iran at home, Khomeini's regime couldn't wait to get its hands on The Shah so Iran could put him on trial. In November 1979, the 78-year old bearded cleric thought he'd found his chance when U.S. President Jimmy Carter invited The Shah to New York for medical attention. With Khomeini's blessing, a group of approximately 500 students demonstrating outside the U.S. embassy in Tehran demanded that the United States extradite The Shah. When Carter refused, the students, some with photos of Khomeini pinned to their shirts, scaled the wall and stormed the compound, seizing approximately 67 American hostages. The captors released 15 hostages, African-Americans and most of the women early on, but 52 remained in captivity for 444 days.

If the eight U.S. Marines had fired on the storming hordes, the outcome may have been very different. The marines guarding the U.S. embassy, however, didn't fire on advancing students because they had been ordered not to load their weapons and to surrender if the perimeter was breached.

Rescued on wings of eagles: The other hostage story

In the midst of Islamic Revolution hysteria stirred by the Ayatollah Khomeini's anti-Western rhetoric of January 1979, and months before the U.S. embassy siege, another hostage story was developing. The Iranian police arrested two American employees working for Electronic Data Systems (EDS) in Tehran. The owner of EDS, Ross Perot (yes, the same one) traveled to the Tehran prison, and committed all available resources to freeing the two men.

When the American diplomatic channels failed, the Texas billionaire organized a rag-tag rescue team comprised of EDS employees and led by retired Green Beret Colonel Arthur "Bull" Simons. The rescue team staged a daring rescue mission from the Tehran jail and managed to escape across the Turkish border. The adventure was captured in Ken Follett's book *On Wings of Eagles* and by a movie of the same name. Unfortunately, the rescue attempt launched by U.S. President Jimmy Carter the next year didn't enjoy the same success.

Carter decided that because his efforts at diplomacy — breaking diplomatic ties and an economic boycott — had gotten him nowhere, he'd resort to military force. On April 24 and 25, 1980, eight helicopters launched from the USS Nimitz off the Iranian coast in the Persian Gulf set to rendezvous with six transport aircraft in the Iranian desert southeast of Tehran at a spot called *Desert One*. An ensuing sandstorm caused two aircraft to collide and burst into flames. The accident killed eight American servicemen, and the mission was aborted. In defiance of Carter, Khomeini released the 52 hostages the following year to Carter's successor Ronald Reagan after Reagan's inauguration on January 20, 1981. Iran had bigger fish to fry, including an invading Iraqi army.

Fighting the Iran-Iraq War

Encouraged by Iran's weakened military and exiled Iranian military officers in Baghdad who convinced the Iraqi president that Iran couldn't last against a full-scale attack more than a few days, Saddam Hussein launched an air assault with French Mirage jets against Iran on September 22, 1980. Saddam hoped to regain the territory of the Shatt al-Arab waterway that Saddam had conceded to Iran five years earlier in the *Algiers Accord*, capture the oil fields of Khuzestan, stem the growing Shiite extremist activity, and incite a revolt against Khomeini.

The war's first two years went well for Saddam, but the Iranian military rebounded and retook most of the lost territory by 1982. The United States, still bitter about the hostage crisis, threw its lot in with Saddam. Reagan sent envoy Donald Rumsfeld to Baghdad, and the United States began providing military and economic support to Iraq. The United States began flagging

Kuwaiti oil tankers to provide safe passage through the Gulf. Khomeini exploited Kurdish unrest inside Iraq to create revolts in Iraqi Kurdistan.

In July 1987, a Kuwaiti oil tanker struck an Iranian mine, and the United States, Britain, and France sent warships to the region. The Americans sank Iranian ships and attacked offshore oil platforms. The following year the United States shot down an Iran Air passenger plane carrying 290 civilians, mistaking it for a military aircraft. The armed conflict that Saddam believed would last just a few days proved to drag on for eight years, bringing two of the Middle East's wealthiest nations to their knees, and depleting the riches and progress that they had made with oil profits over the past quarter of a century. The eight-year struggle cost each country about $100 billion. In human life, the war cost approximately 500,000 human lives, much more than the Lebanese civil war and all the Arab-Israeli wars put together (see Chapter 12).

Remembering Khomeini's "legacy"

Iran's Islamic Revolution of the 1980s was the first of its kind. Khomeini built an intolerant Islamic theocracy that repressed the Iranian people, fought a costly eight-year war with Iraq, and spread Islamic militancy across the region, all in the name of Islam. In the West, this activity earned Khomeini and his regime the reputation of the "epitome of evil" that has only recently been supplanted by Osama bin Laden and the Taliban (see Chapter 15). To many Muslim extremists, Khomeini fashioned the first, true Islamic state — a feat they have tried to emulate again and again. Khomeini's success in taking American hostages, for instance, was replicated by his hand-fed Lebanese protégés, Hezbollah, with whom the United States negotiated in the mid-1980s. Almost certainly, Islamic militants in Southeast Asia in recent years have learned from these earlier successes.

Sitting atop Khomeini's hit list

Anglo-Indian novelist Salman Rushdie made Khomeini's hit list in 1988 upon the publication of *Satanic Verses*. Muslims across the globe set about protesting the book's blasphemous content. A series of violent events included a book-burning demonstration near London, riots in India and Pakistan that left more than 20 dead, and the murder of the book's Japanese translator. Swept up in the euphoria, Khomeini issued a *fatwa* (Islamic injunction) sanctioning the assassination of the novelist and his associates.

Subsequently, a private Islamic foundation placed a bounty on Rushdie's head of $3 million (see Chapter 22), even though Khomeini (or many of the protesters for that matter) probably never read *Satanic Verses*. Rushdie spent the next several years in hiding, his books more popular than ever. Even after Khomeini's death in 1989, the price on the novelist's head remained until 1998, when the Iranian leadership announced the affair was over. Nonetheless, the offer of $3 million for Rushdie's assassination remains open. The author has appeared on the David Letterman show and has met U.S. President Bill Clinton and British Prime Minister Tony Blair.

Iran-Contra Affair: A win-win-win-win situation

In the midst of the Middle Eastern turmoil of the 1980s — the Iranian Revolution, Iranian hostage crisis, Soviet invasion of Afghanistan, and Hezbollah kidnappings — comes a new chapter in the intrigues and convoluted politics of the Middle East: *The Iran-Contra Affair* in 1986. The primary cast members follow:

✔ U.S. government officials, including U.S. Army Colonel Oliver North and National Security Adviser Robert McFarlane under President Ronald Reagan

✔ Hezbollah, the Lebanese Shiite militant organization, holding Western hostages, including a number of Americans

✔ Iranian clerics, who at the time were embroiled in a war with Iraq

✔ American hostages in Lebanon

✔ The Contras, a Nicaraguan militant organization resisting communist Sandanista rule

The United States faced a double dilemma. Congress had cut funding for the U.S.-backed Contras in Central America, and President Reagan had vowed not to negotiate with terrorists and hostage takers. McFarlane devised a brilliant plan to circumvent the system and accomplish the goals of supporting the Contras and releasing the American captives in Lebanon. The United States would sell 120 anti-aircraft and 4,000 antitank missiles to Iran, and in exchange Iran would promise to convince Hezbollah in Lebanon to release the American hostages. The money made from the weapons' sale would go to the Contras to hold them over until Congress came to its senses.

The deal played out, the hostages were released, Iran got its weapons (no doubt throwing Hezbollah a bone), and the Contras received their money: A win-win-win-win situation. Everyone was happy, right? Well everyone but Congress, that is. Well, and Iraq, whom the United States was also supplying with weapons. And, yes, much of the American public. Reagan's approval rating dropped from 67 percent to 46 percent.

Furthermore, in the 1980s, Iran didn't have its hands full enough with an Islamic Revolution at home, taking American hostages, and fighting a war with Iraq, so Khomeini sent 1,000 Pasadaran (Iranian revolutionary guards) to set up training camps in southeastern Lebanon's Beqaa Valley. The Pasadaran recruited and provided young Shiite extremists with military training and Khomeini's religious instruction. The core Hezbollah students, many of whom had graduated from Shiite *madrasas* in Iraq, took these lessons to heart.

As a result, Hezbollah pledged an allegiance to Khomeini and vowed to establish an Islamic state in Iran's own image. To exert militant muscle in Lebanon, Hezbollah turned to suicide bombings, including the car bomb outside the U.S. embassy in Beirut that killed 63 people and a truck bombing at the marine barracks that killed 241 U.S. Marines and 60 French soldiers. Their most effective weapon, however, proved to be kidnapping (see Chapter 16).

After ten years of turmoil, repression, and war, Khomeini died in 1989, leaving a repressed and defeated people, crippled economy, destroyed infrastructure, and authoritarian regime to fend for itself. The Ayatollah's image remains untarnished in the eyes of many of his considerable supporters both inside and outside of Iran. For these loyalists, the revolution has been a great success. The fact that he established an Islamic state in Iran based on sharia outweighs the hardships suffered. Any setbacks during his reign are seen as the work of outside — commonly American or Israeli — forces, which are enemies of Islam, not the result of the cleric's extremist measures.

Coming full circle

Iranian students in 1979 were fed up with secular rule, democracy, the West, and everything it stood for. They had embraced Khomeini and dedicated their lives to the Islamic Revolution. Two decades later, students are once again demonstrating in the streets of Iran. This time they want to oust the corrupt and uncompromising clerics. The students embrace secular values, democracy, and closer ties with the West. Some of the most ardent protests are coming from the very same students who stood outside the U.S. embassy burning American flags and shouting "Death to America" in 1979. Massoumeh Ebtekar, for instance, who'd taken part in storming the U.S. embassy and taking the hostages, became the female spokesperson for the hostage takers. (See Figure 18-3.) Today as the country's first female vice president, she fights for democratic reform against the clerics.

Figure 18-3:
Massoumeh
Ebtekar.

© *REUTER RAYMOND/CORBIS SYGMA*

The power vacuum left in the wake of Khomeini's death allowed the emergence of moderates. As chief of the armed forces and speaker of parliament, Ali Akbar Rafsanjani became Iran's president in 1989. In an attempt to reverse the damage done by Khomeini's regime, Rafsanjani sought to improve relations with the West, boost the economy, and open the way for foreign investment. Hard-line clerics, however, gave very little room for Rafsanjani's political maneuvers.

In 1997, Muhammad Khatami was elected president. Khatami has also taken steps to ease Islamic restrictions, press for democratization, and improve the status of women. But the hard-liners still hold most of the power in Iran, and Khatami and his supporters don't enjoy enough of the power within the government or the military to carry out the reforms.

Somalia

In 1992, the world's eyes focused on Somalia's growing humanitarian crisis. Somalia is shown in Figure 18-4. The century's worst drought exacerbated by civil war left 300,000 dead. Images of starvation in the making — bloat-bellied toddlers, tiny, emaciated infants, more dead than alive, and skeletal adults too weak to shoo away the flies — led the United Nations and the United States to take steps to alleviate the suffering.

Using starvation as a weapon: A humanitarian crisis

In the early 1990s, two major forces struggled for power: The United Somali Congress (USC) primarily comprised the Hawiye clan and the Somali National Movement (SNM) dominated by the Isaaq clan. In Mogadishu, Somalia's capital, the top two USC leaders, General Muhammad Farah Aidid and Ali Mahdi Muhammad fell out, and the USC split into two rival factions. Both militant groups demanded loyalty from the starving population in return for access to food. Rival factions used military force to strangle U.N. supply routes, raid and hoard food supplies, and extort money from relief agencies. Whoever controlled the food controlled the people.

Operation Restore Hope

Washington resolved to send U.S. peacekeeping troops to reopen and stabilize distribution routes for U.N. humanitarian supplies that had been closed by rival clans. When the U.S. Marines first landed in December 1992, both Aidid and Muhammad attempted to coerce the U.S. and U.N. forces (and their food supplies) to recognize the legitimacy of their respective rule. When the United States and United Nations refused to acknowledge Aidid and Muhammad's rule, the warlords became determined to oust the foreign interlopers and resume their practices of old. Figure 18-5 shows U.S. troops in Somalia.

No good deed goes unpunished

From 1992 to 1994, the humanitarian crisis in Somalia drew tons of foreign aid and U.N. peacekeepers to see that it was distributed. Tribal warlords exploited the crisis to further their own political goals.

Increased Saudi, Iranian, and Sudanese support for Aidid brought weapons and Islamic militants trained in Sudan to Somalia. Islamic extremists in Somalia and elsewhere in the Muslim World maintained the U.S. and U.N. foreign aid was little more than a U.S.-Israeli plot to extend Western influence into Somalia and Sudan.

As a result, rival forces looted food-distribution sites and tribal forces clashed with the U.S. and U.N. peacekeepers. Aidid's militants ambushed and killed 24 Pakistani peacekeepers on June 5, 1993.

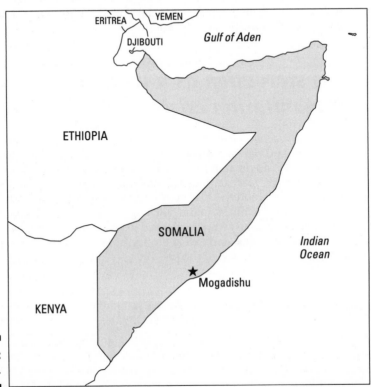

Figure 18-4:
Somalia.

Figure 18-5:
U.S. troops
in Somalia.

The United States quickly realized that Aidid was a major obstacle to stability in Somalia. The Americans became determined to capture him and his henchmen. They had their chance in October 1993 when their intelligence placed two of his ranking officials, Osman Salah and Muhammad Hassan Alawi, at the Olympic Hotel in Mogadishu.

Downing Black Hawks

On October 3, 1993, a U.S. military raid of the Olympic Hotel involved about 100 American ground and air troops. The ground troops reached the hotel and snatched their prey. While leaving the hotel, the troops came under intense enemy fire. The military caravan got lost in the Mogadishu maze of blocked-off streets and took a number of casualties. Aidid's militants shot down three of the UH-60 helicopters (Black Hawks) sent as backup. Two landed within the city, and one made it back to the airport. One helicopter pilot was captured alive (released 10 days later).

The Americans trapped in the city established a perimeter around the first downed aircraft and managed to hold off overwhelming numbers of Aidid's men for 11 hours until a joint Pakistani-American peacekeeping team rescued them. The exuberant Somalis dragged the Americans' dead bodies through the streets. The mission resulted in the deaths of 18 American soldiers (72 wounded) and 300 Somalis (400 injured). By spring of the following year, most of the American troops had withdrawn.

When it rains . . .

After the U.N. peacekeepers pulled out, no one was left to keep the peace, and the warlords resumed their old habits. In 1996, Aidid died, but problems didn't let up.

- ✔ **Floods:** After years of drought, floods caused widespread devastation.
- ✔ **Continued violence:** Mogadishu and southern Somalia continued to suffer from civil war.

In 2000 at a conference held in Djibouti, an interim constitution was established, and a national assembly and president were elected. But the new government's authority is limited and several militias don't recognize it.

Turkey: Politicians, Generals, and Kurds

Turkey's role in regional affairs has been quite different. Although Islamic extremist elements exert considerable influence in Iran and Somalia, Turkey's secular rule has minimized (often brutally) extremism. As a part of NATO, this secular Muslim nation has acted as a staging ground for U.S. military threats into the region. Most notably, American air strikes into Iraq during the Gulf War originated from bases in Turkey.

Kemal Attaturk played no small part in modernizing Turkey, forming a secular government, and paving the way for good relations with the West that have endured to the present (see Chapter 6). Taking a more modern and secular path, however, didn't make Turkey invulnerable to many of the same ethnic, political, and military hardships suffered by other Muslim nations. Turkey is in the process of attempting to rebound from the internal and external strife of recent years. Figure 18-6 shows a map of Turkey.

Overcoming internal strife

Socioeconomic ills in the late 1970s led to political unrest that ended in a military coup and martial law in 1980. General Kenan Evren secured his authority over the government and restored order. In 1982, the general established a new constitution that reinstituted parliament, secured Evran's position as head of state through 1989, and gave the military extended authority in civilian affairs. Martial law was lifted for most of the country in 1987. By this time, the Kurdistan Workers Party (PKK) in southeastern Turkey had launched a guerrilla war to secure Kurdish autonomy. When the Persian Gulf War broke out in 1991, violence in Iraqi Kurdistan exacerbated the situation.

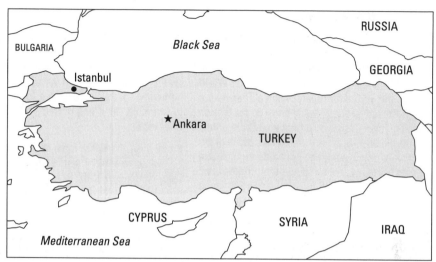

Figure 18-6:
Turkey.

But why did the PKK lash out? After World War I during the Ottoman Empire's breakup, the Treaty of Sevres in 1920 promised the Kurds a homeland. Because of political difficulties, the Kurdish state never took shape, and Kurds in the region have been struggling for independence off and on ever since. Khomeini's Islamic Revolution allowed for brutal campaigns against the Kurds, as did Saddam Hussein's Baathist government. After the Persian Gulf War ended in 1991, one million Kurdish refugees fled to Iran and 500,000 to the Turkish border, but Turkey's military did its best to keep them from entering. The following year an *autonomous region* was established in northern Iraq.

A woman's touch

When discussing gender issues in the Middle East, some wise guy always likes to point out that the Near East has had several female prime ministers, but the United States has yet to have a female president (or even vice president). Golda Meir served as Israeli prime minister from 1969 until 1974, and Benazir Bhutto was Pakistan's prime minister on two occasions in the late 1980s and 1990s. Turkey's first female premier was an economist from the University of Istanbul named Tansu Ciller. She earned her PhD from the University of Connecticut and proved to be an ambitious politician who became prime minister in 1993 but was forced to step down three years later amid numerous scandals.

Kurds in the way

The Ottoman rulers were Turks. When the Ottoman Empire collapsed at the end of World War I, the European superpowers of France and England decided they would divvy up the Turkish spoils. The British would take a sizeable chunk of the old empire, France would take piece of the action, a chunk would be set aside for all those Kurds living in the area so that they could set up their own homeland (Kurdistan), and a tiny piece would even be left over for the Turks. The whole agreement was even put down on paper in the Treaty of Sevres in 1920. But no one ever cleared this with the Turks, who raised a fuss (and an army) and forced everyone back to the bargaining table in 1923. The result was the Treaty of Lausanne that established a larger homeland for the Turks, called Turkey, but failed to mention anything about the Kurds (see Chapter 6).

Since then, the Kurds have remained minorities — even unwanted guests at times — in Turkey, Iraq, Syria, and Iran. In order to realize their dreams of Kurdistan, separatists have often taken to violence. All those countries haven't taken kindly to Kurdish separatist efforts and militancy and have dealt brutally with the Kurds, none more brutally than Iraq and Turkey.

From the mid-1980s through the 1990s in southeastern Turkey, the PKK guerrillas continued to launch violent attacks against government interests. The guerrilla violence earned brutal reprisals from the Turkish military. In 1999, Turkish officials captured PKK's guerrilla leader Abdullah Ocalan and sentenced him to death. Ocalan subsequently asked the PKK to renounce violence. Although violence has since decreased significantly, as recently as 2002, Turkey's human rights abuses against the Kurds have played a huge role in the nation's inability to earn acceptance into the European Union.

Persian Gulf War(s)

As the only Muslim nation currently a member of NATO, Turkey has retained particularly warm relations with the West (although not always with Greece). The United States launched air raids against Iraq from bases in Turkey during the Persian Gulf War (see Chapter 12), but Turkey's participation in the U.S.-led coalition was costly. Turkey's economy suffered a severe blow amounting to billions of dollars in lost tourist revenues and from the sanctions imposed against Iraq, one of Turkey's major trading partners. The influx of Kurdish refugees and increased unrest in southeastern Turkey was equally costly.

Since the war's end, the United States and Britain have used a Turkish air-base at Incirlik to monitor the *no-fly zone* (an area over which Iraqi planes can't pass) in northern Iraq (see Chapter 12). Turkish officials expressed a willingness to participate in George W. Bush's military campaign against Iraq in

2003, but at a price. This time Turkish leaders demanded a war-compensation package — including grants, preferential trading status, and military aid — as well as guarantees that the Kurds in northern Iraq wouldn't be granted independence. On February 6, 2003, the Turkish parliament approved a measure allowing the United States to renovate two seaports and five military posts and bases at a cost of more than $200 million. The plan was to allow the United States access to those bases, but in mid-February the Turkish parliament voted against admitting U.S. troops by a narrow margin. At the last minute, the Turks opted to allow coalition troops use of Turkish airspace.

Part VI
Cultural Contributions of the Middle East

The 5th Wave   By Rich Tennant

©RICH TENNANT

ALONG WITH OTHER SECTS IN THE MIDDLE EAST IS A GROUP OF PEOPLE KNOWN AS THE SARCASTICS.

Oh yeah, I'm really gonna ride that camel across the desert.

Did I put this tent up myself? No, it fell from the sky this way.

No, I'm not selling anything. I just like sitting out in the midday sun surrounded by baskets of fruit hoping someone will talk to me.

In this part . . .

The Middle East seldom gets the credit it deserves for the rich cultural contributions that it's made to the world. Part VI details major and minor Middle Eastern religions. This part further investigates the breadth of Middle Eastern family life. This part also explains the importance language plays in Middle Eastern society and showcases the region's vast literature. And last but not least, this part describes some of the Middle East's contributions to the arts and sciences.

Chapter 19

A Mosaic of Religions

One of the Middle East's most interesting dynamics is religion. Brace yourself! Whether pious or not, anyone you meet in the region may ask you *your* religion. Because Middle Eastern worldviews are often quite different than the West's, many Middle Easterners categorize others by religion. In order for them to understand you, they must first find out your nationality and your religion. Christian minorities I met in the Middle East naturally were pleased to discover I was Christian (a generic term I used for identity purposes). The most curious, however, were Muslims. They, too, were happy to find out that I was Christian. Christians and Jews are *people of the book* (see the section on Islam in this chapter). In general, Muslims respect devotees of any religion, but I wouldn't advise answering atheist or agnostic.

Although your mom probably told you not to discuss religion and politics, that restriction apparently never took hold in the Middle East. The topic of religion, in fact, is quite popular and arises time and again. A drug addict once tried to sell me drugs on the streets of Peshawar, Pakistan. When he found out I wasn't interested, he instantly launched into a parable about Jonah and the whale. Others are genuinely interested in your beliefs. A graduate of a *madrasa* (theological school) I once knew was intrigued by Christianity and requested I send him literature on Christianity. Individuals from engineers to flower vendors often share their religious values in a genuine and friendly manner. Despite the violence surrounding religion that erupts in the Middle East, the respect normally afforded religion in the region can be refreshing.

Because Islam is the predominant religion in the Middle East, the majority of this book deals with Islamic tradition, practices, and history. However, Islam is just the latest manifestation of the religion of Abraham. (For more on who

Exploring the Abrahamic cycle

One central motif passed down in Judaism, Christianity, and Islam is the sacrifice of Abraham's son. One difference lies in which son of Abraham was to be sacrificed. Jews and Christians belief it was Isaac, and most Muslims believe it was Ishmael. By the time that Islam emerged on the scene in the sixth century, a wealth of folklore involving Abraham, Sarah, Hagar, Ishmael, and Isaac was swirling around the Near East in various forms. Islamic culture absorbed a number of variants into its social and religious fabric.

According to Islamic tradition, Abraham is born in Mesopotamia (see Chapter 4). He marries Sarah. At this point, Abraham and Sarah are the only two monotheists (worshippers who believe in one god) on earth. They emigrate westward toward Syria where a tyrant king confronts them and decides to possess Sarah because of her stunning beauty. God intervenes and foils the tyrant's plans. As compensation for his misdeed, the king gives Sarah a maidservant, Hagar. Because Sarah is barren, she permits Hagar to sleep with Abraham so that she can provide him with an heir. When Hagar becomes pregnant, God appears and tells her that her son will be a great leader of 12 sons or nations. Ishmael is born.

Later, while Hagar is still breast-feeding Ishmael, a jealous Sarah drives the two away. In an effort to make peace, Abraham takes Hagar and Ishmael to Mecca, which is a desert at the time. He leaves them and returns to Syria. When Hagar's milk dries up, and they run out of water and are approaching death, the angel

Gabriel arrives and rubs the earth with his heel. Little Ishmael imitates the angel by rubbing his own heel in the same spot. Immediately, water flows from the earth. So much water comes forth that Hagar has to dam the flow. This location is now the famous well of Zamzam.

Throughout the remainder of his life, Abraham continues returning to Mecca to visit his family. Abraham rides his magical horse Buraq back and forth to Mecca, always returning before nightfall so that he can spend his evenings with Sarah. After Ishmael is old enough to run and keep up with his father, Abraham tells Ishmael that he has received a vision from God, instructing the father to sacrifice his son. Ishmael demands that his father do so. He instructs his father to tighten his bonds and protect his clothes so that blood won't soil them and cause Hagar grief. He also tells his father to sharpen the knife so that he will die quickly, and to put him face down because Ishmael fears that if his father looks into his eyes, he won't be able to complete the task at hand. Finally, he tells his father to return his shirt to his mother so that it may offer her some comfort. Then, Ishmael commands his father to proceed.

Abraham does as he is told, but when he turns Ishmael over and tries to slice his son's throat, he finds that God has turned the dull edge of the knife toward his son so that it can cause no harm. At this point God calls out, "Abraham you have already fulfilled your vision." [Q: 37: 103] In Ishmael's place, a ram is slaughtered. In one version of the story, Abraham, his son, the angel Gabriel, and the ram all praise God.

Abraham is and why he's important, see the sidebar, "Exploring the Abrahamic cycle" in this chapter.) Chronologically, Judaism came first, followed by Christianity, and then Islam. Although creation myths in all three begin with Adam and Eve, the religions really take shape with Abraham.

I dedicate this chapter to a discussion of the three major Abrahamic religions: Judaism, Christianity, and Islam. Followers of these three religions all trace their origins back to Abraham.

Judaism

Judaism is the religion of the Jews. The term *ancient Israelites* refers to the Jews of the Hebrew Bible, the chosen people of a god called Yahweh.

Delving into Judaism's background

Two of the earliest adherents of what is called the cult of Yahweh were Abraham and Sarah, who are believed to have migrated from Mesopotamia to Canaan, sometime during the second millennium B.C., where God tested Abraham's faith by ordering him to sacrifice his son Isaac. When Abraham proved his willingness to follow through with the sacrifice, God prevented him from doing so, and Abraham and Isaac sacrificed a lamb in his place.

Promising a covenant: God deals with Abraham

Because of Abraham's devotion, God made a deal with Abraham. The deal, or *covenant*, promised that Abraham's descendents (Jews) would receive the land of Canaan, or Israel, which became known as the *Promised Land*.

Delivering the Ten Commandments: Moses receives God's message

Judaism is a monotheistic religion. The Hebrew Bible tells us that God is a jealous god. Most ancient Israelites weren't as obedient as Abraham, and God punished them for their disobedience. In an effort to set them straight, God routinely punished the Israelites and sent a series of prophets to relay God's messages. Punishments often allowed other nations to conquer the Israelites. On one occasion, God sent Moses to rescue God's people from captivity in Egypt. After successfully escaping from Egypt, perhaps around 1400 to 1200 B.C., while on their way to the Promise Land, God gave Moses Ten Commandments, or the *Decalogue* (ten laws), on tablets of stone. These commandments, prohibiting murder, adultery, theft, polytheism, and lying, among other prescriptions, established an ethical code of conduct for the ancient Israelites to follow.

The temple's destruction and exile

Following a number of Jewish patriarchs and matriarchs who led the Israelites through a minefield of obstacles, King David (c. 1000–961 B.C.) established a unified kingdom of Israel. His son King Solomon succeeded him and built the first Jewish temple in the Jerusalem to house the Ark of the Covenant in which the Ten Commandments were stored. After King Solomon's rule ended in 922 B.C., the kingdom split in two: The northern kingdom of Israel had its capital at Samaria, and the southern kingdom of Judah had its capital in Jerusalem.

Because the Israelites refused to obey divine law, God allowed the Neo-Babylonians to conquer Israel in 586 B.C. and to destroy the first temple. Thousands of Israelites were carted off to Babylon as slaves. The armies of Cyrus defeated Babylonia in 538 B.C., and the Iranian king allowed the return of Jews to Israel and supported the reconstruction of the second temple, which was completed in 516 B.C. (see Chapter 4).

Judaism evolves

In the postexilic period, Judaism began to take a new shape. Although the Torah had been around for a few centuries, religious scholars compiled it during this time. Exposure to Zoroastrianism and other beliefs in Babylonia (see Chapter 20) accounted for new notions of angels, Satan, immortality of the soul, and an afterlife.

The hope of a Messiah

In times of extreme adversity, such as the exile, the Israelites clung to the hope that a savior called the Messiah, meaning the *anointed one,* would arrive to set everything right. The Israelites believed the Messiah would defeat their enemies and restore Israel. Jews began to await the Messiah's coming.

Rabbinic Judaism

After the Romans destroyed the second temple at Jerusalem in 70 A.D. (see Chapter 4), Judaism, as we know it today, began to take form. Rabbis — teachers and scholars of the holy scriptures — emerged as central figures in religious life, and synagogues grew in importance to replace the temple as a central place of worship.

Judaism in the 21st century

Today Israelis (and other Jews worldwide) practice Judaism in a number of forms. For more on Judaism, see *Judaism For Dummies* by Ted Falcon and David Blatner (Wiley Publishing, Inc.).

Orthodox Judaism

Orthodox Jews form a branch that follows strict traditional practices and beliefs. These Jews often devote themselves to prayer, study of the Torah, and adherence to prescribed dietary laws. Men and women are separated in the synagogue.

Reform Judaism

In the 18th century, a type of enlightenment movement spread across Europe that persuaded many Jews to abandon the belief in messianic redemption in favor of individual fulfillment in a secular society. Reform Jews evolving from this movement tend to be more progressive and rely more on individual autonomy than on ritual.

Conservative Judaism

If you think of Orthodox Judaism at one extreme and Reform at the other end, Conservative Judaism lies somewhere in the middle. Conservative Jews believe that Judaism is a constantly evolving belief system that can meet a community's needs. These Jews embrace components of Western modernity, including secular society, while attempting to maintain traditional Jewish practices.

Religious texts

The major sacred texts of the Jews are the following:

- The **Torah,** or the Pentateuch, comprises the first five books of the Hebrew Bible, traditionally attributed to Moses.
- The **Midrash** is the interpretation and commentaries on Jewish scriptures.
- The **Talmud** is the voluminous compilation of Oral Law gathered, interpreted, and commented on by rabbis.
- The **Mishna** is a collection of codified legal interpretations, making up part of the Talmud.

Apart from the first five books of the Torah, the *Tanakh* or Hebrew Bible, comprises 34 additional books. As a whole, the Hebrew Bible essentially comprises the same corpus as the Christian Old Testament, except some of the books are rearranged.

Holidays

Jews celebrate a number of holidays. The following are just five of the most prominent.

- **Hanukkah** is the Festival of Lights, which occurs for eight days in December near Christmas. Jews traditionally light special candles each evening and exchange gifts.

- ✔ **Passover** holiday is best known from the biblical account in Exodus. Jews held in captivity in Egypt who wiped lamb's blood over the doorway were spared God's slaying of all firstborn males. Today the holiday lasts seven to eight days.

- ✔ **Purim** is the festival commemorating Esther's loyalty to the Jewish population living in Persia (see Chapter 4). Jews often exchange food and gifts, or they give alms to the poor during this holiday.

- ✔ **Rosh Hashanah,** or the Jewish New Year, is one of the most important holidays of the year. Jews typically attend services at a synagogue where a *shofar* (ram's horn) is blown to remind devotees of repentance. Orthodox and Conservative Jews celebrate Rosh Hashanah over a period of two days while Reform Jews celebrate it on the first day.

- ✔ **Yom Kippur** means the Day of Atonement. This holiday may be the most important. Set on the Sabbath, Yom Kippur is a 25-hour period when practitioners atone for their sins, in part by fasting, attending the synagogue, and refraining from work.

The Jewish practices, texts, and beliefs of antiquity shaped Christianity in its infancy. The belief in the Messiah, for instance, paves the way for the belief that Christ was indeed the Messiah.

Christianity

Around 30 A.D., a group of Jewish discontents led by Saul (or Paul) splintered off mainstream Judaism and began spreading a religious doctrine of their own throughout the Middle East, Greece, and Rome. The world would never be the same. This Jewish splinter group became known as the Christians.

Exploring Christianity's background

Christians followed a doctrine of monotheism based on the teachings of Jesus Christ of Nazareth in the Roman province of Galilee in Palestine. To Christians, Christ — meaning *anointed one* — was the awaited Jewish Messiah. According to tradition, Jesus' birth to a virgin mother, Mary, was the result of divine intervention, which fulfilled prophecy. Jesus' miracles and teachings earned him a loyal following of 12 disciples as well as the wrath of the Romans. Jesus was crucified and, according to tradition, resurrected three days later. After his death, Christians compiled a corpus of Jesus' teachings along with other religious writings of his followers.

For the first few centuries, Christians suffered persecution under Roman rule. Then in 313 A.D., Roman emperor Constantine I converted to Christianity and established it as the state religion. As a result, Christianity spread westward through Europe and eventually to the Americas. Pockets of Christian communities remain in the Middle East although Armenia is predominately Christian.

Taking shape

As Christianity evolved, Jewish heritage already exposed to Zoroastrianism heavily influenced Christianity, absorbing notions of angels, Satan, resurrection, and an afterlife.

The Holy Trinity

Christianity basically maintains a doctrine of monotheism with a twist.

- ✔ **God the Father:** For Christians, God is Yahweh, the same god the Jews worship. (Later, Europeans who couldn't pronounce *Yahweh*, called him *Jehovah*.)

- ✔ **The Son:** Christians believe Jesus, who was born to a virgin mother, is the Son of God, at once human flesh and divine.

- ✔ **The Holy Spirit:** Christians consider the Holy Ghost or Holy Spirit as a spiritual comforter. The Holy Spirit descended on the apostles in the form of tongues, allowing them to speak in various languages.

The concept of the trinity can be difficult for non-Christians to grasp. Muslims, for instance, sometimes grapple with the concept that Jesus was the Son of God the Father while being God himself. Muslims often ask a number of questions: Is God the father of Himself? How can God have died on the cross? If God is the Father, then who is the mother?

The Savior's crucifixion

Hailing back to Abraham, Christians understand God to have sacrificed his greatest treasure, his Son, in order to wash away the sins of humankind. Whereas Muhammad and Moses can be viewed as reformers and statesmen, Jesus came to be seen a martyr and a savior of humanity. Subsequently, Christians view the cross on which Christ was martyred as a symbol of salvation.

The Golden Rule

Themes of altruism and humanitarianism run through Jesus' teachings. Among the most famous is the *Golden Rule,* which essentially means to *treat others as you would like to be treated* (variations exist in most religions).

Christianity in the 21st century

Throughout history, points of contention arose between various Christian groups, regarding religious authority and doctrine. When differences became too strained, groups splintered off (as they tend to do). Today a number of Christian groups reside in the Middle East.

Catholics

Catholicism is the oldest branch of Christianity. A number of Catholic groups exist in the Middle East. Catholics recognize the pope's authority. For more information, see *Catholicism For Dummies* by Fr. John Trigilio, Jr., and Fr. Kenneth Brighenti (Wiley Publishing, Inc.).

Maronites

The Maronites are an offshoot of Catholicism, who recognize the pope but follow a number of distinct Eastern practices, such as priests marrying and maintaining Syriac as the liturgical language. The Patriarch of Antioch leads the Maronite community, which today resides primarily in Lebanon. Lebanon's president is always a Maronite.

Orthodox Christians

Orthodox Christians differ from Catholics in that they don't obey the pope. A number of Orthodox communities still reside in the Middle East. These Christians use Greek as a liturgical language.

Jacobites (Syrian Orthodox)

Although most Christian groups believe that Christ was at once human and divine, the Jacobites maintain that Christ was entirely divine (monophysite doctrine).

Copts

The Copts are an Egyptian branch of Christianity. Like the Jacobites, the Copts believe that Christ was entirely divine. The Coptic leader is the Patriarch of Alexandria.

Religious texts

Christianity was founded on the scriptures of the Hebrew Bible, which in Christian parlance came to be known as the Old Testament. In addition, a new series of sacred texts was developed called the New Testament.

- ✔ **The Gospels** are four books recording Jesus' life and teachings, often in his own words.
- ✔ **Acts of the Apostles** is an account of the early Palestinian church and the apostle Paul's missionary work and subsequent arrest.
- ✔ **The Epistles** are a number of letters about the early church.

✔ **Revelations** is a apocalyptic text included as the last book in the New Testament.

Apart from the Old and New Testaments, the Apocrypha — a number of Hebrew religious texts — is accepted by the Catholics but considered as noncanonical in Jewish and Protestant traditions.

Holidays

The two most important Christian holidays are the following:

✔ **Christmas:** December 25 has been set as Christmas, the day Christians associate with the birth of Jesus. Because Christian tradition maintains that Jesus was born of humble birth in a manger in Bethlehem, and wise men from the East arrived bearing gifts, today Christmas routinely reflects symbols of mangers, wise men, and gifts. Christians also exchange gifts on Christmas.

✔ **Easter Sunday:** This day commemorates the resurrection of Christ on the third day after his crucifixion (Good Friday). Easter is often characterized by special services at church, giving colored eggs, and family gatherings.

Islam

Muslims see Islam as the third and final Abrahamic religion while Muhammad is the *seal* (last) of a long list of Judeo-Christian (Muslim from their point of view) prophets, including Abraham, Moses, and Jesus.

Investigating Islam's background

In the late sixth century Mecca was a backwater city. Located on the Arabian Peninsula, Mecca was a key trading center on an important caravan route, a desert oasis, and an important spiritual site for pagan pilgrims. The Meccans had no architecture, written literature, or royal heritage worth mentioning. Socially they were organized into a confederation of desert tribes. In 570 A.D., Muhammad was born into the Hashim clan of the ruling Quraysh tribe in Mecca. When his parents died early, he lived with his cousin Ali where his uncle, Ali's father, raised him.

Undergoing a sort of spiritual crisis at the age of 40, Muhammad was on retreat in Hira Cave outside Mecca in search of enlightenment when the Angel Gabriel appeared and whispered revelation from Allah (God) into Muhammad's ear.

The Prophet returned to Mecca and began reciting this revelation, known as the *Quran*. He quickly converted his wife, cousin Ali, and closest friends to Islam, which means *submission* (to Allah). As the religion continued to spread, Muslims didn't see it as a new faith but merely a continuation of the religion of Abraham, the last of the Abrahamic religions after Judaism and Christianity. Because Jews and Christians of Muhammad's time had strayed from God's original messages to those communities, God sent Muhammad to set things right once and for all with an uncorrupted message from God.

An emerging rift

In 632, Muhammad died without naming a successor. While his cousin, Ali, and son-in-law were making funeral arrangements, a council of the Prophet's companions convened without Ali and named the Muhammad's closest friend and father-in-law Abu Bakr *caliph,* or successor. The caliph was at once the spiritual and political leader of the *umma,* Muslim community. After Abu Bakr died, Umar, another companion of the Prophet, became caliph. After a Persian slave murdered Umar in 644, a third of the Prophet's companions named Uthman became caliph. Not until Uthman's execution in 656 did Ali finally get his chance to succeed the Prophet as the fourth caliph. Sunni Muslims look back nostalgically upon these four companions of the Prophet who led the *umma* and call them the *Rightly Guided Caliphs.*

Look closely at the splintering that occurred within the early caliphate between Ali and the other caliphs. As with all struggles for succession, hard feelings between winners and losers affect not only those immediately involved, but also others who get caught up in conflict, even later generations. As you may imagine, Ali's descendents and followers — later known as Shiites (or Shia) — weren't pleased with the developments. Future events later drove a wedge between these two factions, the Shiites, on one hand, and the other three caliphs' followers, the Sunnis.

A power struggle ensued between the Arab tribes. Ali shifted the capital from Medina in Arabia to Kufa, a garrison city in Mesopotamia, where he had more political and military support. Muawiya, a nephew of Uthman and governor of Damascus, contested Ali's authority but couldn't unseat the caliph. In 661, a splinter group of Muslims murdered Ali, the last of the four Rightly Guided Caliphs (see Chapter 5).

Adhering to Islam's five pillars

Five pillars support Islam's religious architecture.

- ✔ **Alms:** *Zakat*, or alms, is intended to be a type of annual charity collected from all Muslims at a rate of 2½ percent of one's wealth and distributed to the needy.

- ✔ **Fasting:** During the month of Ramadan, all healthy adult Muslims are required to fast during daylight hours.

- ✔ **Hajj:** The *Hajj* is the annual pilgrimage to Mecca and is incumbent on all healthy adult Muslims who can afford to travel at least once in their lives.

- ✔ **Prayer:** Muslims are required to pray five times a day at specific hours while facing Mecca.

- ✔ **Shahada:** The *shahada* is the Muslim creed: *There is no god but God.* (Routinely attached to that is a second creed: *and Muhammad was his messenger.*)

Aside from these five pillars, a sixth is sometimes added: *Jihad,* meaning struggle, or holy war (see Chapter 8).

Sharia: Islamic Law

Muslims believe *sharia,* or Islamic law, is divine law. The system of human interpretation of that law is called jurisprudence (*fiqh*). The primary sources for interpreting Islamic law are the Quran, Hadith, and Sunna of the Prophet. (See the section, "Sacred texts" later in this chapter.)

Muslims of the 21st century

Today the two primary classifications of Muslims are Sunni and Shiite. For more information on Islam, see *Islam For Dummies* by Malcolm Clark (Wiley Publishing, Inc.).

Sunnis

Sunnis account for about 90 percent of the Muslim population. The name Sunni originates from the *Sunna,* or tradition, of the Prophet Muhammad. Sunnis believe in the authority of the first four caliphs, and to a lesser degree of subsequent caliphates.

Shiites

Only about 10 percent of the world's Muslims are Shiite. This group doesn't recognize the legitimacy of the first three caliphs, but rather believes Ali is the legitimate heir to the Prophet. As a result, Shiites reject Sunni doctrine and follow the teachings of a number of spiritual leaders, called *imams,* descending from Ali. Shiites live primarily in Iran and Iraq, with smaller groups in Lebanon, Pakistan, and India.

Sacred texts

Because Islam follows Judaism and Christianity chronologically, you may expect the Bible to be one of the sacred texts. Technically it is. However,

Muslims believe that when God handed down the Bible to the prophets, it was a pure, sacred text. Later, Jews and Christians corrupted it. Today the Bible is damaged goods. The following, then, are the most prominent sacred texts in Islam.

- ✔ **Quran:** The Quran is Allah's message that was revealed to the Prophet Muhammad.
- ✔ **Hadith:** The Hadith, or oral traditions, are the Prophet's sayings.
- ✔ **Sunna:** The Sunna, or traditions, are the Prophet's deeds.

Medieval scholars gathered and recorded the Hadith and Sunna in voluminous collections. An entire science is dedicated to studying and validating the authenticity of these traditions.

Holidays

The three most important holidays for Muslims are the following:

- ✔ **Ramadan:** During the lunar month of Ramadan, Muslims fast during daylight hours. When the sun sets, they celebrate by breaking fast and eating special food. Prayers and special recitations of the Quran take place all month.
- ✔ **Id al-Fitr:** Muslims celebrate *Id al-Fitr,* the end of Ramadan, by breaking the fast until next year, wearing new clothes, giving to the poor, and attending Id prayers at the mosque.
- ✔ **Id al-Adha:** At the end of the Hajj, Muslims all around the world celebrate *Id al-Adha.* This holiday is characterized by slaughtering an animal (usually a goat or lamb), giving part of the meat to the poor, eating special food, and visiting friends and family. Gift are also given to children.

Chapter 20

Religions on the Edge

In This Chapter

▶ Understanding how religions on the edge ended up on the edge

▶ Getting to know the religious minorities in the Middle East

▶ Meditating on mysticism in its many forms

For every mainstream or orthodox religion in the history of the Middle East there is a plethora of variant faiths that surface on the edge. Often these religions on the edge have splintered off or parted ways from mainstream faiths over disagreements regarding practices, doctrine, or leadership. Sometimes the dominant religions have snuffed out these alternate faiths or sometimes religions on the edge simply die out due to other factors. This chapter breaks down several religions on the edge into two categories: religious minorities and mysticism.

Religious Minorities

Interestingly enough, in the Medieval period some religious scholars collected data on heterodox faiths and have left records of that compilation. Some of the most vehemently intolerant compilers recorded these variant faiths in encyclopedias of heresies called *heresiographies*. These collections described the *deviant* practices of each faith. Other belief systems lived more or less unhindered by the dominant religious communities although at one time or another, most minorities have suffered from some sort of persecution. This section discusses several religious minorities that you can currently find throughout the Middle East.

Ahmadiyya

At the turn of the 20th century in the Punjab province of India, a new movement developed that came to be known as the *Ahmadiyya*. The movement's Muslim founder Mirza Ghulam Ahmad blended elements of Islam, Christianity, and Hinduism. Followers later believed he was a prophet of God. Considered apostate by many Muslims, the Ahmadiyya movement has been outlawed in Pakistan. The current Ahmadiyya population, most of which live in Pakistan, may be as high as 10 million.

Alawites

As many as 1.8 million Alawites live in Syria with smaller numbers in Lebanon and Turkey. Although Alawites see themselves as Shiites, many mainstream Muslims consider them heretics. This faith originated in the ninth century. Alawite doctrine maintains that Ali, the first Shiite imam (religious leader), was a prophet of God and includes two additional pillars to the five pillars of Islam (see Chapter 19) including devotion to Ali and jihad, or struggle.

Alawites celebrate Christmas in addition to Shiite holidays. Syrian President Bashar al-Assad belongs to this branch, as did his father Hafiz al-Assad.

Baha'is

Bahaullah founded the Baha'i faith in the 19th century. Baha'i doctrine maintains the legitimacy of Judeo-Christian and Muslim prophets, the supremacy of one Creator God, and the unity of all religions.

The administrative center of Baha'ism is in Haifa, Israel, although the majority of the 5 million Baha'is live in Iran and India. During the Islamic Revolution in Iran (see Chapter 18), the extremist leadership carried out a massive campaign of persecution against Baha'is, including murder and imprisonment.

Druze

For fear of religious persecution, the Druze faith has been shrouded in secrecy. The Druze hail their origins back to the tenth-century Egyptian caliph Hakim who assumed power and undertook a path of religious intolerance — relatively rare among Muslim rulers — by persecuting Jews and Christians, and destroying synagogues and churches, including the Church of the Holy Sepulcher in Jerusalem. Hakim also claimed to be a reincarnation of God but was assassinated in 1021.

Like other religions on the edge of Islam, many "mainstream" Muslims do not consider the Druze Muslim. The Druze believe that apart from the exoteric messages of the Bible and the Quran, luminaries from each generation can provide the full meaning of sacred texts. In addition, the Druze faith has its own sacred literature.

Approximately one million Druze live in the Middle East, primarily in Syria, Lebanon, and Jordan. In Israel, the Druze have gained citizenship and serve in the army.

Ismailis

Fleeing from Iran under the British protection after siding with the colonialists, Ismailis resettled in British India. Ismailis comprise a branch of Shiism that has played a prominent role in Islamic history in Egypt (the Fatamids), Iran (the Assassins), and Syria (see Chapter 5). Ismaili doctrine involves a focus on the esoteric teachings passed down orally. Ismailis believe in the infallibility of their *imam* (religious leader), who exists in hiding.

More recently, Ismaili community leaders, the *Aga Khans* (religious leaders), have contributed to the formation of Pakistan and have undertaken education and humanitarian activities in developing nations. Ismaili communities also have at times been severely persecuted. Today Ismailis number approximately 2 million, and pockets of Ismailis exist in India and Pakistan, and to a lesser extent in Syria, Central Asia, Iran, and Yemen.

Mandeans

The Mandean religion dates to the first or second century A.D. Mandean doctrine contains elements of Judaism, Christianity, Islam, and Zoroastrianism. Mandeans have separate sacred texts, and John the Baptist is a central figure. They believe the cosmos is divided into the realm of light and the realm of darkness, and they perform ritual baptisms several times a year. Some 20,000 Mandeans reside in southern Iraq and southwestern Iran.

Zoroastrians

When Islam came on the scene in the seventh century, Zoroastrianism was the predominant religion in Iran. As Islamic rule spread, Zoroastrians moved, fled, assimilated, or converted to Islam. In the tenth century, a community of Zoroastrians migrated to India, where they became known as Parsis. Zoroaster founded this religion about 1800 to 1500 B.C. Zoroastrianism contains the following components.

> ✔ **A Doctrine of Dualism** insists that a constant conflict exists between Ahura Mazda (the Lord of Wisdom) who promotes good and Angra Mainyu (Destructive Spirit) who opts for evil. Humans who align themselves with good reach heaven, and those who choose evil land in hell.

> ✔ **Elaborate purification rituals** performed by priests, or magi.
>
> ✔ **Sacred texts** written in Old and Middle Persian.

Today about 74,000 Zoroastrians live in India and 5,000 in Pakistan. Approximately 45,000 still in Iran have suffered persecution under the Islamic Republic although technically the Islamic Republic's constitution protects them as a protected minority alongside Jews and Christians, who also have been persecuted by the mullas.

Mysticism

Simply put, *mysticism* is the belief system that maintains individuals can have a direct relationship or experience with God without performing external rituals, like praying, fasting, studying texts, attending traditional ceremonies, and so on. You may think of it as a shortcut with little need for formality, often eliminating the need for a middle man (or middle woman for that matter). Mysticism has remained on the edge of orthodoxy because practitioners claim this experience can't be explained in the sacred texts, witnessed, or controlled. Mysticism is often boundless, fluid, and on occasion spontaneous.

For its part, orthodoxy has on occasion tried to reign in mysticism, control or denounce it, and even persecute its followers. Historically, mysticism, or elements of mystical practice, has surfaced in most religions. When strains of mysticism bled into orthodox practice, orthodox leaders often reacted by taking steps to weed it out. Ironically, on other occasions, orthodox members of religion have embraced mysticism. Therefore, depending on the circumstances and perspective, mysticism can be on the edge or at the center of traditional religious practice. The following are three features often associated with mysticism.

> ✔ **Knowledge of God:** Mystics regularly seek esoteric knowledge of God (or the Cosmos, or Universe).
>
> ✔ **Master:** A master, living or deceased, often teaches mysticism to a devotee.
>
> ✔ **Union with God:** One common goal of mysticism has been *Union with God*. Mystics often describe this union as ecstasy.

Historically, mainstream religions often comprised rigid rituals and specific practices, and more often than not, literate, elite males controlled them. The more flexible, less prescribed, mysticism has tended to attract women, and illiterate and poor adherents. The remainder of this chapter discusses a few of the most important dimensions and manifestations of mysticism throughout the Middle East's history.

Asceticism

You've probably seen Hindu ascetics on TV, who wear long, knotted hair, twist themselves into a pretzel, and sit in a glass box at the bottom of swimming pools for hours. Asceticism basically refers to a system of self-denial or self-mortification to attain spiritual realization. The notion of ascetic practices for religious purposes is an old one and cuts across religious and geographical boundaries. You can glean accounts of ascetic practices from a number of sources, including canonical texts (like the Bible) and hagiographies (biographies of saints). A handful of prominent examples of ascetic practice include

- Jesus fasted for 40 days and 40 nights.
- Muhammad first received revelation while on a spiritual retreat at Hira Cave outside Mecca (see Chapter 5).
- Muslim mystics of medieval Iran practiced breath control, sat near fires in the hot sun, and hung upside down all night.
- Christian ascetics on the Arabian Peninsula often retreated to the solitude of caves for long periods of time.
- The Essenes, the authors of the Dead Sea Scrolls, were a Jewish ascetic group that lived an austere, reclusive lifestyle near the Dead Sea (see Chapter 22).

Although mysticism and asceticism need not overlap, mystics frequently undertook the rigors of asceticism in order to free the spirit from the flesh.

Christian mysticism

Like other forms of mysticism, esoteric knowledge and union with God were routinely stressed as goals for Christian mystics. Women regularly turned to mysticism as a form of spiritual expression. One such manifestation for female mystics was to commit to a spiritual marriage with Jesus (or God). In the Medieval period, Christian mystics lived in various parts of the Middle East, including Byzantium (Turkey), Egypt, and Spain. Today Christian mysticism exists in a variety of forms.

Gnosticism

The Gnostics were Judeo-Christian worshippers who were heavily influenced by Neo-platonic thought in late antiquity. Throughout the Middle East, a variety of sects sought intuitive knowledge (*gnosis*) of the divine. The most famous Gnostic texts were discovered near the town of Nag Hammadi in Upper Egypt in 1945. Women in Gnostic communities tended to gain an elevated or equal status to that of men. One Gnostic poem called *The Thunder, Perfect Mind* was written more than 1,600 years ago in the female first person. (See Chapter 22 for more information on the poem.)

Hasidism

Hasidism refers to a branch of Judaism founded in the early 18th century by a Polish rabbi named Israel Baal Shem Tov. Hasidic Judaism mixes mysticism with a commitment to internal and external dimensions of the Torah. Hasidic Jews believe that all Jews, regardless of education or training, can experience a personal relationship with God. The community is based in Israel, but also has a large following in the United States, especially in Brooklyn, New York.

Kabbalism

Kabbalism is a form of Jewish mysticism. Adherents believe that you can tap the universe's esoteric wisdom by following a series of meditative exercises and techniques passed along from master to student. Only a handful of select practitioners earn the chance to study these techniques and gain access to the associated knowledge. Today's Kabbalists trace the belief system's origins back to Abraham. The *Zohar*, a 14th-century Aramaic mystical treatise, is the primary sacred text for Kabbalists.

Sufism

Sufism is Islamic mysticism. Traditionally, Sufis have traced the origins of Sufism back to the Prophet Muhammad who received revelation while on a spiritual retreat in Hira Cave outside Mecca (see Chapter 19). The following three components of Sufism are common although not universal: knowledge of God, spiritual humility or poverty, and union with God. Sufi interpretations of the Quran substantiate their claims. Today Sufism is still practiced in the Middle East.

Chapter 21

The Family: The Hub of Middle Eastern Life

· ·

· ·

Gender issues and family life in the Middle East have been hot topics of debate in the past decade. For example, the Taliban's treatment of women and girls, denying them access to jobs and education, and subjecting them to rape, forced marriages, public beatings, torture, and execution shocked the international community and raised awareness on gender issues. You're also probably familiar with stories about human rights abuses against women in Saudi Arabia, Egypt, Iran, and elsewhere. Honor killings, beatings, polygamy, and female genital mutilation have earned plenty of attention.

Although these issues are certainly of grave concern, more mundane and widespread troubles related not only to women but to populations as a whole — such as overpopulation, lack of education, and health issues — serve as major obstacles to social improvement and development. This chapter discusses various dimensions of gender issues and challenges in the Middle East within the framework of the family and society in general.

Family Dynamics: Love, Honor, and Responsibility

To a large degree, the family unit is the bedrock on which Middle Eastern society is structured. Muslims believe in protecting the family's integrity as essential to maintaining social order.

The family unit

A traditional family unit includes a husband, wife, and children, and also the extended family: grandparents, uncles and aunts, and cousins. The family unit has traditionally been the primary institution to provide economic and emotional support, as well as social and religious values in the Middle East. Because the family unit's reputation and honor has widespread implications for a number of members, the family's honor has commonly superceded individuality (see the "Honor killings" section later in the chapter).

Mom's at the center

Although the mother is regularly in charge of the family unit's day-to-day activities, as is the case in most cultures, patriarchal structures dominate in the Middle East. In many households, little takes place without the mother's approval.

But Dad rules

Notwithstanding the mother's central role in Middle Eastern families, society is still structured so that men are expected to provide and women to bear children.

In the Muslim World, children's names and inheritance originate and pass through male lineage, so the Muslim world is *patrilineal*. Arab sons are named as sons (*bin*) of their fathers. For example, because King Abdullah of Jordan is the late King Hussein's son, he is called Abdullah *bin* Hussein.

A snapshot of a Punjabi kitchen

The dynamics of the extended family unit in the Middle East include children, parents, aunts and uncles, grandparents, and cousins. In the Pakistani province of the Punjab, the family unit typically involves a number of nuclear families living under one roof. Each nuclear family — mom, dad, and a few kids — live in one bedroom. Each bedroom is like a dormitory with one or two beds, a TV, and chest for dishes, clothes, and documents. Toys and other items are stuffed beneath the bed. A general reception room is off the house's front entrance where families can entertain guests. Each family uses a communal bathroom or two, and shares a tiny kitchen.

Punjabi kitchens usually are set up for cooking, not eating. A pair of gas burners sits on the floor, and women crouch to cook entire meals there. The kitchens are extremely small, and each nuclear family takes turns cooking. When the meal is finished, a cloth is spread on the bed or in another dining area, and the nuclear family eats. As one may expect, conflicts between extended family members often break out over a host of day-to-day issues, but the grandfather (and to a lesser extent the grandmother) has a final say in settling disputes.

The ins and outs of marriage

Because the family unit is a central component of Middle Eastern society, marriage is a crucial stage in life. Religious law typically regulates marriage and divorce although secular law and traditions continue to be influential.

Marriage — until death do us part?

In the Middle East, a written contract characterizes marriage. Arranged marriages are still common although modern couples nowadays meet in a variety of ways. Parents often bring first cousins together to wed. Although some children are married at an early age (an Afghan father once tried to marry his 1-year-old daughter to my 9-month-old son), more modern, progressive families tend to hold off weddings until their children have been educated, and until the men have secured gainful employment.

Although Islamic tradition has outlined a number of guidelines for marriage, tribal, ethnic, and local practices often trump Islamic tradition. For example, according to the Quran, a girl has the right to accept or reject a spouse that her parents have selected. In practice, the parents' selection is commonly unquestionable.

Divorce — click your heels three times

Muslim men have a great deal of latitude in divorcing their wives. Even though divorce is uncommon, men don't have to provide an explanation for wanting a divorce. Traditionally, a man needs only to announce three times before witnesses that he divorces his wife. On the other hand, wives have the right to divorce only under certain circumstances: husband's impotency, abandonment, insanity, and apostasy are among them.

Jewish law also allows a man to divorce his wife for any reason. She may have burned his meal, or perhaps the husband has set his sights on a younger, more attractive woman. According to tradition, if the wife has been unfaithful, the husband has to divorce her, like it or not. The wife may obtain a divorce in a few cases, such as if he fails to provide food, clothes, or sexual satisfaction.

Family planning — large families still rule

One of the Middle East's most pressing issues is overpopulation. Development in the region simply can't keep up with population growth rates. The less-educated and more-traditional families continue to have large numbers of children. Many Muslims associate large families with Islamic practice. Educated women, on the other hand, tend to break the cycle of poverty by having fewer children, contributing to the household income, and securing better health-care and education for their own children.

Polygamy — not a common practice

One general misconception in the West about the Middle East is centered on polygamy. The Quran allows a man to take up to four wives, provided he can care for them equally. Western critics routinely cite polygamy as a major factor for the Middle East's social ills. The reality is that polygamy isn't widespread.

Although I've been traveling, studying, and conducting research in the region for 20 years, I've only met two men who had two wives. One was a Kashmiri man who'd been living in the United States for nearly a decade. When his Muslim wife refused to leave Kashmir to join him, he married an American wife. The second was a 50-year old Afghan amputee who'd lost his leg in the war with the Soviets. He liked to brag that he had two wives.

Apart from a few Yemeni Jews who believe in the plurality of wives, the practice has been abandoned for centuries in Judaism.

Women in the workplace

Women have always worked somewhere — in the fields, at home, and in the family business to name just a few locations. Since the 1950s and '60s, economic pressure has forced Near Eastern women from the home and into the workplace. Today you can find working women in the Middle East in a number of varying occupations. Women are sweepers, housewives, lawyers, professors, slaves (or bonded workers), actresses, and politicians.

Education — still lagging behind the boys

Although strides have been made in the past decades, the education of girls still lags behind that of boys at almost every level of society. Contact with the West and internal reflection have increased the awareness that parents need to educate their daughters. Many experts agree that in order for countries in the region to compete in the 21st century, they need an educated female workforce.

The political arena — acting as public servants

Women throughout parts of the Middle East have participated in the political process. Aside from exercising the right to vote in most countries, women have also held ministerial posts or parliamentary seats from Afghanistan to Egypt and Algeria. Female prime ministers have governed in Turkey, Israel, and Pakistan (see Chapters 6 and 14).

For more insight into the lives of Middle Eastern women, check out *The Daughter of Persia*. As a daughter of one of the last Qajar princes, Sattareh Farman Farmaian's book describes her childhood in a small Iranian harem.

Watch out for the fizz: Birth control in soft drinks

Gender issues in the Middle East are complex and multifaceted. Many people, educated and noneducated alike, become defensive when Westerners discuss the treatment of women in Middle Eastern society.

For example, a few years ago I gave a presentation to a group of Pakistani intellectuals — most of whom had traveled, studied, or lived in the United States — on the topic of gender images in Pakistani textbooks. I primarily pointed out the images of girls and women in children's books. After I'd finish the presentation, a 45-minute question-and-answer session turned into an assault on American morals. Some of the comments included

✔ Gender equality, one female educator told me, in America was far from ideal, so why not focus on American textbooks?

✔ The greatest social problem in the United States was the independence given to women, which led to libertinism, which in turn led to infidelity, divorce, teen pregnancy, widowhood, prostitution, and a whole range of other problems (including global warming, I suppose).

✔ All America's social ills could be cured, one man confided in us as he had his barber in the United States, if birth control pills were to become a common ingredient in soft drinks.

✔ Although Pakistan lagged behind the United States in many ways, Pakistan was far superior in morals, particularly with regard to women.

✔ American culture allows young girls to date and have intercourse, which leads to teen pregnancy and all the problems associated with it: abortion, adoption, single motherhood, broken families, divorce, and poverty (don't forget inflation and budget deficits). Pakistani parents, on the other hand, protect their daughters by keeping them safely at home away from boys and mischief.

✔ Because as mothers, women have to sacrifice, one man explained, parents begin training their daughters as girls to the value of sacrifice at an early age. For example, girls eat meals only after their brothers have finished. (One female professor rolled her eyes at this statement.)

In fact, most Pakistanis present were in agreement that the eventual downfall of the United States would stem, not from its Middle Eastern foreign policy, but from the liberalization of its women.

The Lives of Women: Separation and Modesty

In order to maintain social order and retain the family unit's integrity, Muslim society has by and large attempted to protect women from men and from themselves. One noteworthy manifestation of this protection is the tradition of separation of the sexes. For most of their adult lives, women remain segregated from men with the exception of male family members.

The tradition of separation and modesty isn't truly the imposition of the will of men against the will of women. On the contrary, often women are the main propagators of the gender practices. In cases where women remain in seclusion at home, the responsibility of shopping falls squarely on the men. I've known cases where progressive husbands have tried to convince their wives to take an active role in society (travel, shop, meet people, attend functions, and so on), but the female family members resist. When conservative women do leave the home, they often maintain the separation by wearing a veil.

The veil in its many manifestations

The veil is a multifaceted issue that is seldom entirely understood. Western observers predicted that as soon as the Taliban fell in 2001, women would stop wearing the *burqah* (long, all encompassing garment). Despite the disappearance of the Taliban, Afghan women continue to wear this garment today. Some dynamics of the veil in the Middle East worth mentioning include

- ✔ Islamic tradition is the default response given to explain use of the veil although non-Muslim women wear the veil as well.

- ✔ In Morocco, women started wearing the *jallaba* (a dress that entirely covers the women, including the head and face) as protection against foreigners when the French conquered Morocco in the early 20th century.

- ✔ Some women argue that the veil is worn for style.

- ✔ Many women wear the veil as personal preference, modesty, or custom. You can commonly see mothers wearing conservative headdress, and their daughters using much more liberal head coverings, or no veil at all.

- ✔ Some women wear veils as protection against harassment of men, religious police, or other extremists.

When Muslim women leave the house, they select an appropriate garment. Inside the home, traditional families still separate women from the men when guests arrive. Male guests enter a reception room while female guests join the women in other parts of the house.

Gender politics in the extreme

Forces in Muslim society often undertake extreme measures to maintain social order and to protect what they perceive as the honor of the family and of women.

Religious police

Countries like Iran, Saudi Arabia, and Afghanistan under the Taliban have religious police, a body commonly called the Prevention of Vice and the Promotion of Virtue that enforces religious law. Among other duties, these police make sure women conform to accepted religious norms.

In March 2002, Saudi religious police blocked an exit of a burning girls' school, preventing the girls from fleeing the fire because they weren't wearing the appropriate Islamic attire presentable in public. Although 15 girls lie dying in the fire, outside the religious police dutifully busied themselves by beating young girls for not wearing the *abaya* (black robe and headdress). Many Saudis were outraged, and the Saudi government took some steps to reduce the power of the religious police over girls' schools.

Honor killings

Across much of the Middle East, Muslim family members sometimes take the law into their own hands in order to save the family's *honor*. Fathers, brothers, sons, mothers, mothers-in-law, and others resort to violence to enforce appropriate behavior of the women. When the enforcement turns deadly, as is all too often the case, the term *honor killing* is applied. Honor killings are regularly based on suspicion of illicit relations by any female in the family, which is enough to warrant death. Male and female suspects both are commonly killed.

Female genital mutilation

Female genital mutilation, sometimes called female circumcision, is some variation of a surgery that removes the clitoris and/or labia. Although the practice is considered Islamic, Muslims and Christians both carry out female genital mutilation. The practice is common from Yemen to Egypt. Midwives or female family members typically conduct this surgery under unsanitary conditions with razor blades, knives, or scissors.

Parents argue that if their daughters don't undergo this surgery, the girls won't find suitable husbands. The surgery is commonly conducted against the patient/victim's wishes, and occasionally the girl dies as a result. Although governments like Egypt have banned the practice, an estimated 6,000 women and girls undergo the surgery daily.

Chapter 22

Language and Literature

1 can't stress strongly enough the importance of language and linguistics in the Middle East. When I was teaching English to Afghan refugees in Peshawar, Pakistan, in 1987 and 1988, a group of students once asked me if I'd read the Quran. I told them I'd read it twice. They were ecstatic until they realized I'd read the English translation. "Oh," one disappointed student responded, "You have to read it in Arabic." I didn't understand what difference it could make. Boy, was I ever wrong!

About 13 years later while attending a workshop on Afghan textbooks in Islamabad, Pakistan, an Afghan educator asked me what regional languages I knew for my research on Afghan education. I told him I could read Arabic, Persian, Urdu, and some Punjabi among a few others. He shook his head sadly and informed me that if I couldn't read Pashtu, my research was doomed to failure. (A few weeks later I began studying Pashtu at the University of Peshawar.)

Language in the Middle East is tied to ethnicity, religion, politics, identity, and even the military. Hebrew, for instance, had been a dead language for nearly 2,000 years until Jews revived it as a symbol of the unity and survival of the Jewish people in the fledgling Israeli nation in the 20th century.

Although the Quran has been translated into countless languages, the prominence of Arabic in Islamic tradition is unquestionable. The Taliban were an almost entirely Pashtu-speaking entity that attempted to rule by Pashtun tribal code mixed with Islamic tradition at the expense of other ethnic groups. Kurdish speakers have spent more than three quarters of a century attempting to secure a Kurdish homeland in the mountainous region between Iraq and Turkey. Not surprisingly, General Pervez Musharraf gave his first televised speech after seizing power in Pakistan in an October 1999 coup first in English, and then in Urdu. He wanted to justify his actions to the world before explaining them to the nation (not to mention that English is the language of the Pakistani army). These few examples illustrate how ethnicity, religions, politics, identity, and the military are closely linked to Middle Eastern languages and culture.

Language, Ethnicity, and Tradition: You Are What You Speak

A great tension exists between different ethnic groups in the Middle East. In South Asia, for example, Pashtuns, Punjabis, Sindhis, Hazaras, Tajiks, and other groups are in constant conflict. In 1988, I went to a small Afghan hospital in Peshawar to visit one of my Afghan students who'd developed typhoid fever. I was wearing Pakistani clothes, including a *tope*, a Pakistani hat. When I announced to the Pashtun *chokidar* (gatekeeper) in my flawed Urdu of my intentions to visit a patient, he abruptly informed me in his equally flawed Urdu that visiting hours were three hours off. Because I'd walked about 45 minutes to get there, I decided to squat down beside the chokidar, wait, and practice my Urdu on him. After I finally succeeded in getting the reserved Pashtun gatekeeper to talk about his family, tea, upcoming Ramadan holiday, and other small talk, he asked me where I was from. When I told him the United States, he leaped up, shook my hand, expressed his pleasure in meeting me, and informed me that I was free to enter the hospital. He added that he was sorry for the delay, but said, "I thought you were Punjabi."

I design this section on ethnicity, not to express the scope of tension between ethnic groups across the region (an endless topic touched upon throughout the historical sections), but rather to help explain the importance of language and its link to ethnicity.

The importance of Arabic: The language of the Quran

What's an Arab? This question is a good place to start. Arabs are individuals who speak Arabic as a native tongue. For this reason, I say *you are what you speak*. Arabic describes the language they speak, whereas Arab refers to the people. So for instance, you can say an *Arabic* (language) newspaper, but *Arab* food or *Arab* customs.

Even more diverse than the different English dialects spoken in Australia, Ireland, England, Canada, New Zealand, and the United States, Arabic has a vast array of dialects so distinct that an uneducated farmer from Morocco likely couldn't communicate with an illiterate farmer from Lebanon. The literary language of pre-Islamic poetry, the Quran, and classical Arabic literature has survived today in a version called Modern Standard Arabic, or *fusha*. This formal Arabic is in many ways an artificial language because almost no one really grows up speaking Modern Standard Arabic at home (although most Arabs try to convince you their dialect is closest to fusha).

Modern Standard Arabic is used primarily for official speeches, television newscasts, newspapers and magazines, books, and so forth. The language barrier between dialects, therefore, is overcome through the medium of Modern Standard Arabic. If the Moroccan farmer and Lebanese farmer have graduated high school, they're likely well versed in fusha and could communicate with one another, read the newspaper, and comprehend television newscasts from other Arab countries.

Fewer than half the world's Muslims are Arabs. Most Muslims grow up speaking any number of languages other than Arabic. In Iran, most Muslims speak Persian; in Afghanistan, Pushtu, Dari (a dialect of Persian), or Uzbek; in Pakistan, perhaps Sindhi, Baluchi, or Punjabi; in India, Hindi, Kashmiri, or Urdu; in Bangladesh, Bengali. . . You get the picture. Because Muhammad handed down the Quran in Arabic, you can only appreciate the resonant eloquence of the Quran when you recite it. In fact, even today a superb Quranic recitation can drive Muslims to tears.

From the first generation of Muslims, the duty of preserving the Quran has fallen to a Quranic specialist called *hafiz* (meaning *one who memorizes*). These specialists memorize the Quran by heart, recite it, and pass it on orally to others. In this way, Muslims have maintained the holy text's resonant eloquence and assured themselves that no part of the Quran has been altered (a huge concern for Muslims). For these reasons, the prestige of Arabic and oral recitation have remained an essential component of Islamic tradition.

The Muslim dilemma of Arabic stems from the fact that the majority of Muslims don't speak Arabic. Given Arabic's special status in Islamic tradition, the consensus among Muslims is that any translation of the Quran into another language dilutes the meaning and full impact of the Quran's message, not to mention the loss of resonant eloquence that you can only attain in Arabic. Many Muslims believe that reading the Quran in translation to understand it is less of a blessing than reading it in the original Arabic, even if you can't understand the meaning. Therefore, reading for prestige (or blessing) takes precedence over reading for meaning. Today you can find children all across the non-Arab Muslim World reading and reciting the Quran in an almost flawless Arabic under the patient guidance of a mullah (who has normally donated his time) even though these young children don't have a clue what they're saying.

Persian and other Middle Eastern languages

The you-are-what-you-speak paradigm that I present in this chapter works pretty well for Berbers (speaking Berber), Pashtuns (speaking Pashtu), Panjabis (speaking Panjabi), Uzbeks (speaking Uzbek), Kurds (speaking Kurdish) and so on (see Chapter 23). But the pattern begins to break down with Persian. The term Persian generally refers to an Iranian who speaks the Persian language, also known as Farsi. Not all Iranians are Persian though. Some are Arabs, Turkish, Kurdish, or Baluchi. In Tajikistan, most people speak Tajik, which is a dialect of Persian. Also a large number of Afghans speak a dialect of Persian they usually call Dari. In both cases, we refer to those people as Tajiks. Afghan, on the other hand, is a term generally used to refer to any ethnic group in Afghanistan, although some use it to refer specifically to Pashtuns. When we get to Modern Hebrew, the whole theory falls completely apart because the native speakers of Hebrew are Jews, (primarily Israeli Jews). In fact, before the late 19th century, almost no one grew up speaking Hebrew at home.

Waking the dead: The revival of Hebrew

When the Romans destroyed the temple at Jerusalem in 70 A.D., Jews dispersed to the Diaspora (see Chapter 4) ceased speaking Hebrew in everyday life and used it mostly in prayers and literature. The revival of spoken Hebrew is due in great part to Eliezer Ben-Yehuda, who emigrated from Russia to Palestine in 1881, and promoted the use of Hebrew in everyday life. The use of Hebrew became a defining trait of Zionism, and Jewish youngsters in Eastern Europe studied Hebrew when preparing to immigrate to Palestine. Jews returning to Israel in the 20th century spoke Yiddish, Ladino, Arabic, as well as the many languages of their countries of origin. However, intensive efforts were made to teach all of them Hebrew, and the revival of the language became complete. When the State of Israel was founded in 1948, Hebrew was decreed as one of its two official languages (the other one, Arabic, being the language of the Arab Palestinians who remained in Israel). For more about Hebrew, see *Hebrew For Dummies* by Jill Suzanne Jacobs (Wiley Publishing, Inc.).

A Little Background on the Literature of the Middle East

Reading about the Middle East is the next best thing to being there. The considerable literary wealth of the Near East is locked away in a treasure chest at a bookstore or library nearest you. In order to help you unlock this literary treasure chest, I provide a few clues in this section.

Talking the talk: The oral tradition

In the ancient world, people figured out how to speak before they developed a system for writing. Therefore, Middle Easterners first told their tales by word of mouth. Storytellers memorized the best stories and retold them again and again. Some of the best storytellers traveled from village to village, city to city, and told tales for a living. Storytellers also collected various tales from the areas they visited, translated them if necessary, and adapted them as needed for the appropriate contexts. For this reason, the ancient Middle East was replete with entertaining stories and tales about gods and goddesses, creation, heroes, dwarfs, kings and queens, mythical creatures, and adventures of suffering and triumph, all rivaling those of Hollywood today.

Putting pen to paper

About 5,000 years ago, the people of the Near East developed a number of writing systems for documenting an array of items: business dealings, kings' exploits, and other stories — whatever they wanted to record. But not everyone had access to an education or training on how to operate that writing system. Usually reading and writing were skills only acquired by the elite. So converting the majority of people from an oral transmission form of storytelling to a written form was slow. (Even today millions of Middle Easterners can't read well enough to get through a newspaper article.)

From those earliest writing systems (see Chapter 4) to the present, writers have composed countless volumes of texts in a number of languages covering a whole host of genres. The next few sections explore a number of genres and subgenres to give you an idea of what kinds of Middle Eastern texts are available, why they were written, and even a few examples that you may want to check out.

Ancient Literature

The ancient literature is rich and extensive. Much of the extant literature from this period is religious in nature with priests or temple scribes documenting it. Today we call these stories mythology, which is a word reserved for "someone else's" religion that has usually fallen out of use. (For more on the traditional Judeo-Christian religious texts for this period, see Chapter 19.)

Texts began to turn up all across the Middle East in the 19th and 20th centuries. In Babylonia alone, archaeologists and even farmers discovered thousands of cuneiform tablets. Other key discoveries include

✔ **1928:** On the north Syrian coast, a farmer plows up a grave. A subsequent excavation leads to the discovery of a cemetery of vaulted tombs and the ancient city-state of Ugarit (see Chapter 4) where thousands of Ugaritic texts dating back some 3,400 years were safeguarded. Many of the texts are legal or diplomatic documents, dictionaries, and lists of merchandise. Archaeologists find in the main temple's library 15 clay tablets containing Canaanite mythical literature likely transmitted orally for centuries before finally being written down. The stories deal with a number of topics, including a king's search for an heir (*Kirta*), dealing with a son's death, and focusing on the god Baal's triumph over his enemy.

✔ **1945:** Near the town of Nag Hammadi in Upper Egypt, an Arab farmer smashes a clay pot buried near a boulder with his pick. The pot contains the Nag Hammadi Library (which wasn't a library at all but a collection of codices). Around the year 390 A.D., the monks from the St. Pachomius monastery hid these 13 papyrus codices containing some 50 Gnostic texts.

✔ **1947:** At a spot called Qumran on the edge of the Dead Sea in Israel, an Arab teenage goatherd tosses a rock into a cave to scare out a straying goat and hears the crash of a clay container. Upon further investigation, he finds seven scrolls that had been housed in the cave for nearly two millennia. Later searches of other caves at Qumran uncover the existence of numerous leather and papyrus scrolls and fragments written by a community of Jews called Essenes. The scrolls document particular books of the Hebrew Bible, apocrypha, and Essene literature, including devotional poetry, commentaries, and community rules.

The discovery of this ancient literature provides a window into the past, allowing modernity a better understanding of these ancient peoples and their beliefs and culture. Oddly enough, many of the themes of interest today cut across the span of thousands of years to reflect issues that the people of the ancient Middle East were also concerned about, including death, adventure, liberty, creation, friendship, and, in essence, the meaning of life.

Read about some examples of ancient Middle-Eastern literature in the following list:

✔ ***The Assyrian Tree:*** This Parthian (see Chapter 4) poem from the first century B.C. describes an elaborate conversation between a date-palm tree and a goat, each boasting of their superior usefulness, as follows:

> Date palm: "I am better than you in so many ways. They make ships of me and shoes people wear to chase you . . . ropes . . . to tie your legs. I am clubs they hold to break your neck. I am fuel for fires to roast your flesh."

> Goat: "You are worthless, just straw and wood. You are . . . forever in one place. I roam the mountains, and graze in the valleys. I produce milk, which people offer the gods . . . wool for robes. . . . My flesh is eaten by kings and nobles . . . my bones become hand grips on utensils to cut you." [Translated by Dr. Jamsheed Choksy.]

✔ *Enuma Elish:* This Sumerian and Akkadian (see Chapter 4) creation story was composed about 3,000 B.C. and outlines the struggle between two major deities — Tiamat and her consort Kingu who represent huge intermingling bodies of water — and their offspring. One particularly rebellious god, Marduk, kills Tiamat, rips her body apart, and creates the heavens with half and the earth with the other half. Marduk was the patron god of Babylon. Before storytellers wrote this story down, they probably transmitted it orally and specially recited it on the fourth day of the Babylonian New Year.

✔ *Epic of Gilgamesh:* This epic adventure composed about 3,000 B.C. in the language of Akkadian runs some 2,900 lines and covers 11 tablets. The story illuminates the exploits of Gilgamesh, the hero-king in ancient Mesopotamia and his eternal friend Enkidu. When Enkidu dies, Gilgamesh sets off to find the secret of eternal life, but in the end is forced to face his own mortality. The epic includes gods, creatures, and a flood story (predating the biblical account).

✔ *The Thunder, Perfect Mind:* The Gnostic poem of Thunder written more than 1,600 years ago in the female, first person is a fascinating account of contradiction that pries at the very root of our own existence. Thunder is a seductive goddess or female spirit who claims to have been present when God created the world. Thunder is a whore but a holy one. She's a wife and a virgin; a mother, but a daughter. Although she's barren, Thunder has many children. This story is stuff rock songs are made of.

Medieval Literature

The medieval literature is extensive. The genres and subgenres become even more diverse and more interesting.

Pining over poetry

For many of us in the West who didn't grow up in a society that places much value on poetry, getting worked up about a poem isn't easy. But many societies in the medieval Middle East were raised on poetry much the same way that so many modern American children are raised on video games or cartoons.

Pre-Islamic Arabic poetry

In late antiquity and up through the advent of Islam, the pagan Arab tribes couldn't boast of elaborate architecture, written literature, or royal heritage as was the case with their Egyptian and Mesopotamian neighbors. Rather, the Arabs had *language*. The Arabs had mastered a sophisticated system of poetry — guided by elaborate grammatical and lexical refinements in vernacular, rules of meter and rhyme, and themes of pastoral nomadic tradition — that captured Arab tribal identity.

The *qadisa* is an ode, normally up to 100 lines with a single rhyme throughout. Each line was a polished pearl strung together into a flawless string of pearls. Tribal *rawis*, or poets, recited their works of art in public for entertainment or in competition against other poets from opposing tribes. The topic often involved an evocation of a place once visited — not infrequently a camp — or a lost love. The poem recalled vivid details of the scenery, journey, favorite camel or other beasts, as well as combating the elements of nature and praise for the tribe, all which were central components in a Bedouin's life.

Court poetry

As Islam spread throughout the Near East beginning in the seventh century, an appreciation for Arabic poetry also spread. At first, the centers of literary activity were Basra and Kufa (in Iraq) and later Baghdad. Over the next several centuries, Muslim rulers from Spain to Afghanistan sought to attract the most talented poets to their courts, and other languages, such as Persian, became the media of expression. Whereas the pre-Islamic poets had praised their tribes, the new generations of court poets — who at times owed their very existence and subsistence to the patron — composed panegyric poetry, lavishing exquisitely (and at times nauseously) crafted praise for the local ruler (and boy did they pile it on). Although oral recitation continued, the custom of writing in these other cultures and the introduction of paper in the ninth century facilitated the written word.

Ghazal

The origins of *ghazal* poetry can be traced back to classical Arabic poetry. In ghazal, which rarely exceeds 12 lines and has a distinct rhyming pattern, a theme of love, religious devotion, or self-praise runs throughout the poem. Each couplet is an independent unit, and the last line usually includes the poet's pen name. In Iran, this style soon overtook qasida in popularity and became the most popular form of Persian literature. Classical Persian ghazal reached its apex with poets like Sadi and Hafiz.

Homoerotic poetry

Although poets frequently wrote about women, the beloved was often a man. Lacking the company of women, many mystics fought back their lust for young, attractive boys — often referred to as beardless boys — whose beauty was sometimes compared to the *moon* (meaning the face, not *shooting the moon*). The famous Persian poet Jalaluddin Rumi described a reunion with his own male lover, Shamsuddin Tabrizi, as a coupling in which one didn't know who was the lover and who the beloved. After Tabrizi's death at the hands of Rumi's own disciples, Rumi often included the name Tabriz at the end of many of his poems.

Erotic devotion: Persian and Turkish mystical poetry

The fact that mystical poetry characteristically has multiple meanings is among its most interesting features. In an Islamic society where interaction between the sexes outside of marriage was frowned upon, poets wrote erotic verse that also could be construed as devotional love poems to God (or vice versa?). In this way, poets expressed sensual feelings for their beloved in a variety of ways without crossing the bounds into hedonism (although they still earned criticism).

When you think about it, the sexual union of two partners — becoming one in a few fleeting, but blissful moments, when the lovers lose themselves to emotion — could be a perfect description of mystical union with God (or vice versa?). Muslim mystics called Sufis who wrote about *fana*, a temporal union with the beloved, didn't lose the opportunity to exploit this imagery. Sufis wrote about their constant longing for fana, the blissful but short-lived union (while on earth), where, like a drop of water in the ocean, the Sufi would become absorbed in union.

As is the case in Persian and Arabic poetry, Hebrew poetry also elicited sensual emotion between men. The 11th-century Spanish poet, Yishaq ben Mar-Saul, wrote that he was "slain" by a gazelle as beautiful as the moon, with curls of purple, eyes of David, and hair like Adoniah.

The Spanish Conquest: Jewish, Christian, and Muslim literature

In the 11th century, the center of Jewish literary activity shifted from Mesopotamia to Spain, where Arabic and Hebrew literature thrived for centuries. Although the country was divided politically between Christian Spain in the north with its capital at Toledo and Muslim Spain (Andalusia) with its capital at Cordoba, a dynamic interaction between Christian, Muslim, and Jewish thinkers produced some of the most talented thinkers of the period.

The Jewish pen

Back in those days, great minds kept busy. Some of the poets and philosophers had their hands in everything. Take 12th century Abraham ben Meir Ibn Ezra, for instance, who was a poet and philosopher, of course, as well as a grammarian, commentator, and astronomer. He wrote biblical commentary, treatises on ethics, and poetry, you name it. About this same time, Rabbi Judah Ha-Levi also earned a reputation as a poet and philosopher. His mystical poetry flirted with Islamic mysticism, but his magnum opus was *Al-Kuzari*, originally written in Arabic and later translated to Hebrew (*Sefer ha-Kuzari*). This allegorical work describes the conversion of Khazarian king to Judaism.

The Christian pen

Two important Spanish mystics, St. John of the Cross and St. Teresa of Avila, lived in the 16th century. St John wrote a number of mystical works, both in prose and verse. His poem *Dark Night of Soul* describes the painful passage through the darkness and the ineffable joy of encountering God. St. Teresa was a Carmelite nun who wrote a number of works including an autobiography and the *Interior Castle*. In the *Interior Castle*, she describes her vision of the spiritual growth needed to reach union with God. Several months after her death, as the story goes, church leaders exhumed her body. The corpse emitted such a pleasant fragrance, and her body was in such perfect condition that the community decided to lop off body parts to keep as holy relics (she was such a cut up). One church elder allegedly carried around her finger in his pocket.

The Islamic pen

Ibn al-Arabi was a 13th-century literary heavyweight whose Arabic writings have become the most influential and controversial in Islamic mystic spiritual thought. Much of his poetry and prose weave a complex network of spiritual and philosophical thought that elaborates the controversial concept of *wahdat al-wujud* (Oneness of Being). His adorers labeled him the Great Sheikh and the Reviver of Religion; his opponents called him an infidel and apostate. Another complex thinker was Ibn Hazm who was the Cordoba caliph's vizier in the 11th century. According to his son, Ibn Hazm wrote more than 400 books, many on philosophy and jurisprudence.

Ibn Hazm also wrote a book on love in 30 chapters called *The Ring of the Dove*. He deals with such topics as love-at-first sight, correspondence between lovers, fidelity and infidelity, passionate love, and death. Like many good prose writers of his age, he adorned his theoretical discussions on love with autobiographical references, anecdotes, and poetry. Ibn Hazm explained how most of the Andalusian caliphs preferred blonds (guess they had more fun) and how as a youth he even fell in love with a blond slave girl. *The Ring of the Dove* provides an insightful window into 11th-century social life of Muslim Spain.

Adventure and romance stories

Apart from religious and romantic poetry, other genres gained popularity. Storytellers captured tales of adventure and romance on paper. Some of these stories were clearly for entertainment, but at other times the lines between history, myth, and fantasy (and even religion) weren't clearly marked.

Adab literature

During the early Abbasid Caliphate (see Chapter 5), a new genre of literature called *adab* evolved. Adab prose, or sometimes rhyming prose called *saj*, usually sought to entertain or express social or moral commentaries. The ninth-century writer Al-Jahiz, an influential figure in adab literature, wrote the *Book of Animals,* which is considered the first Arabic book on zoology.

A Thousand and One Nights

You've probably heard of *The Arabian Nights,* also called *A Thousand and One Nights,* right? In this story, you get it all — sex, adventure, violence, humor, treachery, romance, sadness, fantasies, genies, imaginary beasts and spirits, and just about anything else you could want in a story. *The Arabian Nights* is really a compendium of a variety of stories bound together inside a larger frame story.

Although no single standardized collection exists, the general story is by and large the same. A king named Shahrayar decides that he has been betrayed by a woman for the last time. He devises a new policy of sleeping with a new virgin every night and having her executed the next morning. The king meets his match, however, in the wise Shahrazad, the vizier's daughter. Determined to save the king and all the remaining virgins in the kingdom, Shahrazad tells part of a riveting story each night before falling asleep. The king is compelled to keep the wise girl alive just one more night in order to find out how the story ends. After completing the former story, however, Shahrazad begins another, and the cycle continues.

One of the stories, "The Tale of Delilah the Swindler," is a masterpiece of structural sophistication that demonstrates the imaginative world of medieval satire and entertainment in Baghdad. Under the surface, the story involves a game of switching disguises and identities as a whole cast of gullible and wily characters appear, disappear, and then reappear in parallel identities. Above the surface, the tale of Delilah teases the sensual sensibilities of the medieval reader with seductive temptations careful never to cross the line into illicit sexuality.

The Shahnama

One of the most famous medieval Persian works is the 11th-century *Shahnama* or *The Epic of Kings.* An author named Ferdowsi from eastern Iran compiled various cycles already in existence and wove them into a modern Persian masterpiece for Sultan Mahmud of Ghazna in Afghanistan. *Shahnama* lists the legendary exploits of Iran's kings from creation to the arrival of Islam. Ferdowsi took 35 years to weave together these episodes that had been transmitted orally for centuries and drawn from written records in Pahlavi (Middle Persian) or Arabic.

Among the most popular stories in the Shahnama is that of "Rustam and Sohrab." Rustam was the handsome, "elephant-bodied" hero who — often with the help of his trusty horse Rakush or the giant magical bird Simurgh — saved Iran time and again from demons or from Iran's archenemies, the Turanians. After a romantic interlude with a beautiful princess named Tahmina, Rustam sires a son, Sohrab. The princess never tells Rustam about his son, and many years later Rustam kills his son on the battlefield.

Do you think beautiful women just grow on trees?

Silly question, huh? Well, according to many Middle Eastern writers, they *did*. The legendary Al-Waqwaq were sexual utopia islands in the narratives of various writers. The 15th-century author Ibn al-Wardi described a complex of islands run by a queen named Damhara who wore clothes woven of gold. Damhara had 4,000 beautiful, virgin handmaidens. Because they were Zoroastrians, their hair was uncovered for all to see. On this island, beautiful women indeed grew on trees. Beautiful, shapely women hung from these fruit-bearing trees by their hair. Their naked bodies exposed hands, feet, breasts, and vulvas, just like those of normal women. Men could simply pick the fruit and have sexual intercourse with the woman until their hearts were content. The only difference was that sexual pleasure exceeded that of normal women, and the former virgin would die a day or two later.

Fighting with pens

Some medieval warriors must have carried pens in one hand and swords in the other. Are you really surprised that soldiers and commanders had desires and needs they wanted to express through the written word just like everyone else? Often these warriors were sophisticated and educated men but whose profession took them to the battlefield, giving their writings an added dimension. The 12th-century Syrian Arab Usama Ibn Munqidh, for instance, wrote poetry and prose, including memoirs of his experiences in Egypt and Syria and in combat against the crusaders. Here is another example:

> **Afghan warrior poet:** Khushhal Khan Khattack was a famous Pushtun chieftain of the Khattack tribe in 17th-century Afghanistan. He spent the first half of his adult life serving the Mughal Empire under Shah Jahan, and dedicated the second half to rallying the Afghan tribes against Shah Jahan's successor and son Aurangzib. Much of his poetry contains barbed attacks against other tribes or against Aurangzib, although other poems describe his affinity for the opposite sex.

Poking fun at the mullas

The Middle Eastern sense of humor is an interesting one. Take a look at this very popular set of funny stories.

> **The exploits of Mulla Nasruddin:** The 13th-century figure Mulla Nasruddin has been the butt of jokes for centuries. Children today in Turkey, Afghanistan, and Iran are familiar with humorous stories of Nasruddin, who plays the role of an educated fool. For example:

> "Mulla Nasruddin loved his donkey. One day a neighbor came running to Nasruddin and out of breath said, 'Mulla Nasruddin, while you were away, your donkey turned up missing.' Nasruddin replied, 'Praise be to Allah! If I'd been on him, I'd be lost too.'"

Mirror of Princes

The *Mirror of Princes* literature was written as training and instructional guides to future rulers — princes, courtiers, and other nobles — as traditionally accepted practices of a good ruler. The great Seljuk vizier Nizam al-Mulk wrote *The Book of Government* (*Siyasat-nameh*) in the 11th century. This Persian treatise contains practical advice on statesmanship, like how to select government officials, how to control them with intelligence, how to deal with grievances, and how to spend leisure time.

Travel literature

Travel literature can be most enlightening and delightful because it provides you access to the double pleasure of experiencing a new culture, but through the eyes of the alien traveler, who is often as awed by the sights as you are. Medieval geographers like Muqaddasi and Idrisi wrote volumes on the peculiar and colorful geography, people, dialect, and customs of the Muslim World (although sometimes they didn't really do the traveling themselves).

The most famous Arab traveler was Abdullah Ibn Batutta, a 21-year-old Moroccan who left his home to perform the Hajj in 1325 and didn't return for nearly a quarter of a century. His journey took him down the east coast of Africa as far as modern day Tanzania, across Oman, through Egypt and Syria, up to Anatolia and the Russian steppe, back down to Afghanistan, India, and all spots in between. After eight years in India, he headed off on a journey to China but was shipwrecked off the coast of India, so he decided to tour Ceylon and Burma along the way. Finally he returned to Morocco in 1349. And you know the best thing about his journeys? He kept a diary.

Travel lit from the other side of the world

Just as Muslims documented their travels, Europeans also kept track of their adventures when they traveled throughout the Middle East. These accounts are often filled with insightful observations that could have only been captured by a Westerner's eye.

At the age 14, an adventurous Italian boy named Niccolao Manucci left Venice, Italy, by sneaking onboard a vessel bound for Smyrna. The next four years he traveled through Turkey and Iran, where he picked up Persian. By the time he was 18, he entered Moghul India, where he met Muslim Prince Dara Shukoh, who immediately put the young Italian in his service at the court. Almost immediately the empire was catapulted into a war of succession, and Manucci found himself on the battlefield of Samugarh where three brothers struggled for the throne. Manucci's adventures spanning over five decades are chronicled in *Mogul India* (*Storia do Mogul*). Hollywood films are made from stories like this one.

Modern Literature

Many of the famous genres in the previous centuries have remained popular even today. But new manifestations and transformations of those old genres only served to create new avenues for expression that enriched the already wealthy literary coffers. Take ghazal, for instance. On the Indian subcontinent, the predominance of Persian gave way to the Urdu ghazal in the 18th century. In India and Pakistan, Urdu ghazal became interwoven with music used by religious devotees at Sufi gatherings (called *qavvali*), by courtesans or by other musicians. Today in Pakistan and India, ghazal's popularity continues in the traditional poetry recitation and in the musical genre of qavvali at shrines and other gatherings as well as in cinema and on cassettes and CDs.

In 1912, Lebanese Christian novelist and poet Khalil Gibran took up residence in New York City, where he wrote in both Arabic and English. Gibran's unique background allowed him to meld East and West into his writings. His most famous piece is *The Prophet,* a selection of 26 poetic essays that narrates a fictional Prophet's final instructions to a group of people on the meaning of life just before he embarks on a journey home.

The novel

The genre of the *novel* became a novel concept in the Middle East. I include two well-known examples.

- ✔ **Satanic Verses:** The negative publicity in 1988 upon the publication of *Satanic Verses* created when Iranian cleric Ayatollah Khomeini sanctioned the assassination of author Salman Rushdie, a subsequent $3 million price placed on Rushdie's head, violent book-burning demonstrations near London, riots in India and Pakistan that left more than 20 dead, and the murder of the book's Japanese translator far outweighed the book's actual contents. Muslim opponents argued that the novel's treatment of a false prophet and a number of prostitutes with the names of the real Prophet's wives amounted to blasphemy. Money can't buy this type of publicity. The novel remained on the *New York Times'* bestseller list until the fall of 1989, and sales skyrocketed.

- ✔ **Umrao Jan Ada:** Mirza Muhammad Hadi Rusva wrote this novel about a 9-year-old girl who is kidnapped from Faizabad and sold to a brothel in 19th-century Lucknow, India. She was trained as a courtesan and mastered Persian and Urdu poetry, singing, and dancing. Life as a courtesan, Umrao Jan recounts, is like that of a goddess, and male clients are worshippers who must bring offerings to the altar. Many years later, she returns to Faizabad and meets her family but finds that the shame of her profession overshadows the reunion. *Umrao Jan Ada* was also made into a popular Hindi movie in 1981.

Autobiographies, memoirs, and firsthand accounts

Autobiographies, memoirs, and firsthand accounts surfaced as powerful devices for personal expression to a wide audience in the 20th century. First-person descriptions of political, religious, and social ordeals in an individual's life engage a reader in a way that other representations can't. Somehow autobiographical accounts allow the writer to share intimate sentiments and experiences creating an empathic relationship with the reader one-on-one. What follows are some great reads:

- ✔ ***The Daughter of Persia:*** As a daughter of one of the last Qajar princes, Sattareh Farman Farmaian grew up in a small Iranian harem. When the Qajar dynasty collapsed and the Pahlavi shah seized power, Sattareh's father told the children that the only legacy he could pass on was education. Indeed she earned an education in the United States and returned to Iran to open the Tehran School of Social Work, the first school of its kind in her country. Caught up in the whirlwind of the Iranian Revolution in 1979, she was arrested and nearly executed.

- ✔ ***The Days:*** Taha Hussein was the renowned blind Egyptian writer who earned a PhD from the Sorbonne and wrote profusely with the help of his adored French wife Suzanne. Aside from novels, he wrote on Arabic literature, Islamic history, and politics. *The Days*, his autobiography, is divided into three parts: his struggles of childhood attempting to cope with blindness in a small village in 20th-century Upper Egypt, his experiences as a university student in Cairo, and his final struggles to overcome all adversity to earn his PhD in France.

- ✔ ***In Search of Identity:*** Hoping to oust the British from Egypt, Anwar Sadat became a German agent during the war. The British arrested him in 1942, but he escaped prison two years later. In 1946, his militant activities against the British landed him once again in prison. In this autobiography, Sadat recalls the years of incarceration as therapeutic, and as an opportunity to return to his roots, to the fundamentals of life, and to emerge with a clear vision of purpose. He finds the experience liberating as he regains an understanding of himself. Sadat, he discovers, was a peasant inextricably linked to the land.

He also undergoes a type of mystical experience, whereby God becomes his best friend. His reliance on, and respect for, the Muslim Brotherhood increases. When Sadat's military colleagues had forgotten him, Brotherhood leader Hassan al-Banna provides Sadat's family ten Egyptian pounds every month. New horizons also open up for Sadat in the world of reading. He reads books, magazines, and newspapers in English and Arabic, and keeps a journal recording quotes from authors that influence him. Sadat even takes advantage of this period to study German.

✔ *Memoirs from the Women's Prison:* Nawal El Saadawi is an Egyptian physician, feminist, and author. From 1979 to 1980, she acted as an adviser for the United Nations in women's programs in Africa and the Near East. Seen as a political opponent for her outspoken views against Anwar Sadat's policies, she landed in prison in 1980. Even in prison she continued to write although she was denied paper and pencil. She found toilet paper and an eyebrow pencil effective tools for note taking (can you imagine what she could do with a bottle of glue and a roll of duct tape?). After her release, she published this book as well as a novel entitled *Woman at Ground Zero* based on her experiences in prison.

✔ *My Life: Autobiography:* Golda Meir was a Russian Jewish immigrant to the United States. She moved to Palestine in 1921. She fought for Zionism until the formation of Israel. She became Israel's foreign minister from 1956 until 1966, and served as Israel's prime minister from 1969 until 1974. Aside from witnessing the birth of Israel and subsequent wars, she describes the turbulence of her personal life.

✔ *Takeover in Tehran:* Massoumeh Ebtekar had taken part in the storming of the U.S. embassy and the taking of hostages, and subsequently became the female spokesperson for the hostage takers. Today as Iran's first female vice president, she fights for democratic reform against the clerics. In her book, she attempts to correct two decades of misconceptions about the takeover.

Read Sadat's autobiography and his experiences, emotions, and struggles in prison from *In Search of Identity* and then read Saadawi's *Memoirs from the Women's Prison.* The comparison is ironic and uncanny.

Looking at the Middle East through Westerners' eyes

Some of the richest observations are those of the Westerners who lived, worked, traveled, or fought in the Middle East:

✔ *Journey to the North of India:* At the age of 22, Lieutenant Arthur Conolly left Moscow with a Russian escort through the Caucasus and Iran in 1829, covertly gathering information on the Russian military presence along the way. After leaving his Russian escort at the Caspian Sea, Conolly disguised himself as an Indian merchant seeking to purchase goods from the bazaars. In 1830, Conolly reached Herat in Afghanistan, and stayed there for two weeks collecting intelligence while posing as a doctor. He then attached himself to a party of Muslim holy men making the 300-mile journey to Kandahar. After become deathly ill in Kandahar, one of the holy men nursed him back to health. He then fled Kandahar after his true identity was discovered. He scouted the strategic Bolan

Pass while traveling with a group of horse dealers. After more than a year on the trail, dusty and sunburned (and probably in need of a hot bath), Conolly reached the British refuge of India (Pakistan today) in the disguise of a bearded Afghan tribesman. Conolly was but the first of many British spies to make similar expeditions.

✔ *Lieutenant in Algeria:* As a French lieutenant in Algeria, Jean Jacques Servan-Schreiber witnessed atrocities of the French-Algerian War. In his book *Lieutenant in Algeria,* Servan-Schreiber describes the conflict as a complex one, in which both sides were at once good and evil. For Servan-Schreiber, no one was inherently evil, but unusual circumstances could awaken the beast inside (see Chapter 15).

✔ *Pages of a Witness:* In December 1859, a Spanish soldier named Pedro Antonio de Alarcon left his native country along with 10,000 fellow soldiers to join the Spanish army in Morocco to fight the Moors (Muslims). Alarcon kept a diary of his adventures into the Campaign of Tetuan.

✔ *Personal Narrative of a Pilgrimage to Al-Madinah and Mecca:* Sir Richard Burton (not Elizabeth Taylor's fifth and sixth husbands) is one of the most fascinating figures of the 19th century. He served in the British army in India, translated *The Arabian Nights* and *The Kama Sutra,* and traveled on the Hajj disguised as an Afghan Pushtun (see Chapter 13). His wife burned his memoirs fearing his obsession with sex would be misinterpreted. Nonetheless, the adventure, dangers, and experiences of the Hajj, which was off limits to non-Muslims, are captured in this personal narrative.

Chapter 23

Arts and Sciences

. . . .

In This Chapter

▶ Studying the Middle East's contribution to the sciences

▶ Realizing that *zero* is *nothing* to take for granted

▶ Enjoying Near Eastern architecture and art

▶ Finding pleasure in today's Middle Eastern music, dancing, and cinema

. . . .

*I*n the past, the Middle East has been home to a number of thriving centers of civilization: Egypt, Iraq, Muslim Spain, and Pakistan. From Spain to Afghanistan, leading medieval scientists, mathematicians, and philosophers developed cutting-edge theories. Many of the finest architectural structures on earth — from the awe-inspiring pyramids at Giza to the breathtaking Hagia Sophia church-mosque in Istanbul — were erected on Middle Eastern soil. Some of the planet's richest art forms were created, and can still be found in the Middle East, including the mosaics at St. George's Church in Jordan, Buddhist statues at Taxila in Pakistan, and elaborate tomb paintings in the Valley of the Queens in Egypt.

In the Middle Ages, kings, sultans, and petty rulers competed to keep a team of the most talented artists and poets in their courts. Today you can still catch street musicians along the promenades of Jerusalem, listen to Kurdish folk music from Iraq, or watch male crossdressers perform at Muslim weddings in Pakistan. This chapter introduces you to some of the region's talent of the past and present, and describes the Middle East's contributions in the fields of science, architecture, art, music, cinema, and beyond.

Science and Philosophy: A Middle East Contribution

Although the West is currently the leader in technology and education, it wasn't always that way. Throughout much of the Medieval period, Baghdad was the splendid center of civilization in the Middle East. At its height, some 1 million people lived in Baghdad.

This city was home to top-notch scholars, poets, artists, mathematicians, philosophers, theologians, and intellectuals. Likewise, Muslim Spain was an intellectual and cultural hub that produced some of the greatest thinkers of the period. A rich interaction between these two centers and the West allowed the Middle East to make lasting contributions in the sciences and philosophy.

Adding it all up: Mathematics

Did you ever wonder about the origin of those numbers that you punch on your calculator? The numerals themselves are called Arabic numerals (although they originated in India of all places). Muslim scholars studied the Greek, Egyptian, Indian, and Babylonian mathematics texts and made revisions and improvements. Look at a couple examples.

- **Algebra:** In the ninth century A.D., Al-Khwarismi (from eastern Iran) first fully developed algebra (*al-jabr* in Arabic).
- **Trigonometry:** In the 13th century, Nasr al-Din al-Tusi made important contributions to trigonometry.

A 15th-century mathematician named Al-Khashi from Uzbekistan also made advances in decimal fractions. Perhaps the most significant contribution of the Middle East was passing along the zero.

Think about Roman numerals. Where's the zero? There isn't one, is there? The number 10 was just a big fat *X*, right? Can you imagine trying to divide 498,491 by 356.2, or cross-multiplying fractions using Roman numerals? What about doing a little algebra with *X*s, *L*s, and *C*s as the numbers? The Greeks weren't much better. They toyed with the idea of a zero, but just couldn't make the commitment.

Today without zeros in our system of numbers, modern astronomy, physics, chemistry, and computers probably wouldn't work. The Arabs ran across the notion of zero in India maybe as early as the fifth century, thought it could be useful, and hung onto it. Around the ninth century, some Europeans picked up on the concept of zero from the Arabs (although some claimed they were making a bid deal over *nothing*) and the rest is history (ah, I mean mathematics).

Pondering over philosophy

The Middle East made great advances in philosophy as well. The following three Middle Easterners are among the best known philosophers in the West.

- ✔ **Ibn Rushd:** The West knew him as Averroes, the 12th-century Spanish philosopher who attempted to reconcile Aristotelian philosophy with Islam. Ibn Rushd's lucid and detailed commentaries on Aristotle became highly influential for later European philosophers.

- ✔ **Ibn Sina:** Known in the West as Avicenna, this 11th-century Persian philosopher and physician wrote texts on the fields of philosophy and medicine. Ibn Sina's philosophy maintained the ontological theme of God's transcendence, but he distinguished between essence and existence. This distinction allowed him to explain in philosophical terms how the universe came into existence within an Islamic framework.

- ✔ **Maimonides:** The 12th-century Jewish philosopher, scholar, and physician from Muslim Spain was perhaps the most important Jewish intellectual in the medieval Middle East. Writing in Arabic, Maimonides attempted, like his Muslim counterparts, to prove complex and puzzling issues in Judaism — like the existence of God and esoteric concepts in the Hebrew Bible — through reason.

Other Muslim philosophers, like Al-Farabi, al-Kindi, and Ibn al-Arabi, also attempted to reconcile philosophy with Islam. Questions of free will, existence, creation, the created-ness of the Quran, God's transcendence, God's anthropomorphism, and prominence of reason over faith (or vice versa) were philosophical issues of contention, debate, dispute, and even persecution at times. In the ninth century, a school of philosophers called the Mutazilites gained the ear of caliph al-Mamun at Baghdad and imposed their philosophy on their opponents through an inquisition (*mihna*).

The Arts and Beyond

If you're heading to the Middle East, make sure you're packin'. Not a gun, silly! A good camera and a bag of film. From every corner and in every nook and cranny, you find spectacular art and architecture to shoot and film.

Art and architecture

Whether you're into the ancient, medieval, or modern world, you can find art and architecture from each time period anywhere people resided or traveled, which was just about everywhere in the Middle East. Read about these few examples to whet your appetite:

✔ **Egypt:** In addition to the pyramids outside of Cairo, the Egyptian Museum in Cairo is a treasure chest of mummies, statues, sarcophagi, weapons, paintings, decorated furniture, masks, scarabs, and thousands of other items. Coptic churches and a museum are rich with Christian art and iconography. The Cities of the Dead are cemeteries in Cairo that have become home to tens of thousands of the city's poorest who've taken up residence there. Some of the tombs date back to medieval times. Luxor's ancient Egyptian temples, giant statues, Avenue of Sphinxes (see Figure 23-1), and subterranean tombs at the Valleys of the Kings and Queens leave you speechless.

✔ **Iran:** The rock reliefs at Bisutun date back to about 500 B.C. (see Chapter 5). The hand-chiseled reliefs on the royal tombs at Naqsh-i Rustam and the palace ruins at Persepolis tease the imagination. Chehel Sotun Palace and the Khaju Bridge at Isfahan (see Figure 23-2), Imam Reza Shrine at Mashhad, and Azadi (Shahyad) Tower in Tehran are well worth the visit. Walk the captivating interior bazaars of Shiraz or Isfahan.

Figure 23-1:
The Avenue of Sphinxes in Luxor.

© Carmen Redondo/CORBIS.

Figure 23-2:
The Khaju
Bridge.

© Paul Almasy/CORBIS.

✔ **Israel and Palestine:** The Old City of Jerusalem is home to countless
  Jewish, Christian, and Muslim sacred sites, such as the Wailing Wall,
  Church of the Holy Sepulcher, and Dome of the Rock. At Bethlehem, you
  can see the Basilica of the Nativity where Christ supposedly was born,
  Jericho the oldest city in the world, the Qumran caves where the Dead
  Sea Scrolls were discovered, and Masada, the mountain hideout where
  Jewish rebels held out against Roman legionnaires for five months.

✔ **Jordan:** Petra, the ancient city carved of stone, is in a class of its own
  (see Chapter 4). You can find beautifully colored mosaics at Mount
  Nebo, St. George's church at Madaba (see Figure 23-3), and at various
  sites in the Roman city of Jerash. If you like medieval castles, you're in
  business. The Roman Amphitheater, the Temple of Hercules, and the
  huge blue mosaic King Abdullah Mosque all lie in downtown Amman.

✔ **Pakistan:** The ancient cities of Harappa and Mohenjo-daro dating back
  to 3000 B.C. are still under excavation. Buddhist stupas, statues, carv-
  ings, and monasteries abound in Taxila and elsewhere. Hindu, Jain, and
  Sikh temples still exist. You can see ornate mosques, tombs, shrines,
  forts, and palaces from the Muslim era. Mughal gardens and parks in
  the region are worth the trip. The Faisal Mosque in Islamabad (see
  Figure 23-4) is among the largest in the world.

Figure 23-3:
The mosaic
floor at St.
George's
Church.

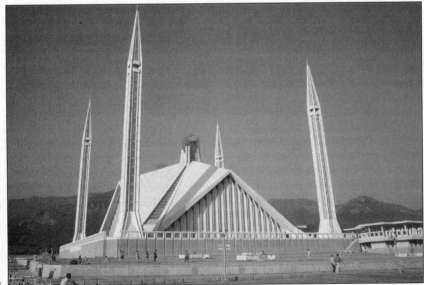

Figure 23-4:
The Faisal
Mosque in
Islamabad.

✔ **Saudi Arabia:** Muslim iconoclasts have succeeded in destroying much of Arabia's ancient art and archaeological treasures. The *kaba* — the ancient square structure that once housed hundreds of pagan statues — still stands although the statues have long been destroyed. The Grand Mosque now surrounds the kaba (although the entire city is off limits to non-Muslims). The ruins of Diraiyah outside Riyadh include reconstructed palaces and mosques.

✔ **Syria and Lebanon:** Visit Syria and Lebanon if you want to visit crusaders' castles. Figure 23-5 shows the Castle of the Knights, which was built in 1031. Palmyra, the ancient caravan city, still has plenty of Canaanite temples, tombs, as well as an amphitheater, colonnade, and other sights to keep you entertained. If you like citadels, mosques, Roman baths, and museums, these two countries are for you.

✔ **Turkey:** Turkey's culture reflects a unique mixture of pagan, Christian, and Muslim art and architecture. An ancient 27-meter-tall Egyptian Obelisk at the Roman Hippodrome — a huge stadium that could hold 100,000 spectators (no women allowed) — was brought to Turkey by Emperor Theodosius I in 390 A.D. The Ottomans converted the splendid Christian Hagia Sophia church into a mosque in 1453, but today it's a museum (see Figure 23-6). You can still find breathtaking Christian frescos and mosaics at Chora. The 16th-century Sulaymaniye Mosque complex at Istanbul may be the greatest sight in the city.

Figure 23-5:
The Castle
of the
Knights in
Syria.

Figure 23-6:
The Hagia
Sophia.

Muslim art

Since the advent of Islam to the present, some conservative Muslims have seen human and animal representations in art as sacrilegious. They have argued that because only God can create, human beings shouldn't attempt to recreate visual images of sentient beings. Such interpretations have occasionally led to campaigns throughout the centuries to deface or destroy artistic images. For this reason, Muslim art has at times taken a unique and creative direction. Mosques, for example, have traditionally been decorated with Quranic passages of ornate calligraphy and geometric or floral patterns.

On the other hand, alternative interpretations found human imagery and Islam completely compatible, provided the images weren't used for worship. Bowls, walls, and carpets as well as paper became canvases for Muslim colorful and intricate human and animal designs. Chinese influence made its way to the Muslim World through the Mongol invasion in the 13th century and helped to shape Persian miniature artwork, which flourished under the patronage of Muslim rulers. Colorful Persian miniature paintings were visual components that accompanied written texts. Miniatures often depicted the religious, legendary, or historical accounts. Battle, adventure, romance, hunting, wedding, and court scenes were among the most popular in Turkey, Iran, Afghanistan, and North India.

An Afghan museum in exile

From about the first century B.C. through the seventh century A.D., the region of Afghanistan and Pakistan was home to the Kushan Empire with its capital at near modern-day Peshawar, Pakistan. Kushan kings, like Kanishka, were Buddhists and patrons of the arts and architecture. Under their patronage, the famous Gandharan school of sculpture, which incorporated classical Roman style techniques, thrived. Today vestiges of Buddhist culture exist, including the breathtaking art — reliefs, busts of Bodhisattvas, and statues of the Buddha with Hindu gods over his shoulders — countless Buddhist stupas and shrines, and monastery ruins are scattered throughout the region. The National Museum in Kabul housed a great deal of the Afghan Buddhist art collection as well as other works of art.

You may remember in 2001 when the Taliban destroyed the 50-meter tall Buddhist statues that had endured two millennia in Bamiyan, Afghanistan. The Taliban had gone on an iconoclast spree all across the country, destroying Buddhist statues and other works of art that sported human or animal images (see Chapter 1), including a smash fest of several priceless items at the National Museum in Kabul. Thanks to looters, smugglers, and art lovers however, much of Afghanistan's art had already been smuggled out of the country before the Taliban got to it. Some estimates indicate as much as 70 percent of Afghanistan's treasures from the National Museum have been plundered and sold on the international market during the past 20 years. A number of these items, including prehistoric stone and bronze artifacts dating back to 3500 B.C., ended up in a *museum-in-exile* in the Swiss Alps.

Calligraphy

Calligraphy in the Middle East developed from a common form of writing Arabic into an art form from about the seventh century. Arabic, Persian, and Urdu calligraphy adorns plates, carpets, drinking vessels, structures such as mosques, and handwritten books of literature and the Quran. Like other art forms, master calligraphers have passed on their skill to willing pupils for centuries. Today calligraphy is still widespread and widely enjoyed.

Performing arts

Do you get the impression from TV that people in the Middle East just attend political rallies or read sacred texts all day? Let me tell you, they don't. Like most everyone else across the globe, Middle Easterners enjoy their leisure time. Whenever appropriate, people sing and dance, attend wedding festivities, watch TV, go to movies, play games, and listen to music. Take a glimpse at some of those activities.

Music and dance

No doubt music and dance have been sources of entertainment and celebration in most cultures for millennia. The following is a little slice of music and dance in the Middle East.

✔ **Belly dancing:** Around midnight in Cairo you can hit the belly-dancing cabarets. They say the cream of the belly-dancing crop doesn't take the stage until about 1 or 2 a.m. You may be surprised, however, to find out that many of "Cairo's best" are actually "Europe's best." Muslim extremists have driven many Muslim women from the stage and driven up the demand for Western belly dancers, whose performance isn't subject to the same Islamic restrictions.

✔ **Enchantment with Indian music:** For all Pakistan's rhetoric against India, popular Pakistani and Afghan culture thrives on Indian music and film. Music shops in Lahore, Pakistan, are stocked with Indian music as Hindi soundtracks blast the bazaars. Pashtun bus drivers in Peshawar adorn their vehicles with posters of female Indian movie stars. One of the first orders of business for the Taliban was to ban the popular Indian music and films. Although the Indian films are likewise banned in Pakistani cinemas, citizens routinely rent and buy pirated DVDs or watch the films on cable and satellite.

✔ **Hijras:** In South Asia, eunuchs and male crossdressers don attractive female clothing, apply makeup, and attend wedding ceremonies as paid singers, dancers, and musicians. In a society where female participants in such ceremonies are kept separate from the men, the attendance of these pseudo-women performers comes in handy.

✔ **An Iranian Madonna:** Before the Iranian Revolution in the 1970s, Googoosh was an Iranian female icon of popular music, not only in Iran but also in Europe. She attended the San Remo Music Festival in 1973 (an honor later experienced by Madonna and Britney Spears). When the Ayatollah Khomeini seized power in 1979, Googoosh was silenced (as were all other female vocalists). In September 2000, she performed before 14,000 screaming admirers at the MCI Center in Washington, D.C.

✔ **Jerash Music Festival:** Every July an international music festival is held in Jordan at the ancient Roman city of Jerash. The festival draws people from all over the region to hear traditional and popular Arab music. The audience sits in ancient stone amphitheaters while musicians perform on stage, pretty much as it was done centuries ago.

✔ **On the street:** Musicians in Jerusalem's streets play violins, accordions, flutes, and other instruments as passersby drop coins into a cup or onto a cloth. Many of these Jewish artists are undoubtedly remnants of the European musical talent that fled to Palestine after World War II.

✔ **Sufis:** From Morocco to Egypt and from Turkey to Kashmir, you can find the Islamic mystics, called Sufis, who often gather in mausoleums or shrines of deceased Muslim saints to perform a special type of worship (see Chapter 20).

✔ **Weddings in Kashmir:** On Golden Dal Lake in Srinagar, wedding celebrations are segregated into two boats: women's and men's. As the gendered crafts travel around the lake, music blares and men dance.

If you're ever invited to a Christian home in Pakistan, you may be in for a treat of Christian folk music. Sephardic Jews, Iranian Kurds, Moroccan Berbers, Uzbek Afghans, and most subcultures have their own variety of folk music. Witnessing authentic folk music firsthand can be a rich and unique experience. Go for it!

Television, cinema, and drama

The modern age has served as a great medium for creative expression of culture, talent, and imagination. Television and cinema cut across time and space to bring that creative expression to audiences all across the globe. Egyptian and Iranian film industries, for instance, are huge. Many movies, TV programs, and plays are sophisticated, artistically shot and directed, and the topics often deal with important and controversial social ills. Check out some of these moving works:

✔ *Googoosh: Iran's Daughter:* Iranian-American filmmaker Farhad Zamani produced this documentary about the female Iranian pop icon who was forced to abandon her career in 1979 with the advent of the Iranian Revolution.

✔ **Indian films:** This media is larger and more influential than you may think. Not only are these films extremely popular among Afghans, Pakistanis, and Bangladeshis, but Indian movies are also widely viewed in the Arab Gulf States.

✔ *Jenin, Jenin:* In 2003, five Israeli soldiers sued Israeli-Arab filmmaker Mohammed Bakri for releasing a 54-minute documentary that portrayed the Israeli Defense Force activities as criminal during a battle for Jenin Refugee Camp in April 2002 (see Chapter 11).

✔ *Jurm, jurm, maila chador:* Much along the lines of the famous Urdu novel, *Umrao Jan Ada* (see Chapter 22), this Punjabi play deals with the story of a young girl who is kidnapped and sold to a brothel in Pakistan. The drama's social message is so compelling that the play has been running at a single theater in Lahore for years.

✔ **Teenage pregnancy:** In 2001, Magdy Ahmed Ali directed an Egyptian film about a 16-year-old girl who becomes pregnant out of wedlock and gives birth to a child in her bathroom. The family arranges to have the young mother circumcised, and the father disconnects the infant's incubator. The film is based on a true story.

If you've never seen a well-made Middle Eastern film, you don't know what you're missing.

Part VII
The Part of Tens

The 5th Wave   By Rich Tennant

Mmmm-naw. I think I can find it without a map.

CAMEL STATI

MAPS to CANAAN sold here

In this part . . .

*P*art VII serves as a tool for keeping track of the
Middle East's rich ethnicity by outlining ten key
ethnic groups. This part also sorts out a lot of the
confusion associated with militant groups by providing a
detailed list of ten of the most important ones. Finally, this
part suggests ten crucial challenges facing the Middle East
in the 21st century.

Chapter 24

Ten Key Ethnic Groups

In This Chapter

▶ Understanding the Middle East's rich cultural diversity

▶ Discovering the region's key ethnic groups

*T*he Middle East is home to a richly diverse environment of several ethnic groups. Each country, region, subculture, and community has an assortment of music, customs, clothes, languages, religions, and food that is equally diverse. To witness this cultural diversity can be a highly rewarding experience. Nothing can quite match mingling with the people, experiencing the culture, tasting the food, beholding the sights, sharing in the customs, listening to the music, and bustling your way through bazaars. This chapter discusses ten key ethnic groups of the Middle East.

Arab

Arabs are native speakers of any number of the various Arabic dialects (see Chapter 22). The Arab World stretches from Morocco in the west to Iraq in the east, and from Syria in the north to Yemen in the southern Arabian Peninsula, encompassing 17 countries: Algeria, Bahrain, Egypt, Iraq, Jordan, Kuwait, Lebanon, Libya, Morocco, Oman, Qatar, Saudi Arabia, Sudan, Syria, Tunisia, the United Arab Emirates, Yemen, and Palestine, which isn't yet an independent country. About 160 out of the 250 million people living in the Arab World are actually Arabs. The overwhelming number of Arabs are Sunni Muslim (85 percent), however, about 10 percent are Shiite Muslim, and a handful are Jewish and Christian Arabs. Traditionally, the term Arab referred to Bedouin (nomadic) populations, but today more than 90 percent of the world's Arabs are sedentary.

Armenians

About 3 million Armenian-speaking people live in Armenia, a country snuggled between Turkey, Georgia, and Iran. About a million more Armenians live in the former Soviet republics. Most Armenians are Christians. During World War I, the Ottomans were responsible for the deaths of 600,000 Armenians, whom the Turks claim aided the Russian army (see Chapter 6).

Ashkenazim

Ashkenazim are one of the two major Jewish ethnic groups living today in Israel, referring to Jews of Eastern and Central European ancestry. Yiddish became the traditional language of Ashkenazi Jews in Europe. Today Ashkenazi food, customs, politics, and religious practices differ from Sephardic customs. (See the "Sephardim" section later in this chapter.)

Bedouin

The Bedouins are Arab nomadic tribes living on the Arabian Peninsula, in Jordan and Israel, and elsewhere. They comprise about 10 percent of the Arab population, and are culturally distinct from sedentary Arabs. Bedouins are a hospitable people traditionally known to herd sheep and camels, moving freely from region to region across borders, and living in black goat-hair tents. In the 20th century, many have abandoned nomadic life and taken up farming or other sedentary occupations, often transporting their livestock in pickup trucks and even earning land rights. Bedouin society is structured into clans and tribes, headed by sheikhs. Most Bedouins are Muslim, although a handful in Palestine and Syria are Christian.

Berbers

Berbers were the people living in North Africa when the Arabs invaded in the seventh century. Today Berbers are Muslims, accounting for some 12 million people throughout Libya, Algeria, Tunisia, and Morocco. Most belong to the Berber ethnic group of loosely knit tribes whose heritage in the region stretches back to 2400 B.C., and Berbers speak any one of a number of Berber dialects. In recent years, a resurgence of Berber pride in their language and heritage has led to conflicts in some regions, particularly in Algeria.

Kurds

Approximately 25 million Kurds live in Syria, Turkey, Iraq, and Iran, generally in mountainous regions. The Kurds are primarily Sunni Muslim. They farm, herd goats and sheep, speak their own language, Kurdish, and have their own customs. In northern Iraq, the United Nations awarded the Kurds their own autonomous region after the Gulf War (see Chapter 18). In the U.S.-led war against Saddam Hussein in 2003, the Kurds joined forces with the United States.

Pashtuns

Pashtu is the first language for about 35 percent of Afghanistan's population, called Pashtuns. The Pashtuns (who also call themselves Pathans) live in tribal areas on the Afghan side of the Pakistani border and spill over into the Pakistani provinces of the North West Frontier Province and Baluchistan. Besides a common language, the Pashtuns share a common culture and frequently religious and political perspectives. Combined, the Pashtuns on both sides of the border constitute a force to be reckoned with (see Chapter 14). Although no official autonomous region for the Pashtuns exists, these tribes do operate with little interference from either the Pakistani or Afghan government in the Pashtun belt resting along both sides of the border. This region, called the *tribal areas*, has for centuries remained an untamed frontier, hostile to outsiders. In 1955, the Pashtuns in Pakistan and Pashtuns in Afghanistan decided they wanted a separate nation, which they would call Pashtunistan. Their bid for an autonomous region was foiled in the 1960s and then again in the 1970s.

Persians

For our purposes, Persian refers to speakers of Persian, which are spread across Iran, Afghanistan, and Tajikistan. In Iran, the Persian dialect is called Farsi (or just plain Persian), while in Tajikistan those speaking Tajik and in Afghanistan speakers of Dari are all called Tajiks. In these three countries, about half the people speak Persian. In Afghanistan, ethnic friction and violence has been a frequent source of tension between Tajiks and Pashtuns.

Sephardim/Oriental Jews

Sephardim, in the strictest sense, refers to the descendents of Jews who migrated from Spain in the Middle Ages. In 1492, Jews (and Muslims) were expelled from Spain. Because many Sephardic Jews settled in the Ottoman Empire and adopted the customs and languages of Oriental Jews already settled there, the term Sephardim has often come to refer to Sephardim/Oriental Jews as opposed to their Ashkenazim counterparts (see "Ashkenazim" earlier in this chapter). A large number of these Sephardic Jews became culturally absorbed into Arabic-speaking environments. After the formation of Israel in 1948, Jews living in some Arab countries underwent various forms of persecution. In 1950, the Israeli Law of Return guaranteed Jews arriving from any nation immediate citizenship. Huge numbers of Sephardic/Oriental Jews, therefore, migrated from these Arab countries to Israel.

Turks

The Turks, of course, speak Turkish. About 80 percent of Turkey's 66 million people are native Turkish speakers. Tribes of Turkic-speaking Sunni Muslims moved from Persia (today Iran) into the region in the 13th century and eventually overthrew the Byzantine Empire in 1453 (see Chapter 5). Today's Turks are mostly Sunni Muslims. Political events in the 20th century have contributed to the unique makeup of Turkish identity. Today Turks hold a mixture of Western, secular, democratic, and Islamic values dear.

Chapter 25

Ten Key Militant Groups

In This Chapter

▶ Understanding the origins and activities of the most prominent militant groups

▶ Following the transformation of some groups from militancy to political activism

*I*n the Middle East, many political groups harbor an extremist ideology and propagate radical propaganda. A militant group is an extremist organization dedicated to achieving its goals through violent struggle. Throughout most of the 20th century, militant groups arose, were repressed and repelled, disappeared, or transformed themselves into legitimate religious or political parties. For example, Yasser Arafat's Palestinian Liberation Organization (PLO) although widely involved in militancy in the 1970s and '80s, evolved into a legitimate political entity (the Palestinian Authority) in the early 1990s and today officially denounces militancy (see Chapter 11). Arafat's secular movement often comes at loggerheads with Islamic militant groups, like Hamas, that seek politico-religious goals.

Many of today's Islamic militant organizations are spinoffs from the Muslim Brotherhood of the mid-20th century. In Egypt, the Muslim Brotherhood was forced to denounce violence and political activities in order to survive as a legitimate religious entity (see Chapter 15). Therefore, those members dedicated to achieving extremist goals through violence branched off from the Brotherhood and formed militant groups, such as Gamaat al-Islamiyya and Egyptian Islamic Jihad. Likewise, Jewish extremist organizations, like Kach and Kahane Chai, in recent years have attempted to distance themselves from militancy in order to gain legitimacy in the political realm.

This chapter details ten key militant groups that maintain an extremist ideology and have employed violence as a means to achieve their goals. As part of the trend, I define the vast majority of the most prominent organizations in politico-religious terms.

Al-Qaeda (International)

No doubt Al-Qaeda has snatched most of the headlines in the past few years. Al-Qaeda means *the base* (or military base) in Arabic. This militant organization has cells in about 60 countries.

✔ **Goals:** Al-Qaeda has many goals. With regard to the United States, Al-Qaeda seeks to diminish American influence in the region, particularly in Israel and Iraq, and oust American troops from sacred Saudi soil (see Chapter 17). Furthermore, Al-Qaeda has designs on all territory in which Muslims had a presence at any time, including Israel and Spain. Finally, the militant network envisions the establishment of a pan-Islamic caliphate, across all Muslim lands along the lines of the Taliban model.

✔ **History:** Osama bin Laden established a network to coordinate efforts of various existing militant organizations in the late 1980s. The Al-Qaeda network funds, recruits, trains, and coordinates Islamic militants and extremist organizations, particularly Sunni contingents across the globe. From 1991, bin Laden ran operations out of Sudan until 1996 when he pulled up stakes and moved camp to Taliban territory in Afghanistan. Al-Qaeda operations ran unimpeded from 1996 until 2001, when the United States retaliated for the September 11, 2001, attacks. In the subsequent U.S. military campaign, the Taliban and Al-Qaeda were forced to flee the cities and rural strongholds and disperse into the tribal environs of Pakistan and Afghanistan.

✔ **Claims to fame (or infamy):**

- **Embassy bombings:** In 1998, Al-Qaeda operatives destroyed U.S. embassies in Nairobi, Kenya and Dar es Salaam, Tanzania. The simultaneous bombings killed 301 people, 12 of which were Americans, and injured 5,000 more.

- **USS Cole:** In 2000, two suicide bombers appearing to stand at attention and salute American sailors crashed a small craft packed with explosives into the hull of the guided missile destroyer USS Cole. The subsequent explosion blew a 40-foot by 40-foot hole in the destroyer's hull, killing 17 sailors and injuring 39 more (see Chapter 17).

- **September 11, 2001:** Al-Qaeda dispatched 19 suicide operatives to hijack four American commercial airliners and fly them into structures in New York and Washington, D.C. Two airliners crashed into the World Trade Center and one into the Pentagon. A fourth jet crashed into an open field in Shanksville, Pennsylvania. More than 3,000 people died in the attacks.

✔ **Leadership:** Bin Laden is Al-Qaeda's leader. On March 2, 2003, Khalid Sheikh Muhammad, a high-ranking officer believed to be the key planner of the September 11, 2001 attacks, was arrested in Rawalpindi, Pakistan, and handed over to U.S. officials.

Al-Qaeda is linked to various other Sunni militant groups including Egyptian Jihad, al-Gamaat al-Islamiyya, and Harakat al-Mujahidin.

Hezbollah (Lebanon)

Hezbollah in Arabic means *The Party of God.*

✔ **Goals:** Hezbollah has vowed to destroy Israel and replicate Ayatollah Khomeini's success through the establishment of an Islamic state in Lebanon.

✔ **History:** A Lebanese Shiite militant movement that called itself *The Party of God* emerged as a major political force in Lebanon around 1982 in the midst of the civil war. A month after the Israeli forces invaded Lebanese territory to stomp out the PLO, Iran's Islamic revolutionary fervor spilled over into Lebanon when Syrian President Hafiz al-Assad agreed to allow 1,000 *Pasadaran* (Iranian revolutionary guards) to set up a training camps in Lebanon's Beqaa Valley. The *Pasadaran* recruited young Shiite extremists from existing militant organizations, including Amal (a Shiite militant group), and provided them with military training and the religious instruction promulgated by Khomeini (see Chapter 18). Core Hezbollah students, many of whom had graduated from Shiite *madrasa*s (theological schools) in southern Iraq, took these teachings to heart.

✔ **Claims to fame (or infamy):** Long before the Sunni Palestinians began to employ the suicide bomb as a weapon of choice against Israelis, Hezbollah and other Shiite groups had experimented with suicide attacks against Western targets in Lebanon.

  • **Kidnapping:** Between 1982 and 1992, Hezbollah and other Shiite factions abducted approximately 50 Western hostages. The captives were often kept blindfolded and in chains for up to five years. Hezbollah released the last of the American hostages in 1992 only after the intervention of Iran and Syria (see Chapter 16).

  • **Suicide bombing:** In April 1983, Hezbollah detonated a suicide car bomb outside the U.S. embassy in Beirut, killing 63 people. Hezbollah carried out a suicide truck bombing at the U.S. Marine barracks in Beirut in October of that same year that killed 241 marines and 60 French soldiers.

  • **Hijacking:** Hezbollah was responsible for the 1985 hijacking of TWA flight 847, in which they tortured and killed American Navy SEAL Robert Stethem.

✔ **Leadership:** Secretary Hassan Nasrullah is often quoted lofting fiery speeches against Israel and the United States.

Hezbollah has succeeded in gaining popularity in Lebanon because of its dedication to protect and secure the rights of Shiites and through the provision of social services to the Shiite community. In 2002, Hezbollah attempted to smuggle a shipment of arms to the Palestinian Authority.

Kach and Kahane Chai (Israel)

Jewish militancy has a long precedence in Israeli history. By 1920, Jews living in Palestine had already formed a secret, loosely organized band of militants known as the Haganah. With an original mission of self-defense, the Arab-Israeli clashes from 1929 to 1939 solidified the group into a unified military unit. Other splinter militant squads, like Irgun and the Stern Gang, carried out bloody attacks against British, Arabs, and even other Jews (see Chapter 6). Kach and Kahane Chai are the two most recent manifestations of Jewish militancy.

- ✔ **Goals:** Kach and Kahane Chai want to restore the biblical state of Israel and drive the Palestinians out of Palestine.

- ✔ **History:** In 1968, Israeli-American Rabbi Meir Kahane formed the Jewish Defense League (JDL). The JDL was involved in plots to attack perceived threats: the PLO, Soviet-bloc nations, Arab states, and moderate Jewish entities. The militant Kach organization grew out of the JDL and Meir Kahane's extremist teachings. In 1990, Palestinian gunmen assassinated Rabbi Kahane in New York. After his father's assassination, Binyamin Kahane founded a spinoff organization called Kahane Chai (meaning *Kahane lives*).

- ✔ **Claim to fame (or infamy):** In 1994, shortly after the Oslo Peace Accords were signed (see Chapter 11), Baruch Goldstein, an American-born Kach militant, murdered 29 Muslims at the Ibrahimi Mosque in Hebron. A month later the Israeli government outlawed both groups.

- ✔ **Leadership:** Binyamin Kahane led the organizations until December 2000 when Palestinian extremists assassinated him and his wife in a drive-by shooting.

In recent years, Kach and Kahane Chai have attempted to gain political legitimacy in Israel by denouncing militancy.

The American FBI arrested two JDL members for allegedly conspiring to bomb King Fahd Mosque near Los Angeles and assassinate Arab-American Congressman Darrel Issa of California in December 2001.

Armed Islamic Group (Algeria)

The most prominent Algerian militant organization is the Armed Islamic Group (GIA), or *Groupes Islamiques Armes*. The GIA played a role in the massacre of tens of thousands of civilians, sometimes slaughtering entire villages, from 1992 to 1998.

- ✔ **Goals:** The GIA wants to defeat the secular government and establish an Islamic state.

- ✔ **History:** The GIA spun off from the Islamic Salvation Front (FIS), a legitimate politico-religious party participating in the parliamentary elections in 1991, after the military cancelled the elections and banned the FIS (see Chapter 15). The GIA became the most prominent Islamic militant organization, which was responsible for slaughtering thousands of innocent civilians. The GIA determined that the entire Algerian society was guilty of abandoning Islam, thus deserving execution. Any individual not praying at the appropriate time, any woman not covering her hair, state employee, farmer, or teacher was fair game.

- ✔ **Claim to fame (or infamy):** Much like the ritual slaughter performed by a Muslim butcher, the GIA became popular for the slitting of its victims' throats.

- ✔ **Leadership:** The GIA is believed to comprise several independent cells.

In 1999, the government granted amnesty to militant groups in an effort to restore peace. Since that time, violence has subsided although extremist militancy continues to claim approximately 100 lives a month.

Al-Gamaat al-Islamiyya (Egypt)

Al-Gamaat al-Islamiyya in the Egyptian dialect — also pronounced Al-Jamat al-Islamiyya — means *the Islamic Group* in Arabic. Al-Gamaat is Egypt's largest militant group.

- ✔ **Goals:** Al-Gamaat al-Islamiyya hopes to overthrow the Egyptian government and establish an Islamic state.

- ✔ **History:** This group spun off from the Egyptian Muslim Brotherhood in the 1970s. In the 1980s, members went to Afghanistan to fight in the jihad against the Soviet Union. Many members have joined Al-Qaeda.

✔ **Claim to fame (or infamy):** On November 17, 1997, six gunmen disguised as police officers descended the cliffs around the Temple of Queen Hatshepsut in Luxor and opened fired on unarmed tourists, most of whom were foreigners from Switzerland, Japan, Germany, Britain, Bulgaria, Colombia, and France, including a 5-year-old British girl. More than 70 died in the attack, including 58 foreign tourists, Egyptian tourists, police, and all six assassins, who turned the guns on themselves when they'd finished with their victims. Representatives for the Al-Gamaat al-Islamiyya promised that there would be more where that came from (see Chapter 15).

✔ **Leadership:** Blind cleric Sheikh Omar Abdul Rahman is the spiritual leader of Gamaat. He's presently serving a life sentence in a U.S. prison for his role in the 1993 bombing of the World Trade Center.

In the 1990s, Egyptian President Hosni Mubarak cracked down on Islamic militants, which included mass arrests, torture, and execution, and succeeded in stemming the tide of violence on Egyptian soil.

Islamic Jihads (Palestine and Egypt)

These groups are actually two separate militant organizations: one based in Egypt and the other in Palestine.

Islamic Jihad (Egypt)

The Egyptian Islamic Jihad shares more in common with Al-Gamaat al-Islamiyya than Palestinian Islamic Jihad.

✔ **Goals:** The Egyptian Islamic Jihad wants to overthrow the Egyptian government and establish an Islamic state. Since merging with Al-Qaeda in June 2001, the Egyptian Islamic Jihad has sought to oust Israel and the United States from the region.

✔ **History:** This group spun off from the Egyptian Muslim Brotherhood in the 1970s. In the 1980s, many members went to Afghanistan to fight in the jihad against the Soviet Union.

✔ **Claim to fame (or infamy):** Islamic Jihad assassinated Egyptian President Anwar Sadat in 1981 because he had made peace with Israel, which the group saw as an act of infidelity.

✔ **Leadership:** Ayman al-Zawahiri and Muhammad Atef were two top leaders of EIJ that joined forces with bin Laden to form the top militant leadership of Al-Qaeda. Al-Zawahiri was jailed in Egypt for his role in Sadat's assassination but later was released. Atef was allegedly killed in the U.S. bombing campaign in Afghanistan in 2001.

In the 1990s, Mubarak's crackdown on Islamic militants, which included mass arrests, torture, and execution, succeeded in stemming the tide of violence on Egyptian soil.

Islamic Jihad (Palestine)

Palestinian Islamic Jihad (PIJ) is based in Damascus, Syria.

✔ **Goals:** Palestinian Islamic Jihad dedicates itself to the destruction of Israel and the establishment of an Islamic state in Palestine.

✔ **History:** Fathi Shikaki formed PIJ in Gaza in the 1970s.

✔ **Claims to fame (or infamy):** PIJ has conducted large-scale suicide-bombing attacks against Israeli civilians and military targets.

✔ **Leadership:** Shikaki was killed in Malta in 1995. Ramadan Shallah leads the most important branch out of Damascus. In February 2003, the FBI arrested Florida college professor Sami Al-Arian on racketeering and conspiracy to commit murder charges. Al-Arian was believed to be the North American leader of PIJ.

The PIJ is much smaller than Hamas, and its strength is unknown.

Hamas (Palestine)

Hamas is an Arabic acronym that stands for *Harakat al-Muqawama al-Islamiyya,* or *Islamic Resistance Movement.* Hamas also is a play on words that means *zeal.* That's why news reports routinely give you a double dose of *Hamas, or Islamic Resistance Movement* whenever they cover the group's exploits. Hamas is Palestine's largest militant organization.

✔ **Goals:** Hamas seeks to wipe out Israel and replace the secular Palestinian Authority with an Islamic state. The militant group opposes Arafat's regime because it's secular and corrupt, and because it has participated in the peace process with Israel.

- ✔ **History:** Hamas split off from the Palestinian branch of the Muslim Brotherhood. Hamas carried out its first suicide bombing in 1993 after Yitzak Rabin and Arafat signed the Oslo Peace Accords.

- ✔ **Claim to fame (or infamy):** In March 2002, a suicide bomber killed 28 Israelis during a Passover seder.

- ✔ **Leadership:** Abdul Aziz al-Rantisi, the spokesman for Hamas, has argued that peace negotiations with the Israelis are a waste of time because the Arabs and the Israelis can't coexist.

Part of Hamas' popularity is due to the organization's extensive social service network of mosques, schools, and health clinics.

Harakat al-Mujahidin (Pakistan and Kashmir)

Harakat al-Mujahidin (Movement of the Holy Warriors) is inextricably intertwined with a number of other militant organizations in the region.

- ✔ **Goals:** Harakat seeks to liberate Kashmir from Indian occupation, merge Kashmir with Pakistan, and create an Islamic state.

- ✔ **History:** Harakat formed in the mid-1980s. Efforts intensified with increased recruitment after the Soviet withdrawal from Afghanistan. Contributions and support from Saudi Arabia, Pakistan, and other Muslim countries enabled Harakat to continue to launch attacks from Pakistan into Indian-held Kashmir throughout the 1990s. The organization's leader from 1998 until 2000 maintained a good working relationship with bin Laden and the Taliban. Harakat ran training camps in eastern Afghanistan and many recruits came from madrasas in Pakistan. In 2000, many of Harakat's members defected to Jaish-i Muhammad, a militant organization operating in the region. Violence in Kashmir has claimed the lives of some 30,000 people since 1990.

- ✔ **Claims to fame (or infamy):**

  - **Kidnapping:** In July 1995, a splinter group called Al-Faran kidnapped and executed five Western tourists in Kashmir.

  - **Hijacking:** In December 1999, Harakat hijacked an Indian airliner, diverted it to Afghanistan, and threatened to execute the 155 passengers unless a number of imprisoned Islamic militants were released from Indian jails. Two of the most notable released militants were Ahmad Omar Sheikh and Maulana Masud Azhar.

- **Execution of Daniel Pearl:** One of the freed militants, Sheikh, was arrested in 2002 for the murder of *Wall Street Journal* journalist Daniel Pearl.

✔ **Leadership:** Fazlur Rahman, head of the Pakistani politico-religious organization Jamiat-i Ulema-i Islami, led Harakat from 1998 until 2000. Faruq Kashmiri currently runs Harakat's operations.

After the September 11, 2001, attacks and the U.S. retaliation against the Taliban, the Pakistani government cracked down on a number of militant groups. Harakat and other militant organizations have reacted by going underground, changing their names, and lashing out against targets in Pakistan.

Jaish-i Muhammad (Pakistan and Kashmir)

In Persian, *Jaish-i Muhammad* (JIM) means the *Army of Muhammad*.

✔ **Goals:** Jaish-i Muhammad seeks to unite Kashmir and Pakistan and establish an Islamic state.

✔ **History:** JIM was born of the militant activities of Jamiat-i Ulema-i Islami and Harakat al-Mujahidin in 2000.

✔ **Claim to fame (or infamy):** The Indian government has blamed JIM and Lashkar-i Tayyiba for the attacks on the Indian parliament in December 2001 that left nine dead. This attack brought India and Pakistan to the brink of nuclear war the following year.

✔ **Leadership:** In December 1999, Islamic militants hijacked an Indian airliner and landed it in Afghanistan. As a result, the Indian government released Pakistani cleric Maulana Masood Azhar from an Indian prison. After his release, he formed JIM.

Pakistan's crackdown on these militant organizations has caused them to go underground, change their names, and turn their attention to targets inside Pakistan.

Kurdistan Workers Party (Turkey)

The Kurdistan Workers Party (PKK), *Partiya Karkeren Kurdistan* in Turkish, is a militant group operating out of southeastern Turkey and northern Iraq.

- ✔ **Goals:** The PKK wants to form a Kurdish state in southeastern Turkey. Since 2000, the PKK has publicly changed its goal to seeking improved rights for Turkish Kurds.

- ✔ **History:** Turkish Kurds formed this militant organization in 1974. From the mid-1980s through the 1990s, the PKK guerrillas continued to launch violent attacks against government interests. The guerrilla violence earned brutal reprisals from the Turkish military.

- ✔ **Claims to fame (or infamy):** The PKK has carried out a number of attacks against diplomatic and commercial targets in Turkey and Western Europe. It also sought to cripple Turkey's tourist industry by bombing popular tourist sites and kidnapping foreign tourists. The rebellion has claimed approximately 35,000 lives since the mid-1980s.

- ✔ **Leadership:** Abdullah Ocalan was PKK's chairman. After his capture in Kenya in 1999, the Turkish government sentenced him to death. From prison, Ocalan called on his organization to renounce violence.

In 2000, the PKK held a conference supporting Ocalan's initiative and committed itself to a new goal of improving the rights of Turkish Kurds.

Chapter 26

Ten Key Challenges

*T*he Middle East's future looks dreary. Almost everywhere you gaze, unrest, violence, oppression, Islamic militancy, widespread poverty and drought, authoritarian regimes, military coups, unequal distributions of wealth, and complications resulting from a colonial legacy plague the Middle East. Several regions are still reeling from war. Suicide bombings and military incursions have become the rule rather than the exception in Palestine and Israel. Nuclear neighbor Pakistan is squaring off with India, and Iran may have its own nuclear arsenal by 2005. Ethnic problems involving the Kurds in Iraq and Turkey, and a number of groups in Afghanistan threaten to inflame further already smoldering tensions. The list goes on.

Although this bleak assessment is accurate, the people's courage, hospitality, and resilience alone should serve as a glimmer of hope. If the Middle East is to rebound and escape the misery and suffering of the past generation, it must overcome a number of challenges. This chapter looks at ten key challenges facing the Middle East. Because most of these challenges are interlinked, the Middle East must tackle them simultaneously.

Assigning the Blame

Over the past several generations, Middle Eastern nations have simply assigned blame for their failures elsewhere. Conspiracy theories abound and take on lives of their own. Few countries or people are willing to accept the blame for their own shortcomings. Instead, Middle Eastern countries conveniently blame Israel, the West, India, foreign conspiracies, women's freedoms, U.S. foreign policy, patriarchal society, Islamic extremists, democracy, communism, politicians, colonialism, secular society, loose morals, the Soviet Union, and almost any other "enemy." Although there's sufficient blame to go around, the Middle Eastern nations and people must begin to take responsibility for their own problems. The Middle East needs a comprehensive strategy for the future that can productively meet the challenges it faces in the 21st century.

Coming into the Nuclear Age

The Middle East has come into the nuclear age, with many implications. The fallout has yet to be measured.

- ✔ An Islamic militant attack on India's parliament in December 2001 that left nine dead brought India and Pakistan to the brink of nuclear war the following year.

- ✔ Pakistani nuclear weapons may find their way into the hands of Islamic militants or into the arsenals of fellow Muslim nations.

- ✔ Islamic militants may possess or may secure dirty radiological bombs. (Dirty bombs are crude radiological weapons that do more damage due to radiation poisoning, than detonation.)

- ✔ Plans of an Iranian nuclear arsenal may already be on the drawing board, and the arsenal can be up and running by 2005.

The United States and coalition forces (including Britain, Australia, and several other nations) undertook the 2003 war on Iraq to disarm Saddam Hussein's weapons of mass destruction, including potential nuclear weapons. What happens when other countries or militants obtain nuclear devices is anyone's guess.

Economic Development and Poverty

The Middle East needs economic development. As discussed in Chapter 10, economic develop will require diversified economies, education, and modernization. In addition, overpopulation contributes to a cycle of poverty and is linked to a host of problems, including lack of education and crime. Development is slow, painstaking, and difficult in the best of times. And we're not in the best of times. The Middle East needs assistance from the international community to succeed.

Ethnic and Religious Pluralism

The Kurds have been struggling for a homeland in the region around northern Iraq and southern Turkey since 1920. Various ethnic conflicts in Afghanistan in the last ten years have resulted in massacres of Pashtuns and Hazaras. Problems with Berbers in North Africa continue to surface. Although you can find religious violence almost anywhere in the region, certain countries, such as Algeria, Egypt, Lebanon, Israel and Palestine, Iraq, Iran, Pakistan, and Kashmir, have had more than their fair share in the past decades. A need to promote ethnic and religious pluralism in the Middle East is long overdue.

Gender Inequity

Gender inequality is still a pressing problem in the Middle East. Honor killings, oppression, and a lack of education, economic independence, and opportunities are just some of the problems (see Chapter 21). Equally troubling is how a lack of female human capital contributes to the cycle of poverty. Many Middle Eastern experts agree that without an educated, female workforce, nations in the region simply can't compete. Furthermore, educated women tend to break the cycle of poverty by having fewer children, contributing to the household income, and securing better health and education for their own children. Until the area attains gender equality, the Middle East will suffer as a victim of its own devices.

Islamic Extremism

Not only does the Middle East suffer from an assortment of social and political ills, but also Islamic extremists oppose almost every treatment to cure those ills: Democracy, secular education, gender equality, population control, economic reform involving Western banking, interest, insurance, and certain aspects of technology are among the obstacles (see Chapter 10). In the past, attempts at appeasing extremism have often only exacerbated the problem. Until the Middle East can overcome these obstacles, the countries can achieve very little improvement.

Military Spending

The eight-year Iran-Iraq War brought the economies of those two oil-rich nations to their knees (see Chapter 12). Iraq's subsequent military buildup contributed to an atmosphere of violence, bloodshed, and starvation over the past decade and a half. In the past generation, Pakistan has invested billions in a nuclear arms race with India even though it can't afford to provide universal education to its children. Many Afghan children are more familiar with weapons and land mines than they are classrooms. Although every nation is entitled to defend itself, military expenditures have strangled many of the region's nations.

Overcoming the Colonial Legacy

The colonial legacy emanating from European mischief in the region has been costly. No doubt problems in Algeria, Libya, Egypt, Israel, Palestine, Lebanon, Syria, Iraq, Iran, Pakistan, and elsewhere have grown out of the wars, occupations, settlements, and oppression at the hands of European powers. Now that the European powers have left, local oppressors have taken their place. New complications have arisen as a result of the earlier colonialism. Middle Eastern countries must develop strategies to overcome these challenges.

Unequal Distribution of Wealth

In Saudi Arabia and other Gulf States, the government, royal families, and/or a handful of elite control most of the wealth derived from oil profits. A more equal land distribution has been a point of contention in Iran, Egypt, and elsewhere. In Pakistan and Afghanistan, semifeudal landlords still operate much the same as they have for centuries. In Pakistan, these landlords often keep many of their tenants in virtual slavery. In many countries in the region, the gap between the wealthy and the abject poor is wide. Until economic reforms take place that address this issue, real socioeconomic progress is unlikely to occur.

Western-Style Democracy

When the West speaks of democracy, much of the Middle East frowns, which is understandable given democracy's poor track record in the region (see Chapter 7). Apart from Israel and Turkey, Western-style democracy has no track record. With a Jewish state opposing Palestinian autonomy and secular Turkey as democratic role models, considerable resistance to democracy as we know it in the West exists in Muslim countries. Unless the region's governments are based on true secular democracy that reflect the will of the population, imagining that any meaningful improvements can be made in their political systems is difficult.

Index

• *I* •

• *M* •

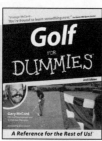

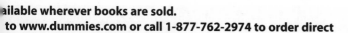

FOR DUMMIES®

Plain-English solutions for everyday challenges

HOME & BUSINESS COMPUTER BASICS

 **PCs For Dummies**
0-7645-0838-5

 **The Flat-Screen iMac For Dummies**
0-7645-1663-9

 **Windows XP All-in-One Desk Reference For Dummies**
0-7645-1548-9

Also available:

Excel 2002 All-in-One Desk Reference For Dummies
(0-7645-1794-5)

Office XP 9-in-1 Desk Reference For Dummies
(0-7645-0819-9)

PCs All-in-One Desk Reference For Dummies
(0-7645-0791-5)

Troubleshooting Your PC For Dummies
(0-7645-1669-8)

Upgrading & Fixing PCs For Dummies
(0-7645-1665-5)

Windows XP For Dummies
(0-7645-0893-8)

Windows XP For Dummies Quick Reference
(0-7645-0897-0)

Word 2002 For Dummies
(0-7645-0839-3)

INTERNET & DIGITAL MEDIA

 **The Internet For Dummies**
0-7645-0894-6

 **eBay For Dummies**
0-7645-1642-6

 **Digital Photography For Dummies**
0-7645-1664-7

Also available:

CD and DVD Recording For Dummies
(0-7645-1627-2)

Digital Photography All-in-One Desk Reference For Dummies
(0-7645-1800-3)

eBay For Dummies
(0-7645-1642-6)

Genealogy Online For Dummies
(0-7645-0807-5)

Internet All-in-One Desk Reference For Dummies
(0-7645-1659-0)

Internet For Dummies Quick Reference
(0-7645-1645-0)

Internet Privacy For Dummies
(0-7645-0846-6)

Paint Shop Pro For Dummies
(0-7645-2440-2)

Photo Retouching & Restoration For Dummies
(0-7645-1662-0)

Photoshop Elements For Dummies
(0-7645-1675-2)

Scanners For Dummies
(0-7645-0783-4)

Get smart! Visit www.dummies.com

- **Find listings of even more Dummies titles**

- **Browse online articles, excerpts, and how-to's**

- **Sign up for daily or weekly e-mail tips**

- **Check out Dummies fitness videos and other products**

- **Order from our online bookstore**

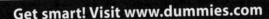

Available wherever books are sold. Go to www.dummies.com or call 1-877-762-2974 to order direct

FOR DUMMIES®

Helping you expand your horizons and realize your potential

GRAPHICS & WEB SITE DEVELOPMENT

Photoshop 7 FOR DUMMIES
A Reference for the Rest of Us!
Deke McClelland
Barbara Obermeier
0-7645-1651-5

Creating Web Pages FOR DUMMIES
A Reference for the Rest of Us!
Bud Smith
Arthur Bebak
0-7645-1643-4

Macromedia Flash MX FOR DUMMIES
A Reference for the Rest of Us!
Gurdy Leete
Ellen Finkelstein
0-7645-0895-4

Also available:

Adobe Acrobat 5 PDF
For Dummies
(0-7645-1652-3)
ASP.NET For Dummies
(0-7645-0866-0)
ColdFusion MX For Dummies
(0-7645-1672-8)
Dreamweaver MX For
Dummies
(0-7645-1630-2)
FrontPage 2002 For Dummies
(0-7645-0821-0)

HTML 4 For Dummies
(0-7645-0723-0)
Illustrator 10 For Dummies
(0-7645-3636-2)
PowerPoint 2002 For
Dummies
(0-7645-0817-2)
Web Design For Dummies
(0-7645-0823-7)

PROGRAMMING & DATABASES

C++ FOR DUMMIES
A Reference for the Rest of Us!
Stephen Randy Davis
0-7645-0746-X

Visual Studio .NET ALL-IN-ONE DESK REFERENCE FOR DUMMIES
7 BOOKS IN 1
0-7645-1626-4

XML FOR DUMMIES
A Reference for the Rest of Us!
Ed Tittel
Natanya Pitts
Frank Boumphrey
0-7645-1657-4

Also available:

Access 2002 For Dummies
(0-7645-0818-0)
Beginning Programming
For Dummies
(0-7645-0835-0)
Crystal Reports 9 For
Dummies
(0-7645-1641-8)
Java & XML For Dummies
(0-7645-1658-2)
Java 2 For Dummies
(0-7645-0765-6)

JavaScript For Dummies
(0-7645-0633-1)
Oracle9*i* For Dummies
(0-7645-0880-6)
Perl For Dummies
(0-7645-0776-1)
PHP and MySQL For
Dummies
(0-7645-1650-7)
SQL For Dummies
(0-7645-0737-0)
Visual Basic .NET For
Dummies
(0-7645-0867-9)

LINUX, NETWORKING & CERTIFICATION

Red Hat Linux 7.3 FOR DUMMIES
A Reference for the Rest of Us!
Jon "maddog" Hall
Paul G. Sery
0-7645-1545-4

TCP/IP FOR DUMMIES
A Reference for the Rest of Us!
Candace Leiden
Marshall Wilensky
0-7645-1760-0

Networking FOR DUMMIES
A Reference for the Rest of Us!
Doug Lowe
0-7645-0772-9

Also available:

A+ Certification For Dummies
(0-7645-0812-1)
CCNP All-in-One Certification
For Dummies
(0-7645-1648-5)
Cisco Networking For
Dummies
(0-7645-1668-X)
CISSP For Dummies
(0-7645-1670-1)
CIW Foundations For
Dummies
(0-7645-1635-3)

Firewalls For Dummies
(0-7645-0884-9)
Home Networking For
Dummies
(0-7645-0857-1)
Red Hat Linux All-in-One
Desk Reference For Dummies
(0-7645-2442-9)
UNIX For Dummies
(0-7645-0419-3)

Available wherever books are sold.
Go to www.dummies.com or call 1-877-762-2974 to order direct